America

Since 1945

Second Edition

America

Since 1945
Second Edition

Edited by

Robert D. Marcus

and

David Burner

State University of New York

at Stony Brook

St. Martin's Press

New York

Preface

In 1971, when we wrote the preface to the first edition of *America Since 1945*, it was easier for us to comprehend the quarter century between 1945 and 1970 as a unit than it is for us to perceive the more than three decades from 1945 as a clear continuity. For all the variety of American experience between 1945 and 1970, certain recurrent themes gave the period a narrative coherence. The presidency always waxed greater; the Cold War was ever a looming presence; prosperity attenuated only by short recessions was the steady experience of most Americans and a visible goal toward which the others could aspire. Now even these few enduring themes have been transformed. Our uncertain present demands a fresh view of our recent past, a new mapping of the road leading to today.

The United States since the end of World War II has contained all the makings of a great historical subject. More powerful yet more vulnerable than ever before, this nation has been not only the world's major military and economic power but also increasingly the center of the world's culture. Having completely terminated their role as European provincials, Americans in this new era have often seemed most awkward at the center of the world's stage, and reviews of their performance, in diplomacy as well as in culture, have varied widely. Rarely a complacent people, Americans have sought eagerly for a perspective on their place in the world.

Keeping in mind this search for a perspective, we have selected articles that deal with—and link together—the most significant political and social events of the past three decades. For example, in foreign affairs the articles include the views of Averell Harriman and Barton Bernstein on the Cold War, David Burner's discussion of John F. Kennedy's foreign policy, and C. D. B. Bryan's account of the effects of the Vietnam war on American life. In the domestic realm we have included not only political articles, such as Garry Wills's reevaluation of Richard Nixon's famous Checkers speech, but also articles that deal with some of the social transformations of the last thirty years—selections from Betty Friedan's *The Feminine Mystique*, Michael Harrington's *The Other America*, and Frances Fox Piven and Richard Cloward's *Regulating the Poor*. Throughout this second edition we have attempted to offer an interesting combination of primary and secondary materials to which end we have included excerpts from such original sources as the Army-McCarthy hearings; the speeches of John F. Kennedy, Lyndon B. Johnson, and Malcolm X; and the Church committee *Report* on the Central Intelligence Agency.

Robert D. Marcus
David Burner

Contents

America

Since 1945

Second Edition

PART ONE

1945-1952

In 1945 World War II ended and the atomic age began. It was a year of high drama: of the final defeat of the Axis powers, the establishment of the United Nations, and the beginning of what people hoped would be a great "American century" in which, under our guidance, the world would know a long era of peace and progress. Americans eagerly awaited demobilization, the sweet harvest of victory. Yet they were uneasy. The great leader, Franklin D. Roosevelt, was dead and in his place a modest ex-haberdasher from Missouri. Victory in Europe had left that continent devastated. Victory over Japan had introduced the world to the horror of nuclear weapons. And in America victory raised the question of whether an economy which had been depressed for a decade would not lapse into the same dismal state from which war production had roused it. Moreover, the unusual homefront harmony had suppressed intense conflicts that would break out again in an era of peace.

Many of the hopes and even more of the fears were realized in the next few years. The United Nations survived, the United States remained the greatest world power, and the domestic economy showed little inclination to slip back into depression. But the image of an "American century" rapidly gave way before the reality of a cold war. New Deal reforms were continued but not expanded, as bipartisan forces vigorously pursued the ideological conflict with the Soviet Union. Amid confusion and ill-feeling the nation rearmed, fought an inconclusive war in Asia, created an economy dependent on military spending, and moved irregularly toward a social order which in the 1950's seemed more stable than in fact it was. In reaction to a threatening world, Americans in 1952 closed ranks behind a popular and decidedly unmilitaristic general whom they hoped—correctly as it turned out—would put the sour era of postwar adjustment behind them.

Russia and the Cold War

AVERELL HARRIMAN

From 1926 when he bargained with Leon Trotsky in Moscow over a manganese concession until 1968 when he conferred in Paris with the North Vietnamese, Averell Harriman has probably been our most experienced and influential representative to the Communist world. His reminiscences are important not only for the insights he has acquired about Communist governments over the years, but for what they reveal about developing American foreign policy.

Harriman never conceived of American-Soviet relations as a struggle to the death between hostile forces, one destined to conquer, the other to die. He had contempt for the crusading cold-warrior mentality in international affairs and strongly criticized Eisenhower's Secretary of State, John Foster Dulles, for taking "the position that Communism was evil and that countries were either for us or against us in our struggle with it."

Harriman's opinions are quite typical of American policy makers in the immediate postwar era. He himself called it "a fairly glorious period, perhaps the most creative period in American foreign policy." The idealism he expresses—as in his account of the Marshall Plan—is undoubtedly genuine. Although some critics such as Barton J. Bernstein (in the next selection) have suggested that those liberal ideals actually defined the world in a way that made the Cold War inevitable, Harriman contends that Stalin's intransigence led to an unavoidable collapse of the wartime alliance.

There has grown a myth about Yalta that somehow or other Roosevelt and Churchill sold out Eastern Europe to Stalin. That wasn't true at all. I can't imagine why Stalin went to such extreme lengths in breaking the Yalta agreements if it had been true that they were so much to his advantage. It was agreed that the people in these countries were to decide on their own governments through free elections. But Stalin didn't permit it.

One wonders why he broke his agreement on Poland so soon. It's rather hard to guess. Personally, I think one of the reasons was that Bierut, the leading member of the Lublin Polish government—the Communist government—was in Moscow on Stalin's return from Yalta. He may have told Stalin that if he carried out his plan for free elections, Bierut and his comrades couldn't deliver Poland. Stalin had the idea that the Red Army would be accepted as a liberating army. In fact, he told me so. In this regard, perhaps the Communist partisans had reported too optimistically to Moscow. At any rate I think the Kremlin leaders were awfully hurt when they found that the Red Army was

3

looked upon by the Poles, the Romanians, and others as a new invading force.

In addition, there appeared to be two schools of thought in the Kremlin hierarchy—the Politburo itself. One is apt to think of the Communist government as one single brain; it isn't. It is made up of men with sometimes differing views; this was true even under Stalin. I was conscious of the fact that members of Politburo even during the war had different views on different subjects. Let me quickly say that there was free discussion in the Politburo on *new* subjects only. On anything Stalin had decided, that was it. That couldn't be questioned. I think it is fair to say that in these discussions about new matters, Stalin listened, smoked his pipe, and walked up and down the room. Then, when he had heard enough, he said, "This is what we are going to do." If anyone left the room with a shrug of his shoulders, he might find himself on the way to Siberia the next afternoon. That may be somewhat of an exaggeration, but I think it's pretty nearly right.

In any event, I feel sure that there was a difference of opinion as to whether it would be wise for the Soviet Union in the immediate postwar period to soft-pedal Communist expansion for a time and continue to collaborate with the Western Allies to get the value of loans and trade, technical assistance, and other cooperation for the terrific job of reconstruction they faced; or whether they should push ahead and use the extraordinary opportunities in the dislocations in Europe and elsewhere to extend Communist control. Stalin once told me, "Communism breeds in the cesspools of capitalists." In this sense, Europe looked as if it were going to be in a mire.

I was so concerned about this that in early 1945, I sent messages about the need to help Western Europe, urging that the recovery of Europe would require much more than most people thought. I said that UNRRA would not be enough, food would not be enough. We would have to supply working capital and raw materials to get trade going again. Imports would be needed for raw materials for industrial production as well as for reconstruction. Without that, there would be vast unemployment and misery, in which the Communists might well take over.

I believe that Stalin hoped to get to the Atlantic, and that was perhaps the reason why he didn't carry out the Yalta agreements. The prospects for Communist takeover simply looked too good.

He said a number of things on different occasions, some of them contradictory, and it is hard to know what he had in mind. After Teheran he sent President Roosevelt a telegram in which, among other things, he said, "Now it is assured that our people will act together, jointly and in friendship, both at the present time and after the completion of the war." This is only one of the many expressions of that kind which gave some indication that he had in mind postwar cooperation. But that didn't happen. Roosevelt died, and I know that before he died he realized that his hopes had not been fully achieved; he knew Stalin had already broken some of the Yalta agreements. I know that from the telegrams I received from him to deliver to Stalin and also from some of the people who talked to him just before his death.[1] . . .

While I was home, I did spend several weeks in San Francisco during the United Nations Conference. At the request of Ed Stettinius, the Secretary of State, I had three off-the-record talks with editors, columnists, and reporters to give them some background on our growing problems with the Soviet government. I told them we would have real difficulties with the Soviet Union in the postwar period. This came as a great shock to many of them. At one meeting, I explained that our objectives and the Kremlin objectives were irreconcilable; they wanted to communize the world, and we wanted a free world. But I added that we would have to find ways to compose our differences if we were to live in peace on this small planet. Two men were so shocked that they got up and left. Some of the press at that time criticized me for being so unkind to what were then known as "our gallant allies," and some even suggested that I should be recalled as Ambassador. It was one of the few times in my experience that members of the press have broken the confidence of an off-the-record talk.

People ask when and why I became convinced we would have difficulties with the Soviets. This judgment developed over a period of time. . . .

A talk I had with Stalin at Potsdam in July 1945 is illuminating. The first time I saw him at the conference I went up to him and said that it must be very gratifying for him to be in Berlin, after all the struggle and the tragedy. He hesitated a moment and then replied, "Czar Alexander got to Paris." It didn't need much of a clairvoyant to guess what was in his mind.

I don't think there is any doubt that, with the strong Communist Parties both in Italy and in France, he would have extended his domination to the Atlantic, if we had not acted to frustrate it. In all probability, the Communist leaders in those countries had reported to Moscow that they could take over, and I think they would have succeeded if we had not helped Western Europe to recover. Some of Western Europe would have had Communist governments under the control of Moscow. One doesn't know what the rest of Europe would have been like, but perhaps some countries would have been something less independent than Finland and allowed to be cautiously neutral at the grace of Moscow.

But that isn't what happened. I know that some young people

1. Mrs. Hoffman wrote me a letter some years later describing her conversation with Roosevelt on March 24, 1945, his last day in Washington:

The President was in his wheel chair as we left the room, and both Mrs. Roosevelt and I walked at his side. He was given a message which I learned later was a cable from you which had been decoded. He read it and became quite angry. He banged his fists on the arms of his wheel chair and said, "Averell is right; we can't do business with Stalin. He has broken every one of the promises he made at Yalta." He was very upset and continued in the same vein on the subject.

These were his exact words. I remembered them and verified them with Mrs. Roosevelt not too long before her death.

think that everything that has been done before them wasn't just right, but we did have a fairly glorious period, perhaps the most creative period in American foreign policy, immediately after the war. It was due to the leadership of President Truman and the effective cooperation of Senator Vandenberg, the Republican Senator from Michigan, who was then Chairman of the Foreign Relations Committee. The undertakings included aid to Greece, which was under Communist attack, and Turkey, which was threatened at that time; the Marshall Plan, which was an extraordinarily ambitious and successful venture in cooperation; and that led to NATO. These things developed one from the other. Public opinion in the West was deeply disturbed by the Czech coup of March 1948 and then the Berlin blockade three months later. . . .

I was involved in the Marshall Plan, in charge of operations in Europe for more than two years. This was a European effort, with United States help. By the way, I should recall that General Marshall's offer of aid was made to all of Europe, including Russia and Eastern Europe. In fact, Molotov came to the meeting of Foreign Ministers of the European countries called in Paris in July 1947 to consider Marshall's offer with a staff of sixty, including senior economists. However, he demanded that each country act independently. He wanted the European nations to reply to the United States along these lines, "Tell us how much money you will give us, and we will divide it on the basis of those who suffered most will get the most. Then each country will look after its own recovery." But Marshall's proposal was that the European countries should cooperate together in a mutual recovery program. Bevin and Bidault, the British and French Foreign Ministers, stood firm for the cooperative concept, and Molotov left in a huff. The Czechs and the Poles had wanted to join the Marshall Plan, but the Kremlin ordered them not to do so.

At that time the Soviets organized the Cominform and declared war on the Marshall Plan, calling it an "American imperialist plot to subjugate Western Europe." Needless to say, that was just exactly the reverse of what we wanted. We wanted a strong, united and independent Europe. Everything that we did was to minimize our role and maximize the cooperative effort of the Europeans. "Self-help and mutual aid" was the slogan. It was amazingly successful—a spirit of cooperation and unity developed within Europe which had never before existed. They abandoned some of the restrictive business and labor practices of the intra-war years and accepted the necessity of an expanding economy as the basis for a rising standard of living. . . .

Now, Western Europe is more vital and dynamic than ever. When De Gaulle was in control, France was, perhaps, a little too nationalistic. But today the Europeans are again moving toward greater integration and closer cooperation. This was part of the objective of the Congress, and certainly of President Truman in initiating the Marshall Plan. . . .

The Berlin blockade in June of 1948 was a startling event and led to the pressure for NATO. You have to remember that never in history has a nation destroyed its armed strength as rapidly as we did after the

Second World War. The demand for bringing the boys home was irresistible. No one was to blame; it was the deep desire of the American people. We thought we had won the war and everyone in the world would want peace. We had the strongest military force in being at the end of the war, but after the Japanese surrendered, it was dissipated. The Russians didn't do that. They strengthened their forces. They developed new weapons. We in Moscow reported to Washington in late 1945 evidence which indicated that Soviet research expenditure was being doubled, that production of certain new weapons and military equipment was continuing at wartime levels, and that combat training for the Red Army was being emphasized.

Although for a time we had a monopoly in nuclear weapons, Stalin ordered the highest priority be given to developing nuclear capability. Much to the surprise of most people at the time, the Soviets exploded their first nuclear device in September 1949.

The Berlin blockade was countered not by direct force. There has been a lot of argument about that at the time and since. People can argue whether Truman's decision was right or wrong—whether to try to drive our forces through and threaten a nuclear attack, or whether to supply Berlin by airlift. In any event, the least provocative of these responses—the airlift—was chosen, and with full British cooperation it was successful. The Soviets lifted the blockade a year later.

We have had difficulty over Berlin ever since, some times more dangerous than others. Of course, one can criticize the arrangements which made Berlin the capital of occupied Germany. Frankly, Ben Cohen and I favored at the time a capital in a new location, where the three zones came together, just north of Magdeburg. I was influenced in part by the appalling way in which the Soviets had stripped Berlin of most everything they could take out, between V-E Day and the Potsdam meeting. The factories, particularly, were emptied of all machinery and machine tools. But these arrangements had been made by the European Advisory Commission in London. They had been accepted by the three Allies and would have been pretty hard to change at Potsdam.

Sometimes I have thought our presence in Berlin was of great value. Other times I have wondered if it was worthwhile. These are things that historians can argue about. But we are there in West Berlin, and the division of Germany continues along the line of the Soviet occupational zone.

Some think that General Eisenhower should have taken Berlin, but if he had done that, our Third Army wouldn't have been in Austria, and Austria, which is a free and independent country, probably would have been occupied largely by the Red Army and might have been turned into a satellite.

These are all questions which one can weigh. It is hard to say what might have been done. If one objective had been gained, something else would have been lost. I think by and large with the Soviet recalcitrance it would have made very little difference.

Some people have even argued that if General Eisenhower had

liberated Prague somehow or other Czechoslovakia would be free today. That's nonsense! The Czech government under President Benes was set up under an agreement in Moscow, negotiated by Benes with Czech party leaders, including the Communists. This government returned to Czechoslovakia from the East, as the Red Army, joined with four or five Czech divisions, advanced. Under the agreement Benes had to take Communists into the government.

I had several talks with Benes when he came to Moscow from London in March 1945 before returning to Czechoslovakia. He told me that he was not too well satisfied with the composition of the new government, but he added, "It might have been worse." Benes was confident he could control the situation in Czechoslovakia as he believed the people would support him. He told me that Stalin had assured him that the Soviets would not interfere in Czech internal affairs.

Unfortunately, Benes was ill in March 1948 when the coup took place. Of course, the Red Army had long since retired. It had withdrawn from Czechoslovakia more than two years earlier. Our troops had also withdrawn long before, so nothing we did in 1945 would have affected the outcome. Whether or not it would have been different if Benes had been well and vigorous, and whether he could have held his own, I don't know. But the Communist coup was successful without the participation of the Red Army, but undoubtedly with Moscow's collusion.

I had long talks with Jan Masaryk in San Francisco in May 1945. He was Benes' Foreign Minister. He told me I must understand that in the United Nations he would have to vote with Molotov. The Soviets were insisting that the Czech government support them in foreign policy. In return, he thought they would have a free hand at home. Unfortunately, it did not work out that way, and Masaryk himself came to a violent end in March 1948.

The Truman period was an exciting period. President Truman was a man of great determination. He was very humble at the start. He said he had not been elected; Roosevelt had been elected, and it was his responsibility to carry out Roosevelt's policies. He did the best he could. Very early he showed that he recognized the unique problems facing the United States in the world, and he had the extraordinary courage to undertake new policies and programs. And I think they were extraordinarily successful.

President Truman proposed in January 1949 the Point Four Program, announcing that since science and technology had developed to such a point that the old enemies of mankind—hunger, misery, poverty, and disease—could be overcome, it was the obligation of the United States and other more technologically advanced nations to help. That concept has moved ahead. There have been some outstanding successes in some ways and in some countries—some disappointments in others. Unfortunately, our development assistance is in rather a low state today —one of the casualties of Vietnam.

There have been lasting constructive results from the Truman period. Germany has revived and has become a strong ally; Japan has revived and is becoming a strong partner. Western Europe is more productive and united than ever. Other countries have made progress as well and are on their way to sustained economic development, for example in Asia, Korea, and Taiwan, and in Latin America, Mexico, Venezuela, and Colombia. There have been disappointments, of course. The developing countries as a whole have not been able to advance as rapidly as had been hoped, and the gap between them and the industrial nations has widened.

China was an enigma. Roosevelt first of all wanted to get the Soviet Union into the war against Japan. There was never any doubt in my mind that Stalin would attack Japan when it suited him. We could not have kept him out. The question was whether that would be soon enough to do us good. Our Chiefs of Staff estimated that it would take eighteen months after the fall of Germany to defeat the Japanese and would require an amphibious landing on the plains of Tokyo. American casualties were estimated to run up near a million with perhaps a couple of hundred thousand killed. This was a grim prospect to President Roosevelt. Yet, if the Russians attacked the Japanese Kwangtung Army in Manchuria, the Japanese strength to defend the home islands would be reduced. President Roosevelt had a deep sense of responsibility to protect American lives, and it was hoped that possibly, with Russia in the war and with American use of Soviet airfields in Siberia, we could bring Japan to surrender without invasion. Therefore, Soviet intervention seemed of vital importance.

It didn't turn out to be important because, unexpectedly, the nuclear bomb became operative and events moved so rapidly. At Yalta, when plans about Soviet entry into the war against Japan were agreed to, the nuclear bomb had not yet been completed, and nobody knew whether it would work. Even five months later at Potsdam, after the first test explosion took place, one of the most distinguished Navy officers bet an apple that it would not go off as a bomb. Of course, after things happen they seem so easy and so obvious that people say, "Why didn't you think of this at the time?"

Apart from Soviet entry into the war, Roosevelt also wanted to get Stalin to accept Chiang Kai-shek's Nationalist government as the government of China. And that, too, was part of the agreements reached at Yalta about the Far East. This was formalized in a treaty negotiated by T. V. Soong, Premier of the Nationalist government, with Stalin six months later. During these negotiations in Moscow I saw T. V. Soong almost every day. He was finally well satisfied, and in fact the world applauded the agreement. . . .

There were certain concessions to the Russians related to the railroads and ports in Manchuria for a thirty-year period, but the important point for Chiang was that the Soviets accepted Chinese sovereignty over the area. Some of us had been concerned when the Russians got into Manchuria they would establish a "Manchurian People's Republic" just as they had the Mongolian People's Republic. The fact that the Soviets accepted Chinese sovereignty was the thing that impressed Chiang.

Curiously, Stalin did not have much respect for Mao Tse-tung. During the war he spoke about him several times, and at one time he called him a "margarine Communist." That created a great deal of puzzlement in Washington. Some didn't know what it means. It would be entirely clear to any dairy farmer what he meant—a fake, not a real product. I gained the impression from several of my talks with Stalin that he was not keen to support Mao Tse-tung in China and that, perhaps, he wanted to see a new group more amenable to Moscow, take over the Chinese Communist Party before he gave his full support.

After the war, in January 1946, he told me that he had "poor contacts with the Communists." He said that the Soviet government's "three representatives in Yenan had been recalled" and that the Soviet influence with the Chinese Communists was not great. I think there is other evidence to that effect. For example, the Red Army not only stripped Manchuria of its industrial machinery for use in the Soviet Union but also blew up facilities such as blast furnaces. However, the Mao Communists were stronger than Stalin thought, and Chiang was weaker. As events developed, Chiang's forces collapsed in 1949, and he was driven out of mainland China.

Some people have said, "We lost China." It just happens that we never owned China. Whatever we had done in China over the years had had only a limited impact. And although it is unfortunate that a government friendly to us did not survive, we could not have involved ourselves in a major war at that time in China. President Truman, in spite of all the initiatives we had taken in other parts of the world, was wise enough to exercise restraint and not become involved in a civil war in mainland China.

So not all the postwar developments were favorable. Some of them did not go as well as we had hoped they might. . . .

President Kennedy handled the Cuban missile crisis with consummate skill and induced Khrushchev to take the offensive missiles out of Cuba. He was able to go on to an agreement with him on a limited test ban. The signing and ratification of the Limited Nuclear Test Ban Treaty marked a high water point in our relations with the Soviet Union. There were of course unsolved critical problems, particularly in regard to Germany and Southeast Asia. But the change in less than a year from the Cuban missile crisis to the test ban was so striking that I believe President Kennedy began to think seriously of a visit to the Soviet Union early in his second term should he be re-elected. But President Kennedy was assassinated three months later.

Within a year new personalities were to take over in Moscow. Khrushchev was removed from office, Brezhnev took his place as Secretary of the Party and Kosygin as Chairman of the Council of Ministers. . . .

QUESTIONS AND ANSWERS

Q—Do you believe that there is anything America could have done to assist Chiang, particularly in the latter period when we did withdraw our support?

A—I don't think so. I went to Chunking to talk with Chiang Kaishek in January 1946. General Marshall was there at the time. Chiang had grave doubts about coming to an agreement for a coalition with the Communists, and he may have been justified in his fears. I asked him why he did not strengthen his government at once by bringing in the Democratic League, which included the leading Chinese intellectuals. They had recently participated in a Consultative Conference which had attempted to reconcile the contending parties. I also asked him why he didn't get rid of some of his warlords and some of the obviously corrupt people around him. He replied that they were the only ones he could count on for support if he brought the Communists into the government.

Perhaps the outcome might have been better if we had had quite a different approach. Looking at things from Moscow, my idea at the time was that we might better accept temporarily a divided China. If we could have prevented Chiang from sending his best troops into Manchuria where they were chewed up, he would have been far better off. It was hopeless for him to expect to take over the rule of Manchuria when he was having difficulty in controlling even the area where his forces were concentrated—southern China.

I also had grave doubts about the attempts to form a coalition government with the Communists. It seemed to me at the time that Chiang was too weak and the Communists too strong for him to have had much of a chance of survival.

In any event, General Marshall was sent out to attempt to mediate between the Nationalists and the Communists, and he did everything he could under his instructions. Despite General Marshall's patience and skill, the reluctance and suspicion of both sides and the inherent weakness of the Kuomintang made successful mediation impossible. . . .

Q—Mr. Ambassador, would you comment on the motivation of Soviet foreign policy? Do you think the motivation is primarily that of power politics and national power concerns, or of Communist ideology, or are they both equally determining factors?

A—It is a combination of both. Stalin had both. He was a Russian imperialist with ambitions similar to the Czars. He was also utterly determined to promote world Communist revolution with the oracle in Moscow. Since Stalin's death the world situation has changed, but the Kremlin still has both motivations. . . .

Q—If you could relive history, what changes would you make in the United States foreign policy during the wartime conferences and what effect that might have had on the future?

A—Well, I don't think much would have been different. You can argue about a lot of different things. People blame Eisenhower for not going to Berlin, but there had been a decision made in which the occupational zones of Germany were set. It was considered important that we should not meet and clash with the Russians, that we should decide in advance the zones each would occupy to avoid that possibility. The agreed zones were considered to be very favorable by our chiefs of staff at the time they were decided upon. They thought the Russians would be much further into Germany than they got and that we would not have gotten as far as we did. It didn't work out that way. I am not critical of them for this, as no one could have foreseen the military events.

Now if we had tried to do what Churchill proposed after V-E Day— stand on the Elbe until there was a political settlement about Eastern Europe—I don't think it would have done any good, and we would then have been held responsible for the cold war. Furthermore, our military plans required a redeployment of our forces in Europe to the Pacific. Churchill wanted to force a political settlement about the areas occupied by the Red Army before we withdrew from the Elbe. But even if we had gotten an agreement and free elections had been held, the governments elected would, in all probability, not have lasted. There was, in fact, a free election in Hungary in 1945 in which the Smallholders party (the small peasants' party) got over 50 per cent of the votes and the Communists only about 18 per cent. The government established after this election lasted only a short time, and the Communists—supported by the Red Army—took over and squeezed out the others.

There was no way we could have prevented any of these events in Eastern Europe without going to war with the Russians. There were a few military people who considered that. This wasn't De Gaulle, but a few French and American officers talked about going in and cleaning them up while we had such superiority in air power. It is perfectly absurd to think the American people would have stood for it, even if the President wanted to do it, which he didn't.

I think it was very important that Roosevelt and Churchill made the effort to come to an agreement with Stalin. One achievement was the establishment of the United Nations. With all the disappointments, it has been effective in many activities during the twenty-five years of its life, although handicapped by the differences that exist between the great powers. The fact that Stalin broke the agreements about Eastern Europe exposed his perfidy and aggressive designs. This aroused the suspicion of the West and eventually led to steps for mutual defense.

There is a group of historians who are now attempting to rewrite the history of that time. Arthur M. Schlesinger, Jr., has pointed out that such attempts to rewrite history have happened frequently in the past. These revisionists are creating myths about what happened and what our objectives were. Some of them take facts out of context and try to build up a case for imagined objectives. Some conveniently overlook Stalin's failure to cooperate, his violation of specific agreements and aggressive actions. Of course, I am not talking about those thoughtful analysts who, with the advantage of hindsight, point out more clearly the significance of events and perhaps mistakes than was possible at the time.

The military alternatives were perhaps more obvious than the political. At the time some people wanted us to go to Vienna, up the Ljubljana Gap, and get there before the Russians, instead of landing in the south of France as we did. Yet as things have turned out, Austria is free today anyway.

Churchill was always very much worried about attempting to cross the Channel. It turned out successfully. It would have been disastrous for the British if it hadn't. Churchill wanted to go at Hitler from the south—"the soft underbelly," as he called it. He didn't want to take the risk of crossing the Channel. Stalin, after having berated and even insulted us for two years for not establishing a second front in Europe by crossing the Channel, said to me after we had successfully landed, "The history of war has never witnessed such a grandiose operation." He added neither Napoleon nor Hitler had dared attempt it. Later, after he had received detailed reports, he spoke to me again about crossing the Channel, as "an unheard of achievement in the history of warfare." The number of men and the vast amount of equipment which had been thrown into France impressed him greatly. He added "the world had never seen an individual operation of such magnitude— an unbelievable accomplishment." He was unconcerned by the fact that he had previously minimized its difficulties and had accused us of cowardice in not having undertaken it before.

Undoubtedly mistakes were made, and undoubtedly many things might have been improved. Your question is an interesting one, and I have thought a lot about it. But the facts are that, although militarily unprepared, we fought a war successfully on two fronts. With our allies in Europe, we completely defeated Hitler, and almost alone we defeated Japan in the Pacific. That was an extraordinary achievement— and particularly as it was done in less than four years. As far as our relations with the Soviet Union since the end of the war are concerned, I doubt whether any different wartime military or political decisions would have had much effect.

The Cold War:
A Revisionist View

BARTON J. BERNSTEIN

*"There is no nation which has
attitudes so pure that they cannot
be bettered by self-examination."*
—John Foster Dulles (1946)

*"We are forced to act in the world
as it is, and not in the world as
we wish it were, or as we would
like it to become."*
—Henry L. Stimson (1947)

*Barton J. Bernstein is one of the "revisionists" whom Averell Harriman
criticizes for "creating myths about what happened [in the Cold War]
and what our objectives were." The revisionist position, expressed repeatedly during the 1960's, holds that Stalin was basically cautious
rather than aggressive in his actions immediately after World War II;
that the United States government, aiming to preserve American access
to a world trading empire, overlooked legitimate Soviet security needs;
and that, possessing preponderant power in the world, America refused
to cooperate with the Soviet Union, forcing the Kremlin into a hostile
posture in Eastern Europe to protect itself from future military threats.*

*Only a small proportion of American diplomatic historians has
totally accepted this analysis of American foreign policy, but the revisionist argument has influenced virtually every student in the field.
The central point of revisionist thinking, that the postwar power of
the United States gave it wider options than the Soviet Union ever had,
seems hard to question. Some theorists also maintain that American
and Soviet social and economic policies would eventually have con-
verged, and that such abrasive conflict between the two ideologies need
not have occurred at all. Yet we know so little of what Stalin was
thinking, and he gave so many contradictory signals that almost any
interpretation is possible. The experience of Vietnam, the breakdown
of monolithic power blocs, both East and West, and the emergence of
"détente" have all provided continuing stimulus for Cold War revisionism.*

Despite some dissents, most American scholars have reached a general consensus on the origins of the Cold War. As confirmed internationalists who believe that Russia constituted a threat to America and its European allies after World War II, they have endorsed their nation's acceptance of its obligations as a world power in the forties and its desire to establish a world order of peace and prosperity. Convinced that only American efforts prevented the Soviet Union from expanding past Eastern Europe, they have generally praised the containment policies of the Truman Doctrine, the Marshall Plan, and NATO as evidence of America's acceptance of world responsibility. While chiding or condemning those on the right who opposed international involvement (or had even urged preventive war), they have also been deeply critical of those on the left who have believed that the Cold War could have been avoided, or that the United States shared substantial responsibility for the Cold War.

Whether they are devotees of the new realism or open admirers of moralism and legalism in foreign policy, most scholars have agreed that the United States moved slowly and reluctantly, in response to Soviet provocation, away from President Franklin D. Roosevelt's conciliatory policy. The Truman administration, perhaps even belatedly, they suggest, abandoned its efforts to maintain the Grand Alliance and acknowledged that Russia menaced world peace. American leaders, according to this familiar interpretation, slowly cast off the shackles of innocence and moved to courageous and necessary policies.

Despite the widespread acceptance of this interpretation, there has long been substantial evidence (and more recently a body of scholarship) which suggests that American policy was neither so innocent nor so nonideological; that American leaders sought to promote their conceptions of national interest and their values even at the conscious risk of provoking Russia's fears about her security. In 1945 these leaders apparently believed that American power would be adequate for the task of reshaping much of the world according to America's needs and standards.

By overextending policy and power and refusing to accept Soviet interests, American policy-makers contributed to the Cold War. There was little understanding of any need to restrain American political efforts and desires. Though it cannot be proved that the United States could have achieved a *modus vivendi* with the Soviet Union in these years, there is evidence that Russian policies were reasonably cautious and conservative, and that there was at least a basis for accommodation.

The author wishes to express his gratitude for generous counsel to Gar Alperovitz, H. Stuart Hughes, Gabriel Kolko, Walter LaFeber, Lloyd Gardner, Allen J. Matusow, Thomas G. Paterson, Athan Theoharis, and Samuel Williamson. Research was conducted with the assistance of grants from the Rabinowitz Foundation, the American Philosophical Society, the Harry S. Truman Library Institute, the Charles Warren Center of Harvard University, and the Institute of American History at Stanford University. Portions of this paper were presented at the Warren Center in November 1967, at the John F. Kennedy Institute at Harvard in 1967–1968, and at the annual meeting of the Southern Historical Association in November 1968.

But this possibility slowly slipped away as President Harry S. Truman reversed Roosevelt's tactics of accommodation. As American demands for democratic governments in Eastern Europe became more vigorous, as the new administration delayed in providing economic assistance to Russia and in seeking international control of atomic energy, policymakers met with increasing Soviet suspicion and antagonism. Concluding that Soviet-American cooperation was impossible, they came to believe that the Soviet state could be halted only by force or the threat of force.

The emerging revisionist interpretation, then, does not view American actions simply as the necessary response to Soviet challenges, but instead tries to understand American ideology and interests, mutual suspicions and misunderstandings, and to investigate the failures to seek and achieve accommodation.

I

During the war Allied relations were often marred by suspicions and doubts rooted in the hostility of earlier years. It was only a profound "accident"—the German attack upon the Soviet Union in 1941 —that thrust that leading anti-Bolshevik, Winston Churchill, and Marshal Josef Stalin into a common camp. This wartime alliance, its members realized, was not based upon trust but upon necessity; there was no deep sense of shared values or obvious similarity of interests, only opposition to a common enemy. "A coalition," as Herbert Feis has remarked, "is heir to the suppressed desires and maimed feelings of each of its members." Wartime needs and postwar aims often strained the uneasy alliance. In the early years when Russia was bearing the major burden of the Nazi onslaught, her allies postponed for two years a promised second front which would have diverted German armies. In December 1941, when Stalin requested recognition of 1941 Russian borders as they had been before the German attack (including the recently annexed Baltic states), the British were willing to agree, but Roosevelt rebuffed the proposals and aroused Soviet fears that her security needs would not be recognized and that her allies might later resume their anti-Bolshevik policies. So distrustful were the Allies that both camps feared the making of a separate peace with Germany, and Stalin's suspicions erupted into bitter accusations in March 1945, when he discovered (and Roosevelt denied) that British and American agents were participating in secret negotiations with the Germans. In anger Stalin decided not to send Vyacheslav Molotov, the Foreign Minister, to San Francisco for the April meeting on the founding of the United Nations Organization.

So suspicious were the Americans and British that they would not inform the Soviet Union that they were working on an atomic bomb. Some American leaders even hoped to use it in postwar negotiations with the Russians. In wartime, American opposition to communism had not disappeared, and many of Roosevelt's advisers were fearful of

Soviet intentions in Eastern Europe. In turn, Soviet leaders, recalling the prewar hostility of the Western democracies, feared a renewed attempt to establish a *cordon sanitaire* and resolved to establish a security zone in Eastern Europe.

Though Roosevelt's own strategy often seems ambiguous, his general tactics are clear: they were devised to avoid conflict. He operated often as a mediator between the British and Russians, and delayed many decisions that might have disrupted the wartime alliance. He may have been resting his hopes with the United Nations or on the exercise of America's postwar strength, or he may simply have been placing his faith in the future. Whatever future tactics he might have been planning, he concluded that America's welfare rested upon international peace, expanded trade, and open markets:

. . . it is our hope, not only in the interest of our own prosperity, but in the interest of the prosperity of the world, that trade and commerce and access to materials and markets may be freer after this war than ever before in the history of the world. . . . Only through a dynamic and soundly expanding world economy can the living standards of individual nations be advanced to levels which will permit a full realization of our hopes for the future.

His efforts on behalf of the postwar world generally reflected this understanding.

During the war Roosevelt wavered uneasily between emphasizing the postwar role of the great powers and minimizing their role and seeking to extend the principles of the Atlantic Charter. Though he often spoke of the need for an open postwar world, and he was reluctant to accept spheres of influence (beyond the Western hemisphere, where American influence was pre-eminent), his policies gradually acknowledged the pre-eminence of the great powers and yielded slowly to their demands. By late 1943 Roosevelt confided to Archbishop Francis Spellman (according to Spellman's notes) that "the world will be divided into spheres of influence: China gets the Far East; the U.S. the Pacific; Britain and Russia, Europe and Africa." The United States, he thought, would have little postwar influence on the continent, and Russia would probably "predominate in Europe," making Austria, Hungary, and Croatia "a sort of Russian protectorate." He acknowledged "that the European countries will have to undergo tremendous changes in order to adapt to Russia; but he hopes that in ten or twenty years the European influence would bring the Russians to become less barbarous."

In 1944 Roosevelt recognized the establishment of zones of influence in Europe. The Italian armistice of the year before had set the pattern for other wartime agreements on the control of affairs of liberated and defeated European nations. When Stalin requested the creation of a three-power Allied commission to deal with the problems of "countries falling away from Germany," Roosevelt and Churchill first rebuffed the Russian leader and then agreed to a joint commission for Italy which would be limited to information gathering. By excluding Russia from sharing in decision-making in Italy, the United States and Great Britain, later concluded William McNeill, "prepared the way for their own exclusion from any but a marginal share in the affairs of Eastern Europe."

When Roosevelt refused to participate in an Anglo-American invasion of southeastern Europe (which seemed to be the only way of restricting Russian influence in that area), Churchill sought other ways of dealing with Russian power and of protecting British interests in Greece. In May 1944 he proposed to Stalin that they recognize Greece as a British "zone of influence" and Rumania as a Russian zone; but Stalin insisted upon seeking Roosevelt's approval and refused the offer upon learning that the United States would not warmly endorse the terms. When the Soviets liberated Rumania in September they secured temporarily the advantages that Churchill had offered. They simply followed the British-American example in Italy, retained all effective power, and announced they were "acting in the interests of all the United Nations." From the Soviet Union, W. Averell Harriman, the American ambassador, cabled, "The Russians believe, I think, that we lived up to a tacit understanding that Rumania was an area of predominant Soviet interest in which we should not interfere. . . . The terms of the armistice give the Soviet command unlimited control of Rumania's economic life" and effective control over political organization.

With Russian armies sweeping through the Balkans and soon in a position to impose similar terms on Hungary and Bulgaria, Churchill renewed his efforts. "Winston," wrote an associate, "never talks of Hitler these days; he is always harping on the dangers of Communism. He dreams of the Red Army spreading like a cancer from one country to another. It has become an obsession, and he seems to think of little else." In October Churchill journeyed to Moscow to reach an agreement with Stalin. "Let us settle our affairs in the Balkans," Churchill told him. "Your armies are in Rumania and Bulgaria. We have interests, missions and agents there. Don't let us get at cross-purposes in small ways." Great Britain received "90 per cent influence" in Greece, and Russia "90 per cent influence" in Rumania, "80 per cent" in Bulgaria and Hungary, and "50 per cent" in Yugoslavia.

In the cases of Hungary and Bulgaria the terms were soon sanctioned by armistice agreements (approved by the United States) which left effective power with the Soviets. "The Russians took it for granted," Cordell Hull, then Secretary of State, wrote later, "that . . . Britain and the United States had assigned them a certain portion of the Balkans, including Rumania and Bulgaria, as their sphere of influence." In December Stalin even confirmed the agreement at a considerable price: he permitted British troops to put down a rebellion in Greece. "Stalin," wrote Churchill later, "adhered strictly and faithfully to our agreement . . . and during all the long weeks of fighting the communists in the streets of Athens, not one word of reproach came from *Pravda* or *Izvestia*."

At Yalta in February 1945 Roosevelt did not seem to challenge

Soviet dominance in east-central Europe, which had been established by the Churchill-Stalin agreement and confirmed by the armistices and by British action in Greece. What Roosevelt did seek and gain at Yalta was a weak "Declaration on Liberated Europe"—that the powers would consult "where in their judgment conditions require" assistance to maintain peace or to establish democratic governments. By requiring unanimity the declaration allowed any one power to veto any proposal that seemed to threaten that power's interests. In effect, then, the declaration, despite its statements about democratic governments, did not alter the situation in Eastern Europe. The operative phrases simply affirmed the principle that the three powers had already established: they could consult together when all agreed, and they could act together when all agreed. At Yalta the broadly phrased statement provoked little discussion—only a few pages in the official proceedings. Presumably the Russians did not consider it a repudiation of spheres of influence, only as rhetoric that Roosevelt wanted for home consumption. Despite later official American suggestions, the Yalta agreement was not a product of Roosevelt's misunderstanding of the Soviet meaning of "democracy" and "free elections." Rather, it ratified earlier agreements, and the State Department probably understood this.

While accepting the inevitable and acknowledging Russian influence in these areas, Roosevelt had not been tractable on the major issue confronting the three powers: the treatment of postwar Germany. All three leaders realized that the decisions on Germany would shape the future relations of Europe. A dismembered or permanently weakened Germany would leave Russia without challenge on the continent and would ease her fears of future invasion. As Anthony Eden, the British Foreign Minister explained, "Russia was determined on one thing above all others, that Germany would not again disturb the peace of Europe. . . . Stalin was determined to smash Germany so that it would never again be able to make war." A strong Germany, on the other hand, could be a partial counterweight to Russia and help restore the European balance of power on which Britain had traditionally depended for protection. Otherwise, as Henry Morgenthau once explained in summarizing Churchill's fears, there would be nothing between "the white snows of Russia and the white cliffs of Dover."

The Allied policy on Germany had been in flux for almost two years. At Teheran in 1943 the Allies had agreed in principle (despite Churchill's reluctance) that Germany should be dismembered, and in 1944 Roosevelt and a reluctant Churchill, much to the distress of Foreign Minister Anthony Eden, had agreed on a loosely phrased version of the Morgenthau Plan for the dismemberment and pastoralization of Germany. Not only would the plan have eliminated German military-industrial potential and thereby allayed Russian fears, but by stripping Germany it would also have provided the resources for Russian economic reconstruction. Churchill, despite his fear of Russia and his desire for Germany as a counterweight on the continent, had temporarily agreed to the plan because it seemed to be a prerequisite for increased American economic aid and promised to eliminate German industry as a postwar rival for the trade that the debt-ridden British economy would need. Many in the State and War Departments charged that the plan was economic madness, that it would leave not only Germany but also much of war-torn Western Europe (which would need postwar German production) without the means for economic reconstruction. (Secretary of the Treasury Morgenthau concluded after discussion with many officials that they wanted a strong Germany as a "bulwark against Bolshevism.") Yielding to the pleas of the War and State Departments, Roosevelt decided upon a plan for a stronger postwar Germany, and Churchill, under pressure from advisers, also backed away from his earlier endorsement of the Morgenthau Plan and again acted upon his fears of an unopposed Russia on the continent. At Yalta, he resisted any agreement on the dismemberment of Germany. Stalin, faced with Anglo-American solidarity on this issue, acceded. The final communiqué patched over this fundamental dispute by announcing that the three powers had pledged to "take such steps including the complete disarmament, demilitarization, and dismemberment of Germany as they deem requisite for future peace and security." The strategy of postponement had triumphed. Unable to reach a substantive agreement, the Big Three agreed to submit these problems (and the related, vital issues of reparations and boundaries) to three-power commissions.

Though Yalta has come to represent the triumph of the strategy of postponement, at the time it symbolized Allied accord. Stalin accepted a limitation of the veto power on certain quasi-judicial issues in the U.N. Security Council; Roosevelt conceded to Russia the return of the Kurile Islands, which stretched between Japan and Siberia, and special rights in Dairen and Port Arthur in Manchuria; Stalin promised to enter the Pacific war within three months of the end of the European conflict. "Stalin," as William McNeill explained, "had conceded something to the British in Yugoslavia; and Churchill had yielded a good deal in Poland."

II

Roosevelt's successor was less sympathetic to Russian aspirations and more responsive to those of Roosevelt's advisers, like Admiral William Leahy, Chief of Staff to the Commander in Chief; Harriman; James Forrestal, Secretary of the Navy; and James F. Byrnes, Truman's choice for Secretary of State, who had urged that he resist Soviet efforts in Eastern Europe. As an earlier self-proclaimed foe of Russian communism, Truman mistrusted Russia. ("If we see that Germany is winning the war," advised Senator Truman after the German attack upon Russia in 1941, "we ought to help Russia, and if Russia is winning we ought to help Germany and in that way kill as many as possible.") Upon entering the White House, he did not seek to follow Roosevelt's tactics of adjustment and accommodation. Only eleven days in the presidency and virtually on the eve of the United Nations conference,

Truman moved to a showdown with Russia on the issue of Poland.

Poland became the testing ground for American foreign policy, as Truman later said, "a symbol of the future development of our international relations." At Yalta the three powers had agreed that the Soviet-sponsored Lublin Committee (the temporary Polish government) should be "recognized on a broader democratic basis with the inclusion of democratic leaders from Poland itself and from Poland abroad." The general terms were broad: there was no specific formula for the distribution of power in the reorganized government, and the procedures required consultation and presumably unanimity from the representatives of the three powers. The agreement, remarked Admiral Leahy, was "so elastic that the Russians can stretch it all the way from Yalta to Washington without ever technically breaking it." ("I know, Bill—I know it. But it's the best I can do for Poland at this time," Roosevelt replied.)

For almost two months after Yalta the great powers haggled over Poland. The Lublin Committee objected to the Polish candidates proposed by the United States and Great Britain for consultation because these Poles had criticized the Yalta accord and refused to accept the Soviet annexation of Polish territory (moving the eastern boundary to the Curzon Line). In early April Stalin had offered a compromise— that about 80 per cent of the cabinet posts in the new government should be held by members of the Lublin Committee, and that he would urge the committee to accept the leading Western candidates if they would endorse the Yalta agreement (including the Curzon Line). By proposing a specific distribution of power, Stalin cut to the core of the issue that had disrupted negotiations for nearly three months, and sought to guarantee the victory he probably expected in Poland. Roosevelt died before replying, and it is not clear whether he would have accepted this 4 to 1 representation; but he had acknowledged that he was prepared to place "somewhat more emphasis on the Lublin Poles."

Now Truman was asked to acknowledge Soviet concern about countries on her borders and to assure her influence in many of these countries by granting her friendly (and probably non-democratic) governments, and even by letting her squelch anti-communist democrats in countries like Poland. To the President and his advisers the issue was (as Truman later expressed Harriman's argument) "the extension of Soviet control over neighboring states by independent action; we were faced with a barbarian invasion of Europe." The fear was not that the Soviets were about to threaten all of Europe but that they had designs on Eastern Europe, and that these designs conflicted with traditional American values of self-determination, democracy, and open markets.

Rushing back to Washington after Roosevelt's death, Harriman found most of FDR's advisers (now Truman's) sympathetic to a tougher approach. At a special White House meeting Harriman outlined what he thought were the Soviet Union's two policies—cooperation with the United States and Great Britain, and the creation of a unilateral security ring through domination of its border states. These policies, he contended, did not seem contradictory to Russian leaders, for "certain elements around Stalin" misinterpreted America's generosity and desire to cooperate as an indication of softness and concluded "that the Soviet Government could do anything that it wished without having any trouble with the United States." Before Roosevelt's death, Harriman had cabled: "It may be difficult . . . to believe, but it still may be true that Stalin and Molotov considered at Yalta that by our willingness to accept a general wording of the declaration on Poland and liberated Europe, by our recognition of the need of the Red Army for security behind its lines, and of the predominant interest of Russia in Poland as a friendly neighbor and as a corridor to Germany, we understood and were ready to accept Soviet policies already known to us."

Harriman wanted the American government to select a few test cases and make the Russians realize they could not continue their present policies. Such tactics, he advised, would place Russian-American relations on a more realistic basis and compel the Soviet Union to adhere to the American interpretation of the issues in dispute. Because the Soviet government "needed our [economic assistance] . . . in their reconstruction," and because Stalin did not wish to break with the United States, Harriman thought Truman "could stand on important issues without running serious risks." As early as January 1944 Harriman had emphasized that "the Soviet Government places the utmost importance on our cooperation" in providing economic assistance, and he had concluded: "it is a factor which should be integrated into the fabric of our overall relations." In early April Harriman had proposed that unless the United States were prepared "to live in a world dominated largely by Soviet influence, we must use our economic power to assist those countries that are naturally friendly to our concepts." In turn, he had recommended "tying our economic assistance directly into our political problems with the Soviet Union.

General George Marshall, the Army Chief of Staff, and Secretary of War Henry Stimson, however, recommended caution. Stimson observed "that the Russians perhaps were being more realistic than we were in regard to their own security," and he feared "that we would find ourselves breaking our relations with Russia on the most important and difficult question which we and Russia have gotten between us." Leahy, though supporting a firm policy, admitted that the Yalta agreement "was susceptible to two interpretations." Secretary of State Edward Stettinius read aloud the Yalta decision and concluded "that this was susceptible of only one interpretation."

Having heard his advisers' arguments, Truman resolved to force the Polish question: to impose his interpretation of the Yalta agreement even if it destroyed the United Nations. He later explained that this was the test of Russian cooperation. If Stalin would not abide by his agreements, the U.N. was doomed, and, anyway, there would not be enough enthusiasm among the American electorate to let the United States join the world body. "Our agreements with the Soviet Union so far . . . [have] been a one-way street." That could not continue, Truman told his advisers. "If the Russians did not wish to join us, they could go to hell." ("FDR's appeasement of Russia is over," joyously wrote Senator Arthur Vandenberg, the Republican leader on foreign policy.) Continuing in this spirit at a private conference with Molotov, the new President warned that economic aid would depend upon Russian behavior in fulfilling the Yalta agreement. Brushing aside the diplomat's contention that the Anglo-American interpretation of the Yalta agreement was wrong, the President accused the Russians of breaking agreements and scolded the Russian Foreign Minister. When Molotov replied, "I have never been talked to like that in my life," Truman warned him, "Carry out your agreement and you won't get talked to like that."

At the United Nations conference in San Francisco, when Anthony Eden, the British Foreign Minister, saw a copy of Truman's "blunt message" about Poland to Stalin, "he could scarcely believe his eyes . . . and cheered loudly," reported Vandenberg. But the policy of firmness was not immediately successful. American-Russian relations were further strained by the disputes at the meeting to create the U.N.—over the veto, the admission of fascist Argentina, and the persistent question of Poland. Despite Soviet objections and Roosevelt's promise at Yalta to exclude Argentina from the U.N., the United States supported the Latin American state's candidacy for membership. In committee Molotov, whom Stalin had sent to establish good will with the new President, tried to block the admission of Argentina until the Lublin Poles were also admitted, but his proposed bargain was overwhelmingly defeated. Later in the plenary session, when only three nations voted with Russia, the Soviets found additional evidence for their fears of an American bloc directed against their interests. The Truman administration's action also gave the Soviets more reason to doubt America's explanations that her interests in Poland were inspired simply by a desire to guarantee representative, democratic governments. Moreover, because of the American bloc and Soviet fears that the U.N. (like the League of Nations) might be used against her, Molotov was at first unwilling to accede to the demands of the United States and the smaller nations who wished to exclude procedural questions before the Security Council from the great power veto.

The Soviets were further embittered when the United States abruptly curtailed lend-lease six days after V-E Day. Though Truman later explained this termination as simply a "mistake," as policy-making by subordinates, his recollection was incomplete and wrong. Leo Crowley, the director of lend-lease, and Joseph Grew, the Under Secretary of State, the two subordinates most closely involved, had repeatedly warned the President of the likely impact of such action on relations with Russia, and the evidence suggests that the government, as Harriman had counseled, was seeking to use economic power to achieve diplomatic means. Termination of lend-lease, Truman later wrote, "should have been done on a gradual basis which would not have made it appear as if somebody had been deliberately snubbed." Yet, despite this later judgment, Truman had four days after signing the order in which to modify it before it was to be implemented and announced, and the lend-lease administrator (in the words of Grew) had made "sure that the President understands the situation." The administrator knew "that we would be having difficulty with the Russians and did not want them to be running all over town for help." After discussing the decision with Truman, Grew, presumably acting with the President's approval, had even contrived to guarantee that curtailment would be a dramatic shock. When the Soviet chargé d'affaires had telephoned Grew the day before the secret order was to become effective, the Under Secretary had falsely denied that lend-lease to Russia was being halted. Harriman, according to Grew's report to the Secretary of State, "said that we would be getting 'a good tough slashback' from the Russians but that we would have to face it."

Presumably to patch the alliance, Truman dispatched to Moscow Harry Hopkin's, Roosevelt's former adviser and a staunch advocate of Soviet-American friendship. Hopkins denied that Truman's action was an American effort to demonstrate economic power and coerce Russia ("pressure on the Russians to soften them up," as Stalin charged). Instead he emphasized that "Poland had become a symbol of our ability to work out our problems with the Soviet Union." Stalin acknowledged "the right of the United States as a world power to participate in the Polish question," but he stressed the importance of Poland to Soviet security. Within twenty-five years the "Germans had twice invaded Russia via Poland," he emphasized. "All the Soviet Union wanted was that Poland should not be in a position to open the gates to Germany," and that required a government friendly to Russia. There was "no intention," he promised, "to interfere in Poland's internal affairs" or to Sovietize Poland.

Through the Hopkins mission, Truman and Stalin reached a compromise: 70 per cent of the new Polish government (fourteen of twenty ministers) should be drawn from the Lublin Committee. At the time there was reason to believe that such heavy communist influence would not lead to Soviet control. Stalin had reaffirmed the pledge of free elections in Poland, and Stanislaw Mikolajczyk, former Prime Minister of the exile government in London and Deputy Prime Minister in the new coalition government, was optimistic. He hoped (in Harriman's words) that "a reasonable degree of freedom and independence can be preserved now and that in time after conditions in Europe can become more stable and [as] Russian turns her attention to her internal development, controls will be relaxed and Poland will be able to gain for herself her independence of life as a nation even though he freely accepts that Poland's security and foreign policy must follow the lead of Moscow."

Truman compromised and soon recognized the new Polish government, but he did not lose his hopes of rolling back the Soviets from their spheres of influence in Eastern Europe. Basing most of his case on the Yalta "Declaration on Liberated Europe" (for which he relied on State Department interpretations), Truman hoped to force Russia to permit representative governments in its zones, and expected that free elections would diminish, perhaps even remove, Soviet authority. Refusing to extend diplomatic recognition to Rumania and Bulgaria, he emphasized that these governments were "neither representative of nor responsive to the will of the people."

"The opportunities for the democratic elements in Rumania and Bulgaria are not less than, say, in Italy, with which the Governments of of the United States and the Soviet Union have already resumed diplomatic relations," replied Stalin, who was willing to exaggerate to emphasize his case. The Russians were demanding a *quid pro quo,* and they would not yield. At Potsdam, in late July, when Truman demanded "immediate reorganization" of the governments of Hungary and Bulgaria to "include representatives of all significant democratic elements" and three-power assistance in "holding . . . free and unfettered elections," Stalin pointed to Greece, again to remind Truman of the earlier agreements. The Russians were "not meddling in Greek affairs," he noted, adding that the Bulgarian and Rumanian governments were fulfilling the armistice agreements while in Greece "terrorism rages . . . against democratic elements." (One member of the American delegation later claimed that Stalin at one point made his position clear, stating that "any freely elected government [in Eastern Europe] would be anti-Soviet and that we cannot permit.") In effect, Stalin demanded that the United States abide by his construction of earlier agreements, and that Truman acknowledge what Roosevelt had accepted as the terms of the sphere-of-influence agreements—that democratic forms and anti-communist democrats of Eastern Europe be abandoned to the larger cause of Russian-American concord.

Though the Allies at Potsdam were not able to settle the dispute over influence in Eastern Europe, they did reach a limited agreement on other European issues. In a "package" deal the Soviets accepted Italy in the U.N. after a peace treaty could be arranged; the United States and Great Britain agreed to set the temporary western border of Poland at the Oder-Neisse line; and the Soviets settled for far less in reparations than they had expected. The decisions on Germany were the important settlements, and the provision on reparations, when linked with American avoidance of offering Russia economic aid, left Russia without the assistance she needed for the pressing task of economic reconstruction.

Russia had long been seeking substantial economic aid, and the American failure to offer it seemed to be part of a general strategy. Earlier Harriman had advised "that the development of friendly relations [with Russia] would depend upon a generous credit," and recommended "that the question of the credit should be tied into our overall diplomatic relations with the Soviet Union and at the appropriate time the Russians should be given to understand that our willingness to cooperate wholeheartedly with them in their vast reconstruction problem will depend upon their behavior in international matters." In January 1945 Roosevelt had decided not to discuss at Yalta the $6 billion credit to the Soviet Union, explaining privately, "I think it's very important that we hold this back and don't give them any promises until we get what we want." (Secretary Morgenthau, in vigorous disagreement, believed that both the President and Secretary of State Stettinius were wrong, and "that if they wanted to get the Russians to do something they should . . . do it nice. . . . Don't drive such a hard bargain that when you come through it does not taste good.") In future months American officials continued to delay, presumably using the prospect of a loan for political leverage. Shortly before Postdam, the administration had secured congressional approval for a $1 billion loan fund which could have been used to assist Russia, but the issue of "credits to the Soviet Union" apparently was never even discussed.

Shunting aside the loan, the United States also retreated from Roosevelt's implied agreement at Yalta that reparations would be about $20 billion (half of which the Soviets would receive); Truman's new Secretary of State, James F. Byrnes, pointed out that the figures were simply the "basis" for discussion. (He was technically correct, but obviously Roosevelt had intended it as a general promise and Stalin had so understood it. Had it not been so intended, why had Churchill refused to endorse this section of the Yalta agreement?) Because Byrnes was unwilling to yield, the final agreement on reparations was similar to the terms that would have prevailed if there had been no agreement: the Soviet Union would fill her claims largely by removals from her own zone. That was the substance of the Potsdam agreement. The Russians also surrendered any hopes of participating in control of the heavily industrialized Ruhr, and confirmed the earlier retreat from the policy of dismemberment of Germany. They settled for an agreement that they could trade food and raw materials from their zone for 15 per cent of such industrial capital equipment from the Western Zones "as is unnecessary for the German peace economy," and that the allies would transfer from the Western Zones "10 percent of such industrial capital equipment as is unnecessary for the German peace economy"—but the agreement left undefined what was necessary for the economy.

Potsdam, like Yalta, left many of the great questions unresolved. "One fact that stands out more clearly than others is that nothing is ever settled," wrote Lord Alanbrooke, Chief of the British Staff, in his diary. As he observed, neither the United States nor Russia had yielded significantly. Russia had refused to move from the areas that her armies occupied, and the United States had been vigorous in her efforts, but without offering economic assistance to gain concessions. Though the atomic bomb may not have greatly influenced Truman's actions in the months before Potsdam, the bomb certainly influenced his behavior at Potsdam. When he arrived he still wanted (and expected) Russian intervention in the Japanese war. During the conference he learned about the successful test at Alamogordo. With Russian intervention no longer necessary, Truman's position hardened noticeably. As sole possessor of the bomb, he had good reason to expect easier future dealings with Stalin. For months Stimson had been counseling that the bomb would be the "master card," and Truman, acting on Stimson's advice, even delayed the Potsdam Conference until a time when he would know about the bomb. On the eve of the conference the President had confided to an adviser, "If it explodes, as I think it will, I'll certainly have a hammer on those boys [the Russians]."

III

At Potsdam President Truman was "delighted" when Stimson brought him the news about the bomb on July 16. Upon learning more about the results of the test, Truman (according to Stimson) said "it gave him an entirely new feeling of confidence and he thanked me for having come to the conference and being present to help him in this way." The President's enthusiasm and new sense of power were soon apparent in his meetings with the other heads of state, for as Churchill notes (in Stimson's words), "Truman was evidently much fortified by something that had happened and . . . he stood up to the Russians in a most emphatic and decisive manner." After reading the full report on the Alamogordo explosion, Churchill said. "Now I know what happened to Truman yesterday. I couldn't understand it. When he got to the meeting after having read this report he was a changed man. He told the Russians just where they got off and generally bossed the whole meeting."

"From that moment [when we learned of the successful test] our outlook on the future was transformed," Churchill explained later. Forced earlier to concede parts of Eastern Europe to the Russians because Britain did not have the power to resist Soviet wishes and the United States had seemed to lack the desire, Churchill immediately savored the new possibilities. The Prime Minister (Lord Alanbrooke wrote in his diary about Churchill's enthusiasm) "was completely carried away . . . we now had something in our hands which would redress the balance with the Russians. The secret of this explosive and the power to use it would completely alter the diplomatic equilibrium. . . . Now we had a new value which redressed our position (pushing out his chin and scowling); now we could say, 'If you insist on doing this or that well . . . And then where were the Russians!'"

Stimson and Byrnes had long understood that the bomb could influence future relations with Russia, and, after the successful test, they knew that Russian entry was no longer necessary to end the Japanese war. Upon Truman's direction, Stimson conferred at Potsdam with General Marshall and reported to the President that Marshall no longer saw a need for Russian intervention. "It is quite clear," cabled Churchill from Potsdam, "that the United States do not at the present time desire Russian participation in the war against Japan."

"The new explosive alone was sufficient to settle matters," Churchill reported. The bomb had displaced the Russians in the calculations of American policy-makers. The combat use of the bomb, then, was not viewed as the only way to end the Far Eastern war promptly. In July there was ample evidence that there were other possible strategies—a noncombat demonstration, a warning, a blockade. Yet, before authorizing the use of the bomb at Hiroshima, Truman did not try *any* of the possible strategies, including the three most likely: guaranteeing the position of the Japanese Emperor (and hence making surrender conditional), seeking a Russian declaration of war (or announcement of intent), or waiting for Russian entry into the war.

As an invasion of the Japanese mainland was not scheduled until about November 1, and as Truman knew that the Japanese were sending out "peace feelers" and that the main obstacle to peace seemed to be the requirement of unconditional surrender (which threatened the position of the Emperor), he could wisely have revised the terms of surrender. At first Under Secretary of State Grew and then Stimson had urged Truman earlier to revise the terms in this way, and he had been sympathetic. But at Potsdam Stimson found that Truman and Byrnes had rejected his advice. As a result the proclamation issued from Potsdam by the United States, Great Britain. and China retained the demand for unconditional surrender when a guarantee of the Emperor's government might have removed the chief impediment to peace.

Nor was Truman willing to seek a Russian declaration of war (or even an announcement of intent). Even though American advisers had long believed that the *threat* of Russian entry might be sufficient to compel Japanese capitulation, Truman did not invite Stalin to sign the proclamation, which would have constituted a statement of Russian intent. There is even substantial evidence that Truman sought to delay Russian entry into the war.

Pledging to maintain the position of the Emperor, seeking a Russian declaration of war (or announcement of intent), awaiting Russian entry—each of these options, as well as others, had been proposed in the months before Hiroshima and Nagasaki. Each was available to Truman. Why did he not try one or more? No *definite* answer is possible. But it is clear that Truman was either incapable or unwilling to reexamine his earlier assumption (or decision) of using the bomb. Under the tutelage of Byrnes and Stimson, Truman had come to assume by July that the bomb should be used, and perhaps he was incapable of reconsidering this strategy because he found no compelling reason not to use the bomb. Or he may have consciously rejected the options because he wanted to use the bomb. Perhaps he was vindictive and wished to retaliate for Pearl Harbor and other atrocities. (In justifying the use of the bomb against the Japanese, he wrote a few days after Nagasaki, "The only language they seem to understand is the one we have been using to bombard them. When you have to deal with a beast you have to treat him as a beast.") Or, most likely, Truman agreed with Byrnes that using the bomb would advance other American policies: it would end the war before the Russians could gain a hold in Manchuria, it would permit the United States to exclude Russia from the occupation government of Japan, and it would make the Soviets more manageable in Eastern Europe. It would enable the United States to shape the peace according to its own standards.

At minimum, then, the use of the bomb reveals the moral insensitivity of the President—whether he used it because the moral implications did not compel a reexamination of assumptions, or because he sought retribution, or because he sought to keep Russia out of Manchuria and the occupation government of Japan, and to make her more manageable in Eastern Europe. In 1945 American foreign policy was not innocent, nor was it unconcerned about Russian power, nor did it assume that the United States lacked the power to impose its will on the Russian state, nor was it characterized by high moral purpose or consistent dedication to humanitarian principles.

IV

Both Secretary of War Stimson and Secretary of State Byrnes had foreseen the importance of the bomb to American foreign policy. To Stimson it had long promised to be the "master card" for diplomacy. After Hiroshima and Nagasaki Byrnes was eager to use the bomb as at least an "implied threat" in negotiations with Russia. and Truman seems to have agreed to a vigorous course in trying to roll back Russian influence in Eastern Europe.

Truman seemed to be rejecting Stimson's recommendations that international control of atomic energy be traded for important Russian concessions—"namely the settlement of the Polish, Rumanian, Yugoslavian, and Manchurian problems." In his report on the Potsdam Conference the day after the second bomb, the President asserted that Rumania, Bulgaria, and Hungary "are not to be the spheres of influence of any one power" and at the same time proclaimed that the United States would be the "trustees" of the atomic bomb.

Following Truman's veiled threat, Byrnes continued his efforts to roll back the Soviet Union's influence. Assisted by a similar protest by the British, who clearly recognized the power of the bomb, he gained postponement of the Bulgarian election, charging that the government was not "adequately representative of important elements . . . of democratic opinion" and that its arrangements for elections "did not insure freedom from the fear of force or intimidation." In Hungary, Russia also acceded to similar Anglo-American demands and postponed the scheduled elections. It is not unreasonable to conclude that the bomb had made the Russians more tractable. "The significance of Hiroshima was not lost on the Russians," Alexander Werth, British correspondent in the Soviet Union, later reported. "It was clearly realized that this was a New Fact in the world's power politics, that the bomb constituted a threat to Russia. . . . Everybody . . . believed that although the two [atomic] bombs had killed or maimed [the] . . . Japanese, their real purpose was, first and foremost, to intimidate Russia."

Perhaps encouraged by his successes in Bulgaria and Hungary, Byrnes "wished to have the implied threat of the bomb in his pocket during the [September] conference" of foreign ministers in London. Stimson confided to his diary that Byrnes "was very much against any attempt to cooperate with Russia. His mind is full of his problems with the coming meeting . . . and he looks to having the presence of the bomb in his pocket . . . as a great weapon to get through the thing he has. He also told me of a number of acts of perfidy . . . of Stalin which they had encountered at Potsdam and felt in the light of those that we would not rely upon anything in the way of promises from them."

The London conference ended in deadlock, disbanding without even a joint communiqué. Despite American possession of the bomb, Molotov would not yield to American demands to reorganize the governments of Bulgaria and Rumania. In turn, he demanded for Russia a role in the occupation government of Japan, but Byrnes rebuffed the proposal. Unprepared for this issue, Byrnes was also unwilling or unable to understand Soviet anxieties about the security of their frontiers, and he pressed most vigorously for the reorganization of the Rumanian government. He would not acknowledge and perhaps could not understand the dilemma of his policy: that he was supporting free elections in areas (particularly in Rumania) where the resulting governments would probably be hostile to the Soviet Union, and yet he was arguing that democracy in Eastern Europe was compatible with Soviet demands for security. Unable to accept that Byrnes might be naive, Molotov questioned the Secretary's sincerity and charged that he wanted governments unfriendly to the Soviet Union. From this, Byrnes could only conclude later, "It seemed that the Soviet Union was determined to dominate Europe."

While the United States in the cases of these Eastern European nations chose to support traditional democratic principles and neither to acknowledge its earlier agreements on spheres of influence nor to respect Russian fears, Byrnes would not admit the similarity between Russian behavior in Rumania and British action in Greece. As part of the terms of his agreement with Churchill, Stalin had allowed the British to suppress a revolutionary force in Greece, and as a result the Greek government could not be accurately interpreted as broadly representative nor as a product of democratic procedures. Yet, as Molotov emphasized, the United States had not opposed British action in Greece or questioned the legitimacy of that government, nor was the United States making a reversal of British imperialism in Greece a condition for the large loan that Britain needed.

Some American observers, however, were aware of this double standard. In the northern Pacific and in Japan, America was to have the deciding voice, but in Eastern Europe, emphasized Walter Lippmann, "we invoke the principle that this is one world in which decisions must not be taken unilaterally." Most Americans did not see this paradox, and Byrnes probably expressed crystallizing national sentiment that autumn when he concluded that the dispute with Russia was a test of whether "we really believed in what we said about one world and our desire to build collective security, or whether we were willing to accept the Soviet preference for the simpler task of dividing the world into two spheres of influence."

Despite Byrnes's views, and although he could not secure a reorganization of the Rumanian government, communist influence was weakened in other parts of Eastern Europe. In Budapest free elections were held and the Communist party was routed; and early in November, just two days after the United States recognized Hungary, the Communists lost in the national elections there. In Bulgaria elections took place in "complete order and without disturbance," and despite American protests, a Communist-dominated single ticket (representing most of the political parties) triumphed.

While the Soviet Union would not generally permit in Eastern Europe conditions that conformed to Western ideals, Stalin was pursuing a cautious policy and seeking accommodation with the West. He was willing to allow capitalism but was suspicious of American efforts at economic penetration which could lead to political dominance. Though by the autumn of 1945 the governments in Russia's general area of influence were subservient in foreign policy, they varied in form and in degree of independence—democracy in Czechoslovakia (the only country in this area with a democratic tradition), free elections and the overthrow of the Communist party in Hungary, a Communist-formed coalition government in Bulgaria, a broadly based but Communist-dominated government in Poland, and a Soviet-imposed government in Rumania (the most anti-Russian of these nations). In all of these countries Communists controlled the ministries of interior (the police) and were able to suppress anti-Soviet groups, including anti-communist democrats.

Those who have attributed to Russia a policy of inexorable expansion have often neglected this immediate postwar period, or they have interpreted it simply as a necessary preliminary (a cunning strategy to allay American suspicions until the American Army demobilized and left the continent) to the consolidation and extension of power in east-central Europe, From this perspective, however, much of Stalin's behavior becomes strangely contradictory and potentially self-defeating. If he had planned to create puppets rather than an area of "friendly governments," why (as Isaac Deutscher asks) did Stalin "so stubbornly refuse to make any concessions to the Poles over their eastern frontiers?" Certainly, also, his demand for reparations from Hungary, Rumania, and Bulgaria would have been unnecessary if he had planned to take over these countries. (America's insistence upon using a loan to Russia to achieve political goals, and the nearly twenty-month delay after Russia first submitted a specific proposal for assistance, led Harriman to suggest in November that the loan policy "may have contributed to their [Russian] avaricious policies in the countries occupied or liberated by the Red Army.")

Russian sources are closed, so it is not possible to prove that Soviet intentions were conservative; nor for the same reason is it possible for those who adhere to the thesis of inexorable Soviet expansion to prove their theory. But the available evidence better supports the thesis that these years should be viewed not as a cunning preliminary to the harshness of 1947 and afterward, but as an attempt to establish a *modus vivendi* with the West and to protect "socialism in one country." This interpretation explains more adequately why the Russians delayed nearly three years before ending dissent and hardening policies in the countries behind their own military lines. It would also explain why the Communist parties in France and Italy were cooperating with the coalition governments until these parties were forced out of the coalitions in 1947. The American government had long hoped for the exclusion of these Communist parties, and in Italy, at least, American intimations of greater economic aid to a government without Communists was an effective lever. At the same time Stalin was seeking to prevent the revolution in Greece.

If the Russian policy was conservative and sought accommodation (as now seems likely), then its failure must be explained by looking beyond Russian actions. Historians must reexamine this period and reconsider American policies. Were they directed toward compromise? Can they be judged as having sought adjustment? Or did they demand acquiescence to the American world view, thus thwarting real negotiations?

There is considerable evidence that American actions clearly changed after Roosevelt's death. Slowly abandoning the tactics of accommodation, they became even more vigorous after Hiroshima. The insistence upon rolling back Soviet influence in Eastern Europe, the reluctance to grant a loan for Russian reconstruction, the inability to reach an agreement on Germany, the maintenance of the nuclear monopoly—all of these could have contributed to the sense of Russian insecurity. The point, then, is that in 1945 and 1946 there may still have been possibilities for negotiations and settlements, for accommodations and adjustments, if the United States had been willing to recognize Soviet fears, to accept Soviet power in her areas of influence, and to ease anxieties.

V

In October 1945 President Truman delivered what Washington officials called his "getting tough with the Russians" speech. Proclaiming that American policy was "based firmly on fundamental principles of righteousness and justice," he promised that the United States "shall not give our approval to any compromise with evil." In a veiled assault on Soviet actions in Eastern Europe, he declared, "We shall refuse to recognize any government imposed on any nation by the force of any foreign power." Tacitly opposing the bilateral trading practices of Russia, he asserted as a principle of American foreign policy the doctrine of the "open door"—all nations "should have access on equal terms to the trade and the raw materials of the world." At the same time, however, Truman disregarded the fact of American power in Latin America and emphasized that the Monroe Doctrine (in expanded form) remained a cherished part of American policy there: ". . . the sovereign states of the Western Hemisphere, without interference from outside the Western Hemisphere, must work together as good neighbors in the solution of their common economic problems."

"Soviet current policy," concluded a secret report by the Deputy Director of Naval Intelligence a few months later, "is to establish a Soviet Monroe Doctrine for the area under her shadow, primarily and urgently for security, secondarily to facilitate the eventual emergence of the USSR as a power which could not be menaced by any other world combination of powers." The report did not expect the Soviets ". . . to take any action during the next five years which might develop into hostilities with Anglo-Americans," but anticipated attempts to build up intelligence and potential sabotage networks, "encouragement of Communist parties in all countries potentially to weaken antagonists, and in colonial areas to pave the way for 'anti-imperialist' disorders and revolutions as a means of sapping the strength of . . . chief remaining European rivals, Britain and France." "Present Soviet maneuvers to control North Iran," the report explained, were conceived to "push . . . from their own oil . . . and closer to the enemy's oil." There was no need to fear military expansion beyond this security zone, suggested the report, for the Soviet Union was economically exhausted, its population undernourished and dislocated, its industry and transportation "in an advanced state of deterioration." Despite suggestions that Soviet policy was rather cautious, Truman was reaching a more militant conclusion. "Unless Russia is faced with an iron fist and strong language," asserted Truman to his Secretary of State in January, "another war is in the making. Only one language do they understand—'how many divisions have you' . . . I'm tired of babying the Soviets."

During the winter months Byrnes, Senator Vandenberg, and John Foster Dulles, a Republican adviser on foreign policy, publicly attacked Russian policies. Vandenberg warned "our Russian ally" that the United States could not ignore "a unilateral gnawing away at the status quo." After these attacks, Churchill, accompanied by the President, delivered at Fulton, Missouri, a speech that announced the opening of the Cold War. "From Stettin in the Baltic to Trieste in the Adriatic, an iron curtain has descended across the Continent," declared the former British war leader. Condemning the establishment of "police governments" in Eastern Europe and warning of "Communist fifth columns or . . . parties elsewhere," Churchill, with Truman's approval, called for an Anglo-American alliance to create "conditions of freedom and democracy as rapidly as possible in all [these] countries." The Soviet Union, he contended, did not want war, only "the fruits of war and the indefinite expansion of their power and doctrines." Such dangers could not be removed "by closing our eyes to them . . . nor will they be removed by a policy of appeasement." While he said that it was "not our duty *at this time* . . . to interfere forcibly in the internal affairs" of Eastern European countries, Churchill implied that intervention was advisable when Anglo-American forces were strengthened. His message was clear: ". . . the old doctrine of the balance of power is unsound. We cannot afford . . . to work on narrow margins, offering temptations to a trial of strength."

This was, as James Warburg later wrote, the early "idea of the containment doctrine . . [and] the first public expression of the idea of a 'policy of liberation,' " which Dulles would later promulgate. Truman's presence on the platform at Fulton implied that Churchill's statement had official American endorsement, and though the President lamely denied afterward that he had known about the contents of the speech, he had actually discussed it with Churchill for two hours. Despite official denials and brief, widespread popular opposition to Churchill's message (according to public opinion polls), American policy was becoming clearly militant. It was not responding to a threat of immediate military danger; it was operating from the position of overwhelming power, and in the self-proclaimed conviction of righteousness.

Undoubtedly Truman also agreed with the former Prime Minister when Churchill said at Fulton:

It would . . . be wrong and imprudent to intrust the secret knowledge of experience of the atomic bomb, which the United States, Great Britain and Canada now share, to the world organization. . . . No one in any country has slept less well in their beds because this knowledge and the method and raw material to apply it are at present . . . in American hands. I do not believe that we should all have slept so soundly had the positions been reversed and some Communist or neo-Fascist state monopolized, for the time being, these dread agencies. . . . Ultimately, when the essential brotherhood of man is truly embodied and expressed in a world organization, these powers may be confided to it.

Here, in classic form, was a theme that would dominate the American dialogue on the Cold War—the assertion of the purity of Anglo-American intentions and the assumption that the opposing power was malevolent and had no justifiable interests, no justifiable fears, and should place its trust in a Pax Americana (or a Pax Anglo-Americana). Under Anglo-American power the world could be transformed, order maintained, and Anglo-American principles extended. Stalin characterized Churchill's message as, "Something in the nature of an ultimatum: 'Accept our rule voluntarily, and then all will be well: otherwise war is inevitable.' "

VI

Churchill's assurances notwithstanding, Russia had reason to fear the atomic bomb, particularly after Byrnes's efforts to use it as an "implied threat." For Byrnes the nuclear monopoly seemed to promise the possibility of creating on American terms a lasting structure of peace. Since this monopoly would last at least seven years, according to his estimates, America could achieve its objectives and presumably avoid an arms race. (A few days after Hiroshima, Byrnes instructed J. Robert Oppenheimer, the nuclear physicist, that "for the time being . . . international agreement was not practical and that he and the rest of the gang should pursue their work [on the hydrogen weapon] full force.")

Byrnes's strategy was briefly and unsuccessfully challenged by another member of the administration, Henry Stimson. Earlier Stimson had hoped that America's possession of the bomb could lead to the offer of a partnership with the Russians in return for a *quid pro quo—*

"the settlement of the Polish, Rumanian, Yugoslavian, and Manchurian problems," and the liberalization of the Soviet regime. Russia would have to roll back her curtain of secrecy and move toward an open society, reasoned Stimson, for "no permanently safe international relations can be established between two such fundamentally different national systems." The bomb, he believed, could not be shared until Russia liberalized her regime, and he hoped that the need for international controls would pry back the lid of secrecy. But his conversations with Harriman at Potsdam had made Stimson pessimistic about Russia's easing her restrictions, and after the bombing of Japan, as he watched Byrnes's strategy unfolding, he moved more strongly toward international cooperation. On September 5 the Secretary of War met with the President, explaining "that both my plan and Byrnes's plan contained chances which I outlined and I said that I thought that in my method there was less danger than in his and also we would be on the right path towards establishment of an international world, while on his plan we would be on the wrong path in that respect and would be tending to revert to power politics."

Rejecting his earlier idea of using possession of the bomb "as a direct lever" to produce "a change in Russian attitudes toward individual liberty," Stimson urged the President to invite the Soviet Union to share the secret "upon a basis of cooperation and trust."

It is true [he wrote to the President] if we approach them now, as I would propose, we may be gambling on their good faith and risk their getting into production of bombs sooner than they would otherwise. To put the matter concisely, I consider the problem of our satisfactory relations with Russia as not merely connected with but virtually dominated by the problem of the atomic bomb. Except for the problem of the control of that bomb, those relations, while vitally important, might not be immediately pressing. The establishment of relations of mutual confidence between her and us could afford to await the slow process of time. But with the discovery of the bomb, they become immediately emergent. *Those relations may be irretrievably embittered by the way in which we approach the solution of the bomb with Russia. For if we fail to approach them now and merely continue to negotiate with them, having this weapon rather ostentatiously on our hip, their suspicions and their distrust of our purposes and motives will increase.*

"The chief lesson I have learned in a long life," concluded Stimson, "is the only way you can make a man trustworthy is to trust him; and the surest way you can make a man untrustworthy is to distrust him and show your distrust." A week after learning that Byrnes planned to use the bomb as an "implied threat," Stimson warned Truman that a direct and forthright approach should be made before using "*express or implied threats* in our peace negotiations."

While Byrnes was at the unsuccessful London conference in mid-September, Stimson was lining up support for his new approach. The President seemed to approve of Stimson's memorandum. Truman "thought that we must take Russia into our confidence," wrote Stimson in his diary. Dean Acheson, the Under Secretary of State, also seemed "strongly on our side in the treatment of Russia," Stimson recorded. Robert P. Patterson, Stimson's Under Secretary who was scheduled to replace the Secretary upon his retirement later in the month, was convinced (in Stimson's words): "The safest way is not to try to keep the secret. It evidently cannot be kept . . . and that being so it is better to recognize it promptly and try to get on [better] terms with the Russians."

At a special cabinet meeting on September 21, Stimson outlined his proposal: "(1) that we should approach Russia at once with an opportunity to share on proper *quid pro quo* the bomb and (2) that this approach to Russia should be to her directly and not through the . . . [United Nations] or a similar conference of a number of states." He received support from Patterson, Robert Hannegan, the Postmaster General, Henry Wallace, the Secretary of Commerce, and Acheson, who was representing the State Department in Byrnes's absence. Explaining that he could not "conceive of a world in which we were hoarders of military secrets from our Allies, particularly this great Ally," Acheson (reported Forrestal) "saw no alternative except to give the full information to the Russians . . . for a *quid pro quo*."

Forrestal, Fred Vinson, the Secretary of the Treasury, Tom Clark, the Attorney General, and Clinton Anderson, the Secretary of Agriculture, opposed sharing the secret. Vinson compared it to the decision at the end of World War I to sink ships, and Anderson emphasized that the President must retain the confidence of the nation in his ability to "handle Russia." He warned that giving up information on atomic energy and the bomb would dangerously weaken that confidence. Forrestal, apparently the most vigorous opponent, objected to any attempt to "buy [Russian] understanding and sympathy. We tried that once with Hitler." Concluding that "trust had to be more than a one-way street," he recommended that the United States exercise "a trusteeship over the . . . bomb on behalf of the United Nations."

Twelve days later, on October 3, Truman publicly announced his decision: the United States would seek international control of atomic energy but would not share the secret of the bomb. Byrnes, who had just returned from the London conference, resisted even this plan: he opposed the sharing of any information with the Russians. Since he believed that his diplomacy had been frustrated by Russian secrecy and suspicions, he did not see how inspection could operate. Convinced that the United States should delay until it had achieved a "decent" peace, he urged the President to stall. He realized that the United States was relying more heavily on the bomb and sharply cutting back conventional forces, and he was unwilling to risk yielding nuclear mastery.

For more than two months the American government delayed even approaching the Russians. "The insistence by the inventors of mankind's most horrible weapon on withholding the secret from their ally has produced a most evident reaction in Moscow," reported the *New York Times*. It also led to Molotov's uneasy public boasting in November that Russia too would develop the bomb. ("We will have atomic energy and many other things too.") Finally, four months after Hiroshima, at the Moscow Conference of Foreign Ministers in late December, Byrnes invited Russia to join in recommending that the United Nations establish a commission on atomic energy.

During the next five months, while the Cold War intensified, the Truman administration organized to formulate a policy. In March it released a preliminary study (the Acheson-Lilienthal report) which sought to minimize the problems of inspection by recommending the establishment of an international Atomic Development Authority (ADA), which would control all significant nuclear activities. The ADA would be established in stages, and at each stage the United States would provide the necessary information, with the specific information on the bomb withheld until the final stage.

Probably this plan would have been unacceptable to the Russians. It would have left the secret of the bomb as an American trust for at least a few years, and it would have meant Russia's relinquishing possible control of a source of great economic potential to an international authority dominated by Western powers. In its emphasis, however, the report also conflicted with the desires of many American officials. It stressed generosity and negotiations when most were emphasizing fear and suspicion. It saw no need for punishment. A violation by any nation, under the proposed arrangements, would have been obvious and would have been a warning to other nations, and all would have returned at that point to big-power politics. The plan emphasized the necessity of international control and was willing to countenance small risks for world security when most emphasized the primacy of American security. ("We should not under any circumstances throw away our gun until we are sure that the rest of the world can't arm against us," asserted Truman.)

The final American plan was formulated and presented by Bernard Baruch, whom Truman had appointed as American representative to the U.N. Atomic Energy Commission. It emphasized "sanctions" and "condign punishments," and called for the elimination of the Security Council veto on matters of atomic energy. The issue of the veto was unnecessary; if any nation violated the treaty after the sharing of atomic energy, what action could be vetoed? In turn, until the nations reached the last stages of the plan, a violation, whatever the situation in the U.N., would lead to the withdrawal of other nations from the plan. Also, rather than following Stimson's advice and first approaching the Soviets privately on control of atomic energy, Baruch insisted upon negotiations in the public forum where positions could easily harden. Lacking the flexibility of the earlier plan but relying upon similar stages, the Baruch plan guaranteed the United States a nuclear monopoly for some years. Thus it left the United States with the option of using the bomb for leverage or even blackmail. While Byrnes and Truman may no longer have wanted to use the bomb as an "implied threat," its value was clear to the Joint Chiefs of Staff who had so counseled Baruch. The atomic bomb, "because of its decisive power is now an essential part of our military strength," explained General Carl

Spaatz, the Air Force Chief of Staff. "Our monopoly of the bomb, even though it is transitory, may well prove to be a critical factor in our efforts to achieve [peace]." Separately the military chiefs had outlined the strategy which the Baruch plan followed: "We should exploit [the nuclear monopoly] to assist in the early establishment of a satisfying peace. . . . It will be desirable for international agreements concerning the atomic bomb to follow the European peace treaties and definitely to precede the time when other countries would have atomic bombs."

Though the Western world generally viewed the plan as magnanimous and interpreted Russia's objections as further evidence of her refusal to negotiate sincerely, the Soviet criticisms were actually quite reasonable. The Baruch plan in its early stages *did* endanger Soviet security. Russia would have had to allow investigations of natural resources and mapping of the interior—thus surrendering a principal military advantage. The Baruch plan, charged Molotov, "proceeds from the desire to secure for the United States the monopolistic possession of the bomb." (Vandenberg had reportedly told Molotov privately, "We have the atomic bomb and we are not going to give it up. We are not going to compromise or trade with you. We are not going to give up our immortal souls.") American leaders, as the Soviets understood, were demanding absolute security for their own nation and refusing to trust Russia at the same time that they were demanding that the Soviets trust the United States and risk the possibility of having the American nuclear monopoly frozen.

The Russian plan, on the other hand, was clearly unacceptable to American leaders. It called for nuclear disarmament and the sharing of secrets first while delaying the establishment of controls. In effect it asked the United States to surrender its nuclear advantage and promised that the nations could thereafter wrestle with the problems of controls. For the Truman administration the Russian plan was further evidence of Soviet insincerity. American leaders could not understand objections to the suspension of the veto, nor, perhaps, why the Soviets feared a plan that could guarantee the American monopoly. Yet Baruch had been explicitly counseled earlier on the advantages of the monopoly, Byrnes had tried to exploit the monopoly, and presumably Truman had understood it. Perhaps because these men so thoroughly believed that their intentions were honorable, that their aim was to establish a just and lasting peace, and that the United States would never use the bomb first, they could not grant the validity of Soviet objections.

Truman and Foreign Policy: The Korean War

WALTER LA FEBER

*Doubts about whether the United States should ever have intervened in
Vietnam have inevitably encouraged reconsideration of our earlier intervention in Korea. There are certain—perhaps superficial—similarities
between the two situations. Both were unpopular wars, demoralizing to
the troops, misunderstood at home, and fought with a mixture of technical brilliance and gross miscalculation. When in Korea the aggressive
American drive northward brought on the subsequent Chinese intervention, American officials, political and military, were caught as unprepared as they were later to be for the Tet offensive of early 1968.
Exactly whom we were fighting—apart from the abstraction of communism—was almost as mysterious in Korea as in Vietnam. And the political repercussions of Korea—the McCarthy era at home—continue to
haunt those who uneasily await the final reaction to Vietnam.*

*Unpopular as it was, the Korean war was relatively short and
quickly forgotten. Americans were satisfied that they had taught the
Communists a lesson—no longer would attempts to absorb (or snatch)
territory go unchallenged. Only with the rise of Cold-War revisionism
in the 1960s was the Korean conflict evaluated afresh. Walter LaFeber,
whose careful study of the Cold War has probably gained a wider acceptance than any other work of revisionism, considers the Korean war
in the context of a global design for an American-sponsored world
order. He suggests that long-range objectives involving Europe, all of
Asia, and the Pacific shaped American policy in Korea. The Communist
adventure in Korea thus provided an opportunity for American policy-
makers to define international power relations for a number of years
thereafter.*

In June 1950, Korea was a Cold War-wracked country which lacked
everything except authoritarian governments, illiteracy, cholera epi-
demics, and poverty. For nearly a century, it had been a pawn in Far
Eastern power plays. In 1905, Japan, after using force to stop a Russian
thrust, had established a protectorate over Korea and in 1910 annexed
that country. When the Japanese surrendered Korea in 1945, it became
a testing ground in the renewed battle between Russia and the United
States. After setting up dependent but Korean-led governments in zones
seized from the Japanese, Russia and the United States evacuated their
occupation armies in 1948 and 1949, respectively. In March 1949, North
Korea and the Soviets signed an agreement for economic cooperation.
Russian military advisers and aid strengthened a formidable 100,000-
man army. American military advisers also remained in the south, but
President Truman encountered difficulty sending large amounts of aid

to Syngman Rhee's government. At the end of June 1950, about $60 million of an allotted $110 million in economic aid had been shipped. Military assistance had scarcely begun. As at the turn of the century, Korea was a prize in the struggle between Russia and countries to the West; and, as in 1904, China, although now a very different China, stood apart from the conflict. Mao's regime devoted itself to internal reconstruction and drawing up plans for a probable invasion of Formosa sometime during 1950.

Mao had little cause to linger over Korean problems; South Korea itself posed no threat to his new government or, apparently, to the remainder of the Communist bloc. MacArthur and Acheson had defined Korea as beyond the perimeter of American military defenses, although not outside the realm of United Nations responsibility. It seemed possible, moreover, that without either Chinese or Russian overt pressure, the South Korean government might crumble. South Korea suffered under Rhee's authoritarian government until the State Department publicly protested his disregard of constitutional rights in early 1950. In an election in May, President Rhee's party collected only forty-eight seats as opposed to one hundred and twenty seats for the other parties; this defeat occurred despite Rhee's arrest of thirty political opponents in "anti-communist" raids just before the election was held. The Korean President pieced together a coalition government that began what promised to be a precarious, perhaps short, struggle to hold power.

On June 7 the northern government of Kim Il Sung attempted to exploit Rhee's problems by initiating an all-out campaign for peaceful reunification of the country through general elections. Rhee attempted to stop the news of this offer from circulating in the South. With that encouragement, the northern government reiterated the proposal on June 19 and intensified its political offensive.

This North Korean initiative apparently fitted within a general strategy which Stalin was designing to counter two threats. In mid-May, Truman announced that discussions on a Japanese peace treaty would receive high priority. The negotiations would particularly consider Japanese independence and the establishment of American military bases on Japan's soil under long-term agreements. The talks, American officials observed, would not be burdened with Russian representation. For Stalin this announcement opened the unhappy prospect of unity between the two greatest industrial nations in the Pacific, perhaps even the extension of a NATO-like organization on the Asian periphery of the Soviet Union. The Sino-Soviet pact in February had singled out Japan as a potential threat to Asian Communism, and this had been followed by the Soviet press accusing Truman with attempting to "draw the Asiatic and Pacific countries into aggressive military blocs, to entangle those countries in the chains of some 'little' Marshall Plan for Asia." On May 30, the Japanese Communist party climaxed weeks of demonstrations with attacks on United States military personnel in Tokyo. If North Korea could unify the country, peacefully or otherwise, the threat of a militarized, western-oriented Japan would be blunted, perhaps neutralized.

The second threat might well have caused Stalin even more concern. Mao's success had not created but probably encouraged revolutions throughout Asia, particularly in Indochina, the Philippines, and Indonesia. The possibility that some of these revolutions might triumph, perhaps following the pattern set by Mao, could weaken Stalin's two-camp premise and loosen his direction over the world Communist bloc. Stalin's view of world matters had become so rigid that he could not accept the nationalist content of these revolts without wrecking his own doctrines and tempering his grip on Soviet and satellite affairs. Malenkov had added to these troubles with his November speech, but by the spring of 1950 (that is, after the Chinese had shown their obstinacy in the Sino-Soviet negotiations and the revolutionary situation had intensified in Asia), Malenkov came back into line. In a speech in March, he no longer talked about the "friendly" nations surrounding Russia, but about a Europe, and especially Germany, which "fascist and revanchist forces," led by the United States, planned to turn into "a military-strategic bridgehead of American aggression." A speech by Molotov the same month was equally aggressive. Stalin had confined the domestic debate; a short and successful war by a Russian-controlled North Korea could intimidate Japan and check the expansive aims and reputation of Mao. On June 25, large numbers of North Korean troops moved across the 38th parallel which divided the country. They followed Soviet-built tanks which had been shipped to Korea during the previous two months.

Attending to family business in Independence, Missouri, when the attack occurred, Truman immediately returned to Washington. He and Acheson assumed the invasion was Russian-directed, perhaps the beginning of an extensive Sino-Soviet thrust. Their initial reaction, however, was carefully measured. They ordered MacArthur in Tokyo to dispatch supplies to the South Korean troops. Then, moving to contain the action, Truman ordered the American Seventh Fleet to sail between China and Formosa, and sent additional assistance to counter-revolutionary forces in the Philippines and Indochina. In a hurriedly called session of the United Nations Security Council, an American resolution branding the North Koreans as aggressors, demanding a cessation of hostilities, and requesting a withdrawal behind the 38th parallel, passed 9–0 with Yugoslavia abstaining. The Soviet Union was not represented, for Yakov Malik continued his boycott to protest the exclusion of Red China. Two days later, as the military situation worsened, Truman ordered American air and naval units into action. That same day, the 27th, the United Nations passed a resolution recommending that its members aid South Korea in restoring peace. This passed 74–1, with Yugoslavia opposing and Egypt and India abstaining. Malik still had not appeared; the rapidity and extent of Truman's reaction had taken the Soviets by surprise.

The day after American units had been committed, the President conferred with Congressional leaders for the first time to inform them of his action. The only strong objection was voiced by Senator Taft who approved of Truman's action but disliked the sending of Americans to war without consulting Congress. Neither then nor later did the President discuss Taft's objection with the full Congress. Two days later, on June 30, Truman made the final commitment. The South Korean army of 65,000 men had suffered heavy losses in the first week of fighting. The President decided that only American ground units could stop the southward flood. In sending these troops Truman emphasized that the United States aimed only "to restore peace there and . . . restore the border." Supporting air attacks were similarly to be limited to the area around the 38th parallel.

Throughout the first week of the war the President carefully refrained from publicly linking the Russians to the attack. He hoped thereby to enable them to stop the aggression without loss of public face. On June 27 Truman dispatched a note to Moscow assuring Stalin that American objectives were limited; the President expressed the hope that the Soviets would help in quickly restoring the *status quo ante bellum*. Truman's immense concern about potential Russian involvement motivated the American statement on June 30 that the United Nations wanted only to restore the parallel as the dividing line, and also resulted in Truman countermanding Air Force directives of July 6 which ordered high-level photo reconnaissance over Russian ports. The Soviets initially responded to Truman's overtures by accusing South Korean forces of invading North Korea. Within ten days this view underwent considerable change. The war was a "civil war among the Koreans," Deputy Minister of Foreign Affairs Andrei Gromyko claimed on July 4. Under these circumstances, Gromyko concluded, the Soviet Union could take no action.

Privately in June and publicly during the late summer, the Truman Administration became less restrained in defining the Soviet role. "In Korea the Russians presented a check which was drawn on the bank account of collective security," Acheson claimed. "The Russians thought the check would bounce. . . . But to their great surprise, the teller paid it." The terms "collective security" and "U.N. action" became the catchwords which supposedly explained and justified Truman's decisions in late June. Both terms were misleading. The United States had no collective security pact in the Pacific in 1950. If the Japanese occupation served as an example of how collective security worked in the abstract, the American exclusion of Australia and Great Britain from control of Japan between 1945 and 1950 twisted collective security to mean unilateralism. As Acheson used the term "collective security," it meant the United States would both define the extent of the "collective" and unilaterally, if necessary, furnish the "security." Nor is there any indication that the President consulted his European or Asian allies before committing American air and naval units on the 27th. This was not the first nor would it be the last time the United States would take unilateral action in an explosive situation without consulting its Western European partners.

As for the sudden American concern to bolster the United Nations, this had not been apparent when the United States acted unilaterally or with some Western powers to establish the Truman Doctrine, the Rio Pact, the Marshall Plan, and NATO. American actions in Korea were consistent with this history, for the United States used the June 27th resolution to establish a military command in Korea that took orders not from the United Nations but from Washington. "The entire control of my command and everything I did came from our own Chiefs of Staff," MacArthur later recalled. "Even the reports which were normally made by me to the United Nations were subject to censorship by our State and Defense Departments. I had no direct connection with the United Nations whatsoever." Sixteen nations finally contributed to "United Nations" forces, but the United States provided 50 percent of the ground forces (with South Korea providing most of the remainder), 86 percent of the naval power, and 93 percent of the air power. In October during the Truman-MacArthur conference at Wake Island, a dozen American officials prepared plans for the reconstruction of *all* Korea without consulting anyone, not even the United Nations or Syngman Rhee.

The American attitude toward the United Nations was exemplified on November 3, 1950 when American delegate John Foster Dulles successfully pushed through the General Assembly a "Uniting for Peace" proposal giving the Assembly the right to make recommendations to United Nations members for collective security measures, including the use of force, if the use of the veto stopped the Security Council from taking action. The resolution also established a permanent "Peace Observation Commission" to report on trouble spots around the world and, finally, invited members to contribute troops that could be used in a United Nations force. This resolution transfigured the United Nations. The organization no longer rested on agreements among the great powers, without which neither the United Nations nor world peace could be viable. Instead power was thrown into a body where Costa Rica had voting power equal to that of the United States or the Soviet Union. Weakening the Soviet veto, the United States also weakened its own. Assuming, however, that it could control the General Assembly, the Administration had taken a calculated risk; it had, to paraphrase Acheson, issued a blank check on the future. After a decade of increased neutralist feelings among the multiplying underdeveloped nations, that check would appear increasingly rubberized.

The United States suffered 142,000 casualties in Korea not for the sake of "collective security" or the United Nations, but because the Executive branch of the government decided that the invasion signaled a direct threat to American interests in both Asia and Europe. Europe, indeed, remained uppermost in the minds of high State Department officials. As the fighting raged in Korea, Acheson devoted increasing amounts of time to the European situation. The State Department had long defined Europe as having first importance. Acheson, moreover, had gotten burned politically and diplomatically when the Korean attack raised questions about his January 12th speech which termed the Communist threat in Asia one of "subversion and penetration," and not "military." This was a rare, probably traumatic, departure from his usual reliance upon military "positions of strength," and he moved quickly to improve the military balance in Europe. . . .

[Meanwhile,] American forces were advancing to greater victories in Korea. What magnifying effects a series of battle losses would have on Republican power and McCarthyism, Democrats did not wish to contemplate. General MacArthur had apparently removed this possibility on September 15 with a brilliant landing at Inchon, back of the North Korean lines, while simultaneously launching a counterattack from the shallow perimeter at Pusan. Within two weeks the United Nations forces joined to cut off large sections of North Korean troops. The Administration's political goals developed accordingly. In late June, Truman reported that the main objective was the restoration of the 38th parallel; on September 1, he told the nation that the Koreans "have a right to be free, independent, and united"; ten days later he approved a National Security Council recommendation that MacArthur should drive the North Koreans north of the 38th and, if encountering no Chinese or Russian troops, to move north of the parallel and prepare for occupation; on September 27, Truman ordered MacArthur north of the parallel; and on October 7, the General Assembly cooperated by endorsing Truman's order 47–5. That day the lead troops of the United States First Cavalry Division crossed into North Korea.

All eyes now turned to China. Throughout July and August, the new Communist government had made little response to the conflict. Recovering from famine, a quarter century of war, and having as her top diplomatic objective the conquest of Formosa, China did not pose an immediate threat to the United Nations forces. In late August, Foreign Minister Chou En-lai made his first important move. At the United Nations, American delegate Warren Austin asked for the open door "within all parts of Korea," and later in the month, Secretary of Navy Francis Matthews applauded "a war to compel co-operation for peace." At this point, Chou reminded the world that "Korea is China's neighbor" and urged that the neighbor's problems be settled "peacefully." Mass anti-American rallies began to appear in Chinese cities. Ten days after the Inchon landing Peking warned India, which had become China's main link with the Western world, that it would not "sit back with folded hands and let the Americans come to the border." After the first remnants of the North Korean troops retreated behind the 38th, Chou formally told India in a dramatic midnight meeting on October 2 that China would attack if United Nations troops moved into North Korea. The United States discounted this threat, believing that it was aimed at influencing upcoming votes on the conflict in the United Nations. MacArthur responded by issuing an ultimatum for the complete surrender of North Korea. On October 7, as the first American troops crossed the border, Chinese troop concentrations on the Manchurian border just across the Yalu River from Korea increased from 180,000 to 320,000. On October 16, a few Chinese "volunteers" crossed the Yalu.

The Truman Administration remained convinced that China would not intervene. Emphasizing, as he had in earlier speeches, that China's immediate concern was with Russian penetration in the north, Acheson commented on national television on September 10, 1950, "I should think it would be sheer madness" for the Chinese to intervene, "and I see no advantage to them in doing it." Acheson later admitted that until late September, American intelligence considered Chinese intervention improbable. On October 9, the danger reached the boiling point when two American F-80 jets strafed a Soviet airfield only a few miles from Vladivostok, a major Russian city close to the Korean border. After the Soviets strongly protested, the United States apologized. Vexed that such a crisis could arise, and angered that he had to back down before Soviet protests just a month before national elections, Truman cancelled a trip to Independence, where he was to watch his sister installed as Worthy Matron in the Order of Eastern Star, and flew to Wake Island to check on MacArthur's policies. In the heavily-censored text of that meeting, little was implied about Russia, but the General assured the President, "We are no longer fearful of [Chinese] intervention. We no longer stand hat in hand." The Chinese, he informed Truman, possessed no air force. They might move 50,000 or 60,000 men across the Yalu, but if these troops attempted to move farther south without air cover, "there would be the greatest slaughter."

Eleven days later, on October 26, the first Chinese prisoner was captured, "so that you began to know, at that point," Acheson later commented, "that something was happening." This realization, however, made little apparent impact on American policies during the next four weeks. On November 21, advanced elements of American troops peered at Chinese sentries stationed several hundred yards across the Yalu. Three days later, MacArthur grandly announced the launching of the end-the-war offensive. At this point the United States government was still not certain whether, in Acheson's words, the Chinese "were committed to a full-scale offensive effort." Two days later, on November 26, the Chinese moved across the river in mass, trapping and destroying large numbers of United Nations troops, including 20,000 Americans and Koreans at the Chosin Reservoir; this outfit finally escaped with 4400 battle casualties and 7000 noncombat casualties, mostly severe cases of frostbite. Three weeks later the retreating United Nations forces once again fought below the 38th parallel, and now it was Chou En-lai who proclaimed his nation's intention of reunifying Korea. "They really fooled us when it comes right down to it; didn't they?" Senator Leverett Saltonstall once asked Acheson. "Yes, sir," the Secretary of State replied.

Throughout September and October the United States had continually assured Peking that Americans never wanted to fight Chinese or threaten in any way China's vital interests. All the Administration wanted, the Secretary of State remarked on November 29, was to "repel the aggressors and restore to the people of Korea their independence." The Chinese retaliated precisely because they interpreted "independence" and Austin's request for "full access" to all Korea to mean the stationing of American power on China's doorstep. From there the United States could exert pressure on both Mao's internal and external policies. China's intense hatred for the West, a hate nurtured by the just-concluded century of western exploitation of China, and Mao's determination to restore Chinese supremacy in Asia made impossible the acceptance of such an American presence. Although historically accustomed to hairsplitting on points of diplomacy, the Chinese failed to see the difference between American presence on the Yalu and American danger to Chinese industries and politics just across the Yalu.

Soviet thinking during November and December was more inscrutable than usual, but Stalin seems to have agreed with the Chinese that the United States could not be allowed to conquer all of Korea. Chinese intervention was a preferred preventive because it would not involve Russian men or large Soviet resources. Stalin meanwhile attempted to use the Chinese successes to pressure the West into reversing German rearmament policies.

In Washington, Administration officials were thoroughly frightened, and Truman's response to the intervention was considerably more explicit than Stalin's. The President reiterated that the United States had no "aggressive intentions toward China," and believed that the Chinese people opposed this sending of troops by their leaders. (This remark was in line with Truman's general theory that Communism anywhere never had popular support.) Because these people could not be heard, the President continued, the aggression must be crushed or "we can expect it to spread throughout Asia and Europe to this hemisphere." As in late June, however, Truman's response was measured. He countermanded MacArthur's order to bomb Chinese troops and supplies in Manchuria. The President finally allowed only the Korean halves of the bridges crossing the Yalu to be bombed, a compromise that infuriated Mac-Arthur and told the Chinese exactly how restrained American retaliation to their intervention would be. In a news conference of November 30, Truman showed signs of losing this restraint. He intimated that the United States would use all the power it possessed to contain the Chinese, and he explicitly did not exclude using atomic bombs. This remark brought [British] Prime Minister Attlee flying to the United States on December 4.

Attlee was not without responsibility for the crises; his government had participated in the decision to send United Nations troops to the Yalu. He now worried that in the newly expanded war Truman would not be able to control the military, and particularly wondered at the spectacle of Truman flying 5000 miles to Wake Island to meet Mac-Arthur who had flown 1900. ("I thought it a curious relationship between a Government and a general," Attlee commented later.) The Prime Minister received Truman's assurances that the United States was not planning to use the bomb. The two men then undertook a full, candid, and most revealing evaluation of the Asian tinderbox.

Both agreed that a general war must be averted and that the United Nations forces should not evacuate Korea unless forced out militarily. Then basic differences emerged. Attlee argued that China's admission to the United Nations could bring her into regular consultations leading to a cease-fire. Acheson doubted that in their present advantageous military position the Chinese would want a cease-fire; if they did and negotiations resulted, Mao would next demand a United Nations seat and concessions on Formosa. The United States had refused to discusss these two items before the intervention and Acheson now was in no mood to reward aggressors. Attlee countered that a cease-fire would make explicit the divisions between China and Russia: "I want them [the Chinese] to become a counterpoise to Russia in the Far East," Attlee argued. If "we just treat the Chinese as Soviet satellites, we are playing the Russian game."

Truman now hardened his earlier view of the Chinese. They were "Russian satellites," and if they succeeded in Korea "it would be Indo-China, then Hong Kong, then Malaya." Acheson interposed that he did not think it mattered whether China was a satellite or not, for she would act like Russia anyway. He believed the invasion into Korea "had design," and, like Truman, adopted the domino theory to warn that any compromise with the Chinese would have a "serious" effect on the Japanese and Philippine islands. Acheson recalled a "saying among State Department officials that with communistic regimes you could not bank good will; they balanced their books every night." Therefore, he argued, the West must develop great military power to stop "this sort of thing from happening in the future." Acheson and Truman also reminded Attlee that the United States could not be "internationalist" in Europe and "isolationist" in Asia; domestic political pressures made that impossible.

At that point Attlee questioned the basic American premise, the fundamental belief that underlay United States policy in Europe as well as Asia. He emphasized that the United Nations must be kept together even if this meant alienating important segments of American public opinion. Whatever the United States and Great Britain did would have to be done through the United Nations, Attlee argued, and this could not be accomplished by the efforts and votes of only the United States and the United Kingdom, "important as we are." Truman and Acheson disagreed; they believed the two nations were "important" enough. By controlling the United Nations forces and now, apparently, the United Nations itself through the "Uniting for Peace" resolution, American officials believed they could keep the American people united, prevent a bigger war in Asia, follow an "internationalist" policy in both Europe and Asia, punish China for moving into Korea by excluding her from the United Nations and Formosa, build up great military power throughout the world, and through it all keep the other United Nations members in agreement with American policies. It was a tall order, so demanding and inflexible that it fixed the American position on China for the next fifteen years.

American intelligence estimates reinforced Truman's and Acheson's views. A December 13 report stated that the Soviet Union hoped to use the war to move American power away from Korea and Formosa, establish China as the dominant power in the Far East and seat her in the United Nations, eliminate American power in Japan, and prevent German rearmament. The Administration expected little help from the United Nations in thwarting these Soviet drives. The most the United Nations could do was brand the Chinese as aggressors, which it did on February 1, 1951 by a vote of 44–7 with 9 abstentions. As the United Nations debated, its forces retreated from the South Korean capital of Seoul.

Although the military situation steadily eroded, not even the other nations in the Western Hemisphere would offer much assistance. The Latin Americans dutifully voted with the United States on resolutions in the United Nations and the Organization of American States, but in the early spring of 1951, when Truman personally appealed to Latin American Foreign Ministers to "establish the principle of sharing our burdens fairly," only Colombia responded with troops. Several other nations sent materiel, but Latin America as a whole failed to see the relevance of Korea to their own economic deprivation and political instability. Later in 1951 a shocked Administration attempted to woo its southern neighbors by extending to them the Mutual Security Program of military aid. Eight nations took the money in 1952 to protect themselves against Communist aggression; this both giver and receiver interpreted to mean preservation of the *status quo*. No other Latin American nation, however, sent men to Korea.

The United States would have to depend primarily upon its own resources in defending what Niebuhr had called "our far-flung lines." In December and January, the President requested emergency powers to expedite war mobilization. Closely following the guidelines suggested in NSC-68, he submitted a $50 billion defense budget; this contrasted with the $13.5 billion budget of six months before. The Administration doubled the number of air groups to ninety-five and obtained new bases in Morocco, Libya, and Saudi Arabia. Army personnel increased 50 percent to 3.5 million men. Truman thereby placed the nation on the Cold War footing on which it would remain, with few exceptions, during the 1950s and 1960s.

The President also embarked the United States upon another costly and momentous journey by committing it to developing and protecting the Western Pacific and Southeast Asia. The riches of the area made it a formidable prize: Burma, Thailand, and Indochina provided rice for much of Asia; Southeast Asia produced nearly 90 percent of the world's natural rubber, 60 percent of the world's tin, and the bulk of Asia's oil. Movements toward independence threw the area into turmoil immediately after the war, but with several exceptions (particularly Vietnam and the Philippines where an Un-Filipino Activities Committee tried to aid the Army in ferreting out the "Huk" rebels), a semblance of order appeared by 1950. Attempted Communist uprisings had been contained in most countries by nationalist elements.

Throughout Asia these anticolonial, nationalist movements had triumphed either peacefully or after short struggles. Vietnam was a tragic exception. There Ho Chi Minh had conducted anti-Japanese underground operations during the war and emerged in 1946 as the leading Communist and nationalist leader. Roosevelt had pressured the French to evacuate Indochina in early 1945. De Gaulle resisted that pressure until the Truman Administration reversed the American policy in order to obtain French cooperation in Europe. After a year of uneasy truce with the French, who were determined to reclaim their control over Indochina, full-scale war broke out in December 1946. The French army moved back into Vietnam carrying large numbers of American lend-lease weapons to eradicate Ho's forces. The Soviets, like the United States, refused to recognize Ho's Republic of Vietnam. Typically distrusting such revolutionaries, Stalin, like Truman, concentrated on European problems in 1946 and early 1947. By 1948 Ho was turning to the Communist Chinese for aid. He had not easily reached this decision, for the Indochinese had historically feared and distrusted their giant neighbor. On January 18, 1950, China recognized Ho's government. The Soviets followed thirteen days later.

After an intensive policy review, the United States fully committed itself to the French cause. On February 6, four and one-half months before the Korean war began, the United States recognized the Bao Dai government which had been established by the French. On June 12, an American military advisory mission prepared to aid the French forces. As early as May, Truman discussed large-scale aid for Bao Dai, and after the Korean conflict, began to pump in aid at the rate of half a billion dollars per year. When French General de Lattre de Tassigny visited Washington in September 1951, the State Department endorsed French war aims and methods.

Although involving itself in the French struggle long before June 1950, the Korean war provided a convenient background as the United States began explaining its commitments in Vietnam. A State Department pamphlet of 1951 defined United States interests as the "much-needed rice, rubber, and tin," but added, "perhaps even more important would be the psychological effect of the fall of Indochina. It would be taken by many as a sign that the force of communism is irresistible and would lead to an attitude of defeatism." The statement concluded that "Communist forces there must be decisively conquered down to the last pocket of resistance," to accomplish this, large amounts of American aid had been given. "Without this aid," the analysis concluded, ". . . it is doubtful whether [Bao Dai and the French] could hold their ground against the Communists."

After mid-1950, Congress began its first systematic aid program to Southeast Asia. The Administration coupled with this economic approach a program for overall military security. The linchpin would necessarily be Japan, the most highly industrialized Asian nation and the only one capable of providing a counterpoise to the Chinese. For three years Truman had failed to write the peace treaty which would cement an independent Japan to the West. The Soviets naturally opposed the pact Truman had in mind, but another intra-Administration dispute between the Defense and State Departments also retarded progress. Defense feared a pact would weaken its hold on Japanese military bases, but State argued that healthy political relations demanded a new agreement.

In March 1950, John Foster Dulles assumed control of the negotiations and almost single-handedly drove the treaty through to a successful conclusion in September 1951. It was a bravura performance. He silenced Defense Department critics by giving them a separate security pact assuring American bases in Japan. Russia was simply excluded from the early, decisive negotiations while Dulles talked only with Japan. When the Soviets finally were asked to participate, Dulles interpreted their proposal as an attempt to dominate the area around Japan; he read out the Russian resolution, one participant later recalled, demonstrated its effect on a map, "took this map dramatically and held it up like this . . . and then threw it on the floor with the utmost contempt. And that made a tremendous impression."

After shrewd parliamentary maneuvering by Dulles, who led the American delegation, and Acheson, who chaired the conference, the treaty was signed by fifty-one nations at a San Francisco conference on September 8, 1951. Russia was not one of the signatories. The treaty restored Japanese sovereignty over the home islands, but not over the Ryukyus (which included the large American base at Okinawa) or the Bonin Islands; these remained in American hands. The agreement allowed Japanese rearmament and "the stationing or retention of foreign armed forces on Japanese territory." In the security pact signed the same day, Japan allowed the stationing of American troops and planes on her soil, but not those of any third power.

The Administration hoped that the treaty would serve as the basis for a long-lasting anti-Communist alliance. For this reason Dulles rode roughshod over demands from American allies and neutrals in Asia who demanded reparations from Japan for her occupation of those countries during World War II. Dulles retained vivid memories of how the Versailles Peace Conference in 1919, in which he had participated as a young economic adviser, had blundered by fastening unreasonably high reparations on Germany. Now, he warned, he would brook no "Carthaginian peace" which would "lead to bitter animosity and in the end drive Japan into the orbit of Russia." Many allies in the Pacific area also urged reparations in order to weaken Japanese war potential; their memories of 1941–1945 matched the vividness of Dulles' recollection of 1919. Dulles solved this problem by negotiating a series of mutual defense treaties to insure the Philippines, Australia, and New Zealand against both reemerging Asian giants, Japan and China. Thirty months before, Acheson had assured Senator Lodge that other than NATO, the Administration contemplated no further regional arrangements. On September 1, 1951 the United States signed with Australia and New Zealand the so-called ANZUS treaty, pledging the security of these two nations and establishing a foreign ministers council for regular consultation.

Because Australia and New Zealand belonged to the British Commonwealth, Great Britain was conspicuous by its absence from ANZUS. As early as March 1914, Winston Churchill, then First Lord of the Admiralty, predicted that with British resources increasingly devoted to Europe, the "white men" in the Pacific would soon have to seek American protection. Thirty-seven years later the British were not as understanding. Angered because Dulles had informed it neither of prior arrangements on the Japanese treaty nor of the discussions of ANZUS, the London government argued that ANZUS derogated British prestige and left the vital British areas of Hong Kong, Malaya, and Burma outside its defensive perimeter. Dulles granted these arguments, but countered that if Britain came in, the French and Dutch would also and thereby transform ANZUS in the eyes of suspicious Asians into a colonial alliance. This argument effectively reduced British influence in the Pacific. "All roads in the Commonwealth lead to Washington," a Canadian official observed.

These negotiations in late 1950 and 1951 determined the geographical extent of the American commitment in the Pacific. During the spring of 1951, with drama and flourishes seldom seen in American history, the military extent of that commitment was decided. In late January, United Nations forces opened a successful drive back to the 38th parallel. As the battle stalemated along the former boundary line, State Department and Pentagon officials cautiously explored the possibility of negotiations with the Chinese on March 20. Three days later General MacArthur issued a personal statement urging that the Red military commanders "confer in the field" with him on surrender; China is "doomed to imminent military collapse," the General proclaimed. Not for the first time had MacArthur undercut his superiors in Washington.

As early as July 1950, he had shown reluctance to accept Truman's decision that Chiang Kai-shek should be contained on Formosa rather than unleashed on the mainland or allowed to ship troops to Korea. A month later, MacArthur sent a message to the annual convention of the Veterans of Foreign Wars, which labeled as "appeasement" any policy that would restrain Chiang. Truman angrily demanded that this message be recalled, and MacArthur complied although it had already been published. The Wake Island conference muted these differences, but the published minutes are embarrassing in their revelation of MacArthur's incredible condescension and Truman's tittering insecurity. Once the President was back in Washington, this insecurity disappeared. After MacArthur again recommended a naval blockade of China, air attacks to level Chinese military and industrial installations, and the use of 30,000 Formosan troops in Korea, Truman patiently explained on January 13 "the political factors" involved in the "world-wide threat" of the Soviet Union which made containment of the Korean war necessary. When MacArthur issued his March 23rd ultimatum, Truman's patience, never inexhaustible, evaporated.

Only the method and timing of relieving the General remained to be decided. On April 5, Representative Joe Martin, the leading Republican in the House, read a letter from MacArthur which charged that "here we fight Europe's war with arms while the diplomats there still fight it with words." "We must win," the letter emphasized. "There is no substitute for victory." The Joint Chiefs of Staff agreed with Truman that MacArthur would have to be relieved immediately; reports from the field indicated that the General was losing the confidence of his men and had already lost confidence in himself. On April 11, the President recalled MacArthur.

Truman knew the political dynamite in the decision. Less than two weeks earlier he had agreed with top advisors that an all-out speaking campaign would have to be undertaken by Cabinet-level officers because the Administration's " 'story' was not reaching the American public." The American people preferred quick victory to containment. This preference was dramatically demonstrated when the General returned to the greatest popular reception in American history. Senator McCarthy expressed the feelings toward Truman of not a few Americans when with characteristic restraint he told a press conference, "The son of a bitch ought to be impeached." Congress warmly received MacArthur's speech before a joint session, then in April and May settled down to investigate the case of the President versus the General.

In a battle of MacArthur versus Truman, the long-range issues tended to be overshadowed by the personalities involved. In Mac-Arthur's case this was not an advantage. Having last set foot in the United States fourteen years before, the General seemed unable or unwilling to grasp the political and social as well as the diplomatic views of his country. He revealed much describing the power he wielded in Japan between 1945 and 1950: "I had not only the normal executive authorities such as our own President has in this country, but I had legislative authority. I could by fiat issue directives." Although he had repeatedly advocated policies which contained the most somber worldwide ramifications, he now admitted having only a "superficial knowledge" of NATO and European affairs.

His basic message was curiously close to Truman's and Niebuhr's in 1948: because Communism posed a threat to all civilization, "you have got to hold every place." Or again, "What I advocate is that we defend every place, and I say that we have the capacity to do it. If you say that we haven't you admit defeat." Like Acheson, he insisted on not putting military power and politics into the intellectual equivalent of a cream separator; in time of war, however, MacArthur demanded the reversal of Acheson's priority: once involved in war, the General argued, the military commander must be supreme over all military and political affairs in his theater, "or otherwise you will have the system that the Soviet once employed of the political commissar, who would run the military as well as the politics of the country." Such a remark cut across the grain of traditional American policies of subordinating military to civilian officials unless the nation was involved in total war. This Mac-Arthur assumed to be the case. When he heard the suggestion of Assistant Secretary of State Dean Rusk that war in Korea must not become a "general conflagration," MacArthur branded it "the concept of appeasement, the concept that when you use force, you can limit the force."

The General believed that by controlling the sea and air no one could "successfully launch an effort against us," but the United States could "largely neutralize China's capability to wage aggressive war and thus save Asia from the engulfment otherwise facing it." He expressed contempt for the Chinese Communists. "Never, in our day, will atomic weapons be turned out of China. They cannot turn out the ordinary weapons." Nor was there threat of Soviet intervention. Time, however, was short. If, as MacArthur once told Forrestal, Europe was a "dying system," and the Pacific would "determine the course of history in the next ten thousand years," victory must be won immediately. The "dreadful slaughter" had to end, MacArthur pleaded; American blood as well as dust is settling in Korea, and the "blood, to some extent" rests "on me." But now, he concluded emotionally, "There is no policy —there is nothing, I tell you, no plan, or anything."

The Administration had a plan, and Acheson outlined it in his testimony after MacArthur finished. Korea must be viewed as part of a "collective security system," Acheson argued. When so viewed two things readily became apparent. First, all-out war in Korea would suck in Russian force to aid Stalin's "largest and most important satellite." "I cannot accept the assumption that the Soviet Union will go its way regardless of what we do," the Secretary of State declared. If Russia did intervene, there could be "explosive possibilities not only for the Far East, but for the rest of the world as well." Unlike MacArthur, Acheson insisted on keeping the European picture uppermost in dealing with Korea. (Truman once added a variant on this: expansion of the war could "destroy the unity of the free nations," the President declared. "We cannot go it alone in Asia and go it with company in Europe.") Second, if Europe and the prevention of Russian entry in force did comprise the main objectives, American forces were not engaged in a "dreadful slaughter," or as Acheson remarked, "a pointless and inconclusive struggle," but had "scored a powerful victory" by dealing "Communist imperialist aims in Asia a severe setback" in preventing the armed conquest of all Korea.

MacArthur lost the argument. He lost it so decisively, moreover, that while negotiations to conclude a stalemated war fitfully began in Korea during the summer of 1951, Acheson accelerated the military buildup of Europe.

To Secure These Rights

THE PRESIDENT'S COMMITTEE
ON CIVIL RIGHTS, 1947

The American Negro Revolution is popularly dated from the Supreme Court's 1955 school desegregation decision, the celebrated Brown v. Board of Education. *But the two main features of the civil rights movement, the militancy of black Americans and the activist role of the federal government, have much earlier origins. The first can be traced at least as far back as W. E. B. DuBois' Niagara Movement of 1908, which later became the National Association for the Advancement of Colored People. Changing circumstances and definitions should not obscure the reality that this was an aggressive organization. The second feature—the concern of the federal government for civil rights—was present as early as the Reconstruction and is evident in the New Deal. Under Franklin Roosevelt new executive policies on appointments, regulations governing hiring in the war industries, and welfare programs came into being. Most significantly, the Supreme Court in those years initiated the series of decisions which inevitably led to the Brown case. And the Democratic party, which in the thirties became the party of black Americans, began to recognize its black constituents.*

The President's Committee on Civil Rights, which Harry S Truman appointed at the end of 1946 in response to a revival of lynching, is another high point of these forgotten years of the civil rights revolution. To read their report 25 years after its formulation is to experience the shock of self-recognition. The Committee saw clearly the vulnerability of the southern system of segregation, recognized covert segregation in the North, and predicted that civil rights would go from a southern to an urban and national problem. Most of all, they saw the expanding role of the federal government as a main force for change. Virtually every piece of civil rights policy enacted in the 1960's is foreshadowed in the recommendations of this report: the civil rights acts and federal election laws, a strengthened civil rights section in the Justice Department, a Fair Employment Practices Act, non-discriminatory administration of federal funds as a condition of receiving them, and much besides. The Committee could not, of course, have prophesied the second phase of the civil rights revolution, the direct action that Martin Luther King would initiate. And of course they could not dream of the day when even King's form of protest would seem too moderate and when the nearly complete enactment of their program after only a generation's delay would seem too little too late.

A PROGRAM OF ACTION: THE COMMITTEE'S RECOMMENDATIONS

THE TIME IS NOW

Twice before in American history the nation has found it necessary to review the state of its civil rights. The first time was during the 15 years between 1776 and 1791, from the drafting of the Declaration of Independence through the Articles of Confederation experiment to the writing of the Constitution and the Bill of Rights. It was then that the distinctively American heritage was finally distilled from earlier views of liberty. The second time was when the Union was temporarily sundered over the question of whether it could exist "half-slave" and "half-free."

It is our profound conviction that we have come to a time for a third re-examintion of the situation, and a sustained drive ahead. Our reasons for believing this are those of conscience, of self-interest, and of survival in a threatening world. Or to put it another way, we have a moral reason, an economic reason, and an international reason for believing that the time for action is now.

THE MORAL REASON

We have considered the American heritage of freedom at some length. We need no further justification for a broad and immediate program than the need to reaffirm our faith in the traditional American morality. The pervasive gap between our aims and what we actually do is creating a kind of moral dry rot which eats away at the emotional and rational bases of democratic beliefs. There are times when the difference between what we preach about civil rights and what we practice is shockingly illustrated by individual outrages. There are times when the whole structure of our ideology is made ridiculous by individual instances. And there are certain continuing, quiet, omnipresent practices which do irreparable damage to our beliefs.

As examples of "moral erosion" there are the consequences of suffrage limitations in the South. The fact that Negroes and many whites have not been allowed to vote in some states has actually sapped the morality underlying universal suffrage. Many men in public and private life do not believe that those who have been kept from voting are capable of self rule. They finally convince themselves that disfranchised people do not really have the right to vote.

Wartime segregation in the armed forces is another instance of how a social pattern may wreak moral havoc. Practically all white officers and enlisted men in all branches of service saw Negro military personnel performing only the most menial functions. They saw Negroes recruited for the common defense treated as men apart and distinct from themselves. As a result, men who might otherwise have maintained the equalitarian morality of their forebears were given reason to look down on their fellow citizens. This has been sharply illustrated by the Army study discussed previously, in which white servicemen expressed great surprise at the excellent performance of Negroes who joined them in the firing line. Even now, very few people know of the successful experiment with integrated combat units. Yet it is important in explaining why some Negro troops did not do well; it is proof that equal treatment can produce equal performance.

Thousands upon thousands of small, unseen incidents reinforce the impact of headlined violations like lynchings, and broad social patterns like segregation and inequality of treatment. There is, for example, the matter of "fair play." As part of its training for democratic life, our youth is constantly told to "play fair," to abide by "the rules of the game," and to be "good sports." Yet, how many boys and girls in our country experience such things as Washington's annual marble tournament? Because of the prevailing pattern of segregation, established as a model for youth in the schools and recreation systems, separate tournaments are held for Negro and white boys. Parallel elimination contests are sponsored until only two victors remain. Without a contest between them, the white boy is automatically designated as the local champion and sent to the national tournament, while the Negro lad is relegated to the position of runner-up. What child can achieve any real understanding of fair play, or sportsmanship, of the rules of the game, after he has personally experienced such an example of inequality?

It is impossible to decide who suffers the greatest moral damage from our civil rights transgressions, because all of us are hurt. That is certainly true of those who are victimized. Their belief in the basic truth of the American promise is undermined. But they do have the realization, galling as it sometimes is, of being morally in the right. The damage to those who are responsible for these violations of our moral standards may well be greater. They, too, have been reared to honor the command of "free and equal." And all of us must share in the shame at the growth of hypocrisies like the "automatic" marble champion. All of us must endure the cynicism about democratic values which our failures breed.

The United States can no longer countenance these burdens on its common conscience, these inroads on its moral fiber.

THE ECONOMIC REASON

One of the principal economic problems facing us and the rest of the world is achieving maximum production and continued prosperity. The loss of a huge, potential market for goods is a direct result of the economic discrimination which is practiced against many of our minority groups. A sort of vicious circle is produced. Discrimination depresses the wages and income of minority groups. As a result, their purchasing power is curtailed and markets are reduced. Reduced markets result in reduced production. This cuts down employment, which of course means lower wages and still fewer job opportunities. Rising fear, prejudice, and insecurity aggravate the very discrimination in employment which sets the vicious circle in motion. . . .

Economic discrimination prevents full use of all our resources. During the war, when we were called upon to make an all-out productive effort, we found that we lacked skilled laborers. This shortage might not have been so serious if minorities had not frequently been denied opportunities for training and experience. In the end, it cost large amounts of money and precious time to provide ourselves with trained persons.

Discrimination imposes a direct cost upon our economy through the wasteful duplication of many facilities and services required by the "separate but equal" policy. That the resources of the South are sorely strained by the burden of a double system of schools and other public services has already been indicated. Segregation is also economically wasteful for private business. Public transportation companies must often provide duplicate facilities to serve majority and minority groups separately. Places of public accommodation and recreation reject business when it comes in the form of unwanted persons. Stores reduce their sales by turning away minority customers. Factories must provide separate locker rooms, pay windows, drinking fountains, and washrooms for the different groups.

Discrimination in wage scales and hiring policies forces a higher proportion of some minority groups onto relief rolls than corresponding segments of the majority. A study by the Federal Emergency Relief Administration during the depression of the Thirties revealed that in every region the percentage of Negro families on relief was far greater than white families:

PER CENT OF FAMILIES ON RELIEF
(MAY, 1934)

	Negro	White
Northern cities	52.2	13.3
Border state cities	51.8	10.4
Southern cities	33.7	11.4

Similarly, the rates of disease, crime, and fires are disproportionately great in areas which are economically depressed as compared with wealthier areas. Many of the prominent American minorities are confined—by economic discrimination, by law, by restrictive covenants, and by social pressure—to the most dilapidated, undesirable locations. Property in these locations yields a smaller return in taxes, which is seldom sufficient to meet the inordinately high cost of public services in depressed areas. The majority pays a high price in taxes for the low status of minorities.

To the costs of discrimination must be added the expensive investigations, trials, and property losses which result from civil rights violations. In the aggregate, these attain huge proportions. The 1943

Detroit riot alone resulted in the destruction of two million dollars in property.

Finally, the cost of prejudice cannot be computed in terms of markets, production, and expenditures. Perhaps the most expensive results are the least tangible ones. No nation can afford to have its component groups hostile toward one another without feeling the stress. People who live in a state of tension and suspicion cannot use their energy constructively. The frustrations of their restricted existence are translated into aggression against the dominant group. Myrdal says:

Not only occasional acts of violence, but most laziness, carelessness, unreliability, petty stealing and lying are undoubtedly to be explained as concealed aggression. . . . The truth is that *Negroes generally do not feel they have unqualified moral obligations to white people.* . . . The voluntary withdrawal which has intensified the isolation between the two castes is also an expression of Negro protest under cover.

It is not at all surprising that a people relegated to second-class citizenship should behave as second-class citizens. This is true, in varying degrees, of all of our minorities. What we have lost in money, production, invention, citizenship, and leadership as the price for damaged, thwarted personalities—these are beyond estimate.

The United States can no longer afford this heavy drain upon its human wealth, its national competence.

THE INTERNATIONAL REASON

Our position in the postwar world is so vital to the future that our smallest actions have far-reaching effects. We have come to know that our own security in a highly interdependent world is inextricably tied to the security and well-being of all people and all countries. Our foreign policy is designed to make the United States an enormous, positive influence for peace and progress throughout the world. We have tried to let nothing, not even extreme political differences between ourselves and foreign nations, stand in the way of this goal. But our domestic civil rights shortcomings are a serious obstacle.

In a letter to the Fair Employment Practice Committee on May 8, 1946, the Honorable Dean Acheson, then Acting Secretary of State, stated that:

. . . the existence of discrimination against minority groups in this country has an adverse effect upon our relations with other countries. We are reminded over and over by some foreign newspapers and spokesmen, that our treatment of various minorities leaves much to be desired. While sometimes these pronouncements are exaggerated and unjustified, they all too frequently point with accuracy to some form of discrimination because of race, creed, color, or national origin. Frequently we find it next to impossible to formulate a satisfactory answer to our critics in other countries; the gap between the things we stand for in principle and the facts of a particular situation may be too wide to be bridged. An atmosphere of suspicion and resentment in a country over the way a minority is being treated in the United States is a formidable obstacle to the development of mutual understanding and trust between the two countries. We will have better international relations when these reasons for suspicion and resentment have been removed.

I think it is quite obvious . . . that the existence of discriminations against minority groups in the United States is a handicap in our relations with other countries. The Department of State, therefore, has good reason to hope for the continued and increased effectiveness of public and private efforts to do away with these discriminations.

The people of the United States stem from many lands. Other nations and their citizens are naturally intrigued by what has happened to their American "relatives." Discrimination against, or mistreatment of, any racial, religious or national group in the United States is not only seen as our internal problem. The dignity of a country, a continent, or even a major portion of the world's population, may be outraged by it. A relatively few individuals here may be identified with millions of people elsewhere, and the way in which they are treated may have world-wide repercussions. We have fewer than half a million American Indians; there are 30 million more in the Western Hemisphere. Our Mexican American and Hispano groups are not large; millions in Central and South America consider them kin. We number our citizens of Oriental descent in the hundreds of thousands; their counterparts overseas are numbered in hundreds of millions. Throughout the Pacific, Latin America, Africa, the Near, Middle, and Far East, the treatment which our Negroes receive is taken as a reflection of our attitudes toward all dark-skinned peoples. . . .

We cannot escape the fact that our civil rights record has been an issue in world politics. The world's press and radio are full of it. This Committee has seen a multitude of samples. We and our friends have been, and are, stressing our achievements. Those with competing philosophies have stressed—and are shamelessly distorting—our shortcomings. They have not only tried to create hostility toward us among specific nations, races, and religious groups. They have tried to prove our democracy an empty fraud, and our nation a consistent oppressor of underprivileged people. This may seem ludicrous to Americans, but it is sufficiently important to worry our friends. The following United Press dispatch from London proves that (*Washington Post,* May 25, 1947):

Although the Foreign Office reserved comment on recent lynch activities in the Carolinas, British diplomatic circles said privately today that they have played into the hands of Communist propagandists in Europe. . . .

Diplomatic circles said the two incidents of mob violence would provide excellent propaganda ammunition for Communist agents who have been decrying America's brand of "freedom" and "democracy."

News of the North Carolina kidnapping was prominently displayed by London papers. . . .

The international reason for acting to secure our civil rights now is not to win the approval of our totalitarian critics. We would not expect it if our record were spotless; to them our civil rights record is only a convenient weapon with which to attack us. Certainly we would like to deprive them of that weapon. But we are more concerned with the good opinion of the peoples of the world. Our achievements in building and maintaining a state dedicated to the fundamentals of freedom have already served as a guide for those seeking the best road from chaos to liberty and prosperity. But it is not indelibly written that democracy will encompass the world. We are convinced that our way of life—the free way of life—holds a promise of hope for all people. We have what is perhaps the greatest responsibility ever placed upon a people to keep this promise alive. Only still greater achievements will do it.

The United States is not so strong, the final triumph of the democratic ideal is not so inevitable that we can ignore what the world thinks of us or our record.

THE COMMITTEE'S RECOMMENDATIONS

I. *To strengthen the machinery for the protection of civil rights, the President's Committee recommends:*

1. The reorganization of the Civil Rights Section of the Department of Justice to provide for:

The establishment of regional offices;

A substantial increase in its appropriation and staff to enable it to engage in more extensive research and to act more effectively to prevent civil rights violations;

An increase in investigative action in the absence of complaints;

The greater use of civil sanctions;

Its elevation of the status of a full division in the Department of Justice.

2. The establishment within the FBI of a special unit of investigators trained in civil rights work.

3. The establishment by the state governments of law enforcement agencies comparable to the federal Civil Rights Section.

4. The establishment of a permanent Commission on Civil Rights in the Executive Office of the President, preferably by Act of Congress; and the simultaneous creation of a Joint Standing Committee on Civil Rights in Congress.

5. The establishment by the states of permanent commissions on civil rights to parallel the work of the federal Commission at the state level.

6. The increased professionalization of state and local police forces.

II. *To strengthen the right to safety and security of the person, the President's Committee recommends:*

1. The enactment by Congress of new legislation to supplement Section 51 of Title 18 of the United States Code which would impose the same liability on one person as is now imposed by that statute on two or more conspirators.

2. The amendment of Section 51 to remove the penalty provision which disqualifies persons convicted under the Act from holding public office.

3. The amendment of Section 52 to increase the maximum penalties that may be imposed under it from a $1,000 fine and a one-year prison term to a $5,000 fine and a ten-year prison term, thus bringing its penalty provisions into line with those in Section 51.

4. The enactment by Congress of a new statute, to supplement Section 52, specifically directed against police brutality and related crimes.

5. The enactment by Congress of an antilynching act.

6. The enactment by Congress of a new criminal statute on involuntary servitude, supplementing Sections 443 and 444 of Title 18 of the United States Code.

7. A review of our wartime evacuation and detention experience looking toward the development of a policy which will prevent the abridgment of civil rights of any person or groups because of race or ancestry.

8. Enactment by Congress of legislation establishing a procedure by which claims of evacuees for specific property and business losses resulting from the wartime evacuation can be promptly considered and settled.

III. *To strengthen the right to citizenship and its privileges, the President's Committee recommends:*

1. Action by the states or Congress to end poll taxes as a voting prerequisite.

2. The enactment by Congress of a statute protecting the right of qualified persons to participate in federal primaries and elections against interference by public officers and private persons.

3. The enactment by Congress of a statute protecting the right to qualify for, or participate in, federal or state primaries or elections against discriminatory action by state officers based on race or color, or depending on any other unreasonable classification of persons for voting purposes.

4. The enactment by Congress of legislation establishing local self-government for the District of Columbia; and the amendment of the Constitution to extend suffrage in presidential elections, and representation in Congress to District residents.

5. The granting of suffrage by the States of New Mexico and Arizona to their Indian citizens.

6. The modification of the federal naturalization laws to permit the granting of citizenship without regard to the race, color, or national origin of applicants.

7. The repeal by the states of laws discriminating against aliens who are ineligible for citizenship because of race, color, or national origin.

8. The enactment by Congress of legislation granting citizenship to the people of Guam and American Samoa.

9. The enactment by Congress of legislation, followed by appropriate administrative action, to end immediately all discrimination and segregation based on race, color, creed, or national origin, in the organization and activities of all branches of the Armed Services.

10. The enactment by Congress of legislation providing that no member of the armed forces shall he subject to discrimination of any kind by any public authority or place of public accommodation, recreation, transportation, or other service or business.

IV. *To strengthen the right to freedom of conscience and expression the President's Committee recommends:*

1. The enactment by Congress and the state legislatures of legislation requiring all groups, which attempt to influence public opinion, to disclose the pertinent facts about themselves through systematic registration procedures.

2. Action by Congress and the executive branch clarifying the loyalty obligations of federal employees, and establishing standards and procedures by which the civil rights of public workers may be scrupulously maintained.

V. *To strengthen the right to equality of opportunity, the President's Committee recommends:*

1. In general:

> The elimination of segregation, based on race, color, creed, or national origin, from American life.

> The conditioning by Congress of all federal grants-in-aid and other forms of federal assistance to public or private agencies for any purpose on the absence of discrimination and segregation based on race, color, creed, or national origin.

2. For employment:

> The enactment of a federal Fair Employment Practice Act prohibiting all forms of discrimination in private employment, based on race, color, creed, or national origin.

> The enactment by the state of similar laws;

> The issuance by the President of a mandate against discrimination in government employment and the creation of adequate machinery to enforce this mandate.

3. For education:

Enactment by the state legislatures of fair educational practice laws for public and private educational institutions, prohibiting discrimination in the admission and treatment of students based on race, color, creed, or national origin.

4. For housing:

The enactment by the states of laws outlawing restrictive covenants;

Renewed court attack, with intervention by the Department of Justice, upon restrictive covenants.

5. For health services:

The enactment by the states of fair health practice statutes forbidding discrimination and segregation based on race, creed, color, or national origin, in the operation of public or private health facilities.

6. For public services:

The enactment by Congress of a law stating that discrimination and segregation, based on race, color, creed, or national origin, in the rendering of all public services by the national government is contrary to public policy;

The enactment by the states of similar laws;

The establishment by act of Congress or executive order of a unit in the federal Bureau of the Budget to review the execution of all government programs, and the expenditures of all government funds, for compliance with the policy of nondiscrimination;

The enactment by Congress of a law prohibiting discrimination or segregation, based on race, color, creed, or national origin, in interstate transportation and all the facilities thereof, to apply against both public officers and the employees of private transportation companies;

The enactment by the states of laws guaranteeing equal access to places of public accommodation, broadly defined, for persons of all races, colors, creeds, and national origins.

7. For the District of Columbia:

The enactment by Congress of legislation to accomplish the following purposes in the District:

Prohibition of discrimination and segregation, based on race, color, creed, or national origin, in all public or publicly-supported hospitals, parks, recreational facilities, housing projects, welfare agencies, penal institutions, and concessions on public property;

The prohibition of segregation in the public school system of the District of Columbia;

The establishment of a fair educational practice program directed against discrimination, based on race, color, creed, or national origin, in the admission of students to private educational institutions;

The establishment of a fair health practice program forbidding discrimination and segregation by public or private agencies, based on race, color, creed, or national origin, with respect to the training of doctors and nurses, the admission of patients to hospitals, clinics, and similar institutions, and the right of doctors and nurses to practice in hospitals;

The outlawing of restrictive covenants;

Guaranteeing equal access to places of public accommodation, broadly defined, to persons of all races, colors, creeds, and national origins.

8. The enactment by Congress of legislation ending the system of segregation in the Panama Canal Zone.

VI. *To rally the American people to the support of a continuing program to strengthen civil rights, the President's Committee recommends:*

A long-term campaign of public education to inform the people of the civil rights to which they are entitled and which they owe to one another.

The most important educational task in this field is to give the public living examples of civil rights in operation. This is the purpose of our recommendations which have gone before. But there still remains the job of driving home to the public the nature of our heritage, the justification of civil rights and the need to end prejudice. This is a task which will require the cooperation of the federal, state, and local governments and of private agencies. We believe that the permanent Commission on Civil Rights should take the leadership in serving as the coordinating body. The activities of the permanent Commission in this field should be expressly authorized by Congress and funds specifically appropriated for them.

Aside from the education of the general public, the government has immediate responsibility for an internal civil rights campaign for its more than two million employees. This might well be an indispensable first step in a large campaign. Moreover, in the armed forces, an opportunity exists to educate men while in service. The armed forces should expand efforts, already under way, to develop genuinely democratic attitudes in officers and enlisted men.

Harry Truman and the Fair Deal

ALONZO L. HAMBY

President Harry S Truman enunciated a program called the Fair Deal that was to be an extension of Franklin Roosevelt's New Deal. The rhetoric of Truman's speeches, especially his inaugural address of 1949, promised much, and Hamby argues that the Fair Deal definitely extended FDR's work. But Truman was by nature a moderate, a border-state politician whose very essence was compromise, and he operated in a period of rapprochement between government and business. Some centers of Democratic strength, notably the urban machines, seem to stand still rather than to grow in social awareness. Did local leaders urge the Truman administration to "go slow" because welfare laws jeopardized their organizations? One historian even asks whether "the Democratic coalition had ceased to be a 'have-not' coalition and had become interested chiefly in maintaining earlier gains." To question the possibilities of policies in the New Deal and Fair Deal is to ask about the possibilities of government today.

"Every segment of our population and every individual has a right to expect from our Government a fair deal," declared Harry S Truman in early 1949. In 1945 and 1946 the Truman administration had almost crumbled under the stresses of postwar reconversion; in 1947 and 1948 it had fought a frustrating, if politically rewarding, battle with the Republican Eightieth Congress. Buoyed by his remarkable victory of 1948 and given Democratic majorities in both houses of Congress, Truman hoped to achieve an impressive record of domestic reform. The president systematized his past proposals, added some new ones, and gave his program a name that would both connect his administration with the legacy of the New Deal and give it a distinct identity. The Fair Deal, while based solidly upon the New Deal tradition, differed from its predecessor in significant aspects of mood and detail. It reflected not only Truman's own aspirations but also a style of liberalism that had begun to move beyond the New Deal during World War II and had come to maturity during the early years of the cold war—"the vital center."

. . .

The legislative goals Truman announced for his administration, while not devised to meet the needs of an abstract theory, were well in tune with the vital-center approach: anti-inflation measures, a more progressive tax structure, repeal of the Taft-Hartley Act, a higher minimum wage, a farm program based on the concepts of abundant production and parity income, resource development and public power programs, expansion of social security, national medical insurance, federal aid to education, extensive housing legislation, and civil rights bills. The president's most controversial request was for authority to increase plant facilities in such basic industries as steel, preferably through federal financing of private enterprise but through outright government construction if necessary. Roundly condemned by right-wing opponents as "socialistic" and soon dropped by the administration, the proposal was actually intended to meet the demands of a prosperous, growing capitalist economy and emerged from the Fair Deal's search for the proper degree of government intervention to preserve the established American economic structure. "Between the reactionaries of the extreme left with their talk about revolution and class warfare, and the reactionaries of the extreme right with their hysterical cries of bankruptcy and despair, lies the way of progress," Truman declared in November 1949.

The Fair Deal was a conscious effort to continue the purpose of the New Deal but not necessarily its methods. Not forced to meet the emergencies of economic depression, given a solid point of departure by their predecessors, and led by a president more prone than FDR to demand programmatic coherence, the Fair Dealers made a systematic effort to discover techniques that would be at once more equitable and more practical in alleviating the problems of unequal wealth and opportunity. Thinking in terms of abundance rather than scarcity, they attempted to adapt the New Deal tradition to postwar prosperity. Seeking to go beyond the New Deal while preserving its objectives, the Truman administration advocated a more sweeping and better-ordered reform agenda. Yet in the quest for political means, Truman and the vital-center liberals could only fall back upon one of the oldest dreams of American reform—the Jacksonian-Populist vision of a union of producing classes, an invincible farmer-labor coalition. While superficially plausible, the Fair Deal's political strategy proved too weak to handle the burden thrust upon it.

The Fair Deal seemed to oscillate between militancy and moderation. New Dealers had frequently gloried in accusations of "liberalism" or "radicalism"; Fair Dealers tended to shrink from such labels. The New Dealers had often lusted for political combat; the Fair Dealers were generally more low keyed. Election campaigns demanded an aggressiveness that would arouse the Democratic presidential party, but the continued strength of the conservative coalition in Congress dictated accommodation in the post-election efforts to secure passage of legislative proposals. Such tactics reflected Truman's personal political experience and instincts, but they also developed naturally out of the climate of postwar America. The crisis of economic depression had produced one style of political rhetoric; the problems of prosperity and inflation brought forth another.

The Fair Deal mirrored Truman's policy preferences and approach to politics; it was no more the president's personal creation, however, than the New Deal had been Roosevelt's. Just as FDR's advisers had formulated much of the New Deal, a group of liberals developed much of the content and tactics of the Fair Deal. For the most part these were the men who had formed a liberal caucus within the administration in early 1947 shortly after the Republican triumph in the congressional elections of 1946, had worked to sway the president toward the left in his policy recommendations and campaign tactics, and had played a significant, if not an all-embracing, role in Truman's victory in 1948. Truman's special counsel, Clark M. Clifford, was perhaps the most prominent member of the group, but Clifford, although a shrewd political analyst, a persuasive advocate, and an extremely valuable administrative chief of staff, was neither the caucus's organizer nor a creative liberal thinker. Others gave the Fair Deal its substance as a program descending from the New Deal yet distinct from it.

. . .

The administration took the next step in April with the introduction in Congress of a new farm program, which had been drawn up under Brannan's direction. The Brannan Plan was difficult and complex in detail, but essentially it was an effort to maintain farm income at the record high level of the war and immediate postwar periods while letting market prices fall to a natural supply-demand level. Brannan thus proposed to continue the New Deal policy of subsidizing the farmers, but he broke dramatically with the New Deal technique of restricting production and marketing in order to achieve artificially high prices.

Many agrarian progressives, including Henry A. Wallace himself, had long been troubled by the price-support mechanisms and had sought methods of unleashing the productive capacity of the farms. Brannan seemed to show the way. He proposed the maintenance of farm income through direct payments to farmers rather than through crop restriction. In order to encourage and protect the family farm, moreover, he recommended supporting a maximum of about $26,100 worth of production per farm. To the consumer he promised milk at fifteen cents a quart, to the dairy farmer a sustained high income. To the Democratic party he offered an apparently ingenious device that would unite the interests of farmers and workers.

Liberals generally were enthusiastic over both the principles and the politics of the Brannan proposals. "The new plan lets growers grow and eaters eat, and that is good," commented Samuel Grafton. "If Brannan is right, the political miracle of 1948 will become a habit as farmers, labor and consumers find common political goals," wrote agricultural columnist Angus MacDonald. James Patton called the Brannan Plan "a milestone in the history of American agriculture," and the *Nation* asserted that the average consumer should devote all his spare time to support of the program.

The plan immediately ran into the opposition of the conservatives who dominated Congress. Republicans feared that the political coalition Brannan was trying to build would entrench the Democrats in power. Large producers, most effectively represented by the powerful Farm Bureau Federation, regarded the plan as discriminatory, and many Democrats with ties to the Farm Bureau refused to support it, among them Senate majority leader Scott Lucas and Clinton Anderson, now the freshman senator from New Mexico. By June it was obvious to most political analysts that the Brannan Plan had no chance of passage in

1949. The administration and most liberals nevertheless remained optimistic. The issue seemed good, the alignment of interests logical and compelling: enough political education and campaigning could revive the scheme and revolutionize American politics.

Both the CIO and the Farmers Union undertook campaigns to spread the message of farmer-labor unity. An article in the *National Union Farmer* typified the effort:

Workers today are in a tough spot. just like farmers. Production has been steadily declining, and that means fewer jobs and lower wages. And that means smaller markets for farm products. This worries everybody but Big Business, but these advocates of scarcity still rule the roost. Monopoly wants less production, less employment, lower wages, fewer family farmers, less collective bargaining, lower farm prices and less competition except for jobs. . . . There is little basic difference between the labor fight against the Taft-Hartley law, and our fight against attempts to tax cooperatives out of existence. . . . Labor's strong objections to 40¢ an hour as a minimum is no different than our equally strong objections to 60% of parity.

Brannan campaigned extensively for his program. "Farm income equals jobs for millions of American workers," he told a labor gathering in a typical effort. "Together, let workers and farmers unite in achieving a full employment, full production economy." The administration sponsored regional farmer-labor conferences around the country. The one attracting the most attention was held in June at Des Moines, Iowa, and featured prominent labor leaders, important Democratic congressmen, and Vice-President Alben Barkley. Other such grass-roots meetings were organized as far east as upstate New York, and the Democratic National Committee prepared a pamphlet on the Brannan Plan for mass distribution. On Labor Day the president devoted two major appearances, one in Pittsburgh and the other in Des Moines, to the Brannan Plan and to farmer-labor unity. "Those who are trying to set these two great groups against each other just have axes of their own to grind," he warned his Pittsburgh audience. "Price supports must . . . give consumers the benefit of our abundant farm production," he told his Des Moines listeners.

Many liberals and Democratic politicians remained convinced that they had an overwhelming political strategy. "In 1950 and '52, the Brannan Plan will be the great issue in the doubtful states," wrote journalist A. G. Mezerik. "After that, Congress will enact a new farm bill—one which is based on low prices for consumers and a high standard of living for family farmers." In early 1950 the Brannan Plan seemed to be gaining popular support. Liberals inside and outside the administration continued to hope for vindication at the polls in November. They could not, of course, foresee the Korean War and the ways in which it would change the shape of American politics.

Even without the Korean War, however, even without the disruptive impact of McCarthyism, it is doubtful that the Brannan Plan would have worked the miracles expected of it. The liberals inside and outside the administration who had created or worked for it assumed that urban and rural groups could be united simply on grounds of mutual self-interest. They failed to understand that these groups were not deeply concerned with *mutual* self-interest; both sides had practiced with some success methods that had taken care of their own self-interest. The rhetoric about urban-rural interdependence was extremely superficial, talked but not deeply felt. Most farm and labor leaders, even those progressive in their outlook, hardly had a basis for communication. The ADA conference of February 1949 included some of the best-informed figures from the unions and the farms. Yet one of the labor leaders had to ask for an explanation "in simple language" of the concept of parity. One of the farm leaders then admitted that he had no idea what the dues check-off was or how it worked. The farm leaders also frankly commented that their constitutents were strongly against such things as a minimum wage applied to farm workers, the extension of social security to cover farm labor and farmers in general, and especially the re-establishment of any sort of price controls. The situation at Des Moines seems to have been much the same. Even some of the Farmers Union officials at the conference were annoyed by the presence of the labor people. "Some farmers wondered if they wern't being sucked in to help the forces of labor fight the Taft-Hartley Act," reported journalist Lauren Soth. Such ideas, of course, were not entirely fanciful. Most of the observers at Des Moines sensed the artificiality of the whole affair, but they continued to hope that further contacts would consummate the union of city and country.

The farm leaders harbored a provincial suspicion of labor, while the reverse was true in the cities. "While labor has given general support to the Brannan plan, I have had the suggestion made, almost ironically, that labor might be given a guaranteed income if such were to be granted to farmers," remarked Jim Loeb in November 1949. Many liberals felt that, as proposed by the administration, the Brannan Plan was too generous. The Chicago *Sun-Times* and the *Nation* agreed that the principles and machinery of the Brannan system were excellent, but both dissented from Brannan's proposal to support farm income at record heights. "The country as a whole should not undertake to support farm income at a higher level than is fair and just," warned the *Sun-Times,* adding that it would always be easier to raise supports than to lower them. Chester Bowles went a step further when he proposed that the whole matter of agricultural subsidies should be tied to urban employment with no supports at all during periods of full employment. Such ideas were hardly the current of a new urban-rural coalition.

Many urban liberals found the plan itself difficult to grasp and could not work up much enthusiasm about it. "Most of us do not understand it completely," admitted Jim Loeb a month and a half after its introduction. A group of ADA leaders had a cordial meeting with Brannan in June 1949 and pledged their support. Actually, however, the ADA did little to promote the program. In the spring of 1950 a Philadelphia liberal wrote to the organization asking for information on the issue, but Violet Gunther, the legislative director, replied that

the ADA had published nothing other than an endorsement in the platform, nor could she think of any group other than the Farmers Union
that might have something available. The *Nation* and the *New Republic* gave only occasional mention to the plan. Most liberals could
heartily endorse and even get excited about Brannan's political objectives, but understanding and identifying with the scheme itself was
quite a different matter.

For a time in early 1950 declining farm prices seemed to generate
a surge of support for the Brannan Plan. At the beginning of June,
Albert Loveland, the undersecretary of agriculture, won the Iowa Democratic senatorial primary on a pro-Brannan platform and thereby
encouraged the administration to believe that the Midwest was moving
in its direction. Just a few weeks later, however, the Korean War began,
creating situations and pressures that doomed most of the Fair Deal.

Even if the Brannan Plan had become law, it is far from certain
that it would have created the dream farmer-liberal coalition. Most
leading agricultural economists, including those of a progressive outlook,
were convinced that the proposal would be unworkable and prohibi-
tively expensive. Some liberal economists condemned its failure to give
the rural poor at least as much aid as the middle-class family farm.
Even assuming that the economists were wrong, there is no guarantee
that a smoothly functioning Brannan program could have performed
the neat trick of uniting the very different cultures of urban liberalism
and rural insurgency; such a feat probably would have required more
than mutual economic benefits. The down-to-earth, church-social ethos
of the Farmers Union would not automatically homogenize with the
sophisticated, intellectual progressivism of the city liberals or the wage-
and-hour, union-shop, reformism of labor.

During 1949 and early 1950 the Truman administration managed a
record of substantial legislative accomplishment, but it consisted almost
entirely of additions to such New Deal programs as the minimum wage,
social security, and public power. The Housing Act of 1949, with its
provisions for large-scale public housing, appeared to be a breakthrough, but weak administration, local opposition, and inadequate
financing subsequently vitiated hopes that it would help the poor.
Acting on his executive authority, Truman took an important step by
forcing the army to agree to a policy of desegregation. The heart of
the Fair Deal, however—repeal of the Taft-Hartley Act, civil rights
legislation, aid to education, national medical insurance, and the Brannan Plan—failed in Congress. Given the power of the well-entrenched
conservative coalition and a wide-spread mood of public apathy about
big new reforms, Truman could only enlarge upon the record of his
predecessor.

Democratic strategists hoped for a mandate in the congressional
elections of 1950. In the spring Truman made a successful whistle-stop
tour of the West and Midwest, rousing party enthusiasm and apparently
demonstrating a solid personal popularity. Loveland's victory provided further encouragement, and in California the aggressive Fair

Dealer Helen Gahagan Douglas won the Democratic nomination for the Senate by a thumping margin. Two incumbent Fair Deal supporters—Frank Graham of North Carolina and Claude Pepper of Florida—lost their senatorial primaries, but, as Southerners who had run afoul of the race issue, they did not seem to be indictors of national trends. Nevertheless, the hope of cutting into the strength of the conservative opposition ran counter to the historical pattern of mid-term elections. The beginning of the Korean War at the end of June destroyed any chances of success.

The most immediate impact of Korea was to refuel an anti-Communist extremism that might otherwise have sputtered out. Senator Joseph R. McCarthy had begun his rise to prominence in February 1950, but he had failed to prove any of his multiple allegations and seemed definitively discredited by the investigations of a special Senate committee headed by Millard Tydings. McCarthy, it is true, was a talented demagogue who should have been taken more seriously by the liberals and the Truman administration in early 1950, but it seems probable that his appeal would have waned more quickly if the cold war with communism had not suddenly become hot. As it was, many of his Senate colleagues rushed to emulate him. In September 1950 Congress passed the McCarran Internal Security Act; only a handful of congressional liberals dared dissent from the overwhelming vote in favor. Truman's subsequent veto was intelligent and courageous, but was issued more for the history books than with any real hope of success. In the subsequent campaign, liberal Democrats, whether they had voted for the McCarran Act or not, found themselves facing charges of softness toward communism.

The war hurt the administration in other ways. It touched off a brief but serious inflation, which caused widespread consumer irritation. By stimulating demand for agricultural products it brought most farm prices up to parity levels and thereby undercut whatever attractiveness the Brannan Plan had developed in rural areas. Finally it removed the Democratic party's most effective spokesman—the president —from active participation in the campaign. Forced to play the role of war leader, Truman allowed himself only one major partisan speech, delivered in St. Louis on the eve of the balloting.

The Fair Deal might have been a winning issue in a nation oriented toward domestic concerns and recovering from an economic recession; it had much less appeal in a country obsessed with Communist aggression and experiencing an inflationary war boom. The reaction against the administration was especially strong in the Midwest. Indiana's Democratic aspirant for the Senate asked Oscar Ewing to stay out of the state. In Iowa, Loveland desperately attempted to reverse his identification with the Brannan Plan. In Missouri the managers of senatorial candidate Thomas C. Hennings, Jr. privately asked White House aides to make Truman's St. Louis speech a foreign policy address that would skip lightly over Fair Deal issues. A few days before the election the columnist Stewart Alsop returned from a Midwestern trip convinced that the region had never been more conservative. Nevertheless, Truman's political advisers, and probably Truman himself, felt that the Fair Deal still had appeal. Given the basic strength of the economy and the victories in Korea that followed the Inchon landing, the White House believed that the Democrats could easily rebut generalized charges of fumbling or softness toward communism. In mid-October the Democratic National Committee and many local leaders were so confident of success that their main concern was simply to get out the vote.

The November results, however, showed a Democratic loss of twenty-eight seats in the House of Representatives and five seats in the Senate. Truman seized every opportunity to remind all who would listen that the numbers were small by traditional mid-term standards. Liberal political analysts, including Kenneth Hechler, a White House staffer, and Gus Tyler of the International Ladies Garment Workers Union, subjected the returns to close scrutiny and all but pronounced a Democratic victory. All the same, most of the Democrats who went under had been staunch Fair Dealers. Republican candidates, including John Marshall Butler in Maryland, Richard M. Nixon in California, Everett McKinley Dirksen in Illinois, and Robert A. Taft in Ohio, scored some of the most spectacular GOP victories by blending right-wing conservatism with McCarthyism. The Midwestern losses were especially disappointing. Hechler argued that the corn-belt vote primarily reflected urban defections and that the Democrats had done comparatively well among farmers. Perhaps so, but for all practical purposes the results put an end to the Brannan strategy of constructing a farmer-labor coalition. Truman was probably more accurate than Hechler when, with characteristic overstatement, he privately expressed his disappointment: "The main trouble with the farmers is that they hate labor so badly that they will not vote for their own interests."

Thereafer, with the Chinese intervention transforming the Korean War into a more serious conflict and with the dismissal of General Douglas MacArthur in April 1951, Truman faced a tough attack from a Republican opposition determined to capitalize upon the frustrations of Korea. Finding it necessary to place party unity above all else, he quietly shelved most of his domestic legislative program and sought to bring the conservative wing of his party behind his military and defense policies. He secretly asked Richard B. Russell of Georgia, the kingpin of the Southern conservatives, to assume the Democratic leadership in the Senate. Russell, content with the substance of power, declined and gave his nod to Ernest W. McFarland of Arizona, an amiable tool of the Southern bloc; Truman made no effort to prevent McFarland's selection as Senate majority leader. The president's State of the Union message was devoted almost entirely to foreign policy and defense mobilization and mentioned social welfare programs only as an afterthought. Subsequently Truman told a press conference that while he supported the Fair Deal as much as ever, "first things come first, and our defense programs must have top priority."

Truman's success in achieving a minimum degree of party unity became apparent in the weeks of investigation and accusation that followed General MacArthur's return to America. Russell, playing the role of parliamentarian-statesman to the hilt and cashing in on his great prestige with senators of both parties, chaired the Senate committee that looked into the MacArthur incident, and he saw to it that the administration was able to deliver a thorough rebuttal to the general. The Northern liberal, Brien McMahon of Connecticut, relentlessly grilled hostile witnesses. The Western representative of oil and gas interests, Robert S. Kerr of Oklahoma, lashed out at MacArthur himself with a vehemence and effectiveness that no other Democrat could match. The tandem efforts of Russell, McMahon, and Kerr demonstrated the new party solidarity, but in terms of the Fair Deal the price was high.

In July 1951 the Federal Power Commission renounced the authority to regulate "independent" (non-pipeline-owning) natural gas producers. The ruling amounted to an adminstrative enactment of a bill, sponsored by Kerr, which Truman had vetoed a year earlier; Truman's close friend and most recent appointee to the Federal Power Commission, Mon Wallgren, cast the deciding vote. Although he talked like a militant liberal in a private conversation with ADA leaders, the president stalled throughout 1951 on repeated demands for the establishment of a Korean War Fair Employment Practices Committee. In December the administration established an ineffective Committee on Government Contract Compliance. Other domestic programs were soft-pedaled to near-invisibility.

Yet even the Korean War was not entirely inimical to reform. Its exigencies forced the army to transform its policy of integration into practice. Korea also provided a test for one of the basic underpinnings of the Fair Deal—Leon Keyserling's philosophy of economic expansion. Truman did not in the end fully embrace Keyserling's policies, but in the main he followed the guidance of his chief economic adviser. The Korean War years demonstrated the extent to which Keyserling's economics diverged from conventional New Deal–World War II Keynesianism and revealed both the strengths and weaknesses of his approach.

From the outbreak of the fighting, most liberals favored either immediate strong economic controls akin to those that had held down inflation in World War II or at least the establishment of stand-by machinery that could impose them rapidly. Truman disliked such measures on the basis of both principle and politics. He and his diplomatic advisers also wanted to signal the Soviet Union that the United States regarded the North Korean attack as a limited challange meriting a limited response. Keyserling's expansionary economics provided an attractive alternative to the liberal clamor for controls. Convinced that extensive controls would put the economy in a strait jacket and retard the expansion necessary to meet both consumer and defense needs and assuming a North Korean defeat in a few months, the administration decided to accept a short-term, war-scare inflation (probably unavoidable in any case) and concentrate on economic growth, which would be underwritten in large measure by tax incentives for business. An expanding economy would be the best long-term answer to inflation:

growth policies could fit a small war into the economy, avoid the social and political strains accompanying wartime controls, and reduce inflationary pressures to a level at which fiscal and monetary policies could contain them. Liberals outside the administration watched with alarm as prices went up, but Truman and Keyserling continued to gamble on a quick end to the war and the development of an economy capable of producing both guns and butter.

Their plan might have worked fairly well had the United States not overreached itself militarily in Korea. The Chinese intervention of November 1950 wrecked hopes of a quick recovery, set off another round of scare buying, and intensified war demands upon the economy. The administration quickly threw up a price-wage control structure, but by the end of February 1951, eight months after the beginning of the Korean conflict, the consumer price index had risen eight per cent (an annual rate of twelve per cent). Keyserling agreed that the new situation necessitated controls, but he accepted them with reluctance and sought to keep them as simple as possible, even at the risk of benefiting profiteers. "We'll never be able to out-control the Russians," he told a Senate committee, "but we can out-produce them." Speaking to an ADA economic conference, he asserted that many liberals, in their opposition to tax breaks for large business and in their demands for stronger controls, were confusing the Korean War with World War II and "engaging merely in hackneyed slogans out of the past."

Most liberals disagreed with Keyserling's emphases. As production was his first imperative, an end to the wage-price spiral was theirs. "Unless we are willing seriously to endanger the basis of existence of the American middle class, we must stop prices from rising," wrote Hans Landsberg in the *Reporter*. The liberals assumed that economic expansion was possible within a framework of rigid, tightly administered controls. Chester Bowles observed that the controlled economy of World War II had turned out a twofold increase in industrial production. John Kenneth Galbraith rejected the idea that Keyserling's expansionary policies could outrun the inflationary pressures they themselves created. The bulk of liberals regarded the administration approach as dangerous, the product of political expediency rather than sound economic analysis.

Neither Keyserling nor the more conventional liberals won a complete victory. Truman, who understood all too well the political dangers of a prolonged inflation, made substantial concessions to the controllers, led by Michael V. DiSalle, head of the Office of Price Stabilization. In the interest of fairness Truman approved a more complex system of price controls than Keyserling thought desirable, giving DiSalle considerable leeway to roll back some prices while approving advances in other areas. By March 1951 inflation was under control; during the final ten months of the year the cost-of-living index increased by less than two and one-half per cent. The waves of scare buying that followed the North Korean attack and the Chinese intervention had subsided. Higher taxes and restraints on credit were beginning to affect consumer buying. The Federal Reserve System, despite opposition from the administration, initiated a stringent monetary policy. Tax breaks for businesses expanding plant facilities presaged increased productive capacity. All these factors, along with the government stabilization program, discouraged an inflationary psychology.

At the time, however, it appeared to most economic observers that the lull was only temporary. Many of the administration's liberal critics refused even to admit the existence of a lull and called for tougher controls as if prices were still skyrocketing. More moderate analysts feared that the impact of large government defense orders would set off another inflationary spiral in the fall. Influenced by such expectations, Truman ostentatiously mounted an anti-inflation crusade, demanding that Congress not only extend his control authority, due to expire on June 30, but actually strengthen it. In fact the Defense Production Act of 1951 weakened the president's powers considerably. Truman signed it reluctantly, comparing it to "a bulldozer, crashing aimlessly through existing pricing formulas, leaving havoc in its wake." A subsequent tax bill failed to meet administration revenue requests and increased the danger of serious inflation.

Yet price stability persisted through 1952, in large measure because defense production, hampered by multiple shortages and bottlenecks, lagged far behind its timetable. In late 1951 these problems and the fear of renewed inflation led Truman to decide in favor of a "stretch-out" of defense production schedules; in doing so he overrode Keyserling's urgings for an all-out effort to break the bottlenecks and concentrate relentlessly upon expansion. Given the serious problems in defense industry, the stretch-out decision may have seemed necessary to Truman, but it also carried the dividend of economic stability.

The president had steered a course between the orthodox liberal obsession with inflation and Keyserling's easy disregard of its perils; perhaps as a result the economy failed to expand at the rate Keyserling had hoped. On balance, however, Truman's approach to the political economy of the Korean War was closer to Keyserling's, and the conflict produced a dramatic economic growth. Before the war the peak gross national product had been $285 billion in 1948; by the end of 1952 the GNP (measured in constant dollar values) had reached a rate of $350 billion. The production index of durable manufactured goods had averaged 237 in 1950; by the last quarter of 1952 it had reached 313. The expansion, even if less than Keyserling had wanted, was breathtaking. Moreover, aside from the probably unavoidable inflation that accompanied the early months of the war, this remarkable growth had occurred in a climate of economic stability. Using a somewhat more orthodox approach than Keyserling preferred, the administration had achieved one of the central goals of the Fair Deal.

In its efforts to carry on with the reforming impulse of the New Deal the Truman administration faced nearly insuperable obstacles. A loosely knit but nonetheless effective conservative coalition had controlled Congress since 1939, successfully defying Franklin Roosevelt long before it had to deal with Truman. Postwar prosperity muted economic liberalism and encouraged a mood of apathy toward new reform breakthroughs, although Truman's victory in 1948 indicated that most of the elements of the old Roosevelt coalition were determined to preserve the gains of the New Deal. The cold war probably made it more difficult to focus public attention upon reform and dealt severe blows to civil liberties. It did, however, give impetus to the movement for Negro equality.

The Fair Deal attempted to adapt liberalism to the new conditions. Under the intellectual leadership of Leon Keyserling it formulated policies that sought to transcend the conflicts of the New Deal era by encouraging an economic growth that could provide abundance for all Americans. With Charles Brannan pointing the way, the Truman administration tried to translate abundance into a political coalition that could provide the votes for its social welfare policies. The political strategy, ambitious but unrealistic, collapsed under the weight of the Korean War. Keyserling's economics, on the other hand, received a lift from Korea; in a period of adversity the Fair Deal was able to achieve at least one of its objectives.

PART TWO

1952-1959

The age of Eisenhower—that era of placidity and order that has already become an object of nostalgia—was shorter than we remember. Eisenhower became President, the Korean war ended, and Joseph Stalin died —all in 1953. But Joseph McCarthy was still a power in the land and the economy sagged immediately after Korea, so that placidity scarcely developed before about 1954. And by 1957 and 1958, beneath the Eisenhower consensus, anxiety stirred over Russian spacecrafts, colonial revolutions, civil-rights disorder, and muckraking journalism—all harbingers of the decade to come.

This short and welcome respite from the strains of war did not bring long-term social stability. In the interchangeable suburbs, Americans were learning new styles of living, new attitudes toward money and family behavior. An economy increasingly based on consumer credit undermined old habits. Meanwhile, the great flux was obscured by public assurances of rooted values and by political stalemate. Yet the decade of the 1950's moved rapidly toward a rendezvous with the new world it was creating. Blacks were increasingly angry; the right wing more sour and disillusioned; the dispirited and invisible poor rising into view of the liberal middle class; adolescents in high school and college finding their own voices (and musical sounds).

Before the decade's end, a fresh spirit of criticism was abroad. The Supreme Court had spoken in a historic school segregation case, and blacks had already discovered the techniques that could force change. Martin Luther King demonstrated their resolve to an uneasy nation at Montgomery in 1955. In John Kennedy, liberals had found a practical hero and the Right a vulnerable enemy. An era of muckraking, which began late in the decade with the writings of C. Wright Mills, John Kenneth Galbraith, Michael Harrington, and others, revealed areas of national shame and failure. The nation would soon come to noisy confrontation over the changes the 1950's had quietly wrought.

Nixon Agonistes:
The Checkers Speech

GARRY WILLS

Nixon-watching, like Johnson-watching and Kennedy-watching, has become a minor national pastime. Men who get to be President usually are highly complex people, and political success at any level often requires a certain amount of evasion, what Richard Nixon himself has called being "devious . . . in the best sense." However understandable evasiveness may be, it is ironic that a large amount of the unflattering reputation for deviousness that has accompanied Nixon throughout his political career comes from his famous "Checkers" speech of 1952— a talk given in defense against charges that the candidate had spent campaign funds on personal needs. ("Checkers" was the Nixons' cocker spaniel, an irrelevant animal Nixon dragged into the speech along with his wife's "cloth" coat.) As Garry Wills shows, this was in many ways the most open moment of Nixon's career, an occasion when he was forced to tear aside the veil of privacy which has been his primary way of handling the ferocious demands of public life. Unlike Lyndon Johnson, Richard Nixon is not comfortable before the crowds.

The Checkers speech ushered in the age of television politics. Estes Kefauver, investigating criminals in 1950, had made himself a household name in a series of nationally televised hearings, but he had not tailored the medium to his ends. Nixon was the first politician to realize the immense possibilities of television and to exploit every subtle popular response the new medium could evoke. Intellectuals have always held the Checkers speech in bad odor, seeing in it a disgusting exhibition of bathos and an unvarnished attempt to manipulate public emotions. But Wills details the tensions and political infighting which surged around the vice-presidential candidate during the week preceding the speech. He argues persuasively that the Checkers speech was both Nixon's only chance to save his career and also a direct confrontation with the presidential candidate, Dwight D. Eisenhower.

One other thing I probably should tell you, because if I don't they'll probably be saying this about me too, we did get something—a gift—after the election. A man down in Texas heard Pat on the radio mention the fact that our two youngsters would like to have a dog. And, believe it or not, the day before we left on this campaign trip we got a message from Union Station in Baltimore saying that they had a package for us. We went down to get it. You know what it was? It was a little cocker spaniel dog in a crate that he sent all the way from Texas. Black and white spotted. And our little girl— Tricia, the six-year-old—named it Checkers. And you know the kids love that dog and I just want to say this right now, that regardless of what they say about it, we're going to keep it.—The Checkers Speech

Riding in the staff bus during Nixon's 1968 campaign, I talked with one of his speech writers about the convention in Miami. Nixon's wooing of Strom Thurmond had been much criticized. But Nixon's man now said the acceptance speech eclipsed everything that went before: "That was so clearly the major event of the convention—a brilliant job. To talk about that convention is, simply, to talk about that speech. What did *you* think of it?" I answered that it reminded me of the Checkers speech. The comment seemed to horrify my interlocutor; and Professor Martin Anderson, traveling with Nixon as an adviser on urban matters, turned around in the seat before us to object: "People forget that the Checkers speech was a political master stroke, an act of political genius!" But I had not forgotten: that was, I assured him, my point.

Professor Anderson's defensiveness was understandable. Nixon has often been sneered at, over the years, for his television speech in the campaign of 1952. The very term "Checkers speech," reducing the whole broadcast to its saccharine doggy-passage, is a judgment in itself. But that broadcast saved Nixon's career, and made history. By the beginning of the 1968 campaign, sixteen years later, it was a journalistic commonplace that Nixon did not appear to advantage on television. His wan first TV encounter with John Kennedy had dimmed the public's earlier impression. But Nixon only risked that debate with Kennedy because he had such a record of success on the TV screen: in the history of that medium, his 1952 speech was probably a greater milestone than the presidential debate that came eight years later. Nixon first demonstrated the political uses and impact of television. In one half hour Nixon converted himself from a liability, breathing his last, to one of the few people who could add to Eisenhower's preternatural appeal— who could gild the lily. For the first time, people saw a living political drama on their TV sets—a man fighting for his whole career and future —and they judged him under that strain. It was an even greater achievement than it seemed. He had only a short time to prepare for it. The show, forced on him, was meant as a form of political euthanasia. He came into the studio still reeling from distractions and new demoralizing blows.

Nixon, naturally, puts the Checkers speech, along with the whole "fund crisis," among the six crises he survived with credit. It belongs there. He probably displayed more sheer nerve in that crisis than in any of the others. As a freshman in Congress, he did not stand to lose so much by the Hiss investigation. He had, moreover, an unsuspected hoard of evidence in that encounter; and he was backed by dedicated men like Father Cronin, while backing another dedicated man, Whittaker Chambers. In the crises he deals with after 1952, he was a Vice-President, in some way speaking for the nation, buoyed by its resources, defending it as much as himself; never totally without dignity. But at the time when he went onto the TV screen in 1952, he was hunted and alone. Nine years later he would write of that ordeal, "This speech was to be the most important of my life. I felt now that it was my battle alone. I had been deserted by so many I had thought were friends but who panicked in battle when the first shot was fired." It was, without exaggeration, "the most searing personal crisis of my life." It was also the experience that took the glitter out of politics for Mrs. Nixon. . . .

The first news story broke on Thursday, September 18. There had been warnings in the Nixon camp all the four preceding days. A newsman in Washington asked Nixon about the fund on Sunday. Monday, three other reporters checked facts with Dana Smith, the administrator of the fund. By Wednesday, Jim Bassett, Nixon's press secretary, heard something was brewing from his old reporter friends. The candidate had just begun his first major tour—a whistlestop north through California; when the train stopped for water around midnight, a worried staff man waited with more rumors. Thursday, it broke: the New York *Post* had a story with the headline, SECRET RICH MEN'S TRUST FUND KEEPS NIXON IN STYLE FAR BEYOND HIS SALARY. The story did not justify that sensational summary, and neither did subsequent investigation. The fund was public, independently audited, earmarked for campaign expenses, and collected in small donations over two years by known Nixon campaign backers. It was neither illegal nor unethical. And the press soon discovered that the Democratic nominee, Adlai Stevenson, had similar funds, only larger in their amount and looser in their administration. Why, then, was so much made of Nixon's fund, and so little of Stevenson's?

Nixon's official explanation, at the time, was his standard charge: the commies were behind it all. By Friday morning, the day after the charge was published, there were hecklers at his train stops to shout "Tell us about the sixteen thousand!" At a town called Marysville, he did tell them. His own version of that speech, included in his book, is more moderate than some others; but even his excerpts seem gamy enough: "You folks know the work that I did investigating Communists in the United States. Ever since I have done that work the Communists and the left-wingers have been fighting me with every possible smear. When I received the nomination for the Vice Presidency I was warned that if I continued to attack the Communists in this government they would continue to smear me. And believe me, you can expect that they will continue to do so. They started it yesterday. They have tried to say that I had taken $16,000 for my personal use." The *they* is conveniently vague throughout. They—i.e., the New York *Post* and other papers—published the charge. Go far enough back up the paragraph, through intervening "theys," and you find that the antecedent is, more immediately, "the Communists in this Government," and, in the first place, "Communists and [broad sweep here] left-wingers." The explanation is beautifully lucid and inclusive (if a little unspecific about the machinery that makes the nation's press perform the communists' bidding): since the publicizing or nonpublicizing of fund scandals is at the disposal of communists, who were (naturally) supporting Adlai Stevenson, the Stevenson fund got (naturally) no publicity like that accorded to Nixon.

Behind this funny explanation, there are scattered but clear indications, in his book, of the true story, a sad one. At one point Nixon asks why his own statement of the "basic facts" about the fund received so little attention from the press. His answer ignores the conspiratorial explanation given eight pages earlier, and supplies four reasons, two of them technical (denials never get as big a play as accusations in the press, news travels east to west and he was in California), and two more substantive: reporters are mainly Democrats (though Nixon admits that publishers are mainly Republicans, which makes for some balance), and "the big-name, influential Washington reporters cover the presidential candidates while the less-known reporters are assigned to the vice presidential candidates." The last reason, the real one, looks like another point of newspaper mechanics—the mere logistics of press assignment; until we ask why that should matter. The answer, in Nixon's own words, is that his own press release "got lost in the welter of news and speculation over whether General Eisenhower would or would not choose to find a new running mate." *That* was the news on Eisenhower's train—because Ike's advisers were known to be searching for a way to dump Nixon, and Ike was a man who at this stage followed his advisers almost blindly. In short, the Nixon fund was a big story because Eisenhower, by his silence and hints and uneasiness, made it one. For no other reason.

It was natural for Eisenhower to acquiesce in a staff decision to drop Nixon. That staff had presented him with Nixon in the first place. (Ike's knowledge of his running mate was very slim—he thought, for instance, he was forty-two rather than thirty-nine.) The General had, in fact, learned of Nixon's choice at exactly the same time Nixon did. When Herb Brownell asked Ike what he thought of Nixon, the presidential nominee expressed surprise that the decision was his to make. He said he would leave the matter to Brownell, provided the latter consulted "the collective judgment of the leaders of the party" (the top man, in military politics, protects himself by putting a subordinate in charge of the operation, under staff scrutiny). So Brownell called a meeting of the party's leaders, and went through the form of considering Taft and others. But then Dewey got up, to speak for the winning camp. Nixon he said, and Nixon it was. That decision made, Brownell went to the phone, dialed Nixon, and had him listen in while, on another phone, he told Eisenhower that the choice had been made.

As the fund story broke, Nixon wondered where Ike stood. Thursday went by, and Friday. No word from the General—to the public, or to Nixon. But the Establishment was at work: the very thing that had made Nixon good "for balance" made him unpalatable in himself, seen through Establishment eyes. He was there to draw in the yokels. If there was any doubt about his ability to do that, no one would feel compunction at his loss: Ike was too valuable a property to be risked with anyone who might hurt him. This was the attitude on Eisenhower's train, and it spread to Nixon's as newsmen jumped over from the main tour to watch the death throes in the smaller one. The machinery of execution made itself visible Saturday morning, when the New York *Herald Tribune*—the voice of the Eastern Establishment—asked for Nixon's resignation from the ticket. It was, Nixon realized, an order. The same voice that had summoned him was now dismissing him. A waiting game had been played for three days to see if he would go without having to be ordered, and Nixon had not gone. The Saturday editorial (written Friday), following so close on the *Post*'s revelation, appearing before Nixon had conferred with Eisenhower, was the first of several "hints" that he was not wanted. Despite his studied deference toward Eisenhower, Nixon makes it clear he was not dense: "The publishers and other top officials of the *Tribune* had very close relations with Eisenhower and" (for which read, *I mean*) "with some of his most influential supporters. I assumed that the *Tribune* would not have taken this position editorially unless it also represented the thinking of the people around Eisenhower. And, as I thought more about it, it occurred to me" (the little light bulb above a cartoon character's head—Nixon must play this role straight) "that this might well be read as" (*obviously had to be*) "the view of Eisenhower himself, for I had not heard from him since the trouble began two days before."

At ten o'clock Friday night a reporter told him the next day's *Herald Tribune* would ask him to resign. Nixon, who had not heard this, was stunned. He summoned his closest advisers, Chotiner and Bill Rogers (who would, after more of Nixon's crises, at last be his Secretary of State). These two had received the editorial an hour and a half earlier, but they were not going to tell him about it till morning—afraid he would lose sleep if he saw it (a judgment events confirmed). He asked for the editorial and read: "The proper course of Senator Nixon in the circumstances is to make a formal offer of withdrawal from the ticket." So that was it. Nixon is quite candid here: "I knew now the fat was in the fire. That sounded like the official word from Eisenhower himself." He spent four hours discussing his options with Chotiner and Rogers. Then, at two in the morning, he told his wife, and went through the whole discussion again with her.

The next day, Saturday, three days after the story broke, with newsmen plaguing him for his decision, he had to brace himself for defiance of the Establishment. It was an all-day job. He asked Chotiner and Rogers to get the ultimatum spelled out, if they could, from Ike's inner circle—Chotiner tried to reach Dewey, Rogers called Fred Seaton. They got no direct answer. But the indirect command was growing more insistent; sharper and sharper "hints" were thrown to the public (and, by this roundabout path, to Nixon). Sherman Adams had summoned a man all the way from Hawaii to join the Eisenhower train, and the man was all too obviously a second-string Nixon: Bill Knowland, tough anticommunist and Californian. Eisenhower had finally spoken too, off the record. The newsmen on his train had taken a poll that came out forty-to-two for dumping Nixon; news of this was passed along to Ike's press secretary (Dewey's press man in the last campaign, Jim Hagerty), along with the newsmen's opinion that Ike might be stalling to arrange a whitewash job for Nixon. Ike did not like such talk; it questioned not only Nixon's honesty, but his. He invited the newsmen into his compartment for a talk off the record—but the main part of it was soon made public. "I don't care if you fellows are forty-to-two against me, but I'm taking my time on this. Nothing's decided, contrary to your idea that this is all a setup for a whitewash of Nixon. Nixon has got to be clean as a hound's tooth." Again, Nixon got the point: "Our little group was somewhat[!] dismayed by reports of Eisenhower's attitude.

I must admit it made me feel like the little boy caught with jam on his face."

By Saturday night, then, the issue was clear: knuckle under, or defy the closest thing modern America has had to a political saint. Nixon, here as in all his crises, claims the decision was made on purely selfless grounds: he was thinking of Ike's own welfare—switching men in mid-campaign might make the General unpopular. (This is like worrying that the Milky Way might go out.) Not that Nixon is insincere in his claim. Politicians are very deft at persuading themselves that the world's best interests just happen to coincide with the advancement of their own careers. He says he put the question to his four advisers (Chotiner, Rogers, Bassett, and Congressman Pat Hillings) this way: "Forget about me. If my staying on the ticket would lead to Eisenhower's defeat, I would never forgive myself. If my getting off the ticket is necessary to assure his victory, it would be worth it, as far as any personal embarrassment to me is concerned. Looking at it this way—should I take the initiative and resign from the ticket at this time?"

But Nixon does not feel obliged to present his friends as men crippled by nobility. Chotiner, for instance, plays straight man here, saying all the "natural" things Nixon is too lofty for: "How stupid can they be? If these damned amateurs around Eisenhower just had the sense they were born with they would recognize that this is a purely political attack . . . This whole story has been blown up out of all proportion because of the delay and indecision of the amateurs around Eisenhower." Not even good old Murray, though, blunt fellow as he is, can be described in this book as attacking the Big Man himself—just the little men around him. When Nixon's friends start criticizing Eisenhower, the veil of anonymity must be lowered over them: "But now, some were beginning to blame Eisenhower, for not making a decision one way or the other." Nixon himself would never dream of questioning his leader: "What had happened during the past week had not shaken my faith in Eisenhower. If, as some of my associates thought, he appeared to be indecisive, I put the blame not on him but on his lack of experience in political warfare and on the fact that he was relying on several equally inexperienced associates. I could see his dilemma."

The decision to be made at this session was simple: obey the order relayed by the *Herald Tribune,* or risk disobedience. But, after a full day of campaigning through Oregon, he sat up with his inner circle, in Portland, debating the matter till three in the morning. Then, left alone, he went over the whole thing in his mind for two more hours. By five o'clock Sunday morning, he had set himself on a course he meant never to abandon: he would not resign. Sunday brought blow on blow meant to shake that resolution. First, there was a long telegram from Harold Stassen, still trying to clear some path for himself. He recommended, for Nixon's own good ("it will strengthen you and aid your career"), that a resignation be sent right off to Ike. Then, that afternoon, Dewey called to give Nixon the decision of "all the fellows here in New York." Dewey had a plan for breaking the stalemate caused by Nixon's refusal to resign and Eisenhower's refusal to back him: Nixon must plead his cause before the people. If the response was big enough, he could stay. And when Dewey said big enough, he meant the impossible—near-unanimity. Nixon reports the ultimatum this way: "You will probably get over a million replies, and that will give you three or four days to think it over. At the end of that time, if it is sixty percent for you and forty percent against you, say you are getting out, as that is not enough of a majority. If it is ninety to ten, stay on." It is no wonder Nixon—or, rather, "some of the members of my staff"—felt wary of this offer: "They feared a concerted campaign might be put under way to stack the replies against me." The whole plan was stacked against him. It started with the presumption that Nixon was through, and with feigned generosity gave him a chance to climb back onto the ticket. If Nixon took the offer and (as was expected) lost, then he must abide by the consequences. It was a brilliant way of forcing resignation on a man who was determined not to resign.

Nixon said he would consider it. Chotiner got in touch with Party Chairman Arthur Summerfield, to find out how the broadcast would be handled. Summerfield said they had offers from some TV sponsors to give Nixon one of their spots. Chotiner naturally protested: Nixon could hardly go on the air to defend himself against the charge of being a messenger boy for California businessmen, and explain this on time given him by some large corporation! He told Summerfield the National Committee would have to buy the time, if they expected any show at all. (Money had already been set aside for two half-hour appearances by the vice-presidential candidate. But now Summerfield was in the unfortunate position of not knowing who would be the candidate: if he gave one of the periods to Nixon, and Nixon failed, that left only one spot for his successor. At $75,000 a throw, these were not shows to be granted easily.)

Nixon had to deliver a scheduled speech that night (Sunday) at the Portland Temple Club. He was still considering the TV broadcast when he came back to his hotel. He knew this contest was not what it appeared—Nixon against the press, or the Democrats, or the people. It was Nixon against Ike—a contest that, as Stevenson would learn twice over, no one can expect to win. Candidates simply do not get 90 percent victories in America—and Nixon was being told to produce that figure or get lost. He was asked to do it in circumstances that told against him. Eisenhower had been presented by his managers as the voice of a purgative honesty meant to remedy corruption. The very fact that this arbiter of morals was silent, that Nixon was sent out to argue on his own, was an implied judgment on him. He would be guilty until proved innocent, and he could not call on the one character witness who, in this set of circumstances, mattered.

Meanwhile, the Eisenhower camp had received no answer to its "offer." Now was the time to turn the screw. No escape was to be left him. The phone rang in Portland. Ike. For the first and last time during the crisis. Giving the ultimatum all his personal weight: "I think you ought to go on a nationwide television program and tell them everything there is to tell, everything you can remember since the day you

entered public life. Tell them about any money you have ever received."
The public self-revelation for which Nixon would be blamed in later
years was being forced on him, against all his own inclinations, personal
and political. By temperament and conditioning, Nixon is reserved,
with Quaker insistence on the right of privacy. Nixon's mother, a
woman of tremendous self-control, later said of the Checkers speech:
"At the point when he gave that itemized account of his personal expenditures, I didn't think I could take it."

Nixon asked Eisenhower if he meant to endorse him. The response
was put in a particularly galling way: "If I issue a statement now backing you up, in effect people will accuse me of condoning wrongdoing."
Ike knew, and Nixon knew he knew, that the results of a vast survey of
Nixon's affairs would be available in a matter of hours. This study had
been going on for three days; Sherman Adams, at the outset of the
scandal, called Paul Hoffman, one of the architects of Eisenhower's
candidacy, and ordered a thorough inquest into Nixon's finances. Hoffman went to the best. He put Price Waterhouse to work checking
Nixon's accounts, and the law firm of Gibson, Dunn and Crutcher went
over all legal aspects of the matter. Fifty lawyers and accountants worked
on a round-the-clock basis. The results of this scrutiny were being com-
piled Sunday night. No wrongdoing would be found. The objective
moral evidence would soon be in Eisenhower's hands. But he refused
to make his own judgment based on this evidence. He wanted the people, who could not know as much as he did, to decide whether Nixon
was honest, and he would follow them. The people, meanwhile, were
waiting to hear Ike's decision so they could follow *him*. Nixon was
caught between two juries, each of which was waiting for the other to
reach a verdict before it would move.

He tried to strike a bargain: if Eisenhower was satisfied with the
TV broadcast, would he *at that point* make a decision to endorse
Nixon? (If he did not, then a victory scored on the TV screen would
be subject to attrition, as lingering or renewed doubts worked on a
situation inexplicably unresolved.) But Ike was not making bargains:
he said he would need three or four days (the same period Dewey had
mentioned) for the popular reaction to be accurately gauged—during
which time, Nixon would presumably be stalled in Los Angeles waiting
for the response, his campaign tour all too noticeably suspended. Nixon
finally blew: "There comes a time when you have to piss or get off the
pot!" But Seraphim piss not, neither Cherubim. The great Cherub sat
blithely there, enthroned on his high pot. Nixon sculpts and prettifies
the unyielding refusal: "One of Eisenhower's most notable characteristics is that he is not a man to be rushed on important decisions."

There was nothing he could do now but go ahead with the show.
And if so, the sooner the better. Chotiner was back on the phone getting
clearance for the $75,000. Sherman Adams and Arthur Summerfield
finally yielded that point around midnight. The press corps had been
alerted, an hour before, that there would be an announcement. It was
one o'clock in the morning when Nixon came down; newsmen thought
this must be it—his resignation. He deliberately built up suspense by

saying he was breaking off—tense pause—his campaign tour. To make a statement over television. Two days from now. Tuesday night. He let them think it might still be his resignation he would announce. The more interest he could generate in the next two days, the bigger his audience on Tuesday night.

That was Monday morning. He got little sleep before he boarded a plane for Los Angeles that afternoon; during the flight, he drafted the first of a series of outlines for his talk. In Los Angeles, he got the reports from Price Waterhouse and Gibson, Dunn in time to put their findings in presentable summary. After midnight, he called his old English and history teachers at Whittier College, with a request that they find some suitable Lincoln quotes for the speech. They phoned two quotes to him by ten o'clock that morning—one witty and one maudlin (he used the latter). Nixon walked the streets with Bill Rogers, discussing approaches he might take. He was keyed up, and thought he just might bring it off.

And then the last blow fell. Tuesday, after a mere four hours of sleep, he kept at his outline resolution, as is his way. He did not go to El Capitan Theater to check the TV set or props or lighting; he wanted every minute for his preparation—it was a pattern familiar to those who have watched Nixon key himself up for a crisis by mood-setting spiritual exercises. And then, with less than an hour before he must leave for the studio, the cruel blow came, shattering his schedule, his carefully programmed psychological countdown. It was Dewey on the phone again, with a last demand: "There has been a meeting of all of Eisenhower's top advisers. They have asked me to tell you that it is their opinion that at the conclusion of the broadcast tonight you should submit your resignation to Eisenhower." The Establishment was taking no chances that its scheme might misfire. Nixon asked if that was the word from the General's own mouth. Dewey answered that the men he spoke of would not have commissioned him to make such a call at such an hour unless they were speaking for the master. (But, as usual, Ike was protected: afterward he could write, "Just before the broadcast Governor Dewey telephoned him from New York reporting the conviction of some of my supporters there"—two can play at that "some of the staff" game—"that he should resign, which the young Senator later said he had feared represented my views." Poor Senator, so fearful, so young, so avuncularly cared for in this retrospective benediction. Those who have called Nixon a master of duplicity should contrast his account of the fund crisis with the smoothed-over version in Eisenhower's book, which does not even mention the "hound's tooth" remark.)

Nixon stalled on the line to Dewey, stalled and wriggled. He said it was too late to change his prepared speech. Dewey said he could, of course, deliver his personal defense and accounting; all he had to do was tack on, at the end, a formal resignation offered to Ike. Nixon said he had to leave for the studio. Dewey: "Can I say you have accepted?" Nixon: "You will have to watch the show to see—and tell them I know something about politics too!"

Nixon had a half hour to tell his staff of this new lightning bolt, get their reaction, shower, shave, dress for the show, making meanwhile his own decision—and trying to collect his wits and memory over the notes for his talk. It had been five days full of pressure, sleeplessness, betrayal, ultimatums—climaxed with the most unsettling demand of all, made when he was at a poise of tension and could be knocked off balance so easily. A whole series of crises. Thursday: answer the charges? Friday: dodge newsmen, or face them; rely on the formal answer or return to the defense again and again; stall or throw oneself upon Ike's mercy? Saturday: heed the *Trib* and resign? Sunday: do the TV show? Monday: what to say on the show? And now, at the last minute, Tuesday: defy Dewey (and, through him, Ike)? Already the strain had shown in Nixon. Sunday in Portland, when Hillings brought a wire from Nixon's mother with the Quaker understated promise of prayers WE ARE THINKING OF YOU, Nixon broke down and cried. "I thought I had better leave the room," Hillings said, "and give him time to compose himself." Chotiner, busy calling party people to get money for the show, remembered "I was more worried about Dick's state of mind than about the Party. He was edgy and irritable."

Even the inner circle could not tell for sure whether Nixon would stand up to the pressure, or give in while he spoke. After reporting Dewey's call, he was silent, his mind working desperately at the problem. During the twenty-five-minute ride to the studio, he went over his notes (on debater-type cards). He had withdrawn to his last ditch, to make an entirely lone stand there. The one thing he demanded in studio arrangements was that even Chotiner and Rogers be kept out. Only his wife would be present, within camera range, visible to Nixon. It is as if he were dramatizing, to himself more than others, the isolation he stood in at this dying moment of defiance.

One of the criticisms made of Nixon's television speech is that the hoarse voice and hurt face, hovering on the edge of tears, were either histrionic or (if unfeigned) disproportionate and "tasteless." But no one who knows the full story can suspect Nixon of acting, or blame him for the tension he felt and conveyed—it would be like blaming a recently flayed man for "indecent exposure." Nixon was deserted, in more ways than he could tell. And he was fighting back with more nerve than anybody knew. Besides concentrating fiercely on his appeal to the audience, which had to succeed if anything else were to follow, he was reaching out across their heads to touch swords in a secret duel with Ike.

And Eisenhower understood. Stewart Alsop, in his useful little book *Nixon and Rockefeller*, quotes from an interview with one who watched Eisenhower's reactions throughout the TV show. The General had to give a speech in Cleveland as soon as Nixon went off the air; the audience for that talk was watching a large screen in the auditorium, while Eisenhower and thirty of his people clustered by the TV set in a backstage office. Even this entourage, predominantly opposed to Nixon, was touched as the show progressed; some wept openly. But Eisenhower was calm, tapping a yellow pad with his pencil, ready to jot down comments on the speech. He took no notes while the talk was in progress, though the tapping stopped twice. Nixon, forced to act like a criminal who must clear himself, deftly made his actions look like those of a man with nothing to fear. And he issued a challenge: the *other* candidates must have something to fear, unless they followed his example. He devoted much of his half hour to this challenge, dictating terms to his accusers. (It is this part of the speech—moving onto the offensive—that so pleased Chotiner.)

Now I'm going to suggest some courses of conduct.

First of all, you have read in the papers about other funds. Now, Mr. Stevenson, apparently, had a couple—one of them in which a group of business people paid and helped to supplement the salaries of state employees. Here is where the money went directly into their pockets.

I think what Mr. Stevenson should do is come before the American people, as I have, and give the names of the people who have contributed to that fund, and give the names of the people who put this money into their pockets at the same time they were receiving money from their state government, and see what favors, if any, they gave out for that.

I don't condemn Mr. Stevenson for what he did. But, until the facts are in there, a doubt will be raised.

As far as Mr. Sparkman is concerned, I would suggest the same thing. He's had his wife on the payroll. I don't condemn him for that. But I think he should come before the American people and indicate what outside sources of income he has had.

I would suggest that under the circumstances both Mr. Sparkman and Mr. Stevenson should come before the American people, as I have, and make a complete statement as to their financial history. If they don't it will be an admission that they have something to hide. And I think you will agree with me.

Because, remember, a man who's to be President and a man who's to be Vice President must have the confidence of all the people. That's why I'm doing what I'm doing, and that's what I suggest that Mr. Stevenson and Mr. Sparkman, since they are under attack, should be doing.

Eisenhower stopped tapping with his pencil—jabbed it, instead, down into the yellow pad—when Nixon said any candidate who did not reveal his finances must have something to hide. Of course, Nixon did not mention Eisenhower, and his phrase about other candidates joining him "since they are under attack" left a loophole for the General. But the overall force of the passage could not be missed. All candidates, he was arguing, should act as he had. That meant *Eisenhower,* too—as Ike realized, and events were to prove. After this all the candidates did make their statements.

There were reasons why it was inconvenient for Eisenhower to make his books public—e.g., the special tax decision on earnings of his *Crusade in Europe.* Besides, as Alsop delicately puts it, "the military rarely get into the habit of making charitable contributions . . ." More important, Nixon was turning the tables on Ike. Eisenhower had brought him to this revelation. Nixon would force the same hard medicine down his mentor's throat.

Yet an even defter stroke followed. Dewey had been vague on how the speech should be judged. He told Nixon to have telegrams addressed to Los Angeles, and measure the talk's impact by their content. This arrangement, besides tying Nixon down for several days, still left the matter with Eisenhower. The real decision would be made by the General, assessing news reaction. Nixon would be left to play games with his switchboard and his mail, unable to vindicate himself if Eisenhower decided the show had not cleared him.

But when it came time for Nixon to mention the sending of telegrams, he said: "I am submitting to *the Republican National Committee* tonight, through this television broadcast, the decision *it is theirs to make* . . . Wire and write *the Republican National Committee* whether you think I should stay or whether I should get off; and whatever *their decision* is, I will abide by it." (Italics added.) The General stabbed again, pencil into pad, a sword struck down as he fenced that image on the screen, and lost. Nixon has always been a party man; his strength lay there. Karl Mundt and Robert Humphreys, manning the Washington headquarters of the National Committee while Chairman Arthur Summerfield traveled with Ike, had routinely issued statements backing Nixon from the very first day of his troubles. Now, by a cool disarming maneuver, Nixon was taking the matter away from the Eastern Establishment and putting it in the hands of men sympathetic to the regulars, to grassroots workers—people who respond in a partisan way to partisan attacks upon one of their own, people most vulnerable to the planned schmaltz and hominess of the Checkers reference, people with small debts of their own and Republican cloth coats. If the decision was theirs to make, then—the real point of the broadcast as Nixon had reshaped it—*it was not Ike's.* It is no wonder that, while others in Cleveland wept, the man who had directed OVERLORD, the largest military operation in the world's history, the *General,* made an angry stab. He knew enough about maneuver to see he was outflanked. Alsop's informant said: "Before that, I'd always liked and admired Ike, of course, but I'd often wondered how smart he really was. After that, I knew Ike got what Dick was getting at right away."

The importance of that decision, redirecting the appeal to the National Committee, explains Nixon's breakdown when he saw he had gone off the air. Under the pressure of the performance, undertaken without rehearsal, using sketchy notes, he had done something rare for him—missed the countdown toward sign-off by a minute or two: "Time had run out. I was cut off just as I intended to say where the National Committee was located and where the telegrams and letters should be sent." He had based everything on this point; he needed every wire that would reach Washington. What if the telegrams were diffused ineffectually about the country, sent to him, to Ike, to TV channels and local campaign offices? He needed a crushing weight of response all directed to one point, and now (he thought) he would not get it. (The wires in fact did go everywhere, but in such breathtaking numbers that all doubt was swept before them.) He threw his cards to the floor in a spasm, told Pat he had failed; when Chotiner came into the studio, elated by the skilled performance, Nixon just shook his head and claimed, "I was an utter flop." Outside the theater, as his car pulled away, an Irish setter friskily rocked alongside barking: Nixon turned,

Bill Rogers would remember, and twisted out a bitter, "At least I won the dog vote tonight." The end, he thought, of the Checkers speech. He was touching bottom. That night he would finally, after all his earlier resistance, resign.

But it took more kicks and blows to bring him to it. During the first hours after his broadcast, others were jubilant and support poured in; but no call came from the General (a wire had been sent off, but was stuck in the traffic-jam of them at Nixon's hotel switchboard—no one called from the Cleveland camp to give Nixon its message). The first notice he had of the telegram came over the news wires—and it brought word of still another ultimatum. Eisenhower did not often lose wars of attrition. They were his kind of battle.

The crowd waiting for Ike in Cleveland was hoarse with shouts and praise for the TV show they had witnessed. Eisenhower's own first comment was to Chairman Summerfield, about the $75,000: "Well, Arthur, you got your money's worth." Hagerty came back from the auditorium and told Eisenhower he could not deliver his prepared talk on inflation with this crowd. He would have to speak to the Nixon issue. The General knew. He had already chosen his strategy. He fashioned its main lines on the yellow pad, and tried it on his advisers. First, a sop to the crowd: "I like courage . . . Tonight I saw an example of courage . . . I have never seen anyone come through in such a fashion as Senator Nixon·did tonight . . . When I get in a fight, I would rather have a courageous and honest man by my side than a whole boxcar full of pussyfooters."

All the praise was a cover, though. Eisenhower was a master of the basics—supply, firepower, and retention of position. After praising Nixon for courage, Ike added that he had not made his mind up on the main subject—whether Nixon would remain on the ticket: "It is obvious that I have to have something more than one single presentation, necessarily limited to thirty minutes, the time allowed Senator Nixon." But if Eisenhower, who had chosen him as his running mate, who had access to the research of the lawyers and accountants, to the advice of top politicians in the party, could not make up his mind after watching the TV show, then how could anyone in the public do so? There is only one explanation for this performance: Ike was determined not to let Nixon take the decision out of his hands. "I am not going to be swayed by my idea of what will get most votes . . . I am going to say: Do I myself believe this man is the kind of man America would like to have for its Vice President?" That is, at one minute he will not be swayed by what the people want and would vote for, and the next minute he is accepting the sacred pledge of finding out what the public wants and will vote for!

Then Eisenhower read them his telegram to Nixon, which shows the real thrust of his remarks: "While technically no decision rests with me, you and I know the realities of the situation require a pronouncement which the public considers decisive." (Or: Get your National Committee support, and see how far it carries you without me.) "My personal decision is going to be based on personal conclusions." (Or: I won't judge you by reaction to your talk—which is what he had promised he *would* do.) "I would most appreciate it if you can fly to see me at once." (Or: Here, Rover.) "Tomorrow evening I will be at Wheeling, W. Va." (Or: Tomorrow *you* will be at Wheeling, W. Va.) Not only was Eisenhower reasserting the personal jurisdiction Nixon had challenged; he wanted a public dramatization of the lines of authority. Having cleared himself with the public, Nixon must appear before a superior tribunal, summoned there to make his defense again, in greater detail, while judgment was pointedly suspended.

Nixon could not submit; yet, once the demand was made public, he could not go further in public defiance, either. He gave in. Rose Woods took down his dictated telegram of resignation.

But he would get in one last blow of his own. The wire was not directed toward Eisenhower, as Dewey had insisted it should be. He addressed it to the National Committee! As Rose Woods went out of the room to send the message, Chotiner followed her and tore off the top sheet of her pad. Rose said she could not have sent it anyway. Nixon is, by his own admission, subject to sharp lapses and lowering of his guard in the emotional depletion that follows on conflict. In four of his book's six crises he finds an example of that pattern: and the example for the fund crisis is his telegram to the National Committee. His loss of grip began the minute the show went off the air and he threw his cards to the floor. " 'What more can he possibly want from me?' I asked . . . I didn't believe I could take any more of the suspense and tension of the past week." Chotiner went to work on him, however, and persuaded him that he could avoid both of the unpalatable things being forced on him—resignation, or compliance with Eisenhower's summons. If he just resumed his interrupted campaign-schedule (next step, Missoula, Montana), the General would have to back down. The wave of public response was already seismic. Nixon reports Chotiner's counsel this way: "Chotiner, particularly, insisted that I not allow myself to be put in the position of going to Eisenhower like a little boy to be taken to the woodshed, properly punished, and then restored to a place of dignity." At this point, there was a call from Ike's camp. Arthur Summerfield, pleased that things had turned out well, was asking for Chotiner—who soon dashed his spirits. Murray said Nixon had just dictated his resignation; he admitted, when Summerfield gasped, that the telegram was torn up—"but I'm not so sure how long it's going to stay torn." Summerfield said things could be smoothed over when Dick reached Wheeling. But Dick was not going to Wheeling: "We're flying to Missoula tonight." Summerfield wanted to know how to head off this disaster—so Chotiner set terms: Nixon will not come unless he is sure of a welcoming endorsement, without further inquisition. This was, of course, a demand that Eisenhower back down on the stated purpose of the summons, which was to go into greater detail than thirty minutes would allow.

Eisenhower, realistic about cutting his losses, saw when this news reached him that the idea of further investigation could not be sustained. He let Summerfield give Nixon's camp the proper assurances.

But Nixon would still be answering a humiliating public call. Just before the plane took off for Missoula, Bert Andrews, who had worked with Nixon all through the Hiss affair, called from the Eisenhower press room in Cleveland: Ike would have no choice now but to receive Nixon warmly; Nixon would have to lose a little face in order to avoid flouting the General's summons. Nixon agreed, and let his staff arrange a flight to Wheeling after the stop at Missoula. Ike was at the airport, to throw his arm around him and call him "my boy"—looking gracious, kind, generous, as if supporting an embattled man rather than picking up strength from a victorious one. The only thing that could resolve the crisis—Ike's blue-eyed smile of benediction—had been bestowed.

But they did not forget the night when they touched swords. There would never be any trust between them. And Nixon had begun a tutelage that would gall him and breed resentment through years of friction and slights.

The Underestimation
of Dwight D. Eisenhower

MURRAY KEMPTON

Dwight Eisenhower was surely among the most beloved of American Presidents. Yet his case is unusual for he was clearly a man loved for what he was rather than for what he did in the White House. And voter affection for the former General did not apparently extend to his adopted party: for six of his eight years in office, Eisenhower faced a Congress in which the Republicans constituted a minority. As Rexford Tugwell has pointed out, he was "the least partisan President" since George Washington. He stood above the political battle—where the people apparently wanted him to stand. And of course this rendered the battle beneath—the world of such men as Vice President Richard Nixon and Senate Majority leader Lyndon Johnson—that much less interesting. Depression and war had meant a generation of political excitement and conflict. After 1952 the pendulum swung, and Americans enjoyed respite from turbulence, sat back, and left things to Ike.

Eisenhower's accomplishments as President were limited but real. He stabilized the Cold War around a potentially disastrous strategy of "massive retaliation" which he had no intention of invoking except in speeches. And he stabilized the New Deal, neither extending it nor cutting it back, therefore making it part of the mainstream of American politics. And he did cool off the sour tensions accumulating over a generation of political stress. What he did not do, the problems that he simply kept in the cooler, nevertheless began to emerge during his second administration. A long list of national needs (that were to define the accomplishments and the failures of the tumultuous sixties) was already pressing for action when Dwight Eisenhower bid his farewell with a prescient warning about the "military-industrial complex" that had grown over-mighty during his own administration. Whether Eisenhower's record deserved the criticism it drew from liberals during the 1950's or whether his presidency merits the encomiums that they are bestowing on him in the war-weary present is the question posed in these readings by Murray Kempton and Richard H. Rovere.

He was a far more complex and devious man than most people realized, and in the best sense of those words.—Richard Nixon, *Six Crises*

The full moment of revelation about the great captains may be possible only for one of the casualties they leave behind them. Richard Nixon was writing in hospital: just once, the resentment whose suppression is the great discipline of his life breaks through and is taken back with that saving clause about the best sense of the word, of course. Yea, though He slay me yet must I depend on Him.

Dwight Eisenhower was as indifferent as Calvin Coolidge, as absolute as Abraham Lincoln, more contained than John Kennedy, more serpentine than Lyndon Johnson, as hard to work for as Andrew Johnson. Historians seem to accept most of these qualities as necessary for greatness; certainly none of them diminish it. But, then, most are accounted sinister by the great mass of civilians, and to confuse civilians and to keep them off his back is the soldier's art. Eisenhower, who understood everything, seems to have decided very early that life is nothing unless it is convenient; to show the living flesh of greatness to one's contemporaries means to show one's face in combat and to be argued about; the only convenient greatness is to appear as a monument.

The most precise description of Eisenhower was rendered in another connection by Edward Lear:

> On the top of the Crumpetty Tree
>   The Quangle Wangle sat,
> But his face you could not see,
>   On account of his Beaver Hat
> For his Hat was a hundred and
>   two feet wide,
>   With ribbons and bibbons on
>   every side
>   And bells, and buttons, and loops,
>   and lace.
> So that nobody ever could see the face
>   Of the Quangle Wangle Quee.

Innocence was Eisenhower's beaver hat, and the ribbons grew longer and more numerous until his true lines were almost invisible. It took a very long watch indeed to catch the smallest glimpse.

"He told Nixon and others, including myself, that he was well aware that somebody had to do the hard-hitting infighting,[1] and he had no objections to it as long as no one expected *him* to do it," Sherman Adams says.

It was the purpose of his existence never to be seen in what he did. When he fired Sherman Adams, his chief of staff, as a political liability in 1958, Adams thought it was Nixon's doing. While he was coldly measuring the gain or loss from dropping Nixon as his 1952 Vice-Presidential candidate, Nixon thought it was Tom Dewey's doing.

When this gesture proved insufficient, Eisenhower accommodated to what was inevitable, if transient, and even offered himself up as battle trophy for Goldwater's brief triumph at the San Francisco convention. It was a situation where, the surreptitiously neat having failed, the heroically messy could hardly succeed. The useless employment of further resources would have been an affront to that superb sense of economy which made Eisenhower a soldier successful just being so immune to notions of glory and to pleasurable anticipations of bleeding.

"He is the most immoral man I have ever known," one of Nelson

---

1. *Definable to the Democrats as the dirty work.*

Rockefeller's captains said not long ago. He was probably wrong; there is always the danger of going overboard in moments when the watcher thinks he has found Eisenhower out. To be absolutely immoral is a perilous excess; being moderate in all things means, after all, being moderate in the expenditure of morality.

No thought was to be uttered undisguised; the face had as many ranges, indeed as many roles as there are sins to commit, because it was an instrument for hinting without ever quite saying. Even the syntax was an instrument. When things were at their stickiest in the Formosa Strait, James Hagerty, his Press Secretary, told the President that the best course would be to refuse to answer any questions at all on the subject if it came up at his press conference.

" 'Don't worry, Jim,' I told him as we went out the door. 'If that question comes up, I'll just confuse them.' "

Those press conferences, his highest achievements as craftsman in masks, seem certain to be half the sport and half the despair of historians; they will give up, one has to assume, and settle for the judgment that he was a man hopelessly confused, it being so difficult to confess that anyone, across so many years, could still so superbly confuse you. The mask he contrived for his comfort has already become the reputation. Generals like MacArthur and Montgomery, as proud of their intelligence as he was appalled by their weakness for theatre, seem to have thought him stupid, as he certainly thought them a little dippy. The other Presidents already evoked most often for comparison with him are General Grant and James Buchanan. But still there abides the mystery of why he never left the country ruined by his laziness, as Buchanan did, or himself ruined by his friends, as Grant did.

The difference in both cases was partly Eisenhower's intelligence, partly his appreciation of those occasions when self-indulgence can produce worse inconveniences, partly that chilliness of his nature which protected him from ever indulging others.

"I could understand it if he played golf all the time with old Army friends, but no man is less loyal to his old friends than Eisenhower," John Kennedy observed when he was a Senator. "He is a terribly cold man. All his golfing pals are rich men he has met since 1945."

"In the evenings when he had no official engagements or on weekends," says Adams, "the President liked to spend his time with old friends whose faces were often seen at Gettysburg—Bill Robinson, the entertaining George Allen, Cliff Roberts, Pete Jones, Bob Woodruff, Al Gruenther, Slats Slater, Freeman Gosden ['Amos' of the famous radio team of Amos and Andy], Sig Larmon."

These Sigs and Petes and Slatses could hardly have been more stimulating than his old Army comrades—of whose intelligence he *does* seem to have entertained the lowest opinion—and, when one member of a salon is granted special distinction as "entertaining," his fellow inmates must be dreary indeed.

But the Sigs and Petes had one substantial advantage; they earned his affection as Casanova made *his* conquests: they were men who paid.

Once, Eisenhower remembers, he had a few days' rest in Scotland on a state trip; and someone, thinking he might be lonely, suggested that he call a few friends to fly over for golf and bridge.

"The idea," he says, "struck me as intriguing, in certain respects the brighest I had heard during the entire trip. Forgetting the time differential, I picked up the telephone and within minutes was talking to Bill Robinson in New York. My call got him out of bed; in New York it was two o'clock in the morning. Without a moment's hesitation he accepted my invitation and a few hours later he and 'Pete' Jones were on their way. I was indeed fortunate to have friends who were such light sleepers."

He lived among strangers; his protective coloration was the appearance of being amiable and innocent. Very seldom does he give himself away: once he said that, when he was President of Columbia, he never went for a walk at night without carrying his service revolver with him. There is surprising hauteur in this image of the most eminent neighbor at large in Morningside Heights; but there is also the grandeur of a man whose dedication it was never to experience a moment on confrontation without the proper weight of means; to him all life was a matter of logistics.

He is revealed best, if only occasionally, in the vast and dreary acreage of his memoirs of the White House years. There he could feel safe in an occasional lapse of guard. For one thing, political history is the opiate of Democrats and he had spent eight years grandly erasing any suggestion from the minds of anyone else that anything he might ever say could be remotely interesting. He had concealed his marvelous intelligence from admirer and critic alike; by now, there was little danger of its being noticed even if confessed; he could be as secure in his memoirs as in his private diary.

The Eisenhower who emerges here intermittently free from his habitual veils is the President most superbly equipped for truly consequential decision we may ever have had, a mind neither rash nor hesitant, free of the slightest concern for how things might look, indifferent to any sentiment, as calm when he was demonstrating the wisdom of leaving a bad situation alone as when he was moving to meet it on those occasions when he absolutely had to.

Of course, we think: That is the way he wants us to see him; he is still trying to fool us; but he won't get away with it this time. And so he has fooled us again, for the Eisenhower who tells us that he never makes an important mistake is telling us for the first time about the real Eisenhower.

There is the sound of trumpets, the fog of rhetoric, then for just a moment the focus of the cold intelligence.

The President-elect goes to Korea.

We used light airplanes to fly along the front and were impressed by the rapidity with which wounded were being brought back for treatment; evacuation was almost completely by helicopter since there were no landing fields for conventional planes in the mountains. Except for sporadic artillery fire and sniping there was little action at the moment, *but in view of the strength of the positions the enemy had developed, it was obvious that any frontal attack would present great difficulties.*

All else would be conversation; one look had decided Eisenhower to fold the war.

Iraq's monarchy has been overthrown, Lebanon's government is collapsing, the British are otherwise committed; President Eisenhower will have to send the Marines.

The basic mission of United States forces in Lebanon was not primarily to fight. Every effort was made to have our landing be as much of a garrison move as possible. In my address I had been careful to use the term 'stationed in' Lebanon. . . . If it had been prudent, I would have preferred that the first battalion ashore disembark at a dock rather than across the beaches. However, the attitude of the Lebanese army was at that moment unknown, and it was obviously wise to disembark in deployed formation ready for any emergency. As it turned out, there was no resistance; the Lebanese along the beaches welcomed our troops. The geographic objectives of the landings included only the city of Beirut and the adjoining airfield.

And, thereunder, he appends this note of explanation:

The decision to occupy only the airfield and capital was a political one which I adhered to over the recommendations of some of the military. If the Lebanese army were unable to subdue the rebels when we had secured their capital and protected their government, I felt, we were backing up a government with so little popular support that we probably should not be there.

There was French Indochina, now of course Vietnam, and this cold intelligence looks upon the French with all the remote distance it would always feel from the romantic poetry of war:

The President is told that the French propose to put 10,000 troops in Dien Bien Phu.

. . . I said, "You cannot do this."

"This will bring the enemy into the open," he said. "We cannot find them in the jungle, and this will draw them out where we can then win."

"The French know military history," I said. "They are smart enough to know the outcome of becoming firmly emplaced and then besieged in an exposed position with poor means of supply and reinforcements."

Never thereafter could he contemplate the war in Indochina except in the frozen tones of a War College report on a maneuver by officers who can henceforth abandon all hope of promotion. The French, he instructs Foster Dulles, have committed the classic military blunder. In Geneva, Dulles is said to have hinted that the United States might use the atom bomb to save the French; there is no evidence that he would have dared transmit that suggestion to a President who plainly would not have trusted him with a stick of dynamite to blow up a fishpond.

Dulles, unhopefully, does transmit a French plea for United States bomber support of the Dien Bien Phu garrison; Eisenhower does not even seem to have noticed it. He had already made up his mind about that:

There were grave doubts in my mind about the effectiveness of such air strikes on deployed troops where good cover was plentiful. Employment of air strikes alone to support French troops in the jungle would create a double jeopardy: *it would comprise an act of war and would also entail the risk of having intervened and lost.*

Sitting with Under Secretary of State Bedell Smith, "I remarked that, if the United States were, unilaterally, to permit its forces to be drawn into conflict in Indochina, and in a succession of Asian wars, the end result would be to drain off our resources and to weaken our overall defensive position."

The French went down; Eisenhower blamed them and the British, who, of course, blamed Dulles.

Then, in his utmost refinement, there is the Eisenhower who supervised the C.I.A.'s U-2 reconnaissance flights over the Soviet Union:

A final important characteristic of the plane was its fragile construction. This led to the assumption (insisted upon by the C.I.A. and the Joint Chiefs) that in the event of mishap the plane would virtually distintegrate. It would be impossible, if things should go wrong, they said, for the Soviets to come into possession of the equipment intact—or, unfortunately, of a live pilot. This was a cruel assumption, but I was assured that the young pilots undertaking these missions were doing so with their eyes wide open and motivated by a high degree of patriotism, a swashbuckling bravado, and certain material inducements.[2]

Then Francis Powers' U-2 was shot down, and Eisenhower, of course, ordered the announcement of the "previously designed 'cover story.'"

Upon which, "Mr. Khrushchev, appearing before the Supreme Soviet once more, announced what to me was unbelievable. The uninjured pilot of our reconnaissance plane, along with much of his equipment intact, was in Soviet hands."

The State Department was still lamely adhering to the cover story. That seemed totally irrational to Eisenhower, who at once ordered a

2. One of the confusions making difficult the full appreciation of Eisenhower's subtlety is the condition that he seems to explain himself in anticlimactic series. For example: "As president of Columbia, I became deeply interested in the educational, financial and public relations aspects of the job." Normally one would expect a college president to be more interested in education than in public relations, and the succession seems anticlimactic. But, with a little thought, one understands that Eisenhower knew he was at Columbia as a public-relations man. In the same way, normal rhetoric would assign the climactic role in the readiness of a soldier to sacrifice his life to "high degree of patriotism"; Eisenhower, with perfect understanding, gives the emphasis to "certain material inducements."

full confession, altering its draft "to eliminate any phrase that seemed to me to be defensive in tone.

"In the diplomatic field," he explained, "it was routine practice to deny responsibility for an embarrassing occurrence when there is even a one percent chance of being believed, but when the world can entertain not the slightest doubt of the facts, there is no point in trying to evade the issue."

And there we have, in Dwight Eisenhower of all unexpected persons, the model of that perfect statesman of Voltaire's ironic dream, the one who could learn nothing from Machiavelli except to denounce Machiavelli.

The precepts are plain to see:

1) Always pretend to be stupid; then when you have to show yourself smart, the display has the additional effect of surprise.

2) Taking the blame is a function of servants. When the orange is squeezed, throw it away.

3) When a situation is hopeless, never listen to counsels of hope. Fold the enterprise.

4) Do nothing unless you know exactly what you will do if it turns out to have been the wrong thing. Walk not one inch forward onto ground which has not been painfully tested by someone else.

5) Never forget the conversation you had with Zhukov about how the Russian army clears minefields. "We march through them," Zhukov had said. It is a useful instruction if applied with the proper economy. Keep Nixon and Dulles around for marching through minefields.

6) Always give an enemy an exit.

7) Never give an ally his head.

8) Assume that your enemies are just as sensible as you are. ("Personally I had always discounted the probability of the Soviets doing anything as 'reaction.' Communists do little on impulse; rather their aggressive moves are invariably the result of deliberate decision.")

9) Lie whenever it seems useful, but stop lying the moment ninety-nine percent of the audience ceases to believe you.

10) Respond only when there is some gain besides honor in meeting the challenge or some serious loss from disregarding it. For example, when Eisenhower was the first candidate for President in memory who indicated that he was unable to pronounce the word "injunction" when discussing the labor problem, I suggested to one of his admirers that he seemed extraordinarily dumb.

"If he's so dumb," was the reply, "why is he such a good bridge player?"

Like all defenses of Dwight Eisenhower, it seemed silly at first; but, with thought one understood its force. Eisenhower spent the Twenties as an officer in garrison; his friends were civilians in towns like Leavenworth, Kansas. He learned to play bridge well because his pay did not cover losing money to civilians. He is equipped to respond to any challenge which seems to him sensible.

He was the great tortoise upon whose back the world sat for eight years. We laughed at him; we talked wistfully about moving; and all the while we never knew the cunning beneath the shell.

I talked to him just once. He was in Denver, getting ready for the 1952 campaign when he would have to run with Republicans like Senator Jenner who had called General Marshall, the chief agent of Eisenhower's promotion, "a living lie." I had thought that anyone so innocent as Eisenhower would be embarrassed by this comradeship and proposed to ask what he thought about what Jenner had said. It seemed cruel to spring any such trap to anyone this innocent, so I told Hagerty that I intended to ask the question.

The time came and I asked, "General, what do you think of those people who call General Marshall a living lie?"

He leaped to his feet and contrived the purpling of his face. How dare anyone say that about the greatest man who walks in America? He shook his finger in marvelous counterfeit of the palsy of outrage.

He would die for General Marshall. He could barely stand to be in the room with anyone who would utter such a profanation. The moment passed when the enlisted man in garrison endures his ordeal as example to the rest of the troops; and suddenly I realized that, in his magnificent rage at me, he had been careful not to mention Senator Jenner at all.

Afterward Hagerty took me over and the General offered the sunshine of his smile; there was not the slightest indication that he was thinking that there was anything for him to forgive or me either. It had simply been the appointed ceremony. I was too dumb to understand him then. It would be ten years before I looked at his picture and realized that the smile was always a grin.

Eisenhower Revisited—
A Political Genius?
A Brilliant Man?

RICHARD H. ROVERE

It has been slightly more than a decade since Robert Frost greeted the dawn of a "next Augustan age . . . of poetry and power" and Dwight D. Eisenhower, ex-President, left Washington for Gettysburg—still an immensely popular figure who, had the law permitted and the spirit and the flesh been willing, could easily have been the man taking the oath of office on January 20, 1961, thus deferring the Augustan age for at least four more years. Eisenhower was held in high esteem for the rest of his life, but throughout most of the sixties those amateurs who sit in more or less professional judgment on Presidents—other politicians, historians, journalists—came more and more into agreement that his eight years in the White House had been a period of meager accomplishment and lackadaisical leadership. The greatest failure, the consensus seemed to be, was one of anticipation. What a prescient statesman could have foreseen in the fifties, the argument runs, was that the ship of state was headed for a sea of troubles, and this the 34th President conspicuously failed to perceive. He lacked foresight and imagination and thus bore considerable responsibility for the difficulties of the three men who succeeded him in the sixties.

Many of those who judged him most harshly until only a few years ago are now having second and third thoughts about the man and his Presidency—thoughts that should ring most agreeably in the ears of those whose faith had never never wavered. Such nay-sayers on the left as Murray Kempton and I. F. Stone are finding virtues in him they failed to detect while he served, and others are making claims for him that not even his partisans made when he sought office or held it. Garry Wills, the eminent Nixonologist, advises us in "Nixon Agonistes" that Eisenhower was "a political genius." Walter Cronkite, who first knew Eisenhower in France during the war and saw him often in subsequent years, recently said that he never thought highly of Eisenhower "either as a general or a President" but that in the post-White House years he discovered that Eisenhower was in actuality a "brilliant" man—indeed, "more brilliant than many brilliant men I have met."

A political genius? A brilliant man? Who ever said or thought that about Eisenhower in his own time? Certainly not Eisenhower himself. It was not that he was lacking in vanity; he had his share, but there is no evidence that he ever thought of himself as possessing a great talent for politics or a towering intellect, and the aspect of his "genius" that Wills calls "realism" would have deterred him from this kind of self-appraisal. He was, and we can be sure that he knew he was, no slouch politically (had he been below average in this respect, he would not have risen in the Army), and he was certainly not lacking in intelligence. But his real strengths lay elsewhere, and the Wills and Cronkite superlatives seem, one has to say, silly.

In the case of Garry Wills, the judgment supports a theory. Wills maintains that Eisenhower all along saw Richard Nixon in the light in which Wills today sees him. In Cronkite's case, the delayed but nontheless dazzling illumination appeared in the course of many meetings he had with Eisenhower while taping some television interviews in the mid-sixties. He asserts his discovery of the ex-President's "brilliance" but does not tell us how it was made manifest.

For my part, I think the revisionist phenomenon as a whole can be rather easily accounted for—though I do not wish to suggest that new judgments are erroneous simply because they are new or, at least, as I see it, obvious in their origins. Seen from 1971, the most important single thing about Dwight D. Eisenhower was that, through luck or good management or some combination of both, *we did not go to war* while he was President. To be sure, we came close on occasion, and his Secretary of State practiced a brand of cold-war diplomacy in which what was called "brinkmanship" at the time—risking war, including nuclear war—was an indispensable strategy. It can also be argued that Dulles's and Eisenhower's Indochina policy made Kennedy's and Johnson's and Nixon's all but inevitable and that, had Eisenhower held office for a third term, he would have found himself at war in Vietnam. The contrary can also be argued, but it does not matter, we were at war when he came to office, and six months later we were out of it, and we did not enter another war during his tenure. Eight years of Eisenhower: seven and a half years of peace. Ten years of Kennedy, Johnson, Nixon: almost ten solid years of war.

What else is there to celebrate about the Eisenhower years? I can think of a few things, but they are of far less consequence and, moreover, they are not blessings of the sort that can be appreciated only in hindsight—unless one chooses to include among them such engineering projects as the St. Lawrence Seaway and the interstate highway system. Though I have myself altered some of my views about Eisenhower over the years, I have felt since 1958 or thereabouts that the country benefited from his first term but would have been better off if he had not had a second. I think I can defend this view in 1971. By 1953 we had made our point in Korea—the expulsion of the invading armies—and it was time for a settlement. It required a Republican President (not necessarily Eisenhower, though of course it helped that he was a successful military man) to end that war on terms short of the "victory" for which Gen. Douglas MacArthur said there was "no substitute." As Harry Truman was to say, he or any other Democrat would have been "lynched" for agreeing to the settlement Eisenhower so cheerfully accepted. It also required a Republican in the White House (though, again, not necessarily Eisenhower) to bring about the downfall of Senator Joe McCarthy.

Eisenhower, to be sure, never took the initiative against McCarthy. He declined to "get into the gutter" with the demagogue, and he tolerated, for a while, a certain amount of high-level appeasement. But the fact remains that 15 months after Eisenhower took office McCarthy was done for. With an active, militant President, the job might have been done somewhat sooner and with less loss of dignity all around. However, a Republican President did not have to be an activist to draw McCarthy's fire. Though nominally a Republican, McCarthy was bound by the nature of his mission in American political life to attack any administration, and when in time he attacked his own party's steward-ship of affairs, resistance was bound to be offered. It tends now to be forgotten that McCarthy scored most of his triumphs when the Demo-crats controlled both the White House and Congress, and he would probably have been more difficult to deal with had they remained in control. It has always seemed to me that the election of Adlai Stevenson in 1952, however desirable it might have been in certain respects, would have prolonged both the Korean war and McCarthyism, and I have reason to think that, in later years, Stevenson believed this, too. The country was bitterly divided in 1952, and 20 years of Democratic governance was one of the causes of disunity.

Putting Eisenhower in the White House seemed a way of promoting national unity, which, though hardly the highest of political values, is not one to be disregarded. But by 1956 Eisenhower had achieved just about all that it was in his power to achieve. The war was over, Mc-Carthy was a spent force and the President had, at the Geneva Summit Conference of 1955, helped negotiate a limited but nonetheless helpful *détente* in the cold war.

The second term was anticlimax almost all the way. It was also rather melancholy and at times squalid. The President was not a well man. The Democrats, growing in power in the Congress and knowing that no one would ever again ride Eisenhower's coattails, were openly seeking to embarrass him and passing bills he felt he had to veto. In midterm, he lost the two men he had relied on most heavily. John Foster Dulles left office and soon died, and Sherman Adams, who was general manager at the White House, had to retire because of a clear conflict of interest. Eisenhower began on his own to practice some of Dulles's peripatetic diplomacy, but it didn't work. In 1960, he started for another summit meeting, in Paris, but Nikita Khrushchev refused to make the final ascent because of the unpleasantness over the U-2 affair. Eisenhower set out for Japan, but for security reasons (rioting anti-American students, etc.) was advised to turn around and go home.

There is more to being a President than entering or ending wars—and more than instituting or failing to institute political and social change. Style and character are important and closely related aspects of leadership. Eisenhowever came to us as a hero—not in the old sense of a man who had displayed great valor but in the newer sense of having been an organizer of victory. His style, though, was anything but heroic. It was in part fatherly, in larger part avuncular. He was not an exhorter —except now and then in campaigns—and as a counselor his perform-ance was as a rule inadequate. He had difficulties with language, par-ticularly when he extemporized. Readers of press-conference texts found his syntax all but impenetrable and often concluded that his thinking was as muddled as the verbatim transcripts. Actually, he was seldom as unclear as he appeared to be when encountered in cold type. Those who listened and watched as he talked were rarely in doubt as to what he was saying. Inflection and expression conveyed much of what seemed missing or mixed up in print. But he was never, to put it mildly, eloquent, never a forceful persuader. He never influenced, or sought to influence, American thought.

Eulogizing Eisenhower in April, 1969, President Nixon said of his late mentor: "For more than a quarter of a century, he spoke with a moral authority seldom equaled in American public life." Nixon did not explain how, when or where the impact of this "moral authority" was felt. Eisenhower was an upright man, a believer in the Protestant ethic he seemed to embody. But the man he twice defeated was no less honorable, and Stevenson had a moral vision that seemed somewhat broader, deeper and less simplistic than Eisenhower's. Do any survivors recall the Eisenhower years as a period notable for elevated standards of morality in public life or elsewhere? In our public life, there were two issues full of "moral" content—McCarthyism and race. On neither did the President personally exercise any of the kind of authority Nixon attributed to him. He was not a McCarthyite or a racist, but he conspicuously failed to engage his personal prestige or that of his office in the struggles against demagogy and racial injustice.

A President can also provide leadership by improving the quality of public life—the quality of the people he appoints and associates himself with, the quality of the acts he and they perform, the quality of the ideas his administration espouses. If in the future, the brief Presidency of Eisenhower's successor is well regarded, it will be largely because of his quest for "excellence." Kennedy brought many first-rate people to Washington, and if one of the lessons they taught us is that first-rate people can sometimes mess things up as badly as third-raters or fourth-raters, it is nevertheless true that some of them performed brilliantly and should continue to serve the Republic for some years to come. No such praise, so far as I am aware, accrues to Eisenhower—except in the case of one institution, the Supreme Court.

He appointed a Chief Justice and four Associate Justices, and all but one of the five (Charles Whittaker, who sat only briefly) served with high distinction. In this respect, Eisenhower's record may be as good as any in history. There was about it, though, a kind of inadvertent quality—as if some architect had achieved splendor while seeking only mediocrity. The President was surprised and in some cases hugely disappointed by the performance of the institution he had created.

In the executive branch, mediocrity was the rule. The one Cabinet member of stature was John Foster Dulles, an imposing man in many ways but also a stiff, self-righteous Calvinist who intensified the cold war as an ideological conflict and sometimes seemed bent on making it a theological one as well—making, as he put it, "the moral force of Christendom . . . felt in the conduct of nations." Nevertheless, Dulles was a man of some intellectual prowess, and nothing of the sort could be said for anyone else in the upper echelons. Eisenhower's measure of expertise in any field was that of the Bitch Goddess: success, usually financial success. Especially in the early days, it was a businessman's administration—to a degree that bred misgivings even in the mind of the first Senator Robert Taft of Ohio, who made no bones about being a spokesman for business but said, when he heard of the first appointments, "I don't know of any reasons why success in business should mean success in public service. . . . Anyone who thinks he can just transfer business methods to government is going to have to learn that it isn't so." Eisenhower's appointments were uninspired and uninspiring; one cannot think of any major office holder whose example might have led any young man or young woman to feel that public life might be a high calling. On the White House staff, there were from time to time highly gifted younger men—Maxwell Rabb, Emmet Hughes, Malcolm Moos—but for the most part they lacked power and visibility, though Moos exerted an influence of a kind when he wrote the line about the "military-industrial complex" into Eisenhower's farewell address.

Still and all, who in 1971 wouldn't exchange a trainload of mediocrities, incompetents and even pickpockets for a speedy end to the war in Vietnam and to the rancor and discord it has created? There may be some survivors of the better-dead-than-Red set, but even a number of these, one suspects, no longer see the conflict in Vietnam as one that compels a choice between extinction and the surrender of American independence. There was peace under Eisenhower, and the question of historical interest to those of us who survived the ensuing decade is whether this indisputable fact is to be ascribed to his stewardship or to luck or to some combination of both. I lean toward the combination theory, with perhaps a heavier emphasis on luck than others might care to make.

The opportunities for military involvement during his tenure were fully as numerous as those of the Kennedy, Johnson and Nixon years. In Asia, there were Korea, the Formosa Strait and Indochina; in Europe, Germany and Hungary; in the Middle East, Suez and Lebanon, and in our own hemisphere, Cuba. In some of these troubled areas, intervention was seriously contemplated; in others, it seemed out of the question from the start. In the Suez crisis of 1956, our policy from the onset was to stay out militarily: we made our disapproval so clear to the British and the French that we were not consulted in the planning stages. Nor was there ever much likelihood of our doing anything about Hungary, which erupted just after Suez in the closing days of the Presidential campaign; the Dulles line on Eastern Europe was always that we stood ready to help in the task of "liberation," but it was never much more than a line, and in moments of crisis behind the Iron Curtain—except when there was trouble in Berlin—we looked the other way. In 1958 in Lebanon, we did, at the request of its beleaguered President, land combat-ready Marine and Army units, but there was no combat and the troops spent their time girl-watching on the beaches they had stormed.

But elsewhere the risks were large. Even before his inauguration, Eisenhower went to Korea in search of peace, and in a matter of months a welcome (though far from satisfactory) settlement was made. Politically, in this country, the credit was all his, and if the whole truth is ever known—it will probably never be—it might turn out that he deserves it all. From what is currently known, his principal strategy seems to have been nuclear blackmail—a threat conveyed to our adversaries that if they dragged their feet much longer in the truce talks while pressing on with the war, this country would not consider itself bound to a reliance on conventional weapons. (Eisenhower was never opposed to the use of atomic weapons on moral grounds. He regarded them simply as explosives, suitable for some demolition jobs and not for others. His later assertions about general war's being "unthinkable" in the atomic age were based not on a moral judgment but a military one. He saw no point in a war no one would survive. But tactical "nukes" were another matter.) Maybe that did it, and maybe not. The truth could only come from the other side, and about all we now have on any other factor is Khrushchev's memory of Chou En-lai later explaining that the Chinese losses in Korea had become militarily insupportable. In any case, with all due respect for and gratitude to Eisenhower, one is compelled to wonder what would have happened—what could have happened—if the Communists had said that they weren't afraid of our bombs and intended to carry on with the war. Did he have a fallback position? If so, was it credible? Or did he, as seems so out of character, stake everything on a wildly dangerous threat of holocaust? These are questions that await answers that may never come. We know only that the war was terminated the following summer.

In Formosa we have what is perhaps the clearest case of prudent management during the Eisenhower Presidency. The danger was that we would be suckered into at least an air and sea war against Communist China, which was, as it still is, insisting on the rightness of its claim to sovereignty over Formosa and all the islands between it and the mainland. Eisenhower was, in 1954 and 1955, under enormous pressure from his own military and diplomatic advisers, among them Dulles, from Congressional Republicans and from many prominent Americans who had supported his candidacy (Henry Luce, for example) to give Chiang Kai-shek every form of assistance he asked for and to help in the defense of every rock in the Formosa Strait—not only to help keep the Generalissimo in his fortress but to aid in preparations for a return to the mainland by the Nationalist armies that had been driven out half a decade earlier. Eisenhower quite clearly had no taste for the entire enterprise. He knew that Chiang alone could never dislodge the Communists, no matter how much materiel we gave him, and he knew, too, that Mao Tse-tung's forces, no matter how many shells they lobbed at the close-in islands, were unequipped for an amphibious invasion of Formosa. So he jollied Chiang with hardware and money and high-level visitors, meanwhile protecting himself with a Congressional resolution and a treaty that pledged direct military assistance to Chiang only if we—not he—determined that Peking's maneuvers in the Formosa Strait were unmistakably preparatory to an assault on Formosa itself.

Had Admiral Radford, then Chairman of the Joint Chiefs, been in control, he might have made that fateful determination a dozen times over. Eisenhower read the cables and studied the maps and found no occasion for invoking those parts of the agreements that could have led to war. His methods were in certain ways dubious—there were questions about the constitutionality of the treaty and the resolution—but at least in the perspective of the present he found a way of averting a war that could have been far costlier than the one we have been in for most of the last decade. There can be little doubt that this was his will and his doing, for, as far as Communist China was concerned, he was the only "dove" in his administration.

Indochina—as always, it is the most complicated of matters. Eisenhower did not get involved militarily, but he may, by his patronage of his Secretary of State and by other words and acts, have made subsequent intervention all but unavoidable. It was Eisenhower who articulated the "domino theory" for Southeast Asia, and we know from his memoirs that on several occasions he seriously considered intervention and was deterred not primarily by political or moral considerations but by military and, to some extent, diplomatic ones. An obvious restraint was our lack of troops and weapons suitable for fighting the kind of war he quite correctly judged it to be. He gave thought to the use of nuclear weapons, and two carriers whose planes had nuclear bombs were in the Tonkin Gulf. But, as Earl Ravenal writes in Foreign Affairs, he "could not identify an appropriate enemy or target to fit the massive nuclear response [and] narrowly declined to intervene."

He considered using ground troops to aid the French but stipulated that under no circumstances would he go it alone—that is, without Asian and European allies. Dulles looked for suitable allies but found none. Had Eisenhower found either the appropriate targets for nuclear retaliation or willing partners in intervention, he might still have come up with an excuse for staying out, for nonintervention seemed almost always his preference; his distaste for war was general and a consistent factor in his reasoning. But it was indisputably under Eisenhower that we made heavy commitments to the powers that were and were to be in Saigon, and it was with Eisenhower's blessing that Dulles set up the Southeast Asia Treaty Organization, at once a political joke and a political disaster.

During his time, Eisenhower was not called upon to make good on any of Dulles's commitments in the region. I think it quite conceivable, however, that had he held office in the early sixties he might have found himself a prisoner of his own past and of then-current events and have followed pretty much the course of his successors. One advantage he had over his successors, though, was confidence in his own military judgment, and this might have saved him, us and the Vietnamese from the horrors that were soon to come.

Eisenhower's two terms fell between the two great Berlin crises—the one brought on by the blockade of the Western Sector in 1948 and the one brought on by the Berlin Wall 10 years ago. There was continuous tension over Germany throughout the fifties, but the dangers of war lessened as NATO, whose supreme command he had left to seek the

Presidency, grew in strength and as circumspection seemed increasingly to prevail in the Kremlin. These were the early days of the world of two nuclear superpowers, and the "balance of terror" would probably have held under any leadership save that of a madman. Though in Europe Dulles made a good many enemies for himself and for his Government, his European diplomacy was always more traditional and more prudent, as witness the Austrian treaty, than his diplomacy elsewhere in the world, and it would, I think, be rather difficult to fault Eisenhower for his handling of American policy in Germany.

In his memoirs, Eisenhower wrote of the Bay of Pigs as a "fiasco" for which "indecision and untimely counterorders" were "apparently responsible." He did not elaborate. But whatever he meant by Kennedy's "indecision," the original conclusion that we should sponsor an invasion came out of the Eisenhower, not the Kennedy, Administration. As he acknowledged, his military and intelligence people had, with his encouragement, armed and trained the forces in exile and, as we learned in the aftermath, completion of the scheme was urged on the new President by such holdovers as Allen Dulles of the C.I.A. and Gen. Lyman Lemnitzer, Chairman of the Joint Chiefs of Staff. Kennedy took responsibility for the bad show of which Eisenhower was the original producer. Eisenhower was lucky enough to be out of office when the rehearsals were over and the performers were ready for the opening. We can only conjecture as to whether he would have called off the whole business or gone about it in some other way. But he surely bears some responsibility for the policy and for the crucial failure of intelligence which led the executors of the policy to believe that the Cuban people would welcome the invaders as liberators and would take up arms to join them.

I have been somewhat surprised in thinking and writing about the Eisenhower years a decade later to discover that we know a good deal less about the Eisenhower Administration than about most recent ones. The historians haven't got around to it yet, and the few memoirists it produced haven't revealed very much except about themselves. Eisenhower's two large volumes were put together mainly with scissors and paste. Richard Nixon's "Six Crises" is all about Richard Nixon. Sherman Adams's "First-Hand Report" is not first-hand at all but second- and third-hand—dealing extensively with large events, such as Indochina and Formosa, about which he knew little and, despite his closeness to the President, was seldom if ever consulted. Robert Murphy's "Diplomat Among Warriors" is a stiff-necked but instructive work, only part of which bears on the Eisenhower period. Emmet Hughes's "Ordeal of Power" is a thoughtful, critical work, but Hughes's experience was limited to two brief tours in the White House as a speechwriter and political consultant. A few journalists—notably Robert J. Donovan in "Eisenhower: The Inside Story"—produced creditable works, more useful on the whole than the memoirs, but the literature by and large is thin.

"The President of the United States," Alfred Kazin wrote in reviewing the first volume of Eisenhower's memoirs, "had to look up the public record that most of us more or less knew in order to find out what happened during his Adminstration." This, I think, comes close to the heart of the matter about Eisenhower. For eight years as President, he presided in the most literal dictionary sense—he occupied the seat of authority. But he exercised authority only when there was no other choice. He headed an administration but he rarely administered. In foreign affairs, he stepped in only on certain European questions and when, as Commander in Chief, he was required to make command decisions. In domestic affairs his temperament was in line with his economics—laissez-faire. Whenever possible, he let the Government run itself—and it was possible a good part of the time.

In fairness, though, it must be recalled that Eisenhower never offered himself as an activist. He never pledged innovation or any sort of basic reform. One cannot quite contend that he was the product of a political "draft," but, at least as much as any chief executive in this century, he had the office thrust upon him. His style was well known to those who engineered his nomination and to those who elected and reelected him. Whatever else may be said in dispraise, he did not betray his trust. He construed it rather narrowly, but in doing so he embodied a long tradition and a specifically Republican tradition.

His command decisions seem, in retrospect, to have been generally wise. He was clear about the hazards of intervention in Asia. However, he deputized Dulles to contract military alliances all over the place—confident, perhaps, that in crises he could prevail as he had in Korea. He deputized much to the other Dulles, Allen, too—and it was under him that the C.I.A. became a force in world affairs and undertook such missions as the overturn of Governments in Iran and Guatemala. Eisenhower was anything but an empire builder—he was by almost any definition an anti-imperialist—but it was while he presided that this country began, if not to acquire new holdings overseas, to use its power in an imperial manner far beyond the Americas.

Domestically, he and we marked time. In the first few years, this was more or less defensible. The country might not have sustained him if he had tried to remake it. Once the Korean war was over and McCarthy's fangs had been drawn, complacency was the dominant American mood, and very few Americans were aware of the large structural faults in many of our institutions. In 1954, the Supreme Court ruled that if we were to be true to ourselves and our pretensions, racism had to be deinstitutionalized, but this was about the only blow to complacency until, in the second term, sputnik went aloft and made some Americans wonder about our educational system. With hindsight, we can see that practically all the problems that bedeviled us in the sixties had been worsening in the fifties. It can be said, to be sure, that nearly all of them predated the fifties by decades, even centuries, and that Eisenhower was no more to blame in such matters than most of his predecessors. And this is only just. He was not a cause of any of our present domestic disorders. Neither, though, did he perceive them or heed the prophets of his time—and there were several—who did perceive them.

What Eisenhower clearly lacked—and this was due as much to the education and experience that had been his lot as a servant of his country as to any deficiency of mind or spirit—was the kind of knowledge of the American condition he might have gained if his background had been in politics rather than in the military. He went through most of the fifties and on into the sixties with an image of this country formed in Kansas *circa* 1910. Nowhere is this so dismayingly clear as in the closing words of the second volume of his memoirs, which was published in a dreadful year for this country, 1965—after his successor had met violent death in Dallas, at a time when violence increasingly characterized our race relations, when the generation gap was widening alongside the credibility gap, when our sons were marching by the tens of thousands into the Vietnam quagmire. In that year, he could bring himself to this apostrophe:

I have unshakable faith that the ideals and the way of life that Western civilization has cherished . . . will flourish everywhere to the infinite benefit of mankind . . . At home . . . our level of education constantly rises . . . opportunity for the properly ambitious boy or girl increases daily. Prospects for the good life were never better, provided only that each continues to feel that he, himself, must earn and deserve these advantages.

Imbued with sense and spirit we will select future leaders [who will] keep a firm, sure hand on the rudder of this splendid ship of state, guiding her through future generations to the great destiny for which she was created.

A good man? Of course. A "brilliant" man? Hardly. "A political genius"? If so, the evidence remains concealed. A good President? Better than average, perhaps, and very useful in his early years. But by and large not what the times required.

The Army-McCarthy Hearings

America's painful adjustment to the Cold War will be forever memorialized by the era to which Joseph McCarthy gave his name. When people do not understand what is happening or what is required of them, when their best instincts and their worst fears are somehow tangled together, then men like Joseph McCarthy have their chance. In the early 1950's there was such a thing as subversion; the problem of disloyalty was real if limited; some spies were discovered in government (although not by Senator McCarthy). But a limited security problem in the hands of an oily demagogue proved to have virtually unlimited political use. McCarthy became a prime agent in the Republican drive to oust the Democrats from a 20-year hold on the federal government. Through accusation or insinuation he retired men from public careers and damaged the reputation of many innocent men in private lives.

Buoyed by these successes, McCarthy took on establishment institutions such as the church and—the case before you—the army.

McCarthy should have selected his victims with more care. Six months after his bout with the army he had been censured by his colleagues in the Senate and his national influence was over. McCarthy had believed that he represented a massive national sentiment which could do battle with every constituted power; and many commentators and politicians, liberal and conservative, had taken him at his word. They were all wrong: when powerful men decided to stop him, he was quickly demolished, and with few political aftereffects.

The Army-McCarthy hearings were on television for 188 hours during their 36-day run from April 22 to June 16, 1954. In David T. Bazelon's description it was "in a fabulously exact sense, the greatest political show on earth." Amid the welter of names, the confusion of charges and countercharges, the points of order and other interruptions, millions of viewers nevertheless got the message. As the Checkers speech showed the way television could save a political career, these hearings showed how it could pitilessly destroy one. The show was unforgettable. McCarthy's sarcasm and disparaging tone of voice lost their customary effectiveness; he went from fame to an alcoholic's death. His flinty adversary, Joseph E. Welch, whose capacity for wit as well as for righteous indignation had thrilled 20 million viewers, was able in his retirement to play a star role as a movie lawyer. The age of television politics was upon us.

Cast of principal characters:

Robert T. Stevens   Secretary of the Army

Senator Joseph R. McCarthy   U.S. Senator, Wisconsin (Rep.)
                                       Chairman, Senate subcommittee

John G. Adams	Counselor for the Army
Joseph N. Welch	Special Counsel for the Army
Senator Karl E. Mundt	U.S. Senator, Kansas (Rep.) Chairman of hearings
Ray H. Jenkins	Chief Counsel, Senate subcommittee
John L. McClellan	U.S. Senator, Arkansas (Dem.) Subcommittee member
Stuart Symington	U.S. Senator, Missouri (Dem.) Subcommittee member
Pvt. G. David Schine	U.S. Army private and former McCarthy aide
Roy M. Cohn	Chief Counsel for Sen. McCarthy

. . .

Secretary STEVENS. Gentlemen of the committee, I am here today at the request of this committee. You have my assurance of the fullest cooperation.

In order that we may all be quite clear as to just why this hearing has come about, it is necessary for me to refer at the outset to Pvt. G. David Schine, a former consultant of this committee. David Schine was eligible for the draft. Efforts were made by the chairman of this committee, Senator Joseph R. McCarthy, and the subcommittee's chief counsel, Mr. Roy M. Cohn, to secure a commission for him. Mr. Schine was not qualified, and he was not commissioned. Selective service then drafted him. Subsequent efforts were made to seek preferential treatment for him after he was inducted.

. .

Before getting into the Schine story I want to make two general comments.

First, it is my responsibility to speak for the Army. The Army is about a million and a half men and women, in posts across this country and around the world, on active duty and in the National Guard and Organized Reserves, plus hundreds of thousands of loyal and faithful civil servants.

Senator McCARTHY. Mr. Chairman, a point of order.

Senator MUNDT. Senator McCarthy has a point of order.

Senator McCARTHY. Mr. Stevens is not speaking for the Army. He is speaking for Mr. Stevens, for Mr. Adams, and Mr. Hensel. The committee did not make the Army a party to this controversy, and I think it is highly improper to try to make the Army a party. Mr. Stevens can only speak for himself. . . .

May I say that, regardless of what the Chair and Mr. McClellan decided, when Mr. Stevens says, "It is my responsibility to speak for the Army," he is not speaking for the Army here. All we were investigating has been some Communists in the Army, a very small percentage, I would say much less than 1 percent. And when the Secretary says that, in effect "I am speaking for the Army," he is putting the 99.9 percent of good, honorable, loyal men in the Army into the position of trying to oppose the exposure of Communists in the Army.

I think it should be made clear at the outset, so we need not waste time on it, hour after hour, that Mr. Stevens is speaking for Mr. Stevens and those who are speaking through him; when Mr. Adams speaks, he is speaking for Mr. Adams and those who are speaking through him, and likewise Mr. Hensel.

I may say I resent very, very much this attempt to connect the great American Army with this attempt to sabotage the efforts of this committee's investigation into communism.

Mr. JENKINS. I again say, Mr. Chairman, there is nothing in this statement from which an inference can be drawn that the Army has become a party in interest to this controversy. We are in accord with the Senator, that the parties in interest are Mr. Stevens, Mr. Adams, and Mr. Hensel.

Senator McCARTHY. If that is understood, then I have no objection. . . .

I speak for the Army today out of a pride and confidence that grows greater every day I spend on the job. There are personal reasons, too, for my pride in the Army and for my resentment of any slur against it or any of the armed services. The 2 oldest of our 4 sons enlisted in the Navy during World War II. Our third son enlisted in 1952 as a private and is now a corporal with the Seventh Army in Europe. He has been overseas 21 months.

Second, I want to affirm here my full belief in the right of Congress to investigate—and that means scrutinizing the activities of the Army or any other department of the executive branch of the Government. The conscientious exercise of this obligation is one of the checks, contemplated by the Constitution, against the possibility of unlimited executive authority by the executive branch of the Government.

As a member of the executive branch, it is my duty to do everything I properly can to help this and other committees of Congress. I have such a profound regard for elective office in this country that it comes very easily for me to cooperate with the Senators, the Representatives, and the committees of Congress.

Let me now turn to the point at issue and first summarize the Schine story. I have been informed that—

1. From mid-July of last year until March 1 of this year, David Schine was discussed between one branch or other of the Department of the Army and Senator McCarthy or members of his staff in more than 65 telephone calls.

2. During the same period, this matter was discussed at approxi-

mately 19 meetings between Army personnel and Senator McCarthy or members of his staff.

3. Requests made on Schine's behalf ranged from several for a direct commission before he was inducted into the Army to many for special assignments, relief from routine duties such as KP, extra time off, and special visitor privileges.

4. From November 10, 1953, to January 16, 1954, Schine, by then a private in the Army, obtained 15 passes from the post. By way of comparison, the majority of other newly inducted personnel obtained three passes during the same period. . . .

About that time these two friends left, and because I wanted Senator McCarthy to restate before Mr. Cohn what he had told me on the courthouse steps, I said, "Let's talk about Schine."

That started a chain of events, an experience similar to none which I have had in my life.

Mr. Cohn became extremely agitated, became extremely abusive. He cursed me and then Senator McCarthy. The abuse went in waves. He would be very abusive and then it would kind of abate and things would be friendly for a few moments. Everybody would eat a little bit more, and then it would start in again. It just kept on.

I was trying to catch a 1:30 train, but Mr. Cohn was so violent by then that I felt I had better not do it and leave him that angry with me and that angry with Senator McCarthy because of a remark I had made. So I stayed and missed my 1:30 train. I thought surely I would be able to get out of there by 2:30. The luncheon concluded——

Mr. JENKINS. You say you were afraid to leave Senator McCarthy alone there with him? Mr. Adams, what did he say? You say he was very abusive.

Mr. ADAMS. He was extremely abusive.

Mr. JENKINS. Was or not any obscene language used?

Mr. ADAMS. Yes.

Mr. JENKINS. Just omit that and tell what he did say which constituted abuse, in your opinion.

Mr. ADAMS. I have stated before, sir, the tone of voice has as much to do with abuse as words. I do not remember the phrases, I do not remember the sentences, but I do remember the violence.

Mr. JENKINS. Do you remember the subject?

Mr. ADAMS. The subject was Schine. The subject was the fact—the thing that Cohn was angry about, the thing that he was so violent about, was the fact that, (1), the Army was not agreeing to an assignment for Schine and, (2), that Senator McCarthy was not supporting his staff in its efforts to get Schine assigned to New York. So his abuse was directed partly to me and partly to Senator McCarthy.

As I say, it kind of came in waves. There would be a period of extreme abuse, and then there would be a period where it would get almost back to normal, and ice cream would be ordered, and then about halfway through that a little more of the same. I missed the 2:30 train, also.

This violence continued. It was a remarkable thing. At first Senator McCarthy seemed to be trying to conciliate. He seemed to be trying to conciliate Cohn and not to state anything contrary to what he had stated to me in the morning. But then he more or less lapsed into silence. Finally, at about 3 o'clock or 10 minutes to 3 we left the restaurant and got in Cohn's car, which was directly in front of the restaurant. Mr. Cohn stated that he was going to give me a ride to the station, which is directly uptown from the courthouse. I had proposed going by subway, but he said, "No, I can get you there quicker."

So we began riding up Fourth Avenue in New York and Cohn's anger erupted again. As it erupted it was directed more on this occasion toward Senator McCarthy than it was to me. As we were riding uptown Senator McCarthy turned around to me and on 2 or 3 occasions during the ride uptown, which took about 15 minutes, he asked me if I could not when I got back to Washington talk to Mr. Stevens and arrange an assignment in New York for Schine.

When we got to 34th Street, which is where————

Mr. Jenkins. What was your reply to that request of the Senator, Mr. Adams?

Mr. Adams. My recollection is that I made no reply. I didn't say much on the ride uptown. It was a little difficult.

Mr. Jenkins. You mean that both you and the Senator had been completely subdued?

Mr. Adams. I had been.

Mr. Jenkins. All right. You were riding uptown in Mr. Cohn's car, being driven by Mr. Cohn, as a matter of fact?

Mr. Adams. Yes sir.

Mr. Jenkins. You were being taken to the station?

Mr. Adams. That is right.

Mr. Jenkins. I will ask you to tell the committee the events of that trip.

Mr. Adams. As I stated, Senator McCarthy said to me 2 or 3 times, or asked me on 2 or 3 occasions if I wouldn't go back to Washington and ask Mr. Stevens to arrange for Schine's assignment in New York. When we got to 34th Street, which is where the turn must be made if you are going to go over to Penn Station, which is on 7th Avenue, we attempted a left turn which was not permitted and a policeman would not permit it and ordered us to go on ahead, which took us under a long tunnel, the tunnel which goes under the Grand Central Station, and we came out about 45th Street or thereabouts going away from the station and I had then 10 or 12 minutes to make the 3:30 train. I complained to Mr. Cohn. I said, "You are just taking me away from the station," and in a final fit of violence he stopped the car in the middle of four lanes of traffic and said, "Get there however you can." So I climbed out of the car in the middle of four lanes of traffic between 46th and 47th Street on Park Avenue, ran across the street and jumped into a cab to try to make the 3:30 train.

Mr. Jenkins. Senator Potter directs me to ask you whether or not you made the train. [Laughter.]

Mr. ADAMS. The 3:30 train was 10 minutes late, so I made it.

Mr. Carr told me a few days later that he didn't think that I should feel badly about the way I was put out of the car because he said I should have been there to see the way Senator McCarthy left the car a few blocks later.

. . .

Mr. JENKINS. Mr. Adams, when did you finally tell Mr. Cohn, if you did so, that Schine in all probability was scheduled for overseas duty?

Mr. ADAMS. On January 13. I was at the Capitol with Mr. Stevens. He was coming up on another appointment. I often use that means of talking to him. He is a very busy man. I jump in his car and ride to his appointment with him. I did it on this occasion. When I got here to the Senate Office Building, instead of going back to the Pentagon as I had originally planned, I told Mr. Stevens that I thought I would go down and see if I could not get back in good with Mr. Cohn and conciliate him because we had been having so much difficulty over Schine.

So I went down to room 101. Mr. Cohn was there and Mr. Carr was there. As I remember, we lunched together in the Senate cafeteria, and everything was peaceful. When we returned to room 101, toward the latter part of the conversation I asked Cohn—I knew that 90 percent of all inductees ultimately face overseas duty and I knew that one day we were going to face that problem with Mr. Cohn as to Schine.

So I thought I would lay a little groundwork for future trouble I guess. I asked him what would happen if Schine got overseas duty.

Mr. JENKINS. You mean you were breaking the news gently, Mr. Adams?

Mr. ADAMS. Yes, sir; that is right. I asked him what would happen if Schine got overseas duty. He responded with vigor and force, "Stevens is through as Secretary of the Army."

I said, "Oh, Roy," something to this effect, "Oh, Roy, don't say that. Come on. Really, what is going to happen if Schine gets overseas duty?"

He responded with even more force, "We will wreck the Army."

Then he said, "The first thing we are going to do is get General Ryan for the way he has treated Dave at Fort Dix. Dave gets through at Fort Dix tomorrow or this week, and as soon as he is gone we are going to get General Ryan for the obscene way in which he has permitted Schine to be treated up there."

He said, "We are not going to do it ourselves. We have another committee of the Congress interested in it."

Then he said, "I wouldn't put it past you to do this. We will start investigations. We have enough stuff on the Army to keep investigations going indefinitely, and if anything like such-and-such double-cross occurs, that is what we will do."

This remark was not to be taken lightly in the context in which it it was given to me. . . .

Senator SYMINGTON. Have you the written instructions that you were going to deliver to the committee?

Mr. ADAMS. It is a letter to the Secretary of Defense from the President of the United States.

This is a letter signed Dwight D. Eisenhower addressed the Honorable, the Secretary of Defense, Washington, D. C.:

DEAR MR. SECRETARY: It has long been recognized that to assist the Congress in achieving its legislative purposes every Executive Department or Agency must, upon the request of a Congressional Committee, expeditiously furnish information relating to any matter within the jurisdiction of the Committee, with certain historical exceptions—some of which are pointed out in the attached memorandum from the Attorney General. This Administration has been and will continue to be diligent in following the principle. However, it is essential for the successful working of our system that the persons entrusted with power over any one of the three great branches of Government shall not encroach upon the authority confided to the others. The ultimate responsibility for the conduct of the Executive Branch rests with the President.

Within this Constitutional framework each branch should cooperate fully with each other for the common good. However, throughout our history the President has withheld information whenever he found that what was sought was confidential or its disclosure would be incompatible with the public interest or jeopardize the safety of the Nation.

Because it is essential to efficient and effective administration that employees of the Executive Branch be in a position to be completely candid in advising with each other on official matters, and because it is not in the public interest that any of their conversations or communications, or any documents or reproductions, concerning such advice be disclosed, you will instruct employees of your Department that in all of their appearances before the Subcommittee of the Senate Committee on Government Operations regarding the inquiry now before it they are not to testify to any such conversations or communications or to produce any such documents or reproductions. This principle must be maintained regardless of who would benefit by such disclosures.

I direct this action so as to maintain the proper separation of powers between the Executive and Legislative Branches of the Government in accordance with my responsibilities and duties under the Constitution. This separation is vital to preclude the exercise of arbitrary power by any branch of the Government. By this action I am not in any way restricting the testimony of such witnesses to what occurred regarding any matters where the communication was directly between any of the principals in the controversy within the Executive Branch on the one hand and a member of the Subcommittee or its staff on the other.

Sincerely,

/s/ DWIGHT D. EISENHOWER

To the letter, sir, is attached a 10-page memorandum from the Attorney General to the President. . . .

Senator MCCARTHY. Mr. Chairman, I must admit that I am somewhat at a loss as to know what to do at the moment. One of the subjects of this inquiry is to find out who was responsible for succeeding and calling off the hearing of Communist infiltration in Government.

That the hearings have been called off, no one can question. I fear that maybe in my mind I was doing an injustice, possibly, to Mr. Adams and Mr. Hensel.

I strongly felt all along that they were the men responsible for it. At this point, I find out there is no way of ever getting at the truth, because we do find that the charges were conceived, instigated, at a meeting which was testified to by Mr. Adams.

Now for some fantastically strange reason, the iron curtain is pulled down so we can't tell what happened at that meeting. I don't think the President is responsible for this. I don't think his judgment is that bad, Mr. Chairman.

There is no reason why any one should be afraid of the facts, of the truth, that came out of that meeting. It is a very important meeting. It doesn't have to do with security matters. It doesn't have to do with national security. It merely has to do with why these charges were filed. . . .

The question is how far can—I am not talking about the present occupant in the White House. But we have a tremendously important question here, Mr. Chairman. That is, how far can the President go? Who all can he order not to testify? If he can order the Ambassador to the U. N. not to testify about something having nothing to do with the U. N., but a deliberate smear against my staff, then any President—and we don't know who will be President in 1956, 1960, 1964—but any President [laughter]—I won't repeat that. Any President can, by an Executive order, keep the facts from the American people. . . .

Now we are getting down to the meat of the case, Mr. Chairman, and that is, who was responsible for the issuance of the smear that has held this committee up for weeks and weeks and weeks, and has allowed Communists to continue in our defense plants, Mr. Chairman, handling top-secret material, as I said before, with a razor poised over the jugular vein of this Nation? Who is responsible for keeping all these Army officers down here and all the Senators tied up while the world is going up in flames?

I do think, Mr. Chairman, that we should go into executive session. I must have a ruling as to what will be behind an iron curtain and what facts we can bring out before I can intelligently question the witnesses. I do think that someone, for his own benefit, should contact the President immediately and point out to him, perhaps, that he and I and many of us campaigned and promised the American people that if they would remove our Democrat friends from the control of this Government, then we would no longer engage in Government by secrecy, whitewash and coverup.

Mr. JENKINS. You will recall, Mr. Cohn, that he testified that you said that if Schine went overseas, Stevens was through as Secretary of the Army?

Mr. COHN. I heard him say that, sir.

Mr. JENKINS. Did you or not?

Mr. COHN. No, sir.

Mr. JENKINS. Did you say anything like that, Mr. Cohn?

Mr. COHN. No, sir, and my recollection is that I did not. I have talked to Mr. Carr who was sitting there the whole time, and he says I did not. . . .

Mr. JENKINS. All right, now you are saying you did not say it, Mr. Cohn?

Mr. COHN. Yes, sir. I am saying I am sure I did not make that statement, and I am sure that Mr. Adams and anybody else with any sense, and Mr. Adams has a lot of sense, could ever believe that I was threatening to wreck the Army or that I could wreck the Army. I say, sir, that the statement is ridiculous.

Mr. JENKINS. I am talking about Stevens being through as Secretary of the Army.

Mr. COHN. That is equally ridiculous, sir.

Mr. JENKINS. And untrue?

Mr. COHN. Yes, sir, equally ridiculous and untrue, I could not cause the President of the United States to remove Stevens as Secretary of the Army.

. . .

Senator McCARTHY. Let me ask you this, Mr. Cohn: Had you something to do with the Hiss case, I believe, also; is that right?

Mr. COHN. I had. What I had to do with the Hiss case is not important enough to mention here, sir.

Senator McCARTHY. Enough to do with it so that you are aware of the facts in the case. Let me ask you this: Are you convinced if it had not been for a congressional committee having exposed the facts in the Hiss case, that Alger Hiss today would be free?

Mr. COHN. Yes, sir. . . .

Senator McCARTHY. Just this one question: Mr. Cohn, do you agree with me that, No. 1, the administration is certainly heading in the right direction so far as getting rid of Communists are concerned, and, No. 2, that it is ridiculous, a complete waste of time to have these exchanges of statements between the White House and this committee, that there is no reason on earth why there should be any contest between the executive department and this committee insofar as exposing Communists, graft, and corruption is concerned, that we all should be heading the same way, there should be none of this silly bickering, fighting about this exposure, that we should be getting the complete cooperation from the executive and that should be flowing both ways, of course?

Senator MUNDT. The Senator's time has expired. You can answer the question.

Senator McCARTHY. Let me finish the question. And if that could be accomplished, a great service could be performed for the country?

Mr. COHN. I am sure of that, sir.

Senator MUNDT. Mr. Welch, you have 10 minutes. After your 10 minutes, we will recess.

Mr. WELCH. Mr. Chairman, ordinarily, with the clock as late as it is I would call attention to it, but not tonight.

Mr. Cohn, what is the exact number of Communists or subversives that are loose today in these defense plants?

Mr. COHN. The exact number that is loose, sir?

Mr. WELCH. Yes, sir.

Mr. COHN. I don't know.

Mr. WELCH. Roughly how many?

Mr. COHN. I can only tell you, sir, what we know about it.

Mr. WELCH. That is 130, is that right?

Mr. COHN. Yes, sir. I am going to try to particularize for you, if I can.

Mr. WELCH. I am in a hurry. I don't want the sun to go down while they are still in there, if we can get them out.

Mr. COHN. I am afraid we won't be able to work that fast, sir.

Mr. WELCH. I have a suggestion about it, sir. How many are there?

Mr. COHN. I believe the figure is approximately 130.

Mr. WELCH. Approximately one-two-three?

Mr. COHN. Yes, sir. Those are people, Mr. Welch——

Mr. WELCH. I don't care. You told us who they are. In how many plants are they?

Mr. COHN. How many plants?

Mr. WELCH. How many plants.

Mr. COHN. Yes, sir; just 1 minute, sir. I see 16 offhand, sir.

Mr. WELCH. Sixteen plants?

Mr. COHN. Yes, sir.

Mr. WELCH. Where are they, sir?

Mr. COHN. Senator McCarthy——

Mr. WELCH. Reel off the cities.

Mr. COHN. Would you stop me if I am going too far?

Mr. WELCH. You can't go too far revealing Communists, Mr. Cohn. Reel off the cities for us.

Mr. COHN. Schenectady, N .Y.; Syracuse, N. Y.; Rome, N. Y.; Quincy, Mass.; Fitchburg, Mass.; Buffalo, N. Y.; Dunkirk, N. Y.; another at Buffalo, N. Y.; Cambridge, Mass.; New Bedford, Mass.; Boston, Mass.; Quincy, Mass.; Lynn, Mass.; Pittsfield, Mass.; Boston, Mass.

Mr. WELCH. Mr. Cohn, you not only frighten me, you make me ashamed when there are so many in Massachusetts. [Laughter.] This is not a laughing matter, believe me. Are you alarmed at that situation, Mr. Cohn?

Mr. COHN. Yes, sir; I am.

Mr. WELCH. Nothing could be more alarming, could it?

Mr. COHN. It certainly is a very alarming thing.

Mr. WELCH. Will you not, before the sun goes down, give those names to the FBI and at least have those men put under surveillance.

Mr. COHN. Mr. Welch, the FBI——

Senator McCARTHY. Mr. Chairman.

Mr. WELCH. That is a fair question.

Senator McCARTHY. Mr. Chairman, let's not be ridiculous. Mr. Welch knows, as I have told him a dozen times, that the FBI has all of this information. The defense plants have the information. The only thing we can do is to try and publicly expose these individuals and hope that they will be gotten rid of. And you know that, Mr. Welch.

Mr. WELCH. I do not know that.

Mr. Cohn, do you mean to tell us that J. Edgar Hoover and the FBI know the names of these men and are doing nothing about them?

Mr. COHN. No, sir. I mean to say—

Mr. WELCH. Do you mean to tell us they are doing something about them?

Mr. COHN. Yes, sir.

Mr. WELCH. What are they doing about them?

Mr. COHN. Here is what they do about them. They notify the Defense Department and the appropriate security——

Mr. WELCH. Don't they put them under surveillance?

Mr. COHN. Appropriate security agencies involved. The FBI gives them full information. It is then up to them, the places where the information goes, to decide whether or not they will act on the FBI information. All the FBI can do is give the information. Their power ends right there.

Mr. WELCH. Cannot the FBI put these 130 men under surveillance before sundown tomorrow?

Mr. COHN. Sir, if there is need for surveillance in the case of espionage or anything like that, I can well assure you that Mr. John Edgar Hoover and his men know a lot better than I, and I quite respectfully suggest, sir, than probably a lot of us, just who should be put under surveillance. I do not propose to tell the FBI how to run its shop. It does it very well.

Mr. WELCH. And they do it, don't they, Mr. Cohn?

Mr. COHN. When the need arises, of course.

Mr. WELCH. And will you tell them tonight, Mr. Cohn, that here is a case where the need has arisen, so that it can be done by sundown tomorrow night?

Mr. COHN. No, sir; there is no need for my telling the FBI what to do about this or anything else.

Mr. WELCH. Are you sure they know every one of them?

Mr. COHN. I would take an oath on it, sir. I think the FBI has complete information about the Communist movement in this country and that would include information about these people.

Mr. WELCH. That being true, Mr. Cohn, can you and I both rest easy tonight?

Mr. COHN. Sir, I certainly agree with you, it is a very disturbing situation.

Mr. WELCH. Well, if the FBI has got a firm grasp on these 130 men, I will go to sleep.

Do you assure me that is so?

Mr. COHN. Sir, I am sure that the FBI does its job well, that it knows all about these people, that it has told the appropriate agencies about these people, and that the failure to act goes elsewhere than in the hands of the FBI.

Mr. WELCH. Just for the purpose of safety, for fear something could be missed somewhere, would you mind, as a patriotic American citizen, sending the 130 names over to the FBI tonight?

Let's be sure we are not taking any chances.

Mr. COHN. I wouldn't mind it at all, sir.

Mr. WELCH. Would you do it, sir?

Senator McCARTHY. Would you yield?

Mr. WELCH. No; I won't yield. I want to find out if he will do it and if he won't, will you do it?

Senator McCARTHY. You asked a question. Will you let me answer it?

Mr. WELCH. I asked it of the witness, sir.

Senator McCARTHY. I want you to know that the FBI has complete access to any files we have, any information we have, at any time.

Mr. Welch knows, I am sure you do, Mr. Welch, that the FBI has no power to order anyone fired. You know that, for example, in the Alger Hiss case, the FBI had furnished all the information and he still rose to be a top man in the State Department. You know, Mr. Welch, that the FBI furnished all the information on the spy Harry Dexter White. You know that despite that fact, Mr. Welch, despite the fact that the FBI had given all of the information, and sent over reports day after day after day, Harry Dexter White, the Communist spy, got to be a top Treasury official. So let's not deceive the American people by blaming the FBI for Communists being in defense plants. . . .

Mr. WELCH. Well, Mr. Chairman, my confidence in the FBI is simply limitless, and I think Mr. Cohn's confidence is similar; is that right, sir?

Mr. COHN. Yes, sir; that is right.

Mr. WELCH. All I am suggesting is that we just nudge them a little and be sure they are busy on these 130.

Would you mind helping nudge them?

Mr. COHN. Sir, you do not have to nudge the FBI about this or about anything else.

Mr. WELCH. Then they have got the whole 130, have they, Mr. Cohn?

Mr. COHN. I am sure of it, sir, and a lot more.

. . .

Mr. WELCH. Then, as a second line of defense, let's send the 130 names to the Department of Defense tonight. Would you mind doing that?

Mr. COHN. Whatever the committee directs on that, sir.

Mr. WELCH. I wish the committee would direct that all the names be sent both to the FBI and to the Department of Defense with extreme suddenness.

Mr. WELCH. Mr. Cohn, tell me once more: Every time you learn of a Communist or a spy anywhere, is it your policy to get them out as fast as possible?

Mr. COHN. Surely, we want them out as fast as possible, sir.

Mr. WELCH. And whenever you learn of one from now on, Mr. Cohn, I beg of you, will you tell somebody about them quick?

Mr. COHN. Mr. Welch, with great respect, I work for the committee here. They know how we go about handling situations of Communist infiltration and failure to act on FBI information about Communist infiltration. If they are displeased with the speed with which I and the group of men who work with me proceed, if they are displeased with the order in which we move, I am sure they will give me appropriate instructions along those lines, and I will follow any which they give me.

Mr. WELCH. May I add my small voice, sir, and say whenever you know about a subversive or a Communist spy, please hurry. Will you remember those words?

Senator McCARTHY. Mr. Chairman.

Mr. COHN. Mr. Welch, I can assure you, sir, as far as I am concerned, and certainly as far as the chairman of this committee and the members, and the members of the staff, are concerned, we are a small group, but we proceed as expeditiously as is humanly possible to get out Communists and traitors and to bring to light the mechanism by which they have been permitted to remain where they were for so long a period of time.

Senator McCARTHY. Mr. Chairman, in view of that question——

Senator MUNDT. Have you a point of order?

Senator McCARTHY. Not exactly, Mr. Chairman, but in view of Mr. Welch's request that the information be given once we know of anyone who might be performing any work for the Communist Party, I think we should tell him that he has in his law firm a young man named Fisher whom he recommended, incidentally, to do work on this committee, who has been for a number of years a member of an organization which was named, oh, years and years ago, as the legal bulwark of the Communist Party, an organization which always swings to the defense of anyone who dares to expose Communists. I certainly assume that Mr. Welch did not know of this young man at the time he recommended him as the assistant counsel for this committee, but he has such terror and such a great desire to know where anyone is located who may be serving the Communist cause, Mr. Welch, that I thought we should just call to your attention the fact that your Mr. Fisher, who is still in your law firm today, whom you asked to have down here looking over the secret and classified material, is a member of an organization, not named by me but named by various committees, named by the Attorney General, as I recall, and I think I quote this verbatim, as "the legal bulwark of the Communist Party." He belonged to that for a sizable number of years, according to his own admission, and he belonged to it long after it had been exposed as the legal arm of the Communist Party.

Knowing that, Mr. Welch, I just felt that I had a duty to respond to your urgent request that before sundown, when we know of anyone serving the Communist cause, we let the agency know. We are now letting you know that your man did belong to this organization for either 3 or 4 years, belonged to it long after he was out of law school.

I don't think you can find anyplace, anywhere, an organization which has done more to defend Communists—I am again quoting the report—to defend Communists, to defend espionage agents, and to aid the Communist cause, than the man whom you originally wanted down here at your right hand instead of Mr. St. Clair.

I have hesitated bringing that up, but I have been rather bored with your phony requests to Mr. Cohn here that he personally get every Communist out of government before sundown. Therefore, we will give you information about the young man in your own organization.

I am not asking you at this time to explain why you tried to foist him on this committee. Whether you knew he was a member of that Communist organization or not, I don't know. I assume you did not, Mr. Welch, because I get the impression that, while you are quite an actor, you play for a laugh, I don't think you have any conception of the danger of the Communist Party. I don't think you yourself would ever knowingly aid the Communist cause. I think you are unknowingly aiding it when you try to burlesque this hearing in which we are attempting to bring out the facts, however.

Mr. WELCH. Mr. Chairman.

Senator MUNDT. Mr. Welch, the Chair should say he has no recognition or no memory of Mr. Welch's recommending either Mr. Fisher or anybody else as counsel for this committee.

I will recognize Mr. Welch.

Senator McCARTHY. Mr. Chairman, I will give you the news story on that.

Mr. WELCH. Mr. Chairman, under these circumstances I must have something approaching a personal privilege.

Senator MUNDT. You may have it, sir. It will not be taken out of your time.

Mr. WELCH. Senator McCarthy, I did not know—Senator, sometimes you say "May I have your attention?"

Senator McCARTHY. I am listening to you. I can listen with one ear.

Mr. WELCH. This time I want you to listen with both.

Senator McCARTHY. Yes.

Mr. WELCH. Senator McCarthy, I think until this moment——

Senator McCARTHY. Jim, will you get the news story to the effect that this man belonged to this Communist-front organization? Will you get the citations showing that this was the legal arm of the Communist Party, and the length of time that he belonged, and the fact that he was recommended by Mr. Welch? I think that should be in the record.

Mr. WELCH. You won't need anything in the record when I have finished telling you this.

Until this moment, Senator, I think I never really gaged your cruelty or your recklessness. Fred Fisher is a young man who went to the Harvard Law School and came into my firm and is starting what looks to be a brilliant career with us.

When I decided to work for this committee I asked Jim St. Clair, who sits on my right, to be my first assistant. I said to Jim, "Pick somebody in the firm who works under you that you would like." He chose Fred Fisher and they came down on an afternoon plane. That night, when he had taken a little stab at trying to see what the case was about, Fred Fisher and Jim St. Clair and I went to dinner together. I then said to these two young men, "Boys, I don't know anything about you except I have always liked you, but if there is anything funny in the life of either one of you that would hurt anybody in this case you speak up quick."

Fred Fisher said, "Mr. Welch, when I was in law school and for a period of months after, I belonged to the Lawyers Guild," as you have suggested, Senator. He went on to say, "I am secretary of the Young Republicans League in Newton with the son of Massachusetts' Governor, and I have the respect and admiration of the 25 lawyers or so in Hale & Dorr."

I said, "Fred, I just don't think I am going to ask you to work on the case. If I do, one of these days that will come out and go over national television and it will just hurt like the dickens."

So, Senator, I asked him to go back to Boston.

Little did I dream you could be so reckless and so cruel as to do an injury to that lad. It is true he is still with Hale & Dorr. It is true that he will continue to be with Hale & Dorr. It is, I regret to say, equally true that I fear he shall always bear a scar needlessly inflicted by you. If it were in my power to forgive you for your reckless cruelty, I will do so. I like to think I am a gentleman, but your forgiveness will have to come from someone other than me.

Senator McCarthy. Mr. Chairman.

Senator Mundt. Senator McCarthy?

Senator McCarthy. May I say that Mr. Welch talks about this being cruel and reckless. He was just baiting; he has been baiting Mr. Cohn here for hours, requesting that Mr. Cohn, before sundown, get out of any department of Government anyone who is serving the Communist cause.

I just give this man's record, and I want to say, Mr. Welch, that it has been labeled long before he became a member, as early as 1944——

Mr. Welch. Senator, may we not drop this? We know he belonged to the Lawyers Guild, and Mr. Cohn nods his head at me. I did you, I think, no personal injury, Mr. Cohn.

Mr. Cohn. No, sir.

Mr. Welch. I meant to do you no personal injury, and if I did, I beg your pardon.

Let us not assassinate this lad further, Senator. You have done enough. Have you no sense of decency sir, at long last? Have you left no sense of decency?

Senator McCarthy. I know this hurts you, Mr. Welch. But I may say, Mr. Chairman, on a point of personal privilege, and I would like to finish it——

Mr. Welch. Senator, I think it hurts you, too, sir.

Senator McCarthy. I would like to finish this.

Mr. Welch has been filibustering this hearing, he has been talking day after day about how he wants to get anyone tainted with communism out before sundown. I know Mr. Cohn would rather not have me go into this. I intend to, however, Mr. Welch talks about any sense of decency. If I say anything which is not the truth, then I would like to know about it.

The foremost legal bulwark of the Communist Party, its front organizations, and controlled unions, and which, since its inception, has never failed to rally to the legal defense of the Communist Party, and individual members thereof, including known espionage agents.

Now, that is not the language of Senator McCarthy. That is the language of the Un-American Activities Committee. And I can go on with many more citations. It seems that Mr. Welch is pained so deeply he thinks it is improper for me to give the record, the Communist-front record, of the man whom he wanted to foist upon this committee. But it doesn't pain him at all—there is no pain in his chest about the unfounded charges against Mr. Frank Carr; there is no pain there about the attempt to destroy the reputation and take the jobs away from the young men who were working in my committee.

And, Mr. Welch, if I have said anything here which is untrue, then tell me. I have heard you and every one else talk so much about laying the truth upon the table that when I hear—and it is completely phony, Mr. Welch, I have listened to you for a long time—when you say "Now, before sundown, you must get these people out of Government," I want to have it very clear, very clear that you were not so serious about that when you tried to recommend this man for this committee.

And may I say, Mr. Welch, in fairness to you, I have reason to believe that you did not know about his Communist-front record at the time you recommended him. I don't think you would have recommended him to the committee, if you knew that.

I think it is entirely possible you learned that after you recommended him.

Senator MUNDT. The Chair would like to say again that he does not believe that Mr. Welch recommended Mr. Fisher as counsel for this committee, because he has through his office all the recommendations that were made. He does not recall any that came from Mr. Welch, and that would include Mr. Fisher.

Senator McCARTHY. Let me ask Mr. Welch. You brought him down, did you not, to act as your assistant?

Mr. WELCH. Mr. McCarthy, I will not discuss this with you further. You have sat within 6 feet of me, and could have asked me about Fred Fisher. You have brought it out. If there is a God in heaven, it will do neither you nor your cause any good. I will not discuss it further. I will not ask Mr. Cohn any more questions. You, Mr. Chairman, may, if you will, call the next witness.

Senator MUNDT. Are there any questions?

Mr. JENKINS. No further questions, Mr. Chairman.

Mr. JENKINS. Senator McCarthy, how do you regard the communistic threat to our Government as compared with other threats with which it is confronted?

. . .

Mr. Jenkins, the thing that I think we must remember is that this is a war which a brutalitarian force has won to a greater extent than any brutalitarian force has won a war in the history of the world before.

For example, Christianity, which has been in existence for 2,000 years, has not convertéd, convinced nearly as many people as this Communist brutalitarianism has enslaved in 106 years, and they are not going to stop.

I know that many of my good friends seem to feel that this is a sort of a game you can play, that you can talk about communism as though it is something 10,000 miles away.

Mr. Jenkins, in answer to your question, let me say it is right here with us now. Unless we make sure that there is no inflltration of our Government, then just as certain as you sit there, in the period of our lives you will see a red world. There is no question about that, Mr. Jenkins. . . .

The Affluent Society

JOHN KENNETH GALBRAITH

John Kenneth Galbraith's The Affluent Society *was one of those rare books whose title gave a name to an era. Rarer still, the book also directly influenced public policy and national opinion. Galbraith enunciated what was called at the time a theory of "qualitative liberalism," the idea that domestic policy had to shift from virtually total emphasis on increasing wealth to a new concern for the quality of life. Galbraith argued that increased production did not automatically translate into progress. Unless care was taken, more goods could mean greater inequality of wealth as well as deterioration of the natural and human environment. For example, if one produced more food but failed to finance adequate sanitation facilities, the result would be more filth, a deteriorating environment, and declining public health.*

Galbraith's ideas were tested in the reform decade of the 1960's as major investment in the public sector—investment in public health, environmental improvement, a revival of state and local government —sought to provide improved services to correct the "social balance" between an individualistic consumer culture and public needs. Public higher education flourished as did improved recreational and cultural facilities, increases in social welfare, and a variety of important public health services. Then, as could have been predicted from Galbraith's own theory, rising inflation began to wipe out gains, with public services suffering and urban blight spreading outward from the center cities to envelop the suburbs in which the majority of the American population now resided. Although Galbraith's analysis was written in the 1950's, it remains worthy of consideration even for the present.

The final problem of the productive society is what it produces. This manifests itself in an implacable tendency to provide an opulent supply of some things and a niggardly yield of others. This disparity carries to the point where it is a cause of social discomfort and social unhealth. The line which divides our area of wealth from our area of poverty is roughly that which divides privately produced and marketed goods and services from publicly rendered services. Our wealth in the first is not only in startling contrast with the meagerness of the latter, but our wealth in privately produced goods is, to a marked degree, the cause of crisis in the supply of public services. For we have failed to see the importance, indeed the urgent need, of maintaining a balance between the two.

This disparity between our flow of private and public goods and services is no matter of subjective judgment. On the contrary, it is the source of the most extensive comment which only stops short of the direct contrast being made here. In the years following World War II, the papers of any major city—those of New York were an excellent example—told daily of the shortages and shortcomings in the elementary municipal and metropolitan services. The schools were old and overcrowded. The police force was under strength and underpaid. The parks and playgrounds were insufficient. Streets and empty lots were filthy, and the sanitation staff was underequipped and in need of men. Access to the city by those who work there was uncertain and painful and becoming more so. Internal transportation was overcrowded, unhealthful, and dirty. So was the air. Parking on the streets had to be prohibited, and there was no space elsewhere. These deficiencies were not in new and novel services but in old and established ones. Cities have long swept their streets, helped their people move around, educated them, kept order, and provided horse rails for vehicles which sought to pause. That their residents should have a nontoxic supply of air suggests no revolutionary dalliance with socialism.

The discussion of this public poverty competed, on the whole successfully, with the stories of ever-increasing opulence in privately produced goods. The Gross National Product was rising. So were retail sales. So was personal income. Labor productivity had also advanced. The automobiles that could not be parked were being produced at an expanded rate. The children, though without schools, subject in the playgrounds to the affectionate interest of adults with odd tastes, and disposed to increasingly imaginative forms of delinquency, were admirably equipped with television sets. We had difficulty finding storage space for the great surpluses of food despite a national disposition to obesity. Food was grown and packaged under private auspices. The care and refreshment of the mind, in contrast with the stomach, was principally in the public domain. Our colleges and universities were severely overcrowded and underprovided, and the same was true of the mental hospitals.

The contrast was and remains evident not alone to those who read. The family which takes its mauve and cerise, air-conditioned, power-steered, and power-braked automobile out for a tour passes through cities that are badly paved, made hideous by litter, blighted buildings, billboards, and posts for wires that should long since have been put underground. They pass on into a countryside that has been rendered largely invisible by commercial art. (The goods which the latter advertise have an absolute priority in our value system. Such aesthetic considerations as a view of the countryside accordingly come second. On such matters we are consistent.) They picnic on exquisitely packaged food from a portable icebox by a polluted stream and go on to spend the night at a park which is a menace to public health and morals. Just before dozing off on an air mattress, beneath a nylon tent, amid the stench of decaying refuse, they may reflect vaguely on the curious unevenness of their blessings. Is this, indeed, the American genius?

In the production of goods within the private economy it has long been recognized that a tolerably close relationship must be maintained between the production of various kinds of products. The output of steel and oil and machine tools is related to the production of automobiles. Investment in transportation must keep abreast of the output of goods to be transported. The supply of power must be abreast of the growth of industries requiring it. The existence of these relationships—coefficients to the economist—has made possible the construction of the input-output table which shows how changes in the production in one industry will increase or diminish the demands on other industries. To this table, and more especially to its ingenious author, Professor Wassily Leontief, the world is indebted for one of its most important of modern insights into economic relationships. If expansion in one part of the economy were not matched by the requisite expansion in other parts—were the need for balance not respected—then bottlenecks and shortages, speculative hoarding of scarce supplies, and sharply increasing costs would ensue. Fortunately in peacetime the market system operates easily and effectively to maintain this balance, and this together with the existence of stocks and some flexibility in the coefficients as a result of substitution, insures that no serious difficulties will arise. We are reminded of the existence of the problem only by noticing how serious it is for those countries—Poland or, in a somewhat different form, India—which seek to solve the problem by planned measures and with a much smaller supply of resources.

Just as there must be balance in what a community produces, so there must also be balance in what the community consumes. An increase in the use of one product creates, ineluctably, a requirement for others. If we are to consume more automobiles, we must have more gasoline. There must be more insurance as well as more space on which to operate them. Beyond a certain point more and better food appears to mean increased need for medical services. This is the certain result of the increased consumption of tobacco and alcohol. More vacations require more hotels and more fishing rods. And so forth. With rare exceptions—shortages of doctors are an exception which suggests the rule—this balance is also maintained quite effortlessly so far as goods for private sale and consumption are concerned. The price system plus a rounded condition of opulence is again the agency.

However, the relationships we are here discussing are not confined to the private economy. They operate comprehensively over the whole span of private and public services. As surely as an increase in the output of automobiles puts new demands on the steel industry so, also, it places new demands on public services. Similarly, every increase in the consumption of private goods will normally mean some facilitating or protective step by the state. In all cases if these services are not forthcoming, the consequences will be in some degree ill. It will be convenient to have a term which suggests a satisfactory relationship between the supply of privately produced goods and services and those of the state, and we may call it social balance.

The problem of social balance is ubiquitous, and frequently it is obtrusive. As noted, an increase in the consumption of automobiles requires a facilitating supply of streets, highways, traffic control, and parking space. The protective services of the police and the highway patrols must also be available, as must those of the hospitals. Although the need for balance here is extraordinarily clear, our use of privately produced vehicles has, on occasion, got far out of line with the supply of the related public services. The result has been hideous road congestion, an annual massacre of impressive proportions, and chronic colitis in the cities. As on the ground, so also in the air. Planes collide with disquieting consequences for those within when the public provision for air traffic control fails to keep pace with private use of the airways.

But the auto and the airplane, versus the space to use them, are merely an exceptionally visible example of a requirement that is pervasive. The more goods people procure, the more packages they discard and the more trash that must be carried away. If the appropriate sanitation services are not provided, the counterpart of increasing opulence will be deepening filth. The greater the wealth the thicker will be the dirt. This indubitably describes a tendency of our time. As more goods are produced and owned, the greater are the opportunities for fraud and the more property that must be protected. If the provision of public law enforcement services do not keep pace, the counterpart of increased well-being will, we may be certain, be increased crime.

The city of Los Angeles, in modern times, is a near-classic study in the problem of social balance. Magnificently efficient factories and oil refineries, a lavish supply of automobiles, a vast consumption of handsomely packaged products, coupled with the absence of a municipal trash collection service which forced the use of home incinerators, made the air nearly unbreathable for an appreciable part of each year. Air pollution could be controlled only by a complex and highly developed set of public services—by better knowledge stemming from more research, better policing, a municipal trash collection service, and possibly the assertion of the priority of clean air over the production of goods. These were long in coming. The agony of a city without usable air was the result.

The issue of social balance can be identified in many other current problems. Thus an aspect of increasing private production is the appearance of an extraordinary number of things which lay claim to the interest of the young. Motion pictures, television, automobiles, and the vast opportunities which go with the mobility, together with such less enchanting merchandise as narcotics, comic books, and pornographia, are all included in an advancing gross national product. The child of a less opulent as well as a technologically more primitive age had far fewer such diversions. The red schoolhouse is remembered mainly because it had a paramount position in the lives of those who attended it that no modern school can hope to attain.

In a well-run and well-regulated community, with a sound school system, good recreational opportunities, and a good police force—in short a community where public services have kept pace with private production—the diversionary forces operating on the modern juvenile may do no great damage. Television and the violent mores of Hollywood and Madison Avenue must contend with the intellectual discipline of the school. The social, athletic, dramatic, and like attractions of the school also claim the attention of the child. These, together with the other recreational opportunities of the community, minimize the tendency to delinquency. Experiments with violence and immorality are checked by an effective law enforcement system before they become epidemic.

In a community where public services have failed to keep abreast of private consumption things are very different. Here, in an atmosphere of private opulence and public squalor, the private goods have full sway. Schools do not compete with television and the movies. The dubious heroes of the latter, not Miss Jones, become the idols of the young. The hot rod and the wild ride take the place of more sedentary sports for which there are inadequate facilities or provision. Comic books, alcohol, narcotics, and switchblade knives are, as noted, part of the increased flow of goods, and there is nothing to dispute their enjoyment. There is an ample supply of private wealth to be appropriated and not much to be feared from the police. An austere community is free from temptation. It can be austere in its public services. Not so a rich one.

Moreover, in a society which sets large store by production, and which has highly effective machinery for synthesizing private wants, there are strong pressures to have as many wage earners in the family as possible. As always all social behavior is part of a piece. If both parents are engaged in private production, the burden on the public services is further increased. Children, in effect, become the charge of the community for an appreciable part of the time. If the services of the community do not keep pace, this will be another source of disorder.

Residential housing also illustrates the problem of the social balance, although in a somewhat complex form. Few would wish to contend that, in the lower or even the middle income brackets, Americans are munificently supplied with housing. A great many families would like better located or merely more houseroom, and no advertising is necessary to persuade them of their wish. And the provision of housing is in the private domain. At first glance at least, the line we draw between private and public seems not to be preventing a satisfactory allocation of resources to housing.

On closer examination, however, the problem turns out to be not greatly different from that of education. It is improbable that the housing industry is greatly more incompetent or inefficient in the United States than in those countries—Scandinavia, Holland, or (for the most part) England—where slums have been largely eliminated and where *minimum* standards of cleanliness and comfort are well above our own. As the experience of these countries shows, and as we have also been learning, the housing industry functions well only in combination with a large, complex, and costly array of public services. These include land purchase and clearance for redevelopment; good neighborhood and city planning, and effective and well-enforced zoning; a variety of financing and other aids to the housebuilder and owner; publicly supported research and architectural services for an industry which, by its nature, is equipped to do little on its own; and a considerable amount of direct or assisted public construction for families in the lowest income brackets. The quality of the housing depends not on the industry, which is given, but on what is invested in these supplements and supports.

The case for social balance has, so far, been put negatively. Failure to keep public services in minimal relation to private production and use of goods is a cause of social disorder or impairs economic performance. The matter may now be put affirmatively. By failing to exploit the opportunity to expand public production we are missing opportunities for enjoyment which otherwise we might have had. Presumably a community can be as well rewarded by buying better schools or better parks as by buying bigger automobiles. By concentrating on the latter rather than the former it is failing to maximize its satisfactions. As with schools in the community, so with public services over the country at large. It is scarcely sensible that we should satisfy our wants in private goods with reckless abundance, while in the case of public goods, on the evidence of the eye, we practice extreme self-denial. So, far from systematically exploiting the opportunities to derive use and pleasure from these services, we do not supply what would keep us out of trouble.

The conventional wisdom holds that the community, large or small, makes a decision as to how much it will devote to its public services. This decision is arrived at by democratic process. Subject to the imperfections and uncertainties of democracy, people decide how much of their private income and goods they will surrender in order to have public services of which they are in greater need. Thus there is a balance, however rough, in the enjoyments to be had from private goods and services and those rendered by public authority.

It will be obvious, however, that this view depends on the notion of independently determined consumer wants. In such a world one could with some reason defend the doctrine that the consumer, as a voter, makes an independent choice between public and private goods. But given the dependence effect—given that consumer wants are created by the process by which they are satisfied—the consumer makes no such choice. He is subject to the forces of advertising and emulation by which production creates its own demand. Advertising operates exclusively, and emulation mainly, on behalf of privately produced goods and services. Since management and emulative effects operate on behalf of private production, public services will have an inherent tendency to lag behind. Automobile demand which is expensively synthesized will inevitably have a much larger claim on income than parks or public health or even roads where no such influence operates. The engines of mass communication, in their highest state of development, assail the eyes and ears of the community on behalf of more beer but not of more schools. Even in the conventional wisdom it will scarcely be contended that this leads to an equal choice between the two.

The competition is especially unequal for new products and services. Every corner of the public psyche is canvassed by some of the nation's most talented citizens to see if the desire for some merchantable product can be cultivated. No similar process operates on behalf of the nonmerchantable services of the state. Indeed, while we take the cultivation of new private wants for granted we would be measurably shocked to see it applied to public services. The scientist or engineer or advertising man who devotes himself to developing a new carburetor, cleanser, or depilatory for which the public recognizes no need and will feel none until an advertising campaign arouses it, is one of the valued members of our society. A politician or a public servant who dreams up a new public service is a wastrel. Few public offenses are more reprehensible.

So much for the influences which operate on the decision between public and private production. The calm decision between public and private consumption pictured by the conventional wisdom is, in fact, a remarkable example of the error which arises from viewing social behavior out of context. The inherent tendency will always be for public services to fall behind private production. We have here the first of the causes of social imbalance.

Social balance is also the victim of two further features of our society—the truce on inequality and the tendency to inflation. Since these are now part of our context, their effect comes quickly into view.

With rare exceptions such as the post office, public services do not carry a price ticket to be paid for by the individual user. By their nature they must, ordinarily, be available to all. As a result, when they are improved or new services are initiated, there is the ancient and troublesome question of who is to pay. This, in turn, provokes to life the collateral but irrelevant debate over inequality. As with the use of taxation as an instrument of fiscal policy, the truce on inequality is broken. Liberals are obliged to argue that the services be paid for by progressive taxation which will reduce inequality. Committed as they are to the urgency of goods (and also, as we shall see, . . . to a somewhat mechanical view of the way in which the level of output can be kept most secure) they must oppose sales and excise taxes. Conservatives rally to the defense of inequality—although without ever quite committing themselves in such uncouth terms—and oppose the use of income taxes. They, in effect, oppose the expenditure not on the merits of the service but on the demerits of the tax system. Since the debate over inequality cannot be resolved, the money is frequently not appropriated and the service not performed. It is a casualty of the economic goals of both liberals and conservatives for both of whom the questions of social balance are subordinate to those of production and, when it is evoked, of inequality.

In practice matters are better as well as worse than this statement of the basic forces suggests. Given the tax structure, the revenues of all levels of government grow with the growth of the economy. Services can be maintained and sometimes even improved out of this automatic accretion.

However, this effect is highly unequal. The revenues of the federal government, because of its heavy reliance on income taxes, increase more than proportionately with private economic growth. In addition, although the conventional wisdom greatly deplores the fact, federal appropriations have only an indirect bearing on taxation. Public services are considered and voted on in accordance with their seeming urgency. Initiation or improvement of a particular service is rarely, except for purposes of oratory, set against the specific effect on taxes. Tax policy, in turn, is decided on the basis of the level of economic activity, the resulting revenues, expediency, and other considerations. Among these the total of the thousands of individually considered appropriations is but one factor. In this process the ultimate tax consequence of any individual appropriation is *de minimus,* and the tendency to ignore it reflects the simple mathematics of the situation. Thus it is possible for the Congress to make decisions affecting the social balance without invoking the question of inequality.

Things are made worse, however, by the fact that a large proportion of the federal revenues are pre-empted by defense. The increase in defense costs has also tended to absorb a large share of the normal increase in tax revenues. The position of the federal government for improving the social balance has also been weakened since World War II by the strong, although receding, conviction that its taxes were at artificial wartime levels and that a tacit commitment exists to reduce taxes at the earliest opportunity.

In the states and localities the problem of social balance is much more severe. Here tax revenues—this is especially true of the General Property Tax—increase less than proportionately with increased private production. Budgeting too is far more closely circumscribed than in the case of the federal government—only the monetary authority enjoys the pleasant privilege of underwriting its own loans. Because of this, increased services for states and localities regularly pose the question of more revenues and more taxes. And here, with great regularity, the question of social balance is lost in the debate over equality and social equity.

Thus we currently find by far the most serious social imbalance in the services performed by local governments. The F.B.I. comes much more easily by funds than the city police force. The Department of Agriculture can more easily keep its pest control abreast of expanding agricultural output than the average city health service can keep up with the needs of an expanding industrial population. One consequence is that the federal government remains under constant pressure to use its superior revenue position to help redress the balance at the lower levels of government.

Finally, social imbalance is the natural offspring of persistent inflation. Inflation by its nature strikes different individuals and groups with highly discriminatory effect. The most nearly unrelieved victims, apart from those living on pensions or other fixed provision for personal security, are those who work for the state. In the private economy the firm which sells goods has, in general, an immediate accommodation to the inflationary movement. Its price increases are the inflation. The incomes of its owners and proprietors are automatically accommodated to the upward movement. To the extent that wage increases are part of the inflationary process, this is also true of organized industrial workers. Even unorganized white collar workers are in a milieu where prices and incomes are moving up. The adaption of their incomes, if less rapid than that of the industrial workers, is still reasonably prompt.

The position of the public employee is at the other extreme. His pay scales are highly formalized, and traditionally they have been subject to revision only at lengthy intervals. In states and localities inflation does not automatically bring added revenues to pay higher salaries and incomes. Pay revision for all public workers is subject to the temptation to wait and see if the inflation isn't coming to an end. There will be some fear—this seems to have been more of a factor in England than in the United States—that advances in public wages will set a bad example for private employers and unions.

Inflation means that employment is pressing on the labor supply and that private wage and salary incomes are rising. Thus the opportunities for moving from public to private employment are especially favorable. Public employment, moreover, once had as a principal attraction a high measure of social security. Industrial workers were subject to the formidable threat of unemployment during depression. Public employees were comparatively secure, and this security was worth an adverse salary differential. But with improving economic security in general this advantage has diminished. Private employment thus has come to provide better protection against inflation and little worse protection against other hazards. Though the dedicated may stay in public posts, the alert go.

The deterioration of the public services in the years of inflation has not gone unremarked. However, there has been a strong tendency to regard it as an adventitious misfortune—something which, like a nasty shower at a picnic, happened to blight a generally good time. Salaries were allowed to lag, which was a pity. This is a very inadequate view. Discrimination against the public services is an organic feature of inflation. Nothing so weakens government as persistent inflation. The public administration of France for many years, of Italy until recent times, and of other European and numerous South American countries have been deeply sapped and eroded by the effects of long-continued inflation. Social imbalance reflects itself in inability to enforce laws, including significantly those which protect and advance basic social justice, and in failure to maintain and improve essential services. One outgrowth of the resulting imbalance has been frustration and pervasive discontent. Over much of the world there is a rough and not entirely accidental correlation between the strength of indigenous communist parties or the frequency of revolutions and the persistence of inflation.

A feature of the years immediately following World War II was a remarkable attack on the notion of expanding and improving public services. During the depression years such services had been elaborated and improved partly in order to fill some small part of the vacuum left by the shrinkage of private production. During the war years the role of government was vastly expanded. After that came the reaction. Much of it, unquestionably, was motivated by a desire to rehabilitate the prestige of private production and therewith of producers. No doubt some who joined the attack hoped, at least tacitly, that it might be possible to sidestep the truce on taxation vis-à-vis equality by having less taxation of all kinds. For a time the notion that our public services had somehow become inflated and excessive was all but axiomatic. Even liberal politicians did not seriously protest. They found it necessary to aver that they were in favor of public economy too.

In this discussion a certain mystique was attributed to the satisfaction of privately supplied wants. A community decision to have a new school means that the individual surrenders the necessary amount, willy-nilly, in his taxes. But if he is left with that income, he is a free man. He can decide between a better car or a television set. This was advanced with some solemnity as an argument for the TV set. The difficulty is that this argument leaves the community with no way of preferring the school. All private wants, where the individual can choose, are inherently superior to all public desires which must be paid for by taxation and with an inevitable component of compulsion.

The cost of public services was also held to be a desolating burden on private production, although this was at a time when the private production was burgeoning. Urgent warnings were issued of the unfavorable effects of taxation on investment—"I don't know of a surer way of killing off the incentive to invest than by imposing taxes which are regarded by people as punitive." This was at a time when the inflationary effect of a very high level of investment was causing concern. The same individuals who were warning about the inimical effects of taxes were strongly advocating a monetary policy designed to reduce investment. However, an understanding of our economic discourse requires an appreciation of one of its basic rules: men of high position are allowed, by a special act of grace, to accommodate their reasoning to the answer they need. Logic is only required in those of lesser rank.

Finally it was argued, with no little vigor, that expanding government posed a grave threat to individual liberties. "Where distinction and rank is achieved almost exclusively by becoming a civil servant of the state . . . it is too much to expect that many will long prefer freedom to security."

With time this attack on public services has somewhat subsided. The disorder associated with social imbalance has become visible even if the need for balance between private and public services is still imperfectly appreciated.

Freedom also seemed to be surviving. Perhaps it was realized that all organized activity requires concessions by the individual to the group. This is true of the policeman who joins the police force, the teacher who gets a job at the high school, and the executive who makes his way up the hierarchy of Du Pont. If there are differences between public and private organization, they are of kind rather than of degree. As this is written the pendulum has in fact swung back. Our liberties are now menaced by the conformity exacted by the large corporation and its impulse to create, for its own purposes, the organization man. This danger we may also survive.

Nonetheless, the postwar onslaught on the public services left a lasting imprint. To suggest that we canvass our public wants to see where happiness can be improved by more and better services has a sharply radical tone. Even public services to avoid disorder must be defended. By contrast the man who devises a nostrum for a nonexistent need and then successfully promotes both remains one of nature's noblemen.

Pilgrimage to Nonviolence

MARTIN LUTHER KING, JR.

A major source of the civil rights movement of the late 1950s and early 1960s was the revival of interest in religion that took place in the United States after World War II. The Reverend Martin Luther King, Jr.'s discussion of the origins of the tactic of nonviolence indicates the depth of religious searching that prepared him for the role he assumed in the Montgomery, Alabama, bus boycott in 1955 and continued until his assassination in 1968. The terms in which King viewed the world, essentially those of a sophisticated Protestant evangelism, gave him a ready communication with white leaders who were responding to a similar intellectual milieu. These common themes made it easier for white churchmen and leaders of public opinion to understand the radically different social experience of black Americans that, combined with such a body of ideas, set the tone of a great social movement for more than a decade after the mid-1950's.

In my senior year in theological seminary, I engaged in the exciting reading of various theological theories. Having been raised in a rather strict fundamentalist tradition, I was occasionally shocked when my intellectual journey carried me through new and sometimes complex doctrinal lands, but the pilgrimage was always stimulating, gave me a new appreciation for objective appraisal, and critical analysis, and knocked me out of my dogmatic slumber.

Liberalism provided me with an intellectual satisfaction that I had never found in fundamentalism. I became so enamored of the insights of liberalism that I almost fell into the trap of accepting uncritically everything it encompassed. I was absolutely convinced of the natural goodness of man and the natural power of human reason.

A basic change in my thinking came when I began to question some of the theories that had been associated with so-called liberal theology. Of course, there are aspects of liberalism that I hope to cherish always: its devotion to the search for truth, its insistence on an open and analytical mind, and its refusal to abandon the best lights of reason. The contribution of liberalism to the philological-historical criticism of biblical literature has been of immeasurable value and should be defended with religious and scientific passion.

But I began to question the liberal doctrine of man. The more I observed the tragedies of history and man's shameful inclination to choose the low road, the more I came to see the depths and strength of sin. My reading of the works of Reinhold Niebuhr made me aware of the complexity of human motives and the reality of sin on every level of man's existence. Moreover, I came to recognize the complexity of man's social involvement and the glaring reality of collective evil. I realized that liberalism had been all too sentimental concerning human nature and that it leaned toward a false idealism.

I also came to see that the superficial optimism of liberalism concerning human nature overlooked the fact that reason is darkened by sin. The more I thought about human nature, the more I saw how our tragic inclination for sin encourages us to rationalize our actions. Liberalism failed to show that reason by itself is little more than an instrument to justify man's defensive ways of thinking. Reason, devoid of the purifying power of faith, can never free itself from distortions and rationalizations.

Although I rejected some aspects of liberalism, I never came to an all-out acceptance of neo-orthodoxy. While I saw neo-orthodoxy as a helpful corrective for a sentimental liberalism, I felt that it did not provide an adequate answer to basic questions. If liberalism was too optimistic concerning human nature, neo-orthodoxy was too pessimistic. Not only on the question of man, but also on other vital issues, the revolt of neo-orthodoxy went too far. In its attempt to preserve the transcendence of God, which had been neglected by an overstress of his immanence in liberalism, neo-orthodoxy went to the extreme of stressing a God who was hidden, unknown, and "wholly other." In its revolt against overemphasis on the power of reason in liberalism, neo-orthodoxy fell into a mood of antirationalism and semifundamentalism, stressing a narrow uncritical biblicism. This approach, I felt, was inadequate both for the church and for personal life.

So although liberalism left me unsatisfied on the question of the nature of man, I found no refuge in neo-orthodoxy. I am now convinced that the truth about man is found neither in liberalism nor in neo-orthodoxy. Each represents a partial truth. A large segment of Protestant liberalism defined man only in terms of his essential nature, his capacity for good; neo-orthodoxy tended to define man only in terms of his existential nature, his capacity for evil. An adequate understanding of man is found neither in the thesis of liberalism nor in the antithesis of neo-orthodoxy, but in a synthesis which reconciles the truths of both.

During the intervening years I have gained a new appreciation for the philosophy of existentialism. My first contact with this philosophy came through my reading of Kierkegaard and Nietzsche. Later I turned to a study of Jaspers, Heidegger, and Sartre. These thinkers stimulated my thinking; while questioning each, I nevertheless learned a great deal through a study of them. When I finally engaged in a serious study of the writings of Paul Tillich, I became convinced that existentialism, in spite of the fact that it had become all too fashionable, had grasped certain basic truths about man and his condition that could not be permanently overlooked.

An understanding of the "finite freedom" of man is one of the permanent contributions of existentialism, and its perception of the anxiety and conflict produced in man's personal and social life by the perilous and ambiguous structure of existence is especially meaningful for our time. A common denominator in atheistic or theistic existential-ism is that man's existential situation is estranged from his essential nature. In their revolt against Hegel's essentialism, all existentialists contend that the world is fragmented. History is a series of unrecon-ciled conflicts, and man's existence is filled with anxiety and threatened with meaninglessness. While the ultimate Christian answer is not found in any of these existential assertions, there is much here by which the theologian may describe the true state of man's existence.

Although most of my formal study has been in systematic theology and philosophy, I have become more and more interested in social ethics. During my early teens I was deeply concerned by the problem of racial injustice. I considered segregation both rationally inexplicable and morally unjustifiable. I could never accept my having to sit in the back of a bus or in the segregated section of a train. The first time that I was seated behind a curtain in a dining car I felt as though the curtain had been dropped on my selfhood. I also learned that the in-separable twin of racial unjustice is economic injustice. I saw how the systems of segregation exploited both the Negro and the poor whites. These early experiences made me deeply conscious of the varieties of injustice in our society.

Not until I entered theological seminary, however, did I begin a serious intellectual quest for a method that would eliminate social evil. I was immediately influenced by the social gospel. In the early 1950s I read Walter Rauschenbusch's *Christianity and the Social Crisis,* a book which left an indelible imprint on my thinking. Of course, there were points at which I differed with Rauschenbusch. I felt that he was a victim of the nineteenth-century "cult of inevitable progress," which led him to an unwarranted optimism concerning human nature. More-over, he came perilously close to identifying the Kingdom of God with a particular social and economic system, a temptation to which the church must never surrender. But in spite of these shortcomings, Rauschenbusch gave to American Protestantism a sense of social re-sponsibility that it should never lose. The gospel at its best deals with the whole man, not only his soul but also his body, not only his spirit-ual well-being but also his material well-being. A religion that professes a concern for the souls of men and is not equally concerned about the slums that damn them, the economic conditions that strangle them, and the social conditions that cripple them, is a spiritually moribund religion.

After reading Rauschenbusch, I turned to a serious study of the social and ethical theories of the great philosophers. During this period I had almost despaired of the power of love to solve social problems. The turn-the-other-cheek and the love-your-enemies philosophies are valid, I felt, only when individuals are in conflict with other individuals; when racial groups and nations are in conflict, a more realistic ap-proach is necessary.

Then I was introduced to the life and teachings of Mahatma Gandhi. As I read his works I became deeply fascinated by his campaigns of nonviolent resistance. The whole Gandhian concept of *satya-graha* (*satya* is truth which equals love and *graha* is force; *satyagraha* thus means truth-force or love-force) was profoundly significant to me. As I delved deeper into the philosophy of Gandhi, my skepticism concerning the power of love gradually diminshed, and I came to see for the first time that the Christian doctrine of love, operating through the Gandhian method of nonviolence, is one of the most potent weapons available to an oppressed people in their struggle for freedom. At that time, however, I acquired only an intellectual understanding and appreciation of the position, and I had no firm determination to organize it in a socially effective situation.

When I went to Montgomery, Alabama, as a pastor in 1954, I had not the slightest idea that I would later become involved in a crisis in which nonviolent resistance would be applicable. After I had lived in the community about a year, the bus boycott began. The Negro people of Montgomery, exhausted by the humiliating experiences that they had constantly faced on the buses, expressed in a massive act of nonco-operation their determination to be free. They came to see that it was ultimately more honorable to walk the streets in dignity than to ride the buses in humiliation. At the beginning of the protest, the people called on me to serve as their spokesman. In accepting this responsibility, my mind, consciously or unconsciously, was driven back to the Sermon on the Mount and the Gandhian method of nonviolent resistance. This principle became the guiding light of our movement. Christ furnished the spirit and motivation and Gandhi furnished the method.

The experience in Montgomery did more to clarify my thinking in regard to the question of nonviolence than all of the books that I had read. As the days unfolded, I became more and more convinced of the power of nonviolence. Nonviolence became more than a method to which I gave intellectual assent; it became a commitment to a way of life. Many issues I had not cleared up intellectually concerning nonviolence were now resolved within the sphere of practical action.

My privilege of traveling to India had a great impact on me personally, for it was invigorating to see firsthand the amazing results of a nonviolent struggle to achieve independence. The aftermath of hatred and bitterness that usually follows a violent campaign was found nowhere in India, and a mutual friendship, based on complete equality, existed between the Indian and British people within the Commonwealth.

I would not wish to give the impression that nonviolence will accomplish miracles overnight. Men are not easily moved from their mental ruts or purged of their prejudiced and irrational feelings. When the underprivileged demand freedom, the privileged at first react with bitterness and resistance. Even when the demands are couched in nonviolent terms, the initial response is substantially the same. I am sure that many of our white brothers in Montgomery and throughout the South are still bitter toward the Negro leaders, even though these leaders have sought to follow a way of love and nonviolence. But the nonviolent approach does something to the hearts and souls of those committed to it. It gives them new self-respect. It calls up resources of strength and courage that they did not know they had. Finally, it so stirs the conscience of the opponent that reconciliation becomes a reality.

More recently I have come to see the need for the method of non-violence in international relations. Although I was not yet convinced of its efficacy in conflicts between nations, I felt that while war could never be a positive good, it could serve as a negative good by prevent-ing the spread and growth of an evil force. War, horrible as it is, might be preferable to surrender to a totalitarian system. But I now believe that the potential destructiveness of modern weapons totally rules out the possibility of war ever again achieving a negative good. If we assume that mankind has a right to survive, then we must find an al-ternative to war and destruction. In our day of space vehicles and guided ballistic missiles, the choice is either nonviolence or nonexis-tence.

I am no doctrinaire pacifist, but I have tried to embrace a realistic pacifism which finds the pacifist position as the lesser evil in the cir-cumstances. I do not claim to be free from the moral dilemmas that the Christian nonpacifist confronts, but I am convinced that the church cannot be silent while mankind faces the threat of nuclear annihilation. If the church is true to her mission, she must call for an end to the arms race.

Some of my personal sufferings over the last few years have also served to shape my thinking. I always hesitate to mention these experi-ences for fear of conveying the wrong impression. A person who con-stantly calls attention to his trials and sufferings is in danger of develop-ing a martyr complex and impressing others that he is consciously seeking sympathy. It is possible for one to be self-centered in his self-sacrifice. So I am always reluctant to refer to my personal sacrifices. But I feel somewhat justified in mentioning them in this essay because of the influence they have had upon my thought.

Due to my involvement in the struggle for the freedom of my peo-ple, I have known very few quiet days in the last few years. I have been imprisoned in Alabama and Georgia jails twelve times. My home has been bombed twice. A day seldom passes that my family and I are not the recipients of threats of death. I have been the victim of a near-fatal stabbing. So in a real sense I have been battered by the storms of persecution. I must admit that at times I have felt that I could no longer bear such a heavy burden, and have been tempted to retreat to a more quiet and serene life. But every time such a temptation ap-peared, something came to strengthen and sustain my determination. I have learned now that the Master's burden is light precisely when we take his yoke upon us.

My personal trials have also taught me the value of unmerited suffering. As my sufferings mounted I soon realized that there were two ways in which I could respond to my situation—either to react with bitterness or seek to transform the suffering into a creative force. I decided to follow the latter course. Recognizing the necessity for suffering, I have tried to make of it a virtue. If only to save myself from bitterness, I have attempted to see my personal ordeals as an opportunity to transfigure myself and heal the people involved in the tragic situation which now obtains. I have lived these last few years with the conviction that unearned suffering is redemptive. There are some who still find the Cross a stumbling block, others consider it foolishness, but I am more convinced than ever before that it is the power of God unto social and individual salvation. So like the Apostle Paul I can now humbly, yet proudly, say, "I bear in my body the marks of the Lord Jesus."

The agonizing moments through which I have passed during the last few years have also drawn me closer to God. More than ever before I am convinced of the reality of a personal God. True, I have always believed in the personality of God. But in the past the idea of a personal God was little more than a metaphysical category that I found theologically and philosophically satisfying. Now it is a living reality that has been validated in the experiences of everyday life. God has been profoundly real to me in recent years. In the midst of outer dangers I have felt an inner calm. In the midst of lonely days and dreary nights I have heard an inner voice saying, "Lo, I will be with you." When the chains of fear and the manacles of frustration have all but stymied my efforts, I have felt the power of God transforming the fatigue of despair into the buoyancy of hope. I am convinced that the universe is under the control of a loving purpose, and that in the struggle for righteousness man has cosmic companionship. Behind the harsh appearances of the world there is a benign power. To say that this God is personal is not to make him a finite object besides other objects or attribute to him the limitations of human personality; it is to take what is finest and noblest in our consciousness and affirm its perfect existence in him. It is certainly true that human personality is limited, but personality as such involves no necessary limitations. It means simply self-consciousness and self-direction. So in the truest sense of the word, God is a living God. In him there is feeling and will, responsive to the deepest yearnings of the human heart: *this* God both evokes and answers prayer.

The past decade has been a most exciting one. In spite of the tensions and uncertainties of this period something profoundly meaningful is taking place. Old systems of exploitation and oppression are passing away; new systems of justice and equality are being born. In a real sense this is a great time to be alive. Therefore, I am not yet discouraged about the future. Granted that the easygoing optimism of yesterday is impossible. Granted that we face a world crisis which leaves us standing so often amid the surging murmur of life's restless sea. But every crisis has both its dangers and its opportunities. It can spell either salvation or doom. In a dark, confused world the Kingdom of God may yet reign in the hearts of men.

The Texture of Poverty

MICHAEL HARRINGTON

The poor, Michael Harrington urges us, "need an American Dickens to record the smell and texture and quality of their lives." Yet his own brilliant mixture of reporting and social analysis served the essential purpose of encouraging a compassionate view of the poor, which meant first forcing people to see them. The book remains curiously stirring— what we might expect from a novel, but not from a book which constantly quotes the findings of empirical social science.

The Other America, from which this excerpt by Harrington is taken, was one of several muckraking social-science works that forced a new perspective on poverty in modern America. John Kenneth Galbraith in The Affluent Society had pointed to the persistence of poverty amid affluence and questioned whether economic growth alone would eradicate it. Robert Lampman and Gabriel Kolko demonstrated that the New Deal had not significantly changed the distribution of wealth. All these writers cleave the path for a new liberal program that, ironically, undermined the claims of older liberals that the New Deal had reformed the economy in the interest of poorer Americans.

Harrington's book continues to be the most vital of the many polemics that muckraked American society in the late fifties and the sixties. It was an important book because it helped launch a war on poverty which, for all its shortcomings, has made a real difference. For one thing the poor are no longer so invisible or politically powerless. They make themselves known despite official efforts to eliminate the word "poverty" from the national vocabulary. This is not to say that they may never become "invisible" again: The job that Harrington did in the early sixties (like Dickens' a century before) will clearly need constant redoing.

I

There are perennial reasons that make the other America an invisible land.

Poverty is often off the beaten track. It always has been. The ordinary tourist never left the main highway, and today he rides interstate turnpikes. He does not go into the valleys of Pennsylvania where the towns look like movie sets of Wales in the thirties. He does not see the company houses in rows, the rutted roads (the poor always have bad roads whether they live in the city, in towns, or on farms), and everything is black and dirty. And even if he were to pass through such a place by accident, the tourist would not meet the unemployed men in the bar or the women coming home from a runaway sweatshop.

Then, too, beauty and myths are perennial masks of poverty. The traveler comes to the Appalachians in the lovely season. He sees the hills, the streams, the foliage—but not the poor. Or perhaps he looks at a run-down mountain house and, remembering Rousseau rather than seeing with his eyes, decides that "those people" are truly fortunate to be living the way they are and that they are lucky to be exempt from the strains and tensions of the middle class. The only problem is that "those people," the quaint inhabitants of those hills, are undereducated, underprivileged, lack medical care, and are in the process of being forced from the land into a life in the cities, where they are misfits.

These are normal and obvious causes of the invisibility of the poor. They operated a generation ago; they will be functioning a generation hence. It is more important to understand that the very development of American society is creating a new kind of blindness about poverty. The poor are increasingly slipping out of the very experience and consciousness of the nation.

If the middle class never did like ugliness and poverty, it was at least aware of them. "Across the tracks" was not a very long way to go. There were forays into the slums at Christmas time; there were charitable organizations that brought contact with the poor. Occasionally, almost everyone passed through the Negro ghetto or the blocks of tenements, if only to get downtown to work or to entertainment.

Now the American city has been transformed. The poor still inhabit the miserable housing in the central area, but they are increasingly isolated from contact with, or sight of, anybody else. Middle-class women coming in from Suburbia on a rare trip may catch the merest glimpse of the other America on the way to an evening at the theater, but their children are segregated in suburban schools. The business or professional man may drive along the fringes of slums in a car or bus, but it is not an important experience to him. The failures, the unskilled, the disabled, the aged, and the minorities are right there, across the tracks, where they have always been. But hardly anyone else is.

In short, the very development of the American city has removed poverty from the living, emotional experience of millions upon millions of middle-class Americans. Living out in the suburbs it is easy to assume that ours is, indeed, an affluent society.

This new segregation of poverty is compounded by a well-meaning ignorance. A good many concerned and sympathetic Americans are aware that there is much discussion of urban renewal. Suddenly, driving through the city, they notice that a familiar slum has been torn down and that there are towering, modern buildings where once there had been tenements or hovels. There is a warm feeling of satisfaction, of pride in the way things are working out: the poor, it is obvious, are being taken care of.

The irony in this . . . is that the truth is nearly the exact opposite to the impression. The total impact of the various housing programs in postwar America has been to squeeze more and more people into existing slums. More often than not, the modern apartment in a towering building rents at $40 a room or more. For, during the past decade and a half, there has been more subsidization of middle- and upper-income housing than there has been of housing for the poor.

Clothes make the poor invisible too: America has the best-dressed poverty the world has ever known. For a variety of reasons, the benefits of mass production have been spread much more evenly in this area than in many others. It is much easier in the United States to be decently dressed than it is to be decently housed, fed, or doctored. Even people with terribly depressed incomes can look prosperous.

This is an extremely important factor in defining our emotional and existential ignorance of poverty. In Detroit the existence of social classes became much more difficult to discern the day the companies put lockers in the plants. From that moment on, one did not see men in work clothes on the way to the factory, but citizens in slacks and white shirts. This process has been magnified with the poor throughout the country. There are tens of thousands of Americans in the big cities who are wearing shoes, perhaps even a stylishly cut suit or dress, and yet are hungry. It is not a matter of planning, though it almost seems as if the affluent society had given out costumes to the poor so that they would not offend the rest of society with the sight of rags.

Then, many of the poor are the wrong age to be seen. A good number of them (over 8,000,000) are sixty-five years of age or better; an even larger number are under eighteen. The aged members of the other America are often sick, and they cannot move. Another group of them live out their lives in loneliness and frustration: they sit in rented rooms, or else they stay close to a house in a neighborhood that has completely changed from the old days. Indeed, one of the worst aspects of poverty among the aged is that these people are out of sight and out of mind, and alone.

The young are somewhat more visible, yet they too stay close to their neighborhoods. Sometimes they advertise their poverty through a lurid tabloid story about a gang killing. But generally they do not disturb the quiet streets of the middle class.

And finally, the poor are politically invisible. It is one of the cruelest ironies of social life in advanced countries that the dispossessed at the bottom of society are unable to speak for themselves. The people of the other America do not, by far and large, belong to unions, to fraternal organizations, or to political parties. They are without lobbies of their own; they put forward no legislative program. As a group, they are atomized. They have no face; they have no voice. . . .

II

Out of the thirties came the welfare state. Its creation had been stimulated by mass impoverishment and misery, yet it helped the poor least of all. Laws like unemployment compensation, the Wagner Act, the various farm programs, all these were designed for the middle third in the cities, for the organized workers, and for the upper third in the country, for the big market farmers. If a man works in an extremely low-paying job, he may not even be covered by social security or other welfare programs. If he receives unemployment compensation, the payment is scaled down according to his low earnings.

One of the major laws that was designed to cover everyone, rich and poor, was social security. But even here the other Americans suffered discrimination. Over the years social security payments have not even provided a subsistence level of life. The middle third have been able to supplement the Federal pension through private plans negotiated by unions, through joining medical insurance schemes like Blue Cross, and so on. The poor have not been able to do so. They lead a bitter life, and then have to pay for that fact in old age.

Indeed, the paradox that the welfare state benefits those least who need help most is but a single instance of a persistent irony in the other America. Even when the money finally trickles down, even when a school is built in a poor neighborhood, for instance, the poor are still deprived. Their entire environment, their life, their values, do not prepare them to take advantage of the new opportunity. The parents are anxious for the children to go to work; the pupils are pent up, waiting for the moment when their education has complied with the law.

Today's poor, in short, missed the political and social gains of the thirties. They are, as Galbraith rightly points out, the first minority poor in history, the first poor not to be seen, the first poor whom the politicians could leave alone.

The first step toward the new poverty was taken when millions of people proved immune to progress. When that happened, the failure was not individual and personal, but a social product. But once the historic accident takes place, it begins to become a personal fate.

The new poor of the other America saw the rest of society move ahead. They went on living in depressed areas, and often they tended to become depressed human beings. In some of the West Virginia towns, for instance, an entire community will become shabby and defeated. The young and the adventurous go to the city, leaving behind those who cannot move and those who lack the will to do so. The entire area becomes permeated with failure, and that is one more reason the big corporations shy away.

Indeed, one of the most important things about the new poverty is that it cannot be defined in simple, statistical terms. Throughout this book a crucial term is used: aspiration. If a group has internal vitality, a will—if it has aspiration—it may live in dilapidated housing, it may eat an inadequate diet, and it may suffer poverty, but it is not impoverished. So it was in those ethnic slums of the immigrants that played such a dramatic role in the unfolding of the American dream. The people found themselves in slums, but they were not slum dwellers.

But the new poverty is constructed so as to destroy aspiration; it is a system designed to be impervious to hope. The other America does not contain the adventurous seeking a new life and land. It is populated by the failures, by those driven from the land and bewildered by the city, by old people suddenly confronted with the torments of loneliness and poverty, and by minorities facing a wall of prejudice.

In the past, when poverty was general in the unskilled and semiskilled work force, the poor were all mixed together. The bright and the dull, those who were going to escape into the great society and those who were to stay behind, all of them lived on the same street. When the middle third rose, this community was destroyed. And the entire invisible land of the other Americans became a ghetto, a modern poor farm for the rejects of society and of the economy.

It is a blow to reform and the political hopes of the poor that the middle class no longer understands that poverty exists. But, perhaps more important, the poor are losing their links with the great world. If statistics and sociology can measure a feeling as delicate as loneliness (and some of the attempts to do so will be cited later on), the other America is becoming increasingly populated by those who do not belong to anybody or anything. They are no longer participants in an ethnic culture from the old country; they are less and less religious; they do not belong to unions or clubs. They are not seen, and because of that they themselves cannot see. Their horizon has become more and more restricted; they see one another, and that means they see little reason to hope.

Galbraith was one of the first writers to begin to describe the newness of contemporary poverty, and that is to his credit. Yet because even he underestimates the problem, it is important to put his definition into perspective.

For Galbraith, there are two main components of the new poverty: case poverty and insular poverty. Case poverty is the plight of those who suffer from some physical or mental disability that is personal and individual and excludes them from the general advance. Insular poverty exists in areas like the Appalachians or the West Virginia coal fields, where an entire section of the country becomes economically obsolete.

Physical and mental disabilities are, to be sure, an important part of poverty in America. The poor are sick in body and in spirit. But this is not an isolated fact about them, an individual "case," a stroke of bad luck. Disease, alcoholism, low IQ's, these express a whole way of life. They are, in the main, the effects of an environment, not the biographies of unlucky individuals. Because of this, the new poverty is something that cannot be dealt with by first aid. If there is to be a lasting assault on the shame of the other America, it must seek to root out of this society an entire environment, and not just the relief of individuals.

But perhaps the idea of "insular" poverty is even more dangerous. To speak of "islands" of the poor (or, in the more popular term, of "pockets of poverty") is to imply that one is confronted by a serious, but relatively minor, problem. This is hardly a description of a misery that extends to 40,000,000 or 50,000,000 people in the United States. They have remained impoverished in spite of increasing productivity and the creation of a welfare state. That fact alone should suggest the dimensions of a serious and basic situation.

And yet, even given these disagreements with Galbraith, his achievement is considerable. He was one of the first to understand that there are enough poor people in the United States to constitute a subculture of misery, but not enough of them to challenge the conscience and the imagination of the nation.

Finally, one might summarize the newness of contemporary poverty by saying: These are the people who are immune to progress. But then the facts are even more cruel. The other Americans are the victims of the very inventions and machines that have provided a higher living standard for the rest of the society. They are upside-down in the economy, and for them greater productivity often means worse jobs; agricultural advance becomes hunger.

In the optimistic theory, technology is an undisguised blessing. A general increase in productivity, the argument goes, generates a higher standard of living for the whole people. And indeed, this has been true for the middle and upper thirds of American society, the people who made such striking gains in the last two decades. It tends to overstate the automatic character of the process, to omit the role of human struggle. (The CIO was organized by men in conflict, not by economic trends.) Yet it states a certain truth—for those who are lucky enough to participate in it.

But the poor, if they were given to theory, might argue the exact opposite. They might say: Progress is misery.

As the society became more technological, more skilled, those who learn to work the machines, who get the expanding education, move up. Those who miss out at the very start find themselves at a new disadvantage. A generation ago in American life, the majority of the working people did not have high-school educations. But at that time industry was organized on a lower level of skill and competence. And there was a sort of continuum in the shop: the youth who left school at sixteen could begin as a laborer, and gradually pick up skill as he went along.

Today the situation is quite different. The good jobs require much more academic preparation, much more skill from the very outset. Those who lack a high-school education tend to be condemned to the economic underworld—to low-paying service industries, to backward factories, to sweeping and janitorial duties. If the fathers and mothers of the contemporary poor were penalized a generation ago for their lack of schooling, their children will suffer all the more. The very rise in productivity that created more money and better working conditions for the rest of the society can be a menace to the poor.

But then this technological revolution might have an even more disastrous consequence: it could increase the ranks of the poor as well as intensify the disabilities of poverty. At this point it is too early to make any final judgment, yet there are obvious danger signals. There are millions of Americans who live just the other side of poverty. When a recession comes, they are pushed onto the relief rolls. (Welfare payments in New York respond almost immediately to any economic decline.) If automation continues to inflict more and more penalties on the unskilled and the semiskilled, it could have the impact of permanently increasing the population of the other America.

Even more explosive is the possibility that people who participated in the gains of the thirties and the forties will be pulled back down into poverty. Today the mass-production industries where unionization made such a difference are contracting. Jobs are being destroyed. In the process, workers who had achieved a certain level of wages, who had won working conditions in the shop, are suddenly confronted with impoverishment. This is particularly true for anyone over forty years of age and for members of minority groups. Once their job is abolished, their chances of ever getting similar work are very slim.

It is too early to say whether or not this phenomenon is temporary, or whether it represents a massive retrogression that will swell the numbers of the poor. To a large extent, the answer to this question will be determined by the political response of the United States in the sixties. If serious and massive action is not undertaken, it may be necessary for statisticians to add some old-fashioned, pre-welfare-state poverty to the misery of the other America.

Poverty in the 1960's is invisible and it is new, and both these factors make it more tenacious. It is more isolated and politically powerless than ever before. It is laced with ironies, not the least of which is that many of the poor view progress upside-down, as a menace and a threat to their lives. And if the nation does not measure up to the challenge of automation, poverty in the 1960's might be on the increase.

There are mighty historical and economic forces that keep the poor down; and there are human beings who help out in this grim business, many of them unwittingly. There are sociological and political reasons why poverty is not seen; and there are misconceptions and prejudices that literally blind the eyes. The latter must be understood if anyone is to make the necessary act of intellect and will so that the poor can be noticed.

Here is the most familiar version of social blindness: "The poor are that way because they are afraid of work. And anyway they all have big cars. If they were like me (or my father or my grandfather), they could pay their own way. But they prefer to live on the dole and cheat the taxpayers."

This theory, usually thought of as a virtuous and moral statement, is one of the means of making it impossible for the poor ever to pay their way. There are, one must assume, citizens of the other America who choose impoverishment out of fear of work (though, writing it down, I really do not believe it). But the real explanation of why the poor are where they are is that they made the mistake of being born to the wrong parents, in the wrong section of the country, in the wrong industry, or in the wrong racial or ethnic group. Once that mistake has been made, they could have been paragons of will and morality, but most of them would never even have had a chance to get out of the other America.

There are two important ways of saying this: The poor are caught in a vicious circle; or, The poor live in a culture of poverty.

In a sense, one might define the contemporary poor in the United States as those who, for reasons beyond their control, cannot help themselves. All the most decisive factors making for opportunity and advance are against them. They are born going downward, and most of them stay down. They are victims whose lives are endlessly blown round and round the other America.

Here is one of the most familiar forms of the vicious circle of poverty. The poor get sick more than anyone else in the society. That is because they live in slums, jammed together under unhygienic conditions; they have inadequate diets, and cannot get decent medical care. When they become sick, they are sick longer than any other group in the society. Because they are sick more often and longer than anyone else, they lose wages and work, and find it difficult to hold a steady job. And because of this, they cannot pay for good housing, for a nutritious diet, for doctors. At any given point in the circle, particularly when there is a major illness, their prospect is to move to an even lower level and to begin the cycle, round and round, toward even more suffering.

This is only one example of the vicious circle. Each group in the other America has its own particular version of the experience, and these will be detailed throughout this book. But the pattern, whatever its variations, is basic to the other America.

The individual cannot usually break out of this vicious circle. Neither can the group, for it lacks the social energy and political strength to turn its misery into a cause. Only the larger society, with its help and resources, can really make it possible for these people to help themselves. Yet those who could make the difference too often refuse to act because of their ignorant, smug moralisms. They view the effects of poverty—above all, the warping of the will and spirit that is a consequence of being poor—as choices. Understanding the vicious circle is an important step in breaking down this prejudice.

There is an even richer way of describing this same, general idea: Poverty in the United States is a culture, an institution, a way of life.

There is a famous anecdote about Ernest Hemingway and F. Scott Fitzgerald. Fitzgerald is reported to have remarked to Hemingway, "The rich are different." And Hemingway replied, "Yes, they have money." Fitzgerald had much the better of the exchange. He understood that being rich was not a simple fact, like a large bank account, but a way of looking at reality, a series of attitudes, a special type of life. If this is true of the rich, it is ten times truer of the poor. Everything about them, from the condition of their teeth to the way in which they love, is suffused and permeated by the fact of their poverty. And this is sometimes a hard idea for a Hemingway-like middle-class America to comprehend.

The family structure of the poor, for instance, is different from that of the rest of the society. There are more homes without a father, there are less marriage, more early pregnancy and if Kinsey's statistical findings can be used, markedly different attitudes toward sex. As a result of this, to take but one consequence of the fact, hundreds of thousands, and perhaps millions, of children in the other America never know stability and "normal" affection.

Or perhaps the policeman is an even better example. For the middle class, the police protect property, give directions, and help old ladies. For the urban poor, the police are those who arrest you. In almost any slum there is a vast conspiracy against the forces of law and order. If someone approaches asking for a person, no one there will have heard of him, even if he lives next door. The outsider is "cop," bill collector, investigator (and, in the Negro ghetto, most dramatically, he is "the Man").

While writing this book, I was arrested for participation in a civil-rights demonstration. A brief experience of a night in a cell made an abstraction personal and immediate: the city jail is one of the basic institutions of the other America. Almost everyone whom I encountered in the "tank" was poor: skid-row whites, Negroes, Puerto Ricans. Their poverty was an incitement to arrest in the first place. (A policeman will be much more careful with a well-dressed, obviously educated man who might have political connections than he will with someone who is poor.) They did not have money for bail or for lawyers. And, perhaps most important, they waited their arraignment with stolidity, in a mood of passive acceptance. They expected the worst, and they probably got it.

There is, in short, a language of the poor, a psychology of the poor, a world view of the poor. To be impoverished is to be an internal alien, to grow up in a culture that is radically different from the one that dominates the society. The poor can be described statistically; they can be analyzed as a group. But they need a novelist as well as a sociologist if we are to see them. They need an American Dickens to record the smell and texture and quality of their lives. The cycles and trends, the massive forces, must be seen as affecting persons who talk and think differently.

I am not that novelist. Yet in this book I have attempted to describe the faces behind the statistics, to tell a little of the "thickness" of personal life in the other America. Of necessity, I have begun with large groups: the dispossessed workers, the minorities, the farm poor, and the aged. Then, there are three cases of less massive types of poverty, including the only single humorous component in the other America. And finally, there are the slums, and the psychology of the poor.

Throughout, I work on an assumption that cannot be proved by Government figures or even documented by impressions of the other America. It is an ethical proposition, and it can be simply stated: In a nation with a technology that could provide every citizen with a decent life, it is an outrage and a scandal that there should be such social misery. Only if one begins with this assumption is it possible to pierce through the invisibility of 40,000,000 to 50,000,000 human beings and to see the other America. We must perceive passionately, if this blindness is to be lifted from us. . . .

III

There are few people in the United States who accept Rousseau's image of the "noble savage," of primitive, untutored man as being more natural than, and superior to, his civilized descendants. Such an idea could hardly survive in a society that has made technological progress one of its most central values. There are occasional daydreams about "getting away from it all," of going to an idyllic countryside, but these are usually passing fancies.

Yet, there is a really important remnant of Rousseau's myth. It is the conviction that, as far as emotional disturbance and mental disease go, the poor are noble savages and the rich are the prime victims of tension and conflict.

There are the literature of the harried executive, the tales of suburban neurosis, the theme of the danger of wealth and leisure. It is not so much that anyone says that the poor are healthy in spirit because they are deprived of material things. Rather, the poor are just forgotten, as usual. The novels and the popular sociology are written by the middle class about the middle class, and there is more than a little strain of self-pity. The result is an image in which personal maladjustment flourishes at the top of the society, the price the well-off pay for their power. As you go down the income scale, this theory implies, life becomes more tedious and humdrum, if less upset. (However, it should be noted that the white-collar strata have the chronicler of their quiet desperation in Paddy Chayevsky.)

The truth is almost exactly opposite to the myth. The poor are subject to more mental illness than anyone else in the society, and their disturbances tend to be more serious than those of any other class. This conclusion has emerged from a series of studies made over the past few decades.. There is still considerable controversy and disagreement with regard to the reasons behind this situation. But the fact itself would seem to be beyond dispute.

Indeed, if there is any point in American society where one can see poverty as a culture, as a way of life, it is here. There is, in a sense, a personality of poverty, a type of human being produced by the grinding, wearing life of the slums. The other Americans feel differently than the rest of the nation. They tend to be hopeless and passive, yet prone to bursts of violence; they are lonely and isolated, often rigid and hostile. To be poor is not simply to be deprived of the material things of this world. It is to enter a fatal, futile universe, an America within America with a twisted spirit.

Perhaps the most classic (but still controversial) study of this subject is the book *Social Class and Mental Illness* by August B. Hollingshead and F. C. Redlich. Published in 1958, it summarizes a careful research project in New Haven, Connecticut. It is an academic, scholarly work, yet its statistics are the description of an abyss.

Hollingshead and Redlich divided New Haven into five social classes. At the top (Class I) were the rich, usually aristocrats of family as well as of money. Next came the executives and professionals more newly arrived to prestige and power. Then, the middle class, and beneath them, the workers with decent paying jobs. Class V, the bottom class, was made up of the poor. About half of its members were semiskilled, about half unskilled. The men had less than six years of education, the women less than eight.

As it turned out, this five-level breakdown was more revealing than the usual three-class image of American society (upper, middle, and lower). For it showed a sharp break between Class V at the bottom and Class IV just above it. In a dramatic psychological sense, the skilled unionized worker lived much, much closer to the middle class than he did to the world of the poor. Between Class IV and Class V, Hollingshead and Redlich found a chasm. This represents the gulf between working America, which may be up against it from time to time but which has a certain sense of security and dignity, and the other America of the poor.

Perhaps the most shocking and decisive statistic that Hollingshead and Redlich found was the one that tabulated the rate of treated psychiatric illness per 100,000 people in New Haven. These are their results:

Classes I and II	556 per 100,000
Class III	538
Class IV	642
Class V	1,659

From the top of society down to the organized workers, there are differences, but relatively small ones. But suddenly, when one crosses the line from Class IV to Class V, there is a huge leap, with the poor showing a rate of treated psychiatric illness of almost three times the magnitude of any other class.

But the mental suffering of the poor in these figures is not simply expressed in gross numbers. It is a matter of quality as well. In Classes I and II, 65 percent of the treated psychiatric illness is for neurotic problems, and only 35 percent for the much graver disturbances of psychoses. But at the bottom, in Class V, 90 percent of the treated illness is for psychosis, and only 10 percent for neurosis. In short, not only the rate but also the intensity of mental illness is much greater for the poor.

One of the standard professional criticisms of Hollingshead and Redlich is that their figures are for treated illness (those who actually got to a doctor or clinic) and do not indicate the "true prevalence" of mental illness in the population. Whatever merits this argument has in relation to other parts of the study, it points up that these particular figures are an understatement of the problem. The higher up the class scale one is, the more likely that there will be recognition of mental illness as a problem and that help will be sought. At the bottom of society, referral to psychiatric treatment usually comes from the courts. Thus, if anything, there is even more mental illness among the poor than the figures of Hollingshead and Redlich indicate.

The one place where this criticism might have some validity is with regard to the intensity of emotional disturbance. Only 10 percent of the poor who received treatment are neurotics, yet the poor neurotic is the least likely person in the society to show up for treatment. He can function, if only in an impaired and maimed way. If there were something done about this situation, it is quite possible that one would find more neurosis in the other America at the same time as one discovered more mental illness generally.

However, it is not necessary to juggle with statistics and explanations in order to corroborate the main drift of the New Haven figures. During the fifties the Cornell University Department of Psychiatry undertook an ambitious study of "Midtown," a residential area in New York City. The research dealt with a population of 170,000 from every social class, 99 percent of them white. (By leaving out the Negroes, there probably was a tendency to underestimate the problem of poverty generally, and the particular disabilities of a discriminated minority in particular.) The goal of the study was to discover "true prevalence," and there was interviewing in depth.

The Cornell scholars developed a measure of "mental health risk." They used a model of three classes, and consequently their figures are not so dramatic as those tabulated in New Haven. Yet they bear out the essential point: the lowest class had a mental health risk almost 40 percent greater than the highest class. Once again the world of poverty was given definition as a spiritual and emotional reality.

The huge brute fact of emotional illness in the other America is fairly well substantiated. The reasons behind the fact are the subject of considerable controversy. There is no neat and simple summary that can be given at the present time, yet some of the analyses are provocative for an understanding of the culture of poverty even if they must be taken tentatively.

One of the most interesting speculations came from the Cornell study of "Midtown" in New York City. The researchers developed a series of "stress factors" that might be related to an individual's mental health risk. In childhood, these were poor mental health on the part of the parents, poor physical health for the parents, economic deprivation, broken homes, a negative attitude on the part of the child toward his parents, a quarrelsome home, and sharp disagreements with parents during adolescence. In adult life, the stress factors were poor health, work worries, money worries, a lack of neighbors and friends, marital worries, and parental worries.

The Cornell team then tested to see if there was any relationship between these factors and mental health. They discovered a marked correlation. The person who had been subjected to thirteen of these stress factors was three times more likely to be mentally disturbed than the person who had felt none of them. Indeed, the researchers were led to conclude that the sheer number of stress factors was more important than the quality of stresses. Those who had experienced any three factors were of a higher mental risk than those who had experienced two.

If the Cornell conclusions are validated in further research, they will constitute an important revision of some widely held ideas about mental health. The Freudian theory has emphasized the earliest years and the decisive trauma in the development of mental illness (for example, the death of a parent). This new theory would suggest a more cumulative conception of mental illness: as stress piles upon stress over a period of time, there is a greater tendency toward disturbance. It would be an important supplement to the Freudian ideas.

But if this theory is right, there is a fairly obvious reason for the emotional torment of the other America. The stress factors listed by the Cornell study are the very stuff of the life of the poor: physical illness, broken homes, worries about work and money, and all the rest. The slum, with its vibrant, dense life hammers away at the individual. And because of the sheer, grinding, dirty experience of being poor, the personality, the spirit, is impaired. It is as if human beings dilapidate along with the tenements in which they live.

However, some scholars have attempted to soften the grimness of this picture with a theory about "drift." The poor, they argue, have a high percentage of disturbed people, not because of the conditions of life in the urban and rural slums, but because this is the group that gets all the outcasts of society from the rest of the classes. If this thesis were true, then one would expect to find failures from the higher classes as a significant group in the culture of the poor.

Hollingshead and Redlich tested this theory in New Haven and did not find any confirmation for it. The mentally impaired poor had been, for the most part, born poor. Their sickness was a product of poverty, instead of their poverty being a product of sickness. Similarly, in the Midtown study, no evidence was turned up to indicate that the disturbed poor were the rejects from other classes. There are some exceptions to this rule: alcoholics, as noted before, often tend to fall from a high position into the bitterest poverty. Still, current research points to a direct relationship between the experience of poverty and emotional disturbance.

And yet, an ironic point turned up in the Midtown research. It was discovered that a certain kind of neurosis was useful to a minority of poor people. The obsessive-compulsive neurotic often got ahead; his very sickness was a means of advancement out of the other America and into the great world. And yet, this might only prepare for a later crisis. On the lower and middle rungs of business society, hard work, attention to detail, and the like are enough to guarantee individual progress. But if such a person moves across the line, and is placed in a position where he must make decisions, there is the very real possibility of breakdown.

IV

Someone in trouble, someone in sorrow, a fight between neighbors, a coffin carried from a house, were things that coloured their lives and shook down fiery blossoms where they walked.—Sean O'Casey

The feelings, the emotions, the attitudes of the poor are different. But different from what? In this question there is an important problem of dealing with the chaotic in the world of poverty.

The definition makers, the social scientists, and the moralists come from the middle class. Their values do not include "a fight between neighbors" as a "fiery blossom." Yet that is the fact in the other America. (O'Casey was talking about Ireland; he might as well have been describing any slum in the United States.) Before going on and exploring the emotional torment of the poor, it would be well to understand this point.

Take the gangs. They are violent, and by middle-class standards they are antisocial and disturbed. But within a slum, violence and disturbance are often norms, everyday facts of life. From the inside of the other America, joining a "bopping" gang may well not seem like deviant behavior. It could be a necessity for dealing with a hostile world. (Once, in a slum school in St. Louis, a teacher stopped a fight between two little girls. "Nice girls don't fight," she told them. "Yeah," one of them replied, "you should have seen my old lady at the tavern last night.")

Indeed, one of the most depressing pieces of research I have ever read touches on this point. H. Warren Dunham carefully studied forty catatonic schizophrenics in Chicago in the early forties. He found that none of them had belonged to gangs or had engaged in the kind of activity the middle class regards as abnormal. They had, as a matter of fact, tried to live up to the standards of the larger society, rather than conforming to the values of the slum. "The catatonic young man can be described as a good boy and one who has all the desirable traits which all the social agencies would like to inculcate in the young men of the community."

The middle class does not understand the narrowness of its judgments. And worse, it acts upon them as if they were universal and accepted by everyone. In New Haven, Hollingshead and Redlich found two girls with an almost identical problem. Both of them were extremely promiscuous, so much so that they eventually had a run-in with the police. When the girl from Class I was arrested, she was provided with bail at once, newspaper stories were quashed, and she was taken care of through private psychotherapy. The girl from Class V was sentenced to reform school. She was paroled in two years, but was soon arrested again and sent to the state reformatory.

James Baldwin made a brilliant and perceptive application of this point to the problem of the Negro in a speech I heard not long ago. The white, he said, cannot imagine what it is like to be Negro: the danger, the lack of horizon, the necessity of always being on guard and watching. For that matter, Baldwin went on, the Negro problem is really the white problem. It is not the Negro who sets dark skin and kinky hair aside as something fearful, but the white. And the resolution of the racial agony in America requires a deep introspection on the part of the whites. They must discover themselves even more than the Negro.

This is true of all the juvenile delinquents, all the disturbed people, in the other America. One can put it baldly: their sickness is often a means of relating to a diseased environment. Until this is understood, the emotionally disturbed poor person will probably go on hurting himself until he becomes a police case. When he is finally given treatment, it will be at public expense, and it will be inferior to that given the rich. (In New Haven, according to Hollingshead and Redlich, the poor are five times more likely to get organic therapy—including shock treatment—rather than protracted, individual professional care.)

For that matter, some of the researchers in the field believe that sheer ignorance is one of the main causes of the high rate of disturbance among the poor. In the slum, conduct that would shock a middle-class neighborhood and lead to treatment is often considered normal. Even if someone is constantly and violently drunk, or beats his wife brutally, people will say of such a person, "Well, he's a little odd." Higher up on the class scale an individual with such a problem would probably realize that something was wrong (or his family would). He will have the knowledge and the money to get help.

One of the researchers in the field who puts great stress on the "basic universals" of the Freudian pattern (mother figure, father figure, siblings) looks upon this factor of ignorance as crucial. He is Dr. Lawrence Kubie. For Dr. Kubie, the fundamental determinants of mental health and illness are the same in every social class. But culture and income and education account for whether the individual will handle his problem; whether he understands himself as sick; whether he seeks help, and so on. This theory leaves the basic assumptions of traditional psychoanalysis intact, but, like any attempt to deal with the poor, it recognizes that something is different.

For the rich, then, and perhaps even for the better-paid worker, breakdowns, neurosis, and psychosis appear as illness and are increasingly treated as such. But the poor do not simply suffer these disturbances; they suffer them blindly. To them it does not appear that they are mentally sick; to them it appears that they are trapped in a fate.

PART THREE

The 1960's

When John F. Kennedy was inaugurated in 1961, the second youngest man ever elected President replaced the oldest man ever to serve in the office. The generation that came of age in the era of World War I was giving way to a breed shaped by World War II—men like Richard Nixon, Robert McNamara, William Westmoreland, Norman Mailer, Barry Goldwater. Kennedy's young administration stirred the nation far beyond what any of his policies would have suggested. A new generation may not always have fresh perspectives, but it is bound to have a new style, and even that is exciting.

But that generation paced a hard path. Assassinations, disorders, disastrous foreign adventures, and an accidental President obscured its record before its policies had a chance to bear fruit. Many of Kennedy's ideas resulted in legislation only after his death when Lyndon Johnson pushed his program for a "Great Society" through Congress. By then a generation even younger than the Kennedy administration had burst upon the national political scene, before anyone had even adjusted to the hard brilliance of the men who swept in early in the decade. The 1960's were years of extraordinary self-consciousness. The awareness of self was so sharp—my people, my generation, my "thing"—that the nation became almost ungovernable in traditional ways. Everyone had to be met directly (the process of "confrontation"), had to be self-directed (black power, women's liberation, student power), yet had to fit into a more crowded and interdependent nation (computerized data banks, tax records, the desire for law and order).

Americans—to their credit—have never been an easy people to govern. This old, near anarchic virtue asserted itself more strongly than ever in the 1960's, and strongest of all among the newest generation. The decade ended with accomplishments that would have astonished men of a generation before: the abolition of legal segregation, widespread government-financed medical and educational services, the longest economic boom in our history, men on the moon. Yet it also finished amidst potential chaos with the legitimacy of nearly every major institution—political parties, churches, universities, corporations, the government itself—deeply eroded.

The year 1968 was the climax of this history, a turning point that did not turn. The youngest generation fell back in disarray, the men who depended for inspiration largely on the New Deal vanished from the national scene, and an administration that described itself as conservative came to power. But whatever they called themselves, the new Nixon bureaucrats were another group of the hard young men—now growing old—who had come out of World War II; on many issues their conservatism reached farther forward than had the Kennedy liberalism of 1960—to which they often turned for their rhetoric.

The Feminine Mystique

BETTY FRIEDAN

Women have always been a majority treated like a minority: discriminated against in politics, in schools, and on the job, condescended to in nearly every social relationship, scoffed at for almost every aspiration. It is true that certain benefits have accompanied this second-class citizenship. Millions of women enjoyed the advantage of being discounted as a force in society, took the pleasures of prosperity and apparently paid few of the tangible costs in meaningless work or early death. But women as a group have suffered from a remarkably consistent discrimination, and throughout the industrialized countries they have fought back, winning a place for themselves in the economic, cultural, and political worlds.

But something went wrong in the United States in the twentieth century; while women in other countries increasingly found satisfying careers outside the home, American women seemed to be retreating. More of them worked, but at less demanding or rewarding jobs. And they had more children than their peers in other countries. Safely ensconced in the growing suburbs after World War II, apparently uninterested in politics or a career, they seemed calm and safe—the envy, one assumed, of the world. But they had one problem. "The Problem," Betty Friedan called it, "that has no name": more and more of them were miserable. The bored housewife syndrome became a national parlor game, broadcast through the mass media, discussed in countless living rooms and doubtless in as many bedrooms. Betty Friedan brought the problem into the open in her influential The Feminine Mystique *(1963), a book that heralded a new assertiveness on the part of American women such as had not been seen since the women's suffrage movement.*

In part, this new militancy reflects the general climate of political activism in the 1960's; in part it grows from new opportunities open to women. But clearly much of it is a direct and understandable response to the peculiar circumstances of the postwar era, whose attitude toward woman's role Betty Friedan has captured in vigorous polemic.

In the early 1960's *McCall's* has been the fastest growing of the women's magazines. Its contents are a fairly accurate representation of the image of the American woman presented, and in part created, by the large-circulation magazines. Here are the complete editorial contents of a typical issue of *McCall's* (July, 1960):

1. A lead article on "increasing baldness in women," caused by too much brushing and dyeing.
2. A long poem in primer-size type about a child, called "A Boy Is A Boy."

3. A short story about how a teenager who doesn't go to college gets a man away from a bright college girl.

4. A short story about the minute sensations of a baby throwing his bottle out of the crib.

5. The first of a two-part intimate "up-to-date" account by the Duke of Windsor on "How the Duchess and I now live and spend our time. The influence of clothes on me and vice versa."

6. A short story about a nineteen-year-old girl sent to a charm school to learn how to bat her eyelashes and lose at tennis. ("You're nineteen, and by normal American standards, I now am entitled to have you taken off my hands, legally and financially, by some beardless youth who will spirit you away to a one-and-a-half-room apartment in the Village while he learns the chicanery of selling bonds. And no beardless youth is going to do that as long as you volley to his backhand.")

7. The story of a honeymoon couple commuting between separate bedrooms after an argument over gambling at Las Vegas.

8. An article on "how to overcome an inferiority complex."

9. A story called "Wedding Day."

10. The story of a teenager's mother who learns how to dance rock-and-roll.

11. Six pages of glamorous pictures of models in maternity clothes.

12. Four glamorous pages on "reduce the way the models do."

13. An article on airline delays.

14. Patterns for home sewing.

15. Patterns with which to make "Folding Screens—Bewitching Magic."

16. An article called "An Encyclopedic Approach to Finding a Second Husband."

17. A "barbecue bonanza," dedicated "to the Great American Mister who stands, chef's cap on head, fork in hand, on terrace or back porch, in patio or backyard anywhere in the land, watching his roast turning on the spit. And to his wife without whom (sometimes) the barbecue could never be the smashing summer success it undoubtedly is . . ."

There were also the regular front-of-the-book "service" columns on new drug and medicine developments, child-care facts, columns by Clare Luce and by Eleanor Roosevelt, and "Pots and Pans," a column of readers' letters.

The image of woman that emerges from this big, pretty magazine is young and frivolous, almost childlike; fluffy and feminine; passive; gaily content in a world of bedroom and kitchen, sex, babies, and home. The magazine surely does not leave out sex; the only passion, the only pursuit, the only goal a woman is permitted is the pursuit of a man. It is crammed full of food, clothing, cosmetics, furniture, and the physical bodies of young women, but where is the world of thought and ideas, the life of the mind and spirit? In the magazine image, women do no work except housework and work to keep their bodies beautiful and to get and keep a man.

This was the image of the American woman in the year Castro led a revolution in Cuba and men were trained to travel into outer space; the year that the African continent brought forth new nations, and a plane whose speed is greater than the speed of sound broke up a Summit Conference; the year artists picketed a great museum in protest against the hegemony of abstract art; physicists explored the concept of anti-matter; astronomers, because of new radio telescopes, had to alter their concepts of the expanding universe; biologists made a breakthrough in the fundamental chemistry of life; and Negro youth in Southern schools forced the United States, for the first time since the Civil War, to face a moment of democratic truth. But this magazine, published for over 5,000,000 American women, almost all of whom have been through high school and nearly half to college, contained almost no mention of the world beyond the home. In the second half of the twentieth century in America, woman's world was confined to her own body and beauty, the charming of man, the bearing of babies, and the physical care and serving of husband, children, and home. And this was no anomaly of a single issue of a single women's magazine.

I sat one night at a meeting of magazine writers, mostly men, who work for all kinds of magazines, including women's magazines. The main speaker was a leader of the desegregation battle. Before he spoke, another man outlined the needs of the large women's magazine he edited:

Our readers are housewives, full time. They're not interested in the broad public issues of the day. They are not interested in national or international affairs. They are only interested in the family and the home. They aren't interested in politics, unless it's related to an immediate need in the home, like the price of coffee. Humor? Has to be gentle, they don't get satire. Travel? We have almost completely dropped it. Education? That's a problem. Their own education level is going up. They've generally all had a high-school education and many, college. They're tremendously interested in education for their children—fourth-grade arithmetic. You just can't write about ideas or broad issues of the day for women. That's why we're publishing 90 per cent service now and 10 per cent general interest.

Another editor agreed, adding plaintively: "Can't you give us something else besides 'there's death in your medicine cabinet'? Can't any of you dream up a new crisis for women? We're always interested in sex, of course."

At this point, the writers and editors spent an hour listening to Thurgood Marshall on the inside story of the desegregation battle, and its possible effect on the presidential election. "Too bad I can't run that story," one editor said. "But you just can't link it to woman's world."

As I listened to them, a German phrase echoed in my mind—"*Kinder, Kuche, Kirche,*" the slogan by which the Nazis decreed that women must once again be confined to their biological role. But this was not Nazi Germany. This was America. The whole world lies open to American women. Why, then, does the image deny the world? Why does it limit women to "one position, one role, one occupation"? Not long ago, women dreamed and fought for equality, their own place in the world. What happened to their dreams; when did women decide to give up the world and go back home?

A geologist brings up a core of mud from the bottom of the ocean and sees layers of sediment as sharp as a razor blade deposited over the years—clues to changes in the geological evolution of the earth so vast that they would go unnoticed during the lifespan of a single man. I sat for many days in the New York Public Library, going back through bound volumes of American women's magazines for the last twenty years. I found a change in the image of the American woman, and in the boundaries of the woman's world, as sharp and puzzling as the changes revealed in cores of ocean sediment.

In 1939, the heroines of women's magazine stories were not always young, but in a certain sense they were younger than their fictional counterparts today. They were young in the same way that the American hero has always been young: they were New Women, creating with a gay determined spirit a new identity for women—a life of their own. There was an aura about them of becoming, of moving into a future that was going to be different from the past. The majority of heroines in the four major women's magazines (then *Ladies' Home Journal, McCall's, Good Housekeeping, Woman's Home Companion*) were career women—happily, proudly, adventurously, attractively career women —who loved and were loved by men. And the spirit, courage, independence, determination—the strength of character they showed in their work as nurses, teachers, artists, actresses, copywriters, saleswomen— were part of their charm. There was a definite aura that their individuality was something to be admired, not unattractive to men, that men were drawn to them as much for their spirit and character as for their looks.

These were the mass women's magazines—in their heyday. The stories were conventional: girl-meets-boy or girl-gets-boy. But very often this was not the major theme of the story. These heroines were usually marching toward some goal or vision of their own, struggling with some problem of work or the world, when they found their man. And this New Woman, less fluffily feminine, so independent and determined to find a new life of her own, was the heroine of a different kind of love story. She was less aggressive in pursuit of a man. Her passionate involvement with the world, her own sense of herself as an individual, her self-reliance, gave a different flavor to her relationship with the man. The heroine and hero of one of these stories meet and fall in love at an ad agency where they both work. "I don't want to put you in a garden behind a wall," the hero says. "I want you to walk with me hand in hand, and together we could accomplish whatever we wanted to" ("A Dream to Share," *Redbook,* January, 1939).

These New Women were almost never housewives; in fact, the stories usually ended before they had children. They were young because the future was open. But they seemed, in another sense, much older, more mature than the childlike, kittenish young housewife heroines today. One, for example, is a nurse ("Mother-in-Law," *Ladies' Home Journal*, June, 1939). "She was, he thought, very lovely. She hadn't an ounce of picture book prettiness, but there was strength in her hands, pride in her carriage and nobility in the lift of her chin, in her blue eyes. She had been on her own ever since she left training, nine years ago. She had earned her way, she need consider nothing but her heart."

One heroine runs away from home when her mother insists she must make her debut instead of going on an expedition as a geologist. Her passionate determination to live her own life does not keep this New Woman from loving a man, but it makes her rebel from her parents; just as the young hero often must leave home to grow up. "You've got more courage than any girl I ever saw. You have what it takes," says the boy who helps her get away ("Have a Good Time, Dear," *Ladies' Home Journal*, May 1939).

Often, there was a conflict between some commitment to her work and the man. But the moral, in 1939, was that if she kept her commitment to herself, she did not lose the man, if he was the right man. A young widow ("Between the Dark and the Daylight," *Ladies' Home Journal*, February, 1939) sits in her office, debating whether to stay and correct the important mistake she has made on the job, or keep her date with a man. She thinks back on her marriage, her baby, her husband's death . . . "the time afterward which held the struggle for clear judgment, not being afraid of new and better jobs, of having confidence in one's decisions." How can the boss expect her to give up her date! But she stays on the job. "They'd put their life's blood into this campaign. She couldn't let him down." She finds her man, too—the boss!

These stories may not have been great literature. But the identity of their heroines seemed to say something about the housewives who, then as now, read the women's magazines. These magazines were not written for career women. The New Woman heroines were the ideal of yesterday's housewives; they reflected the dreams, mirrored the yearning for identity and the sense of possibility that existed for women then. And if women could not have these dreams for themselves, they wanted their daughters to have them. They wanted their daughters to be more than housewives, to go out in the world that had been denied them.

It is like remembering a long-forgotten dream, to recapture the memory of what a career meant to women before "career woman" became a dirty word in America. Jobs meant money, of course, at the end of the depression. But the readers of these magazines were not the women who got the jobs; career meant more than job. It seemed to mean doing something, being somebody yourself, not just existing in and through others.

I found the last clear note of the passionate search for individual identity that a career seems to have symbolized in the pre-1950 decades in a story called "Sarah and the Seaplane," (*Ladies' Home Journal,* February, 1949). Sarah, who for nineteen years has played the part of docile daughter, is secretly learning to fly. She misses her flying lesson to accompany her mother on a round of social calls. An elderly doctor houseguest says: "My dear Sarah, every day, all the time, you are committing suicide. It's a greater crime than not pleasing others, not doing justice to yourself." Sensing some secret, he asks if she is in love. "She found it difficult to answer. In love? In love with the good-natured, the beautiful Henry [the flying teacher]? In love with the flashing water and the lift of wings at the instant of freedom, and the vision of the smiling, limitless world? 'Yes,' she answered, 'I think I am.' "

The next morning, Sarah solos. Henry "stepped away, slamming the cabin door shut, and swung the ship about for her. She was alone. There was a heady moment when everything she had learned left her, when she had to adjust herself to be alone, entirely alone in the familiar cabin. Then she drew a deep breath and suddenly a wonderful sense of competence made her sit erect and smiling. She was alone! She was answerable to herself alone, and she was sufficient.

" 'I can do it!' she told herself aloud. . . . The wind blew back from the floats in glittering streaks, and then effortlessly the ship lifted itself free and soared." Even her mother can't stop her now from getting her flying license. She is not "afraid of discovering my own way of life." In bed that night she smiles sleepily, remembering how Henry had said, "You're my girl."

"Henry's girl! She smiled. No, she was not Henry's girl. She was Sarah. And that was sufficient. And with such a late start it would be some time before she got to know herself. Half in a dream now, she wondered if at the end of that time she would need someone else and who it would be."

And then suddenly the image blurs. The New Woman, soaring free, hesitates in midflight, shivers in all that blue sunlight and rushes back to the cozy walls of home. In the same year that Sarah soloed, the *Ladies' Home Journal* printed the prototype of the innumerable paeans to "Ocupation: Housewife" that started to appear in the women's magazines, paeans that resounded throughout the fifties. They usually begin with a woman complaining that when she has to write "housewife" on the census blank, she gets an inferiority complex. ("When I write it I realize that here I am, a middle-aged woman, with a university education, and I've never made anything out of my life. I'm just a housewife.") Then the author of the paean, who somehow never is a housewife (in this case, Dorothy Thompson, newspaper woman, foreign correspondent, famous columnist, in *Ladies' Home Journal,* March, 1949), roars with laughter. The trouble with you, she scolds, is you don't realize you are expert in a dozen careers, simultaneously. "You might write: business manager, cook, nurse, chauffeur, dressmaker, interior decorator, accountant, caterer, teacher, private secretary—or just put down philanthropist. . . . All your life you have been giving away your energies, your skills, your talents, your services, for love." But still, the housewife complains, I'm nearly fifty and I've never done what I hoped to do in my youth—music—I've wasted my college education.

Ho-ho, laughs Miss Thompson, aren't your children musical because of you, and all those struggling years while your husband was finishing his great work, didn't you keep a charming home on $3,000 a year, and make all your children's clothes and your own, and paper the living room yourself, and watch the markets like a hawk for bargains? And in time off, didn't you type and proofread your husband's manuscripts, plan festivals to make up the church deficit, play piano duets with the children to make practicing more fun, read their books in high-school to follow their study? "But all this vicarious living—through others," the housewife sighs. "As vicarious as Napoleon Bonaparte," Miss Thompson scoffs, "or a Queen. I simply refuse to share your self-pity. You are one of the most successful women I know."

As for not earning any money, the argument goes, let the housewife compute the cost of her services. Women can save more money by their managerial talents inside the home than they can bring into it by outside work. As for woman's spirit being broken by the boredom of household tasks, maybe the genius of some women has been thwarted, but "a world full of feminine genius, but poor in children, would come rapidly to an end. . . . Great men have great mothers."

And the American housewife is reminded that Catholic countries in the Middle Ages "elevated the gentle and inconspicuous Mary into the Queen of Heaven, and built their loveliest cathedrals to 'Notre Dame—Our Lady.' . . . The homemaker, the nurturer, the creator of children's environment is the constant recreator of culture, civilization, and virtue. Assuming that she is doing well that great managerial task and creative activity, let her write her occupation proudly: 'housewife.' "

In 1949, the *Ladies' Home Journal* also ran Margaret Mead's *Male and Female*. All the magazines were echoing Farnham and Lundberg's *Modern Woman: The Lost Sex*, which came out in 1942, with its warning that careers and higher education were leading to the "masculinization of women with enormously dangerous consequences to the home, the children dependent on it and to the ability of the woman, as well as her husband, to obtain sexual gratification."

And so the feminine mystique began to spread through the land, grafted onto old prejudices and comfortable conventions which so easily give the past a stranglehold on the future. Behind the new mystique were concepts and theories deceptive in their sophistication and their assumption of accepted truth. These theories were supposedly so complex that they were inaccessible to all but a few initiates, and therefore irrefutable. It will be necessary to break through this wall of mystery and look more closely at these complex concepts, these accepted truths, to understand fully what has happened to American women.

The feminine mystique says that the highest value and the only commitment for women is the fulfillment of their own femininity. It says that the great mistake of Western culture, through most of its history, has been the undervaluation of this femininity. It says this femininity is so mysterious and intuitive and close to the creation and origin of life that man-made science may never be able to understand it. But however special and different, it is in no way inferior to the nature of man; it may even in certain respects be superior. The mistake, says the mystique, the root of women's troubles in the past is that women envied men, women tried to be like men, instead of accepting their own nature, which can find fulfillment only in sexual passivity, male domination, and nurturing maternal love.

But the new image this mystique gives to American women is the old image: "Occupation: housewife." The new mystique makes the housewife-mothers, who never had a chance to be anything else, the model for all women; it presupposes that history has reached a final and glorious end in the here and now, as far as women are concerned. Beneath the sophisticated trappings, it simply makes certain concrete, finite, domestic aspects of feminine existence—as it was lived by women whose lives were confined, by necessity, to cooking, cleaning, washing, bearing children—into a religion, a pattern by which all women must now live or deny their femininity.

Fulfillment as a woman had only one definition for American women after 1949—the housewife-mother. As swiftly as in a dream, the image of the American woman as a changing, growing individual in a changing world was shattered. Her solo flight to find her own identity was forgotten in the rush for the security of togetherness. Her limitless world shrunk to the cozy walls of home.

The transformation, reflected in the pages of the women's magazines, was sharply visible in 1949 and progressive through the fifties. "Femininity Begins at Home," "It's a Man's World Maybe," "Have Babies While You're Young," "How to Snare a Male," "Should I Stop Work When We Marry?" "Are You Training Your Daughter to be a Wife?" "Careers at Home," "Do Women Have to Talk So Much?" "Why GI's Prefer Those German Girls," "What Women Can Learn from Mother Eve," "Really a Man's World, Politics," "How to Hold On to a Happy Marriage," "Don't Be Afraid to Marry Young," "The Doctor Talks about Breast-Feeding," "Our Baby Was Born at Home," "Cooking to Me is Poetry," "The Business of Running a Home."

By the end of 1949, only one out of three heroines in the women's magazines was a career woman—and she was shown in the act of renouncing her career and discovering that what she really wanted to be was a housewife. In 1958, and again in 1959, I went through issue after issue of the three major women's magazines (the fourth, *Woman's Home Companion*, had died) without finding a single heroine who had a career, a commitment to any work, art, profession, or mission in the world, other than "Occupation: housewife." Only one in a hundred heroines had a job; even the young unmarried heroines no longer worked except at snaring a husband.

These new happy housewife heroines seem strangely younger than the spirited career girls of the thirties and forties. They seem to get younger all the time—in looks, and a childlike kind of dependence. They have no vision of the future, except to have a baby. The only active growing figure in their world is the child. The housewife heroines are forever young, because their own image *ends* in childbirth. Like Peter Pan, they must remain young, while their children grow up with the world. They must keep on having babies, because the feminine mystique says there is no other way for a woman to be a heroine. Here is a typical specimen from a story called "The Sandwich Maker" (*Ladies' Home Journal*, April, 1959). She took home economics in college, learned how to cook, never held a job, and still plays the child bride, though she now has three children of her own. Her problem is money. "Oh, nothing boring, like taxes or reciprocal trade agreements, or foreign aid programs. I leave all that economic jazz to my constitutionally elected representative in Washington, heaven help him."

The problem is her $42.10 allowance. She hates having to ask her husband for money every time she needs a pair of shoes, but he won't trust her with a charge account. "Oh, how I yearned for a little money of my own! Not much, really. A few hundred a year would have done it. Just enough to meet a friend for lunch occasionally, to indulge in extravagantly colored stockings, a few small items, without having to appeal to Charley. But, alas, Charley was right. I had never earned a dollar in my life, and had no idea how money was made. So all I did for a long time was brood, as I continued with my cooking, cleaning, cooking, washing, ironing, cooking."

At last the solution comes—she will take orders for sandwiches from other men at her husband's plant. She earns $52.50 a week, except that she forgets to count costs, and she doesn't remember what a gross is so she has to hide 8,640 sandwich bags behind the furnace. Charley says she's making the sandwiches too fancy. She explains: "If it's only ham on rye, then I'm just a sandwich maker, and I'm not interested. But the extras, the special touches—well, they make it sort of creative." So she chops, wraps, peels, seals, spreads bread, starting at dawn and never finished, for $9.00 net, until she is disgusted by the smell of food, and finally staggers downstairs after a sleepless night to slice a salami for the eight gaping lunch boxes. "It was too much. Charley came down just then, and after one quick look at me, ran for a glass of water." She realizes that she is going to have another baby.

"Charley's first coherent words were 'I'll cancel your lunch orders. You're a mother. That's your job. You don't have to earn money, too.' It was all so beautifully simple! 'Yes, boss,' I murmured obediently, frankly relieved." That night he brings her home a checkbook; he will trust her with a joint account. So she decides just to keep quiet about the 8,640 sandwich bags. Anyhow, she'll have used them up, making sandwiches for four children to take to school, by the time the youngest is ready for college.

The road from Sarah and the seaplane to the sandwich maker was traveled in only ten years. In those ten years, the image of American woman seems to have suffered a schizophrenic split. And the split in the image goes much further than the savage obliteration of career from women's dreams.

In an earlier time, the image of woman was also split in two—the good, pure woman on the pedestal, and the whore of the desires of the flesh. The split in the new image opens a different fissure—the feminine woman, whose goodness includes the desires of the flesh, and the career woman whose evil includes every desire of the separate self. The new feminine morality story is the exorcising of the forbidden career dream, the heroine's victory over Mephistopheles: the devil, first in the form of a career woman, who threatens to take away the heroine's husband or child, and finally, the devil inside the heroine herself, the dream of independence, the discontent of spirit, and even the feeling of a separate identity that must be exorcised to win or keep the love of husband and child.

In a story in *Redbook* ("A Man Who Acted Like a Husband," November, 1957) the child-bride heroine, "a little freckle-faced brunette" whose nickname is "Junior," is visited by her old college roommate. The roommate Kay is "a man's girl, really, with a good head for business . . . she wore her polished mahogany hair in a high chignon, speared with two chopstick affairs." Kay is not only divorced, but she has also left her child with his grandmother while she works in television. This career-woman-devil tempts Junior with the lure of a job to keep her from breast-feeding her baby. She even restrains the young mother from going to her baby when he cries at 2 A.M. But she gets her comeuppance when George, the husband, discovers the crying baby uncovered, in a freezing wind from an open window, with blood running down its cheek. Kay, reformed and repentant, plays hookey from her job to go get her own child and start life anew. And Junior, gloating at the 2 A.M. feeding—"I'm glad, glad, glad I'm just a housewife" starts to dream about the baby, growing up to be a housewife, too.

With the career woman out of the way, the housewife with interests in the community becomes the devil to be exorcised. Even PTA takes on a suspect connotation, not to mention interest in some international cause (see "Almost a Love Affair," *McCall's,* November, 1955). The housewife who simply has a mind of her own is the next to go. The heroine of "I Didn't Want to Tell You" (*McCall's,* January, 1958) is shown balancing the checkbook by herself and arguing with her husband about a small domestic detail. It develops that she is losing her husband to a "helpless little widow" whose main appeal is that she can't "think straight" about an insurance policy or mortgage. The betrayed wife says: "She must have sex appeal and what weapon has a wife against that?" But her best friend tells her: "You're making this too simple. You're forgetting how helpless Tania can be, and how grateful to the man who helps her . . ."

"I couldn't be a clinging vine if I tried," the wife says. "I had a better than average job after I left college and I was always a pretty independent person. I'm not a helpless little woman and I can't pretend to be." But she learns, that night. She hears a noise that might be a burglar; even though she knows it's only a mouse, she calls helplessly to her husband, and wins him back. As he comforts her pretended panic, she murmurs that, of course, he was right in their argument that morning. "She lay still in the soft bed, smiling sweet, secret satisfaction, scarcely touched with guilt."

The end of the road, in an almost literal sense, is the disappearance of the heroine altogether, as a separate self and the subject of her own story. The end of the road is togetherness, where the woman has no independent self to hide even in guilt; she exists only for and through her husband and children.

Coined by the publishers of *McCall's* in 1954, the concept "togetherness" was seized upon avidly as a movement of spiritual significance by advertisers, ministers, newspaper editors. For a time, it was elevated into virtually a national purpose. But very quickly there was sharp social criticism, and bitter jokes about "togetherness" as a substitute for larger human goals—for men. Women were taken to task for making their husbands do housework, instead of letting them pioneer in the nation and the world. Why, it was asked, should men with the capacities of statesmen, anthropologists, physicists, poets, have to wash dishes and diaper babies on weekday evenings or Saturday mornings when they might use those extra hours to fulfill larger commitments to their society?

Significantly, critics resented only that men were being asked to share "woman's world." Few questioned the boundaries of this world for women. No one seemed to remember that women were once thought to have the capacity and vision of statesmen, poets, and physicists. Few saw the big lie of togetherness for women.

Consider the Easter 1954 issue of *McCall's* which announced the new era of togetherness, sounding the requiem for the days when women fought for and won political equality, and the women's magazines "helped you to carve out large areas of living formerly forbidden to your sex." The new way of life in which "men and women in ever-increasing numbers are marrying at an earlier age, having children at an earlier age, rearing larger families and gaining their deepest satisfaction" from their own homes, is one which "men, women and children are achieving together . . . not as women alone, or men alone, isolated from one another, but as a family, sharing a common experience."

The picture essay detailing that way of life is called "a man's place is in the home." It describes, as the new image and ideal, a New Jersey couple with three children in a gray-shingle split-level house. Ed and Carol have "centered their lives almost completely around their children and their home." They are shown shopping at the supermarket, carpentering, dressing the children, making breakfast together. "Then Ed joins the members of his car pool and heads for the office."

Ed, the husband, chooses the color scheme for the house and makes the major decorating decisions. The chores Ed likes are listed: putter around the house, make things, paint, select furniture, rugs and draperies, dry dishes, read to the children and put them to bed, work in the garden, feed and dress and bathe the children, attend PTA meetings, cook, buy clothes for his wife, buy groceries.

Ed doesn't like these chores: dusting, vacuuming, finishing jobs he's started, hanging draperies, washing pots and pans and dishes, picking up after the children, shoveling snow or mowing the lawn, changing diapers, taking the baby-sitter home, doing the laundry, ironing. Ed, of course, does not do these chores.

For the sake of every member of the family, the family needs a head. This means Father, not Mother. . . . Children of both sexes need to learn, recognize and respect the abilities and functions of each sex. . . . He is not just a substitute mother, even though he's ready and willing to do his share of bathing, feeding, comforting, playing. He is a link with the outside world he works in. If in that world he is interested, courageous, tolerant, constructive, he will pass on these values to his children.

There were many agonized editorial sessions, in those days at *McCall's*. "Suddenly, everybody was looking for this spiritual significance in togetherness, expecting us to make some mysterious religious movement out of the life everyone had been leading for the last five years—crawling into the home, turning their backs on the world—but we never could find a way of showing it that wasn't a monstrosity of dullness," a former *McCall's* editor reminisces. "It always boiled down to, goody, goody, goody, Daddy is out there in the garden barbecuing. We put men in the fashion pictures and the food pictures, and even the perfume pictures. But we were stifled by it editorially.

"We had articles by psychiatrists that we couldn't use because they would have blown it wide open: all those couples propping their whole weight on their kids but what else could you do with togetherness but child care? We were pathetically grateful to find anything else where we could show father photographed with mother. Sometimes, we used to wonder what would happen to women, with men taking over the decorating, child care, cooking, all the things that used to be hers alone. But we couldn't show women getting out of the home and having a career. The irony is, what we meant to do was to stop editing for women as women, and edit for the men and women together. We wanted to edit for people, not women."

But forbidden to join man in the world, can women be people? Forbidden independence, they finally are swallowed in an image of such passive dependence that they want men to make the decisions, even in the home. The frantic illusion that togetherness can impart a spiritual content to the dullness of domestic routine, the need for a religious movement to make up for the lack of identity, betrays the measure of women's loss and the emptiness of the image. Could making men share the housework compensate women for their loss of the world? Could vacuuming the living-room floor together give the housewife some mysterious new purpose in life?

In 1956, at the peak of togetherness, the bored editors of *McCall's* ran a little article called "The Mother Who Ran Away." To their amazement, it brought the highest readership of any article they had ever run. "It was our moment of truth," said a former editor. "We suddenly realized that all those women at home with their three and a half children were miserably unhappy."

But by then the new image of American woman, "Occupation:

housewife," had hardened into a mystique, unquestioned and permitting no questions, shaping the very reality is distorted.

By the time I started writing for women's magazines, in the fifties, it was simply taken for granted by editors, and accepted as an immutable fact of life by writers, that women were not interested in politics, life outside the United States, national issues, art, science, ideas, adventure, education, or even their own communities, except where they could be sold through their emotions as wives and mothers.

Politics, for women, became Mamie's clothes and the Nixons' home life. Out of conscience, a sense of duty, the *Ladies' Home Journal* might run a series like "Political Pilgrim's Progress," showing women trying to improve their children's schools and playgrounds. But even approaching politics through mother love did not really interest women, it was thought in the trade. Everyone knew those readership percentages. An editor of *Redbook* ingeniously tried to bring the bomb down to the feminine level by showing the emotions of a wife whose husband sailed into a contaminated area.

"Women can't take an idea, an issue, pure," men who edited the mass women's magazines agreed. "It had to be translated in terms they can understand as women." This was so well understood by those who wrote for women's magazines that a natural childbirth expert submitted an article to a leading woman's magazine called "How to Have a Baby in a Atom Bomb Shelter." "The article was not well written," an editor told me, "or we might have bought it." According to the mystique, women, in their mysterious femininity, might be interested in the concrete biological details of having a baby in a bomb shelter, but never in the abstract idea of the bomb's power to destroy the human race.

Such a belief, of course, becomes a self-fulfilling prophecy. In 1960, a perceptive social psychologist showed me some sad statistics which seemed to prove unmistakably that American women under thirty-five are not interested in politics. "They may have the vote, but they don't dream about running for office," he told me. "If you write a political piece, they won't read it. You have to translate it into issues they can understand—romance, pregnancy, nursing, home furnishings, clothes. Run an article on the economy, or the race question, civil rights, and you'd think that women had never heard of them."

Maybe they hadn't heard of them. Ideas are not like instincts of the blood that spring into the mind intact. They are communicated by education, by the printed word. The new young housewives, who leave high school or college to marry, do not read books, the psychological surveys say. They only read magazines. Magazines today assume women are not interested in ideas. But going back to the bound volumes in the library, I found in the thirties and forties that the mass-circulation magazines like *Ladies' Home Journal* carried hundreds of articles about the world outside the home. "The first inside story of American diplomatic relations preceding declared war"; "Can the U.S. Have Peace After This War?" by Walter Lippmann; "Stalin at Midnight," by Harold Stassen; "General Stilwell Reports on China"; articles about the last days of Czechoslovakia by Vincent Sheean; the persecution of Jews in Germany; the New Deal; Carl Sandburg's account of Lincoln's assassination; Faulkner's stories of Mississippi, and Margaret Sanger's battle for birth control.

In the 1950's they printed virtually no articles except those that serviced women as housewives, or described women as housewives, or permitted a purely feminine identification like the Duchess of Windsor or Princess Margaret. "If we get an article about a woman who does anything adventurous, out of the way, something by herself, you know, we figure she must be terribly aggressive, neurotic," a *Ladies' Home Journal* editor told me. Margaret Sanger would never get in today.

In 1960, I saw statistics that showed that women under thirty-five could not identify with a spirited heroine of a story who worked in an ad agency and persuaded the boy to stay and fight for his principles in the big city instead of running home to the security of a family business. Nor could these new young housewives identify with a young minister, acting on his belief in defiance of convention. But they had no trouble at all identifying with a young man paralyzed at eighteen. ("I regained consciousness to discover that I could not move or even speak. I could wiggle only one finger of one hand." With help from faith and a psychiatrist, "I am now finding reasons to live as fully as possible.")

Does it say something about the new housewife readers that, as any editor can testify, they can identify completely with the victims of blindness, deafness, physical maiming, cerebral palsy, paralysis, cancer, or approaching death? Such articles about people who cannot see or speak or move have been an enduring staple of the women's magazines in the era of "Occupation: housewife." They are told with infinitely realistic detail over and over again, replacing the articles about the nation, the world, ideas, issues, art and science; replacing the stories about adventurous spirited women. And whether the victim is man, woman or child, whether the living death is incurable cancer or creeping paralysis, the housewife reader can identify. . . .

A baked potato is not as big as the world, and vacuuming the living room floor—with or without makeup—is not work that takes enough thought or energy to challenge any woman's full capacity. Women are human beings, not stuffed dolls, not animals. Down through the ages man has known that he was set apart from other animals by his mind's power to have an idea, a vision, and shape the future to it. He shares a need for food and sex with other animals, but when he loves, he loves as a man, and when he discovers and creates and shapes a future different from his past, he is a man, a human being.

This is the real mystery: why did so many American women, with the ability and education to discover and create, go back home again, to look for "something more" in housework and rearing children? For, paradoxically, in the same fifteen years in which the spirited New Woman was replaced by the Happy Housewife, the boundaries of the human world have widened, the pace of world change has quickened, and the very nature of human reality has become increasingly free from biological and material necessity. Does the mystique keep American woman from growing with the world? Does it force her to deny reality, as a woman in a mental hospital must deny reality to believe she is a queen? Does it doom women to be displaced persons, if not virtual schizophrenics, in our complex, changing world?

It is more than a strange paradox that as all professions are finally open to women in America, "career woman" has become a dirty word; that as higher education becomes available to any woman with the capacity for it, education for women has become so suspect that more and more drop out of high school and college to marry and have babies; that as so many roles in modern society become theirs for the taking, women so insistently confine themselves to one role. Why, with the removal of all the legal, political, economic, and educational barriers that once kept woman from being man's equal, a person in her own right, an individual free to develop her own potential, should she accept this new image which insists she is not a person but a "woman," by definition barred from the freedom of human existence and a voice in human destiny?

The feminine mystique is so powerful that women grow up no longer knowing that they have the desires and capacities the mystique forbids. But such a mystique does not fasten itself on a whole nation in a few short years, reversing the trends of a century, without cause. What gives the mystique its power? Why did women go home again?

Kennedy: A Cold Warrior

DAVID BURNER

John Fitzgerald Kennedy was one of the most attractive men ever to be President of the United States. He was, Norman Mailer once wrote, "our leading man." His confidence that he could "get the nation moving again," his handsome and stylish wife, photogenic children, and appealing and able associates touched chords in American society which his predecessor, for all the love and respect he generated, could not (and would not have wished to) reach. Kennedy was as passionately loved and hated as any president in our history. And especially, he was the hero of the new men—in the professions, the universities, business and government—who were reaching positions of leadership in the American scene, a new generation "born in this century."

David Burner's discussion of Kennedy and his presidential term recognizes this élan and its vital—if intangible—effect on American culture. Nevertheless, Burner's account of Kennedy is no part of the hagiography that began to appear after his assassination. While the writer has an admiration for Kennedy, this is clearly a "revisionist" account of his administration, sharply aware of its failings as well as its successes. A president who both stalled and spurred civil rights, who both eased and intensified the Cold War, who tended to allow events to move to a crisis but then responded superbly to the emergency, JFK will never be easy to evaluate.

John F. Kennedy came to the office of President as a spokesman for the Cold War at its most sophisticated point. The nation had acquired, during a decade of atomic diplomacy, an intelligence and temperament that enabled it to live with some coolness amidst the continuing strategies and extraordinary technological complex of nuclear confrontation. The language of that intelligence was Kennedy's: he could speak crisply about the dangers of a missile gap, the need for innovation in nuclear weaponry, the advantages of flexible response over massive retaliation. He combined a fascination for military technology with a feeling for military dash and elitism; a naval hero who had survived a bizarre shipwreck, a reader of James Bond novels, he was intrigued by the knowledge that we had it within our ability to fly a specially trained army from New Jersey to Asia in two days, and he admired the Green Berets, telling them to wear their insignia proudly.

The flaws in the temperament of the Cold War strategists are easy to define. In our recent rediscovery of high political emotion, we have learned to condemn past administrations for bringing to desperately human facts little more than the calculations of a computerized intelligence. But that temperament had its special strengths of nerve and patience; and in its quickness to perceive complications, its analytical dislike of ideological formulas, it carried the seeds of its own liquidation. Kennedy was both in person and in time a figure central to that paradox; the Cold War as an assured attitude of mind would not long survive his presidency. Like other technicians of the conflict, from George F. Kennan and Dean Acheson onwards, the President did not want to talk the anti-Communist ideology of the Right—that would be too simplistic and would distract us from the details of power and the diversities in local situation with which our strategies had to cope. Yet if we were to forbear obsessions about the existence of a monolithic international communism and instead think of peasant revolutions and emergent nationalism and tension among Communist states, then we were obliged to prepare for a time when the world quasi war would no longer be necessary, and at that instant to effect quick disengagements. But Kennedy would not himself live to preside over a policy finally twisted and broken with self-contradiction, as it pursues in Vietnam a conflict that its own habit of careful calculation puts into question; and a conflict for which it cannot allow itself a satisfyingly belligerent and chauvinistic rhetoric, for it does not believe in such rhetoric.

Kennedy's unconscious part in all this was to an extent a matter of his sophistication in rhetoric, his insistence during the 1960 campaign, for example, that the developing split between China and Russia should dominate our view of communism. After Kennedy, critics could no longer condemn the mentality of the Cold War for its simplicity; they would need to rebut the complex and highly qualified understanding it had reached. Kennedy had something else to do with the psychology of the decade. He contributed to the youth movement that by the later sixties succeeded in making a major statement against the structures of American power. His appeals to idealism and to sacrifice struck a responsive chord, and beyond these intangibles his administration attracted young people into lives of public service. Kennedy also gave cover and encouragement to the civil rights workers in the South, the early activists of liberation and communalism. Yet even in all this the bite of mind that he brought to nuclear diplomacy was also the verve of his domestic politics. The call to arms was cool and tempered: Kennedy once told a group of White House reporters that he had little faith anything he could do would solve America's problems. He seemed to believe in human depravity.

Though many of John Kennedy's beliefs grew out of the 1950s, his personal manner had set him far apart from other politicians of that decade: he disdained the cronyism of the Senate, the cant of national politicians, and the naïveté of the professional liberals. Toward such things he showed an aristocrat's aloofness, even an arrogance born of having money, brains, good looks, the right education, a war hero's record, a beautiful wife, and a father ambitious for his son. Kennedy's temperament, detached from some accepted values and without illusions, was quite compatible with a manipulation of the electorate. When he first entered presidential politics in 1956 as a candidate for the vice-presidency, he let his adviser Ted Sorenson circulate a memorandum arguing that a Catholic candidate would strengthen rather than harm a national ticket. In 1959 he told a group of Pennsylvanians that if he went into the convention with many delegates and then were denied the nomination, the Democratic party would risk alienating Catholics and losing the election. Such incidents foreshadowed the opportunistic way Kennedy would use his Catholicism in the 1960 campaign, and they created a lasting impression of Kennedy as a man in a hurry.

Kennedy's coolness of manner protected his integrity. Never possessed of a political street personality, he winced at the thought of displaying his emotions. His critical mistake at the 1956 Democratic Convention, where he sought the vice-presidency, was in not visiting Hubert Humphrey to win favor—or so one account has it. The chosen candidate, Estes Kefauver, indulged in a tearful meeting with the sentimental Humphrey that would have been foreign to Kennedy's temper. Senator Kennedy, who had lost potential votes by declaring against high price supports for farmers, barely missed the vice-presidential nomination in 1956, and perhaps he did not try very hard. But it was a lucky thing: a place on the losing ticket would have spoiled his perfect record at the polls, and he was free to win a record-breaking reelection victory from Massachusetts voters in 1958.

Kennedy's record in the House and Senate had been marred by his failure to speak out against the demagogic Senator Joseph McCarthy—a failure especially to be noted in the author of *Profiles in Courage;* he missed the important censure vote because of sickness and did not arrange to pair with some member opposed to censure. He did not lead in introducing new legislation. Yet he was an independent man, usually given to an honest expression of his political views. He supported the St. Lawrence Seaway, despite its unpopularity in Massachusetts; though a decorated veteran, he condemned the powerful American Legion on the floor of the House; an Irishman, he was the only Democratic congressman in his state not to request a pardon for James Michael Curley, the former governor and congressman popular among the Irish in Massachusetts and then serving a term in prison. Kennedy had about him an air of freshness and unpredictability. He was both Irish and a Harvard graduate; he was wealthy, yet was presumed a political underdog because of his religion. His coolness of manner even hinted at a new type of popular hero.

The success of Senator Kennedy and other congressional Democrats in the elections of 1958—a crucial moment in the realignment of forces that was to change the politics of the era—gave political expression to an awareness of things wrong with American society. Older conservatives such as Senators William Knowland, John Bricker, and William Jenner disappeared from national life, and many of the new faces of the sixties first appeared in the Congress that met the following year. The Russian space achievement in sending two sputniks across the sky in 1957 had particularly shocked the country. American scientific education became a major campaign issue for Democrats, and was intensified by the crowding of the enormous postwar generation into inadequate school facilities across the nation. Publicists pointed to still more failures in American society: the coexistence of poverty and affluence; alleged corporate control over American foreign policy; uninhabitable suburbs under-supplied with libraries, parks, and privacy; and a conformity that threatened boredom and demoralization among the very class of technicians and businessmen who might have supplied America with new initiatives. While not all of these were politically effective issues, they contributed to a growing unease.

Most of all, the sluggish economy injured Republican candidates. The Eisenhower administration had discovered the means to prevent depression, but it seemed powerless to avoid repeated recessions, to stem inflation, or even to achieve a national economic growth rate at levels then prevailing in Western Europe or the Soviet Union. That failure came at a bad time. For a rise in productivity for each man-hour created surplus labor that demanded an economy expansive enough to supply it with jobs, while accumulating social needs and programs in health, welfare, and education required a richer economy yielding tax receipts adequate to finance them.

Though Democrats, including Senator Kennedy, blamed the inaction on Treasury Secretary George Humphrey's strong influence with Eisenhower, the cause cut deeper, for the peculiar way the economy had solved some of its older problems had generated new ones. Trusts had settled down into a permanent state to which economists gave the ugly name "oligopoly"; large firms were attempting to run their sectors of the economy not for the venturesome efforts of competition but for the comforts of profits at high prices. Much of the labor problem had been solved by wage increases to a unionized elite of protected workers, often in the same enterprises that were also organized into oligopoly. Gains in wages for the protected workers were passed on to consumers in the form of a general rise in prices. The situation of the unemployed meanwhile remained static because surplus capital was being consumed in the form of inflation long before it turned to new production and new jobs. Investments in plants and equipment shrank; late in the decade investments in the United States for these crucial items were one-eighth those of European countries in proportion to population.

The Eisenhower administration was too firmly grounded in the business community to press for serious changes in economic policy. Undoubtedly, it sincerely desired to stem price increases, but it could make no move at all when business, particularly the steel industry, resisted. The conditions of the late 1950s pose curious questions about the history of fiscal and economic policy. It is a standard assumption that the forces of business and the political Right have tended to favor economic opportunity over social justice. Yet the 1950s present the spectacle of a business-dominated government that seems to have restrained economic growth, while the liberal forces of the late fifties and the early sixties made growth their major domestic objective. Although such influences as simple hostility to the new economics also shaped its thinking, the business community—and its allies in the Republican party —took far longer than most economists, politicians, and publicists to recover from the trauma of the Great Depression.

While unemployment rates went as high as 7.5 percent, their political impact on organized labor, an elite working in heavy industry and participating in Eisenhower prosperity, was remarkably small. But conservative business groups politicized labor in the 1958 elections by placing the open or nonunion shop ("right to work" law) on the ballot in several states. And nonorganized workers were not going to continue being thankful for the absence of outright depression when a sharp recession in 1957–1958 was followed by a weak recovery of only twenty-five months, retarded afresh by a lengthy steel strike, and that in turn coasting into new recession in 1960–1961.

Disadvantaged groups in America suffered most from these economic slackenings. Negroes were flooding into urban ghettos, Indians and Mexicans were lost in self-perpetuating poverty, and growing numbers of elderly men and women were living out useless lives in decaying rooms or becoming medical indigents in hospitals that lacked not simply adequate medical care but often rudimentary cleanliness. Such people, as Michael Harrington pointed out in an unforgettable term, were "invisible" in the 1950s. In part this meant that they were physically shut away: in hospitals, on reservations, in migrant workers' camps, on the other side of freeways, or in inner cities abandoned by the middle class. But they were also politically invisible, without organized groups among themselves or representation through any other group, such as the Democratic party fixed to its institutional base in the unions. The fifties lacked an intellectual as well as a workers' Left; and this means not so much that the country was deprived of the specific policies such a Left might have achieved but that the conservative administration was able to be much more conservative, having no articulate opponent able to compel concessions from it.

John Kennedy knew his times well and believed he could cope with their problems. His near success in winning the vice-presidential nomination in 1956, and his enormous victory in the 1958 Massachusetts Senate race, made him a serious candidate for the presidency in 1960. The absence of other strong Democratic candidates was another advantage for Kennedy. Some party professionals thought he alone might pull back into the Democratic party the many Catholic voters who had deserted it in 1952 and 1956. Nevertheless, the party's leaders worried about his religion and his youthfulness. Since Al Smith's crushing defeat in 1928 still haunted the party, Kennedy would first have to show in the primaries that he could attract solid support from Protestants. His unimpressive victory over Hubert Humphrey in the early Wisconsin primary did not prove the point, for that state had too many Catholic voters. West Virginia, where he was scheduled to contest the persistent Humphrey on May 10, would be the crucial field of the preconvention campaign.

Kennedy's advisers told him to play down the religious issue in West Virginia. But average West Virginians, Kennedy instinctively believed, knew they were being tested and that their vote, above all else, would be interpreted by the nation at large as a repudiation or an endorsement of bigotry. Humphrey vehemently attacked the candidate's wealth, but West Virginians, like other Americans, admire wealth; and besides, Kennedy appeared moved by what he saw of poverty in the state. Kennedy himself repeatedly drew attention to his religion; he used the issue in a way that his opponent could not, managing to make it a matter of sportsmanship. West Virginia, a state 95 percent Protestant and only 4 percent black, cast 61 percent of its Democratic primary vote for Kennedy.

The victory in West Virginia carried Kennedy to a first-ballot nomination in Los Angeles. The Democratic Convention in that city was graced by Senator Eugene McCarthy's eloquent plea for the nomination of Adlai E. Stevenson, twice defeated as the party's presidential candidate: "Do not reject this man who made us all proud to be called Democrats. . . ." But Stevenson's candidacy, which he suspected was engineered by the Johnson people in an effort to head off the main contender, irritated Kennedy. When a close election seemed in the offing, why did Stevenson let liberals rally in an impossible drive against the front-runner? For him and for Eleanor Roosevelt the reason was to keep Kennedy aware that his record needed to be more daring. But the Senator believed Stevenson's bid to be a hopeless and egotistical gesture certain to endanger party unity, and the venture by the Stevenson forces did not stop Kennedy from offering the vice-presidency to a man unpopular among northern liberals—Lyndon Baines Johnson.

Much has been written about the selection of Johnson, who had held second place in the presidential balloting. Most of the accounts treat the offer and the acceptance as spontaneous and even impulsive; this may be true but both men, who respected each other considerably, must also have been calculating the likelihood for months: such a ticket would certainly be the strongest one imaginable. The Republican candidate, Richard Nixon, knowing this, had anticipated the ticket. The least measurable issue of the campaign, Kennedy's religion, presented the worst handicap in the South, where the Texas Protestant Johnson would greatly aid the ticket. Johnson was well regarded among farmers, businessmen, and conservative independents in the rest of the country many of whom might have been expected to lean toward Nixon. Such voters would be attracted by Johnson's prudent legislative record, his willingness to cooperate with Eisenhower, and his universally acknowledged political skill at leading the Democratic party in the Senate. True, Johnson's candidacy would not be good news to labor and the liberals— but where else could they go? Nixon, they had decided long ago, was beyond redemption. Apparently the vice-presidency also suited the ambitions of Johnson, who had offered to run with Stevenson in 1956; the office would lift him above a confining Southern identity, which had stood in the way of the presidential nomination.

Johnson went on to conduct a superbly professional campaign. Kennedy, in Norman Mailer's image, was a young professor whose manner was adequate for the classroom, but whose mind was off in some intricacy of the Ph.D. thesis he was writing; the man was always a touch too aloof from the candidate. Johnson, on the other hand, gave all of himself: he was "a political animal, he breathed like an animal, sweated like one, you knew his mind was entirely absorbed with the compendium of political fact and maneuver." On his brilliant campaign trips through the South, Johnson demanded order and precision: the rostrum had to be exactly 52 inches high when he spoke, the band must blast the first note of "The Yellow Rose of Texas" the second he finished speaking, the train must pull away from the station at the syllable of farewell. The content of Johnson's message as he sped from one small town to another—"God bless yuh, Rocky Bottom. Ah wish ah could stay an' do a little sippin' an' whittlin' with yuh. . . . God bless yuh, Gaffney"— seemed to clash oddly with the technical skill of the performance and the abrupt manners of the candidate among his advisers but apparently spoke to his audience.

Kennedy's Republican opponent, Vice-President Nixon, was a strong candidate. Much more attuned to the country's politics than Dwight Eisenhower, he had been an active and partisan Vice-President, urging his administration to take a more progressive view on civil rights, the economy, and public education. He was effective on television and welcomed the chance to debate Kennedy. Newspaper editors and publishers generally favored Nixon, and his campaign chest more than matched Kennedy's. His greatest fault was one that John Kennedy spotted easily: Nixon lacked taste. He fabricated sentimentality and sought a level of communication much below his capacity.

Nixon's campaign was fated to a series of misfortunes. His running mate, Henry Cabot Lodge, proved to be an unenthusiastic campaigner. A preconvention meeting at Governor Nelson Rockefeller's New York apartment was interpreted by many Republican conservatives as a capitulation to Rocky's liberal domestic views. Early in the campaign, Nixon suffered an infected knee and was hospitalized for two weeks; later, still underweight and in a weakened condition, he caught a bad case of the flu. Despite the loss in time, he insisted on fulfilling a pledge to visit all fifty states, spending valuable hours in Alaska when he should have been barnstorming downstate Illinois. Instead of benefiting from Eisenhower's projected meeting with Khrushchev at Paris in the spring of 1960, Nixon shared with the administration the embarrassment of being caught in the act of espionage; a short time before, an American U-2 high-altitude reconnaissance plane had been shot down deep in Russian territory. Thereby the Republican slogan of peace and prosperity, already in doubt because of the continuing recession, suffered a further loss of credibility. In August, Eisenhower was none too helpful when he carelessly told a reporter who had asked him what major administration decisions Nixon had participated in: "If you give me a week, I might think of one." And Nixon could not make good use of Eisenhower in the closing weeks of the campaign, for the President's doctors advised against it. When the Reverend Norman Vincent Peale, Nixon's New York pastor, condemned Kennedy on religious grounds, the minister in fact lent strength to the argument that a vote for a Catholic was a vote for freeing politics of the sterile religious issue. The incident gave Kennedy an opportunity dramatically to convince an audience of Houston ministers that they had no call to fear him. Worst of all, a series of television debates demolished the myth of Kennedy's youthful inexperience and placed the haggard Nixon in the role of defending a passive administration. The Vice-President had counted on his ability: there was the effective "kitchen debate" of 1959 with Khrushchev in Moscow; and in a television speech of the 1952 campaign, when Nixon defended himself against dubious allegations of financial misconduct and evoked the name of his dog, Checkers, he had proved his mastery of television. He could not strike hard, since he thought it unwise to evoke memories of his ruthlessness in anti-Communist investigation during the McCarthy era, and in any case Kennedy kept him off balance.

Once Eisenhower had set the depression psychosis to rest, the nation was ready to venture beyond tranquillity to a more exciting economics of expansion, and this the young Kennedy offered it. Economic experiment came to seem not only possible but necessary if America was to maintain a position of world leadership. The Cold War, which for so long had hampered experimentation, now encouraged it, for Russia was embarked on a phase of economic competition with the United States. Khrushchev's threat "We will bury you," by which he signified economic triumph, illustrates that the Cold War was shifting from direct confrontation to a struggle for the Third World, whose need for development meant that the United States and Russia had to compete as models of productivity. Kennedy, by shrewdly emphasizing a missile gap and Castro's victory in Cuba, and by linking the issues of national prestige and economic growth, implied that Nixon—part of a well-intentioned but ineffective administration—could not solve these difficulties. The two party platforms, an aggressive Democratic document and a defensive Republican one, seemed to restate the difference between the candidates.

During the campaign Kennedy rarely attacked the substance of the Eisenhower foreign policies. But citing a supposed missile gap, he urged that we catch up with Russia technologically, particularly in space. With problems like Cuba and Laos in mind, Kennedy also called for a new look for the army. A one-sided reliance on nuclear weapons—the "bigger bang for the buck" philosophy of Eisenhower's Defense Secretary Charles E. Wilson—denied us any flexibility of choice, Kennedy argued. Faced with a war of national liberation, we were restricted to the alternatives of doing nothing or threatening a nuclear strike, and that threat could not be carried out except at a catastrophic price. Perhaps, of course, Eisenhower and Dulles never really thought nuclear war to be an option. Conceivably they believed that no aggressive military move by Russia was likely and that our opposition to localized revolts would have to take nonmilitary form. Eisenhower himself talked of peace and offered his "open skies" disarmament proposal; his own enormous prestige enabled him stubbornly to resist enlarged military appropriations and to criticize influential generals and admirals as "parochial." Kennedy, on the other hand, proposed that the nation complement its nuclear arsenal with a well-financed, innovative armed force and an improved stock of conventional weapons. He was capitalizing on a debate in the Pentagon itself; for such army leaders as Maxwell Taylor and Matthew Ridgway were calling for a more mobile and sophisticated force capable of fighting in limited kinds of unrest such as that in Laos and the Congo. Kennedy's kinetic charm (he talked too fast for most people to grasp his arguments) and his confidence in fathoming the complexity of public problems cast him as a man with a more sophisticated, more dashing, and more effective response to the familiar problems of the fifties. He defeated Nixon by 303 to 219 electoral votes and by a hairsbreadth in the popular vote. Even the electoral vote in truth should have been closer: alleged fraud in counting the close returns in Illinois and Texas cast deep suspicion on the Kennedy victory in those states. Any Democrat should have won easily given the recession and the strength of his party. It is puzzling that Kennedy did not do better. Whether his religion helped or harmed him is questionable. The Survey Research Center of the University of Michigan, and other similar organizations, found that the issue cost him 2 percent of the popular vote but helped him in crucial states with substantial Catholic blocs and large electoral votes.

In the course of his presidency, Kennedy would eventually articulate a foreign policy of restraint and accommodation, and bring the Cold War almost to the point of its terminating in explicit agreements and implicit understandings. Yet he came to the office with a remarkable bellicosity. John Kennedy, Congressman and Senator from 1947 to 1960, was a product and, like almost everyone of that era, a prisoner to some extent of the Cold War. He had matured from its earlier rhetoric—he apologized for blaming the loss of China on the Truman administration —he had profited from its growing sophistication, and he hoped, with Eisenhower, for an eventual accommodation with Russia. But he was of two minds, for he also appeared to believe that communism would continue to be America's implacable foe. In Kennedy's years in the House of Representatives, that body had habitually voted overwhelmingly for resolutions calling on the peoples of eastern Europe to revolt against their Communist rulers; and Kennedy had joined in these votes. Anticommunism, moreover, was a strong tradition of Kennedy's own family and church. In the first television debate with Nixon he endorsed a devil theory of communism.

President Kennedy's selection of advisers like Dean Rusk for State, Robert McNamara for Defense, and Walt Rostow and McGeorge Bundy as White House aides showed he was not ready for a foreign policy like that of Adlai Stevenson, who had been almost alone in believing, as early as 1956, that the Cold War might conceivably be liquidated. Kennedy chose his staff from organization men who held positions demanding great technical competence in government, business, or university bureaucracies. He finally rejected independent figures like Senator William Fulbright, his own initial favorite for the post of State. Rusk, who became a strong, and stubborn, Secretary of State, failed at first to provide leadership. McNamara, a man of some genius, talked of "cost-effectiveness" and "flexible response," but rarely if ever disagreed with a unanimous decision of the Joint Chiefs of Staff. Hawkish former Secretary of State Dean Acheson gave his approval to the Kennedy appointments, recommending Rusk after warning that the selection of

Stevenson for State would be a "terrible disaster" and that of Fulbright a "mistake." If the year 1960 had a tone in foreign policy, it was set by the publication of Herman Kahn's *On Thermonuclear War,* which Kennedy studied closely. Kahn, who thought war likely and described how we could survive, argued that if Russia braced for a nuclear attack and America did not, our world position would be weakened.

The beliefs on foreign policy that Kennedy carried with him into office are caught for history in the Bay of Pigs fiasco. The Eisenhower administration, to be sure, had prepared the way for anti-Communist guerrillas to invade Cuba. More than a thousand Cuban refugees, trained by America's Central Intelligence Agency, awaited commands at a coffee plantation high in the Guatemalan mountains. To cancel the planned invasion and disperse the men, who would tell tales, might say to the world that the new administration in Washington was weak. To some degree, events generated their own momentum, and Kennedy received misinformation and bad advice from the CIA. He had also seen that the increasingly dictatorial Castro had deceived many liberals, and he had his own jingoistic campaign rhetoric to live with. Finally, the bureaucracies of government, during the Bay of Pigs and later in the Vietnam escalations, discouraged criticism and "rocking the boat"; here Kennedy might have been saved by the visceral liberals his temperament could not abide. Still, it was absurd to suppose that the well-entrenched Castro could be overthrown without the active support of the United States Air Force, Army, and Navy; and to make an abortive attempt would be disastrous. Cuba, as Senator Fulbright observed, was after all a thorn in the flesh, not a dagger in the heart. The important creditable part of the President's role came in restraining the militarists who wanted an all-out attack when it was plain that the landing had failed.

How could a hardheaded pragmatist like Kennedy have been misled by advisers he hardly even knew? It was perhaps a part of his competitive temper that drove him almost to court crisis; in the inaugural, for instance, he had declaimed, "Before my term has ended we shall have to test anew whether a nation organized and governed such as ours can endure." He repeatedly declared America to be at the most critical point in its history. In those days he even gave serious thought to a planned assassination of Castro, according to a source perhaps inaccurate, Senator George Smathers. In 1962 he told the journalist Stewart Alsop that a nuclear war in the next decade stood an even chance. Some part of the decision to place our prestige on the line with the guerrilla invaders, however, must also have been based on the faulty premise that because communism was totalitarian the people who lived under it yearned for freedom and would revolt at the first opportunity. And since communism was evil, the rebels would succeed. They failed miserably. Their CIA-directed strategy included every blunder imaginable: the wrong landing place, inadequate air cover, munitions and equipment piled in a single boat, and an underestimation of the enemy's strength.

In the short term, the Bay of Pigs possibly taught Kennedy the wrong lesson: it firmed his resolve to expect and be prepared for future encounters, and he redoubled his efforts to increase military spending. Though he also pushed the Alliance for Progress, seeking to reconstruct Latin America economically, he discounted arguments that building up an arsenal of conventional weapons would itself be a provocative act demanding a like response from the Soviets.

The first years of the Kennedy administration were a brief but dangerous period in international relations. During these times the old policy of threatening a massive nuclear retaliation existed perilously alongside a new problem, the national liberation movements. In Asia, in Africa, and in Latin America, in countries like Laos, the Congo, and Cuba, dynamic revolutionary forces were challenging the world balance of power. In the fresh context of the sixties, irresponsible third powers might precipitate the ultimate conflict between Russia and the United States.

In the long, tense confrontation over Berlin that lasted throughout 1961, Kennedy seemed to believe that an actual war could break out, that Russian determination might force war. Such was his impression from talking with Khrushchev at the summit meeting held in Vienna in June 1961; the Russian leader said that before the end of the year his country would sign a treaty with East Germany banning us from West Berlin. The encounter deeply troubled Kennedy, and shortly afterward he spurred fallout shelter construction, increased draft quotas, and called up military reserve units. For some years Russia had appeared to be ahead in space, in industrial growth, in long-range missiles; and it seemed that Communist imperialism was making progress almost everywhere in the world except Western Europe, where, since NATO and the Marshall Plan, communism had stopped its advance. At Vienna Khrushchev sharply challenged Kennedy even in Europe, demanding that the West sign a German peace treaty or quit Berlin. Stiffened by the hard-line opinion of Dean Acheson that Berlin was a "simple conflict of wills," Kennedy saw Khrushchev's "ultimatum" as an audacious effort to upset the one area of the world where America was incontestably ahead.

Khrushchev eventually compromised on Western Europe, constructing the Berlin wall and withdrawing the deadline of January 1, 1962, for western acquiescence. In the long run, the wall was a propaganda triumph for the West. But international tension continued to tighten in 1962. The previous summer and fall Kennedy had sped his plan for building fallout shelters. America's increased defense spending provoked a comparable rise in Russia. In response to Khrushchev's resumption of atmospheric nuclear testing in the fall of 1961, Kennedy followed suit the next April. In Africa, Russia and Communist China slipped from the toehold they had gained around the turn of the decade. The United Nations was instrumental in preserving the new Congo nation and in blocking a Soviet-American clash there; and Kennedy scored a coup by an order denying arms to South Africa as long as it should practice hard racial separation. On the other hand, although Khrushchev managed to effect a neutralization of Laos, indigenous Communist movements were gaining ground in South Vietnam, Cambodia, and the Philippines. In reaction, Kennedy, appealing to American pride, competitiveness, anticommunism, and respect for technology, secured enormous congressional appropriations for military purposes and for the race to the moon, which the President promised to reach before the end.of the decade.

Then in the autumn of 1962 the world came as close as it ever has come to destruction. During the preceding summer Khrushchev had decided to place long-range nuclear missiles in Cuba. Once again, the Central Intelligence Agency failed Kennedy on Cuba; Senator Kenneth Keating of New York, using Cuban refugees as his source, seemed to be able to guess more about the missiles than the administration. Not until mid-October was it known definitely in Washington that Russian missiles in Cuba were aimed at principal American cities. The immediate reaction was one of astonishment. Nowhere else in the world outside its own borders had Russia set up such missiles. The tactical advantage was slight; Russian submarines equipped with similar weapons had been passing close to American shores for many years. But from a diplomatic standpoint the interference in an area so patently within America's sphere of influence was flagrant.

At first Kennedy's advisers considered every alternative course of action, but soon two groups coalesced, one advising an air strike and the other some kind of blockade. The Joint Chiefs favored the more warlike course, even though it would probably kill Soviet technicians. Robert Kennedy persuasively argued against a surprise air attack on the grounds that it conflicted with our national traditions and brought to mind Pearl Harbor. Eventually the view prevailed that the less risky course, the quarantine, should be pursued initially; stronger actions could be commenced later should they become necessary. Kennedy moved the blockade as close to Cuba as he dared so that Khrushchev would have time to consider all the implications it presented. After some indecision the Kremlin decided to respect the blockade, as soon as the first ship with launching equipment turned away, the world was safe—for a time. Kennedy had heightened the confrontation by refusing Khrushchev's offer to remove the missiles if we would dismantle our own obsolete ones in Turkey. A diplomatic settlement was worked out whereby Russia removed all missiles from Cuba, and America promised to respect that country's territorial integrity. Some critics have faulted Kennedy for making the missile confrontation a public affair. He might have given Khrushchev a private ultimatum. Public exposure gave the Russian leader an opportunity to appear temperate in the face of world opinion. But Kennedy had grown beyond the Bay of Pigs affair, gaining courage and restraint.

It is said that the missile crisis scared Khrushchev; in the condescending vocabulary of the Chief of Staff Maxwell Taylor, it made him "tractable." It undoubtedly scared Kennedy, too. But the missile crisis, which might have blown up the world, instead cleared the air.

A sudden realization dawned that in an age of national revolutionary movements such as Castro's Cuba, direct nuclear confrontation was no longer thinkable. Nineteen sixty-three was to be the year of the great international thaw. The United States and the Soviet Union, locked in nuclear stalemate, established a "hot line" to guard against future misunderstandings. In June the President delivered a moving speech at American University, calling for a new era of harmony and mutual progress with Russia. The Test Ban Treaty of 1963, which Kennedy drove through the Senate in face of stiff opposition from the Pentagon, was his one great positive accomplishment in foreign policy. The Soviets broke with the Chinese on the issue of peaceful coexistence and publicly stressed the need to avoid nuclear war, while the United States made arrangements to sell wheat to Russia. Kennedy himself was said to be tiring of Dean Rusk's clichéd rhetoric and hard-line ideas. In the long run, the missile crisis perhaps simply quickened the shift of the Cold War from confrontation between the superpowers to less cataclysmic "wars of national liberation," but the immediate effect was a loosening of tension.

On other issues as well, Kennedy began his presidential years unimpressively, and matured only as experience and circumstances compelled. Sobered by his meager margin of victory in 1960, he had arranged harmony meetings with Nixon and Eisenhower even before taking office, and he gave continuity to government (and continued conservative policies) by keeping on officials such as J. Edgar Hoover of the FBI and Allen Dulles of the CIA. After Congress convened in 1961 Kennedy forced a change in the size of the House Rules Committee, and thereby opened up the possibility that controversial legislation might at least reach the floor. But again his margin of victory was so slight that in the months ahead he rarely challenged Congress on important issues: federal aid to education floundered on religious controversy; a new cabinet department of urban affairs failed to win approval; foreign aid was cut drastically, owing to successive administration blunders. The Trade Expansion Act of 1962 was the one early achievement, but it was not of major importance, despite the publicity given it. Kennedy, it seemed, would endorse Jefferson's dictum: "Great innovations should not be forced on slender majorities."

The lack of programs of Kennedy's first year in the presidency is especially to be noted with respect to the great domestic issue of the sixties, the one for which he is honored most—that of civil rights. Actually, the President entered office with an undistinguished record on the question of race. Twice he had voted with the South on the Civil Rights Bill of 1957: on the abortive effort to return the bill to Mississippi Senator James Eastland's Judiciary Committee; and on the successful O'Mahoney amendment guaranteeing jury trials in criminal contempt cases—and so ensuring, in effect, that southern white defendants in civil rights cases would be tried by southern white juries. In the vice-presidential balloting of 1956 Kennedy had received support from such sources as Arkansas Governor Orville Faubus, and in the late fifties the governors of Alabama and Mississippi had urged his presidency. At a time when Kennedy was giving no more account of himself than this, Richard Nixon was calling for a strong civil rights bill and speaking against discrimination in jobs and housing.

Kennedy's campaign of 1960 was also unpromising on the question. When in January he listed the "real issues of 1960," he omitted civil rights—and this from a candidate who during the campaign declared, quoting Franklin D. Roosevelt, that the presidency is "above all, a place of moral leadership." Along with Nixon he did make many campaign promises to the cause of racial equality, and he even phoned a message of consolation to Mrs. Martin Luther King, whose husband had been imprisoned in an Atlanta jail. Dr. King's early release was probably attributable to a phone call from Robert Kennedy to an Atlanta judge. But in his inaugural President Kennedy mentioned civil rights only briefly and in the most general terms.

Fearing loss of support for other programs, Kennedy sponsored virtually no new rights legislation in 1961 and 1962, relying instead on executive action. He did not appear to sense the explosive potential of the racial situation. Had he understood it better, he would never have appointed his brother Attorney General, for that office bore the responsibility of enforcing civil rights laws and it would have been politically astute to choose for it a man of independent reputation.

Yet the Department of Justice brought about much of the concrete gains the Kennedy administration achieved on racial matters. Believing that once southern Negroes voted, their political power would secure other rights, Bobby Kennedy introduced many new federal lawsuits in behalf of the Negro franchise. The Justice Department also saw to it that transportation facilities became almost entirely desegregated in the South. (In 1962, however, the Federal Aviation Agency awarded a $2 million grant to build an airport with segregated restaurants and rest rooms in Jackson, Mississippi.) Though he had earlier urged the Negro leader Ralph Abernathy to hold back the freedom riders, the Attorney General in May 1961 dispatched 600 federal marshals to Alabama to protect them. Vice-President Lyndon Johnson, who chaired the Committee on Equal Employment, took another approach: intimate with the art of persuasion, he urged government contractors to hire more Negro workers. But Johnson came to realize that coercion would be needed, and in 1963 the Vice-President delivered strong civil rights speeches in Gettysburg and Detroit.

President Kennedy avoided the ultimate sanction, that of forcing desegregation by the withholding of federal funds. In the fall of 1962, two years after criticizing Eisenhower for failing, "by a stroke of the presidential pen," to eliminate discrimination in federally assisted housing, the President did issue such an order, sandwiching it between major news releases so that it received minimal publicity; but administrative interpretations then softened even this forward step. President Kennedy decried "straight-from-the-shoulder platitudes" on civil rights, not comprehending that this was a place where presidential exhortation might be of some value. Whatever progress the Justice Department made in 1961 and in 1962, the President wiped out some of it by appointing several segregationists to lifetime positions on southern district courts; they exhibited little enthusiasm for enforcing the Supreme Court school desegregation decision of 1954.

Then, in the last year of his life, Kennedy—and the churches and much of the nation—awakened to the moral crisis that the civil rights movement had long been seeking to publicize. Events compelled him to act, but he acted in a manner that brought credit to his presidency. In the fall of 1962 he had enforced with federal troops the enrollment of James Meredith at the University of Mississippi, employing radio and television to call on southerners to obey the law. The following spring, when Governor George Wallace attempted to prevent the court-ordered entrance of Vivian Malone and James Hood into the University of Alabama, the President's pronouncement went beyond the issue of obedience to law, where federal declarations in crises of illegal resistance to integration had typically placed themselves, and spoke to the moral question. (Earlier, Kennedy had borrowed Lincoln's birthday from the Republicans by inviting several hundred Negro leaders to the White House.) In May of 1963 Kennedy moved in troops to quell brutal repression in Birmingham, Alabama, where police had used dogs, fire hoses, and electric cattle prods against Negroes. In June he gave a moving speech on civil rights and he finally sent new legislation to Congress. The President proposed a limited ban on discrimination in public places, asked for powers enabling the Justice Department to sue for school desegregation where an aggrieved citizen asked its help, and urged a broad provision authorizing the government to withhold funds for federally assisted programs where discrimination occurred. But it contained no proposal for mandatory fair employment practices and failed to resurrect the unsuccessful Part III of the 1957 bill giving the Justice Department power to intervene in all civil rights cases. Kennedy also took a step backward when he gave tax reform priority over civil rights legislation, reasoning that a stronger economy would help the Negro more than anything else. And certainly the President feared southern congressional power. Some critics even charged that there was an unstated agreement with the South, gaining votes on other bills in exchange for stalling on civil rights. But just before he was killed the President secured an agreement from congressional leaders that would probably have assured passage of a strong civil rights act early in 1964.

Kennedy's claim to be celebrated as a champion of Negro rights is precarious. Though the great Negro leader, the Reverend Martin Luther King, Jr., granted in June 1963 that Kennedy had perhaps done "a little more" than Eisenhower, King added that "the plight of the vast majority of Negroes remains the same." The following August 250,000 people participated in the March on Washington to be counted in favor of civil rights legislation and to hear King speak: "I have a dream that one day on the red hills of Georgia the sons of former slaves and the sons of former slaveowners will be able to sit together at the table of brotherhood. . . . I have a dream that one day even the State of Mississippi, a desert state sweltering with the heat of injustice and oppression, will be transformed into an oasis of freedom and justice. . . . I have a dream that one day the State of Alabama . . . will be transformed into a situation where little black boys and black girls will be able to join hands with little white boys and girls and walk together as sisters and brothers." Despite Kennedy's failure to share King's vision, in few places did his death arouse such sorrow as in the Negro communities. And subsequent efforts to pass effective legislation gained from being construed as a memorial to the martyred President; the first law easily went through Congress early in 1964 and soon others followed.

The pattern of initiative in race relations during the Kennedy years generally repeated itself in the President's handling of the economy. Kennedy in the 1960 campaign had criticized the Republicans for not maintaining a high rate of economic growth and for lapsing into recessions from fear of employing advanced economic policies. In office, however, the new President at first proceeded cautiously, endorsing in practice the economic policies he had earlier condemned. Unemployment remained substantial in 1961 and 1962. Certainly many real obstacles held Kennedy back from economic experimentation: the adverse balance of payments discouraged expansive policies; a severe break in the stock market in May 1962 evoked distrust of the President in the economic community; he was wary of the image of "reckless spender" that the Republicans had tried to fix on the Democrats; and the congressional seniority system rewarded conservatives of long service. Kennedy did succeed in holding down the cost of living, and in 1961 he supported a boost in Social Security payments and the minimum wage to end the "Eisenhower recession" of 1960–1961. These techniques were similar to those Eisenhower himself had used when the economy faltered.

Kennedy evidently believed in such tools as deficit spending, a tax cut, and easy credit, but he thought the powerful and independent Federal Reserve Board might rebel at a novel program. But when the economy later in 1962 ceased its recovery from the earlier recession, the President and his able Republican Treasury Secretary, Douglas Dillon, decided to follow a truly radical economic policy. For the first relatively prosperous time in American history an administration proposed the deliberate unbalancing of the budget through tax reduction as a means of stimulating growth. It was a great victory for the university economists who had sought to influence the President. According to Ted Sorenson, Kennedy became convinced by a speech they prepared for him to deliver at the Economic Club of New York in December. He also believed that a tax cut was an indirect means of helping the poor, the black, and the cities—and the stock market, which had moved downward the preceding spring. If the tax policy should give new life to the economy, Congress might do something to redress the imbalance between public squalor and private affluence. Early in 1963 Kennedy proposed a $10 billion tax cut, despite a record-breaking peacetime deficit. The unbalanced budget troubled the business community, but it disliked high taxes even more and supported the President. After the Kennedy recommendations became law early in 1964, the pace of economic growth quickened, and before our extensive involvement in Vietnam, prosperity without serious inflation briefly seemed within reach. In a sense, then, it was Kennedy's tax policy, which led to a $30 billion enlargement of Gross National Product that made possible the harvest of Great Society legislation.

Businessmen generally responded well to the economic policies of the Kennedy-Johnson years, though many of them continued to distrust the government's sympathy toward labor. Kennedy obtained tax credits and a liberal depreciation allowance for business in 1962, and reduced corporate income taxes by 20 percent in 1963. But he soon found himself in a confrontation with a powerful segment of business. Early in the Kennedy administration, which had vigorously pursued an anti-inflation policy, the steel industry attempted to raise prices. The act was a major embarrassment for the government, for when Labor Secretary Arthur Goldberg, anxious to avoid a critical strike that might delay economic recovery, had employed his experience in negotiation to persuade labor to keep its wage demands down, he had repeated an assurance given by industry leaders that prices would be held steady. When Roger Blough, President of U.S. Steel, appeared at the White House at 5:45 P.M. on April 10, 1962, to announce that press releases of an industry-wide price rise were just then being distributed, the President was furious. He quoted his father as having said that steelmen were "sons of bitches," and then launched an almost unprecedented attack on a major American industry. The President withdrew defense contracts and threatened antitrust action and new antitrust laws; he used every major branch of the government to bring the steel companies into line. Secretary of Commerce Luther Hodges, himself a businessman, gave Kennedy full support. The President addressed the people bluntly: "In this serious hour in our nation's history, when we are confronted with grave crises in Berlin and Southeast Asia . . . , the American public will find it hard, as I do, to accept a situation in which a tiny handful of steel executives whose pursuit of private power and profit exceeds their sense of public responsibility can show such utter contempt of the interests of 185 million Americans." Kennedy over-played by having the FBI take some uncertain role, but by and large it was a handsome demonstration of presidential power in the service of the public interest. Big Steel, following the lead of some smaller companies, rescinded the price increase. Arthur Krock observed afterward that presidential anger "must be reserved for those rare occasions when the office and the nation as well as the man are basically offended"; the steel episode was such an occasion.

Made confident by successes in foreign affairs and hopeful of improving domestic life, Kennedy gave promise by 1963 of fashioning a stronger presidency. Then Kennedy, two years and ten months after becoming President, went to Dallas. In a typical but foolish gesture, the President sat in an open car moving slowly through the streets of the hostile southern city. In the previous presidential campaign, even Lyndon Johnson had been spat upon in Dallas, and a woman had hit

Ladybird on the head with a placard. And only weeks before, Adlai Stevenson had been physically abused there. The man who almost certainly shot and killed Kennedy, Lee Harvey Oswald, was a refugee of the political Left; but he might easily have been a right-wing fanatic or any lunatic with a grudge against the government. The President's body was flown home to Washington, where the next day, November 23, 1963, a Roman Catholic mass was held in the White House for the first time —something bigots had feared. Chief Justice Earl Warren, reporting swiftly for an investigation panel of eminent but busy men, uncovered no evidence of a conspiracy, and subsequent efforts to find one have proved unconvincing.

A summary view of the Kennedy administration would be out of focus if it concentrated heavily on how much legislation passed through Congress. Such a view could not take into account the times and the might-have-beens—or the possibility that the death of Kennedy provided the national temper needed for the passage of the Kennedy program. This is not to say that the domestic achievements of the thousand days were unimpressive. When Kennedy promised in the presidential campaign to get the country moving again he was referring principally to the economy. As a result of Kennedy's recommendations, the national economy became brilliantly active. Kennedy's belated leadership in the civil rights movement must not be discounted. But the President also made the White House a home for the arts, and he even promised that America would reach the moon before the decade was finished. Important legislation surmounted the Congressional deadlock of the early sixties, including the Peace Corps and drug labeling; and critical beginnings were made on problems of water and air pollution, area redevelopment, and manpower training. Finally, Kennedy acted intelligently in crises: Ole Miss, the University of Alabama, Birmingham, the steel episode, the Cuban missile crisis, and—at least by refusing to compound errors—the Bay of Pigs.

What made the Kennedy years most memorable, besides the event that brought them to a premature conclusion, was something quite intangible. The ambiance of the administration was more significant than its actual legislative record. In attempting to answer various social needs that the New Deal had failed to meet and that had enlarged and multiplied in twenty years of political stasis during hot and cold war, President Kennedy implied that the country could no longer simply go its ordinary way. It required a more intense and faster pace, and a call to moral arms—in the rhetoric of the campaign, a "new frontier." John and Jacqueline Kennedy placed a high and racy fashion of living before a people of growing affluence. It can be granted that much of the Kennedy style fed upon glittering, banal values, that the President's record displays naïveté as often as sophistication, that Kennedy's own taste was often trivial and dull, and that estimates of him are colored by his romance with the intellectuals. But the Kennedy manner gave sharper edge to American life, created expectations still unfulfilled, gave encouragement to civil rights workers, and contributed something to an awakening among America's youth.

Certain forces of the Kennedy era were moving toward a fundamental reconsideration of American society. The issues here are hard to characterize: broadly speaking, they are cultural rather than economic; they relate to race, education, health, the environment, public safety, attitudes toward youth and the quality of life. They are founded, most of them, in the economic and social concern that American liberalism has carried down from the New Deal. The emergence of the racial question in the Kennedy years, however, would bring radical acts of civil disobedience and militant protest by the young, as well as new strivings for social reconstructions and innovative conceptions of community. A cultural politics, which the President scarcely intended, was spawned in the Kennedy years.

The John F. Kennedy Inaugural Address

John F. Kennedy set proud goals for his administration in 1961, promising that "a new generation of Americans" would march forth to do battle with "the common enemies of man: tyranny, poverty, disease and war itself." But the Kennedy administration was to be a brief one —two years and ten months from the "trumpet summons" of the inauguration to the muffled drums and caissons marching slowly up Pennsylvania Avenue in November 1963. This foreshortened story of beginnings and promises, then, is a hard one to interpret. Were the hopes real? Was the vitality an illusion? Was there substance behind the glittering style? Was the New Frontier a beckoning horizon or an armed border, a fresh direction or only a new rhetoric? The answers remain "blowing in the wind"—a phrase directly from the Kennedy era.

Kennedy's inaugural address set the tone for his administration as few such addresses have ever done. The elevation, the magnetic tone of dedication and of hope comes across in the way of words chiseled in granite. Thousands, perhaps millions, of Americans have read these words on Kennedy's tombstone in Arlington National Cemetery. Yet a close reading of this famous speech reveals subtle counterthemes that suggest possible answers to the questions that were subsequently raised after John F. Kennedy's death: about his place in American history, his administration's continuity, or discontinuity, with his predecessors' policies, and the substance lodged beneath the glittering language. Ask yourself what the various publics listening to this speech would have understood by it. What would a civil rights worker have derived from it? A conservative congressman? A Pentagon policy planner? The Soviet foreign ministry? John F. Kennedy was never easy to evaluate, and his untimely death left a legacy of controversy and unanswered questions surrounding him that history may never resolve.

We observe today not a victory of party but a celebration of freedom—symbolizing an end as well as a beginning—signifying renewal as well as change. For I have sworn before you and Almighty God the same solemn oath our forebears prescribed nearly a century and three quarters ago.

The world is very different now. For man holds in his mortal hands the power to abolish all forms of human poverty and all forms of human life. And yet the same revolutionary beliefs for which our forebears fought are still at issue around the globe—the belief that the rights of man come not from the generosity of the state but from the hand of God.

We dare not forget today that we are the heirs of that first revolution. Let the word go forth from this time and place, to friend and foe alike, that the torch has been passed to a new generation of Americans—born in this century, tempered by war, disciplined by a hard and bitter peace, proud of our ancient heritage—and unwilling to witness or permit the slow undoing of those human rights to which this nation has always been committed, and to which we are committed today at home and around the world.

Let every nation know, whether it wishes us well or ill, that we shall pay any price, bear any burden, meet any hardship, support any friend, oppose any foe to assure the survival and the success of liberty.

This much we pledge—and more.

To those old allies whose cultural and spiritual origins we share, we pledge the loyalty of faithful friends. United, there is little we cannot do in a host of cooperative ventures. Divided, there is little we can do—for we dare not meet a powerful challenge at odds and split asunder.

To those new states whom we welcome to the ranks of the free, we pledge our word that one form of colonial control shall not have passed away merely to be replaced by a far more iron tyranny. We shall not always expect to find them supporting our view. But we shall always hope to find them strongly supporting their own freedom—and to remember that, in the past, those who foolishly sought power by riding the back of the tiger ended up inside.

To those peoples in the huts and villages of half the globe struggling to break the bonds of mass misery, we pledge our best efforts to help them help themselves, for whatever period is required—not because the communists may be doing it, not because we seek their votes, but because it is right. If a free society cannot help the many who are poor, it cannot save the few who are rich.

To our sister republics south of our border, we offer a special pledge —to convert our good words into good deeds—in a new alliance for progress—to assist free men and free governments in casting off the chains of poverty. But this peaceful revolution of hope cannot become the prey of hostile powers. Let all our neighbors know that we shall join with them to oppose aggression or subversion anywhere in the Americas. And let every other power know that this Hemisphere intends to remain the master of its own house.

To that world assembly of sovereign states, the United Nations, our last best hope in an age where the instruments of war have far outpaced the instruments of peace, we renew our pledge of support—to prevent it from becoming merely a forum for invective—to strengthen its shield of the new and the weak—and to enlarge the area in which its writ may run.

Finally, to those nations who would make themselves our adversary, we offer not a pledge but a request: that both sides begin anew the quest for peace, before the dark powers of destruction unleashed by science engulf all humanity in planned or accidental self-destruction.

We dare not tempt them with weakness. For only when our arms are sufficient beyond doubt can we be certain beyond doubt that they will never be employed.

But neither can two great and powerful groups of nations take comfort from our present course—both sides overburdened by the cost of modern weapons, both rightly alarmed by the steady spread of the deadly atom, yet both racing to alter that uncertain balance of terror that stays the hand of mankind's final war.

So let us begin anew—remembering on both sides that civility is not a sign of weakness, and sincerity is always subject to proof. Let us never negotiate out of fear. But let us never fear to negotiate.

Let both sides explore what problems unite us instead of belaboring those problems which divide us.

Let both sides, for the first time, formulate serious and precise proposals for the inspection and control of arms—and bring the absolute power to destroy other nations under the absolute control of all nations.

Let both sides seek to invoke the wonders of science instead of its terrors. Together let us explore the stars, conquer the deserts, eradicate disease, tap the ocean depths and encourage the arts and commerce.

Let both sides unite to heed in all corners of the earth the command of Isaiah—to "undo the heavy burdens . . . [and] let the oppressed go free."

And if a beach-head of cooperation may push back the jungle of suspicion, let both sides join in creating a new endeavor, not a new balance of power, but a new world of law, where the strong are just and the weak secure and the peace preserved.

All this will not be finished in the first one hundred days. Nor will it be finished in the first one thousand days, nor in the life of this Administration, nor even perhaps in our lifetime on this planet. But let us begin.

In your hands, my fellow citizens, more than mine, will rest the final success or failure of our course. Since this country was founded, each generation of Americans has been summoned to give testimony to its national loyalty. The graves of young Americans who answered the call to service surround the globe.

Now the trumpet summons us again—not as a call to bear arms, though arms we need—not as a call to battle, though embattled we are —but a call to bear the burden of a long twilight struggle, year in and year out, "rejoicing in hope, patient in tribulation"—a struggle against the common enemies of man: tyranny, poverty, disease and war itself.

Can we forge against these enemies a grand global alliance, North and South, East and West, that can assure a more fruitful life for all mankind? Will you join in that historic effort?

In the long history of the world, only a few generations have been granted the role of defending freedom in its hour of maximum danger. I do not shrink from this responsibility—I welcome it. I do not believe that any of us would exchange places with any other people or any other generation. The energy, the faith, the devotion which we bring to this endeavor will light our country and all who serve it—and the glow from that fire can truly light the world.

And so, my fellow Americans: ask not what your country can do for you—ask what you can do for your country.

My fellow citizens of the world: ask not what America will do for you, but what together we can do for the freedom of man.

Finally, whether you are citizens of America or citizens of the world, ask of us here the same high standards of strength and sacrifice which we ask of you. With a good conscience our only sure reward, with history the final judge of our deeds, let us go forth to lead the land we love, asking His blessing and His help, but knowing that here on earth God's work must truly be our own.

The Port Huron Statement

STUDENTS FOR A DEMOCRATIC SOCIETY

The radical tradition in America is a series of episodes, not a continuous story. Where conservatives and liberals never cease reaching back for real or imaginary forbears, radicals have generally insisted on forgetting the history of radicalism as the first act in any new beginning. In the early 1960's, when the Students for a Democratic Society spread from campus to campus, drawing together activists in the civil rights and peace movements, the group received compliments for precisely this tendency to forget the radical past. It was "pragmatic," "non-ideological," and "non-programmatic." The movement worried little about its intellectual underpinnings; its main concern was action. The Port Huron Statement, drawn up at the first SDS convention in 1962, achieved wide circulation on the campuses as an "agenda for a generation."

The document, written principally by Tom Hayden, is impressive in surprising ways. Its tentative assertions, social science language, and generally nationalistic and cooperative stance contrast sharply with the image of campus militancy of the later 1960's. In its quiet way, however, it states the main themes of the youth political movement: rejection of bureaucracy, anti-communism, alienation, and the lack of community. It is clearly the beginning of a quest, not a set of final answers. Where that quest led was one of the fascinating subjects of the decade. It raises the inevitable question—to what extent did the young radicals relive the experience of earlier radicals because they began by rejecting its lessons?

INTRODUCTION: AGENDA FOR A GENERATION

We are people of this generation, bred in at least modest comfort, housed now in universities, looking uncomfortably to the world we inherit.

When we were kids the United States was the wealthiest and strongest country in the world; the only one with the atom bomb, the least scarred by modern war, an initiator of the United Nations that we thought would distribute Western influence throughout the world. Freedom and equality for each individual, government of, by, and for the people—these American values we found good, principles by which we could live as men. Many of us began maturing in complacency.

As we grew, however, our comfort was penetrated by events too troubling to dismiss. First, the permeating and victimizing fact of human degradation, symbolized by the Southern struggle against racial bigotry, compelled most of us from silence to activism. Second, the enclosing fact of the Cold War, symbolized by the presence of the Bomb, brought awareness that we ourselves, and our friends, and millions of abstract "others" we knew more directly because of our common peril, might die at any time. We might deliberately ignore, or avoid, or fail to feel all other human problems, but not these two, for these were too immediate and crushing in their impact, too challenging in the demand that we as individuals take the responsibility for encounter and resolution.

While these and other problems either directly oppressed us or rankled our consciences and became our own subjective concerns, we began to see complicated and disturbing paradoxes in our surrounding America. The declaration "all men are created equal . . ." rang hollow before the facts of Negro life in the South and the big cities of the North. The proclaimed peaceful intentions of the United States contradicted its economic and military investments in the Cold War status quo.

We witnessed, and continue to witness, other paradoxes. With nuclear energy whole cities can easily be powered, yet the dominant nation-states seem more likely to unleash destruction greater than that incurred in all wars of human history. Although our own technology is destroying old and creating new forms of social organization, men still tolerate meaningless work and idleness. While two-thirds of mankind suffers undernourishment, our own upper classes revel amidst superfluous abundance. Although world population is expected to double in forty years, the nations still tolerate anarchy as a major principle of international conduct and uncontrolled exploitation governs the sapping of the earth's physical resources. Although mankind desperately needs revolutionary leadership, America rests in national stalemate, its goals ambiguous and tradition-bound instead of informed and clear, its democratic system apathetic and manipulated rather than "of, by, and for the people."

Not only did tarnish appear on our image of American virtue, not only did disillusion occur when the hypocrisy of American ideals was discovered, but we began to sense that what we had originally seen as the American Golden Age was actually the decline of an era. The worldwide outbreak of revolution against colonialism and imperialism, the entrenchment of totalitarian states, the menace of war, overpopulation, international disorder, supertechnology—these trends were testing the tenacity of our own commitment to democracy and freedom and our abilities to visualize their application to a world in upheaval.

Our work is guided by the sense that we may be the last generation in the experiment with living. But we are a minority—the vast majority of our people regard the temporary equilibriums of our society and world as eternally-functional parts. In this is perhaps the outstanding paradox: we ourselves are imbued with urgency, yet the message of our society is that there is no viable alternative to the present. Beneath the reassuring tones of the politicians, beneath the common opinion that America will "muddle through," beneath the stagnation of those who have closed their minds to the future, is the pervading feeling that there simply are no alternatives, that our times have witnessed the exhaustion not only of Utopias, but of any new departures as well.

Feeling the press of complexity upon the emptiness of life, people are fearful of the thought that at any moment things might be thrust out of control. They fear change itself, since change might smash whatever invisible framework seems to hold back chaos for them now. For most Americans, all crusades are suspect, threatening. The fact that each individual sees apathy in his fellows perpetuates the common reluctance to organize for change. The dominant institutions are complex enough to blunt the minds of their potential critics, and entrenched enough to swiftly dissipate or entirely repel the energies of protest and reform, thus limiting human expectancies. Then, too, we are a materially improved society, and by our own improvements we seem to have weakened the case for further change.

Some would have us believe that Americans feel contentment amidst prosperity—but might it not be better be called a glaze above deeply-felt anxieties about their role in the new world? And if these anxieties produce a developed indifference to human affairs, do they not as well produce a yearning to believe there *is* an alternative to the present, that something *can* be done to change circumstances in the school, the workplaces, the bureaucracies, the government? It is to this latter yearning, at once the spark and engine of change, that we direct our present appeal. The search for truly democratic alternatives to the present, and a commitment to social experimentation with them, is a worthy and fulfilling human enterprise, one which moves us and, we hope, others today. On such a basis do we offer this document of our convictions and analysis: as an effort in understanding and changing the conditions of humanity in the late twentieth century, an effort rooted in the ancient, still unfulfilled conception of man attaining determining influence over his circumstances of life. . . .

THE STUDENTS

In the last few years, thousands of American students demonstrated that they at least felt the urgency of the times. They moved actively and directly against racial injustices, the threat of war, violations of individual rights of conscience and, less frequently, against economic manipulation. They suceeded in restoring a small measure of controversy to the campuses after the stillness of the McCarthy period. They succeeded, too, in gaining some concessions from the people and institutions they opposed, especially in the fight against racial bigotry.

The significance of these scattered movements lies not in their success or failure in gaining objectives—at least not yet. Nor does the significance lie in the intellectual "competence" or "maturity" of the students involved—as some pedantic elders allege. The significance is in the fact the students are breaking the crust of apathy and overcoming the inner alienation that remain the defining characteristics of American college life.

If student movements for change are still rareties on the campus scene, what is commonplace there? The real campus, the familiar campus, is a place of private people, engaged in their notorious "inner emigration." It is a place of commitment to business-as-usual, getting ahead, playing it cool. It is a place of mass affirmation of the Twist, but mass reluctance toward the controversial public stance. Rules are accepted as "inevitable," bureaucracy as "just circumstances," irrelevance as "scholarship," selflessness as "martyrdom," politics as "just another way to make people, and an unprofitable one, too."

Almost no students value activity as citizens. Passive in public, they are hardly more idealistic in arranging their private lives: Gallup concludes they will settle for "low success, and won't risk high failure." There is not much willingness to take risks (not even in business), no settling of dangerous goals, no real conception of personal identity except one manufactured in the image of others, no real urge for personal fulfillment except to be almost as successful as the very successful people. Attention is being paid to social status (the quality of shirt collars, meeting people, getting wives or husbands, making solid contacts for later on); much, too, is paid to academic status (grades, honors, the med school rat race). But neglected generally is real intellectual status, the personal cultivation of the mind.

"Students don't even give a damn about the apathy," one has said. Apathy toward apathy begets a privately-constructed universe, a place of systematic study schedules, two nights each week for beer, a girl or two, and early marriage; a framework infused with personality, warmth, and under control, no matter how unsatisfying otherwise.

Under these conditions university life loses all relevance to some. Four hundred thousand of our classmates leave college every year.

But apathy is not simply an attitude; it is a product of social institutions, and of the structure and organization of higher education itself. The extracurricular life is ordered according to *in loco parentis* theory, which ratifies the Administration as the moral guardian of the young.

The accompanying "let's pretend" theory of student extracurricular affairs validates student government as a training center for those who want to spend their lives in political pretense, and discourages initiative from the more articulate, honest, and sensitive students. The bounds and style of controversy are delimited before controversy begins. The university "prepares" the student for "citizenship" through perpetual rehearsals and, usually, through emasculation of what creative spirit there is in the individual.

The academic life contains reinforcing counterparts to the way in which extracurricular life is organized. The academic world is founded on a teacher-student relation analogous to the parent-child relation which characterizes *in loco parentis*. Further, academia includes a radical separation of the student from the material of study. That which is studied, the social reality, is "objectified" to sterility, dividing the student from life—just as he is restrained in active involvement by the deans controlling student government. The specialization of function and knowledge, admittedly necessary to our complex technological and social structure, has produced an exaggerated compartmentalization of study and understanding. This has contributed to an overly parochial view, by faculty, of the role of its research and scholarship, to a discontinuous and truncated understanding, by students, of the surrounding social order; and to a loss of personal attachment, by nearly all, to the worth of study as a humanistic enterprise.

There is, finally, the cumbersome academic bureaucracy extending throughout the academic as well as the extracurricular structures, contributing to the sense of outer complexity and inner powerlessness that transforms the honest searching of many students to a ratification of convention and, worse, to a numbness to present and future catastrophes. The size and financing systems of the university enhance the permanent trusteeship of the administrative bureaucracy, their power leading to a shift within the university toward the value standards of business and the administrative mentality. Huge foundations and other private financial interests shape the under-financed colleges and universities, not only making them more commercial, but less disposed to diagnose society critically, less open to dissent. Many social and physical scientists, neglecting the liberating heritage of higher learning, develop "human relations" or "morale-producing" techniques for the corporate economy, while others exercise their intellectual skills to accelerate the arms race.

Tragically, the university could serve as a significant source of social criticism and an initiator of new modes and molders of attitudes. But the actual intellectual effect of the college experience is hardly distinguishable from that of any other communications channel—say, a television set—passing on the stock truths of the day. Students leave college somewhat more "tolerant" than when they arrived, but basically unchallenged in their values and political orientations. With administrators ordering the institution, and faculty the curriculum, the student learns by his isolation to accept elite rule within the university, which prepares him to accept later forms of minority control. The real function of the educational system—as opposed to its more rhetorical function of "searching for truth"—is to impart the key information and styles that will help the student get by, modestly but comfortably, in the big society beyond.

THE SOCIETY BEYOND

Look beyond the campus, to America itself. That student life is more intellectual, and perhaps more comfortable, does not obscure the fact that the fundamental qualities of life on the campus reflect the habits of society at large. The fraternity president is seen at the junior manager levels; the sorority queen has gone to Grosse Pointe; the serious poet burns for a place, any place, to work; the once-serious and never-serious poets work at the advertising agencies. The desperation of people threatened by forces about which they know little and of which they can say less; the cheerful emptiness of people "giving up" all hope of changing things; the faceless ones polled by Gallup who listed "international affairs" fourteenth on their list of "problems" but who also expected thermonuclear war in the next few years; in these and other forms, Americans are in withdrawal from public life, from any collective effort at directing their own affairs.

Some regard these national doldrums as a sign of healthy approval of the established order—but is it approval by consent or manipulated acquiescence? Others declare that the people are withdrawn because compelling issues are fast disappearing—perhaps there are fewer bread-lines in America, but is Jim Crow gone, is there enough work and work more fulfilling, is world war a diminishing threat, and what of the revolutionary new peoples? Still others think the national quietude is a necessary consequence of the need for elites to resolve complex and specialized problems of modern industrial society—but, then, why should *business* elites help decide foreign policy, and who controls the elites anyway, and are they solving mankind's problems? Others, finally, shrug knowingly and announce that full democracy never worked anywhere in the past—but why lump qualitatively different civilizations together, and how can a social order work well if its best thinkers are skeptics, and is man really doomed forever to the domination of today?

There are no convincing apologies for the contemporary malaise. While the world tumbles toward final war, while men in other nations are trying desperately to alter events, while the very future qua future is uncertain—America is without community, impulse, without the inner momentum necessary for an age when societies cannot successfully perpetuate themselves by their military weapons, when democracy must be viable because of the quality of life, not its quantity of rockets.

The apathy here is, first *subjective*—the felt powerlessness of ordinary people, the resignation before the enormity of events. But subjective apathy is encouraged by the *objective* American situation—the actual structural separation of people from power, from relevant knowledge, from pinnacles of decision-making. Just as the university influences the student way of life, so do major social institutions create the circumstances in which the isolated citizen will try hopelessly to understand his world and himself.

The very isolation of the individual—from power and community and ability to aspire—means the rise of a democracy without publics. With the great mass of people structurally remote and psychologically hesitant with respect to democratic institutions, those institutions themselves attenuate and become, in the fashion of the vicious circle, progressively less accessible to those few who aspire to serious participation in social affairs. The vital democratic connection between community and leadership, between the mass and the several elites, has been so wrenched and perverted that disastrous policies go unchallenged time and again.

POLITICS WITHOUT PUBLICS

The American political system is not the democratic model of which its glorifiers speak. In actuality it frustrates democracy by confusing the individual citizen, paralyzing policy discussion, and consolidating the irresponsible power of military and business interests.

A crucial feature of the political apparatus in America is that greater differences are harbored within each major party than the differences existing between them. Instead of two parties presenting distinctive and significant differences of approach, what dominates the system is a natural interlocking of Democrats from Southern states with the more conservative elements of the Republican party. This arrangement of forces is blessed by the seniority system of Congress which guarantees congressional committee domination by conservatives—ten of 17 committees in the Senate and 13 of 21 in the House of Representatives are chaired currently by Dixiecrats.

The party overlap, however, is not the only structural antagonist of democracy in politics. First, the localized nature of the party system does not encourage discussion of national and international issues: thus problems are not raised by and for people, and political representatives usually are unfettered from any responsibilities to the general public except those regarding parochial matters. Second, whole constituencies are divested of the full political power they might have: many Negroes in the South are prevented from voting, migrant workers are disenfranchised by various residence requirements, some urban and suburban dwellers are victimized by gerrymandering, and poor people are too often without the power to obtain political representation. Third, the focus of political attention is significantly distorted by the enormous lobby force, composed predominantly of business interests, spending hundreds of millions each year in an attempt to conform facts about productivity, agriculture, defense, and social services, to the wants of private economic groupings.

What emerges from the party contradiction and insulation of privately-held power is the organized political stalemate: calcification dominates flexibility as the principle of parliamentary organization, frustration is the expectancy of legislators intending liberal reform, and Congress becomes less and less central to national decision-making especially in the area of foreign policy. In this context, confusion and blurring is built into the formulation of issues, long-range priorities are not discussed in the rational manner needed for policy-making, the politics of personality and "image" become a more important mechanism than the construction of issues in a way that affords each voter a challenging and real option. The American voter is buffeted from all directions by pseudo-problems, by the structurally-initiated sense that nothing political is subject to human mastery. Worried by his mundane problems which never get solved, but constrained by the common belief that politics is an agonizingly slow accommodation of views, he quits all pretense of bothering.

A most alarming fact is that few, if any, politicians are calling for changes in these conditions. Only a handful even are calling on the President to "live up to" platform pledges; no one is demanding structural changes, such as the shuttling of Southern Democrats out of the Democratic Party. Rather than protesting the state of politics, most politicians are reinforcing and aggravating that state. While in practice they rig public opinion to suit their own interests, in word and ritual they enshrine "the sovereign public" and call for more and more letters. Their speeches and campaign actions are banal, based on a degrading conception of what people want to hear. They respond not to dialogue, but to pressure: and knowing this, the ordinary citizen sees even greater inclination to shun the political sphere. The politician is usually a trumpeter to "citizenship" and "service to the nation," but since he is unwilling to seriously rearrange power relationships, his trumpetings only increase apathy by creating no outlets. Much of the time the call to "service" is justified not in idealistic terms, but in the crasser terms of "defending the free world from communism"—thus making future idealistic impulses harder to justify in anything but Cold War terms.

In such a setting of status quo politics, where most if not all government activity is rationalized in Cold War anti-communist terms, it is somewhat natural that discontented, super-patriotic groups would emerge through political channels and explain their ultra-conservatism as the best means of Victory over Communism. They have become a politically influential force within the Republican Party, at a national level through Senator Goldwater, and at a local level through their important social and economic roles. Their political views are defined generally as the opposite of the supposed views of communists: complete individual freedom in the economic sphere, non-participation by the government in the machinery of production. But actually "anti-communism" becomes an umbrella by which to protest liberalism, internationalism, welfareism, the active civil rights and labor movements. It is to the disgrace of the United States that such a movement should become a prominent kind of public participation in the modern world—but, ironically, it is somewhat to the interests of the United States that such a movement should be a public constituency pointed toward realignment of the political parties, demanding a conservative Republican Party in the South and an exclusion of the "leftist" elements of the national GOP.

THE ECONOMY

American capitalism today advertises itself as the Welfare State. Many of us comfortably expect pensions, medical care, unemployment compensation, and other social services in our lifetimes. Even with one-fourth of our productive capacity unused, the majority of Americans are living in relative comfort—although their nagging incentive to "keep up" makes them continually dissatisfied with their possessions. In many places, unrestrained bosses, uncontrolled machines, and sweatshop conditions have been reformed or abolished and suffering tremendously relieved. But in spite of the benign yet obscuring effects of the New Deal reforms and the reassuring phrases of government economists and politicians, the paradoxes and myths of the economy are sufficient to irritate our complacency and reveal to us some essential causes of the American malaise.

We live amidst a national celebration of economic prosperity while poverty and deprivation remain an unbreakable way of life for millions in the "affluent society," including many of our own generation. We hear glib references to the "welfare state," "free enterprise," and "shareholder's democracy" while military defense is the main item of "public" spending and obvious oligopoly and other forms of minority rule defy real individual initiative or popular control. Work, too, is often unfulfilling and victimizing, accepted as a channel to status or plenty, if not a way to pay the bills, rarely as a means of understanding and controlling self and events. In work and leisure the individual is regulated as part of the system, a consuming unit, bombarded by hard-sell, soft-sell, lies and semi-true appeals to his basest drives. He is always told that he is a "free" man because of "free enterprise." . . .

THE MILITARY-INDUSTRIAL COMPLEX

The most spectacular and important creation of the authoritarian and oligopolistic structure of economic decision-making in America is the institution called "the military-industrial complex" by former President Eisenhower—the powerful congruence of interest and structure among military and business elites which affects so much of our development and destiny. Not only is ours the first generation to live with the possibility of world-wide cataclysm—it is the first to experience the actual social preparation for cataclysm, the general militarization of American society. In 1948 Congress established Universal Military Training, the first peacetime conscription. The military became a permanent institution. Four years earlier, General Motors' Charles E. Wilson had heralded the creation of what he called the "permanent war economy," the continuous use of military spending as a solution to economic problems unsolved before the post-war boom, most notably the problem of the seventeen million jobless after eight years of the New Deal. This has left a "hidden crisis" in the allocation of resources by the American economy.

Since our childhood these two trends—the rise of the military and the installation of a defense-based economy—have grown fantastically. The Department of Defense, ironically the world's largest single organization, is worth $160 billion, owns 32 million acres of America and employs half the 7.5 million persons directly dependent on the military for subsistence, has an $11 billion payroll which is larger than the net annual income of all American corporations. Defense spending in the Eisenhower era totaled $350 billions and President Kennedy entered office pledged to go even beyond the present defense allocation of 60 cents from every public dollar spent. Except for a war-induced boom immediately after "our side" bombed Hiroshima, American economic prosperity has coincided with a growing dependence on military outlay—from 1941 to 1959 America's Gross National Product of $5.25 trillion included $700 billion in goods and services purchased for the defense effort, about one-seventh of the accumulated GNP. This pattern has included the steady concentration of military spending among a few corporations. In 1961, 86 percent of Defense Department contracts were awarded without competition. The ordnance industry of 100,000 people is completely engaged in military work; in the aircraft industry, 94 percent of 750,000 workers are linked to the war economy; shipbuilding, radio and communications equipment industries commit 40 percent of their work to defense; iron and steel, petroleum, metal-stamping and machine shop products, motors and generators, tools and hardware, copper, aluminum and machine tools industries all devote at least 10 percent of their work to the same cause.

The intermingling of Big Military and Big Industry is evidenced in the 1,400 former officers working for the 100 corporations who received nearly all the $21 billion spent in procurement by the Defense Department in 1961. The overlap is most poignantly clear in the case of General Dynamics, the company which received the best 1961 contracts, employed the most retired officers (187), and is directed by a former Secretary of the Army. A *Fortune* magazine profile of General Dynamics said: "The unique group of men who run Dynamics are only incidentally in rivalry with other U.S. manufacturers, with many of whom they actually act in concert. Their chief competitor is the USSR. The core of General Dynamics' corporate philosophy is the conviction that national defense is a more or less permanent business." Little has changed since Wilson's proud declaration of the Permanent War Economy back in the 1944 days when the top 200 corporations possessed 80 percent of all active prime war-supply contracts.

MILITARY-INDUSTRIAL POLITICS

The military and its supporting business foundation have found numerous forms of political expression, and we have heard their din endlessly. There has not been a major Congressional split on the issue of continued defense spending spirals in our lifetime. The triangular relations of the business, military, and political arenas cannot be better expressed than in Dixiecrat Carl Vinson's remarks as his House Armed Services Committee reported out a military construction bill of $808 million throughout the 50 states, for 1960-61: "There is something in this bill for everyone," he announced. President Kennedy had earlier acknowledged the valuable anti-recession features of the bill.

Imagine, on the other hand, $808 million suggested as an anti-recession measure, but being poured into programs of social welfare: the impossibility of receiving support for such a measure identifies a crucial feature of defense spending—it is beneficial to private enterprise, while welfare spending is not. Defense spending does not "compete" with the private sector; it contains a natural obsolescence; its "confidential" nature permits easier boondoggling; the tax burdens to which it leads can be shunted from corporation to consumer as a "cost of production." Welfare spending, however, involves the government in competition with private corporations and contractors; it conflicts with immediate interests of private pressure groups; it leads to taxes on business. Think of the opposition of private power companies to current proposals for river and valley development, or the hostility of the real estate lobby to urban renewal; or the attitude of the American Medical

Association to a paltry medical care bill; or of all business lobbyists to foreign aid; these are the pressures leading to the schizophrenic public-military, private-civilian economy of our epoch. The politicians, of course, take the line of least resistance and thickest support: warfare, instead of welfare, is easiest to stand up for: after all, the Free World is at stake (and our constituency's investments, too). . . .

THE STANCE OF LABOR

Amidst all this, what of organized labor, the historic institutional representative of the exploited, the presumed "countervailing power" against the excesses of Big Business? The contemporary social assault on the labor movement is of crisis proportions. To the average American, "big labor" is a growing cancer equal in impact to Big Business—nothing could be more distorted, even granting a sizeable union bureaucracy. But in addition to public exaggerations, the labor crisis can be measured in several ways. First, the high expectations of the newborn AFL-CIO of 30 million members by 1965 are suffering a reverse unimaginable five years ago. The demise of the dream of "organizing the unorganized" is dramatically reflected in the AFL-CIO decision, just two years after its creation, to slash its organizing staff in half. From 15 million members when the AFL and CIO merged, the total has slipped to 13.5 million. During the post-war generation, union membership nationally has increased by four million—but the total number of workers has jumped by 13 million. Today only 40 percent of all non-agricultural workers are protected by any form of organization. Second, organizing conditions are going to worsen. Where labor now is strongest—in industries—automation is leading to an attrition of available work. As the number of jobs dwindles, so does labor's power of bargaining, since management can handle a strike in an automated plant more easily than the older mass-operated ones.

More important, perhaps, the American economy has changed radically in the last decade, as suddenly the number of workers producing goods became fewer than the number in "nonproductive" areas— government, trade, finance, services, utilities, transportation. Since World War II "white collar" and "service" jobs have grown twice as fast as have "blue collar" production jobs. Labor has almost no organization in the expanding occupational areas of the new economy, but almost all of its entrenched strength in contracting areas. As big government hires more, as business seeks more office workers and skilled technicians, and as growing commercial America demands new hotels, service stations and the like, the conditions will become graver still. Further, there is continuing hostility to labor by the Southern states and their industrial interests—meaning "runaway" plants, cheap labor threatening the organized trade union movement, and opposition from Dixiecrats to favorable labor legislation in Congress. Finally, there is indication that Big Business, for the sake of public relations if nothing more, has acknowledged labor's "right" to exist, but has deliberately tried to contain labor at its present strength, preventing strong unions from helping weaker ones or from spreading to unorganized sectors of the economy. Business is aided in its efforts by proliferation of "right-to-work" laws at state levels (especially in areas where labor is without organizing strength to begin with), and anti-labor legislation in Congress.

In the midst of these besetting crises, labor itself faces its own problems of vision and program. Historically, there can be no doubt as to its worth in American politics—what progress there has been in meeting human needs in this century rests greatly with the labor movement. And to a considerable extent the social democracy for which labor has fought externally is reflected in its own essentially democratic character: representing millions of people, not millions of dollars; demanding their welfare, not eternal profit.

Today labor remains the most liberal "mainstream" institution— but often its liberalism represents vestigial commitments, self-interestedness, unradicalism. In some measure labor has succumbed to institutionalization, its social idealism waning under the tendencies of bureaucracy, materialism, business ethics. The successes of the last generation perhaps have braked, rather than accelerated labor's zeal for change. Even the House of Labor has bay windows: not only is this true of the labor elites, but as well of some of the rank-and-file. Many of the latter are indifferent unionists, uninterested in meetings, alienated from the complexities of the labor-management negotiating apparatus, lulled to comfort by the accessibility of luxury and the opportunity of long-term contracts. "Union democracy" is not simply inhibited by labor-leader elitism, but by the related problem of rank-and-file apathy to the tradition of unionism. The crisis of labor is reflected in the co-existence within the unions of militant Negro discontents and discriminatory locals, sweeping critics of the obscuring "public interest" marginal tinkering of government and willing handmaidens of conservative political leadership, austere sacrificers and business-like operators, visionaries and anachronisms—tensions between extremes that keep alive the possibilities for a more militant unionism. Too there are seeds of rebirth in the "organizational crisis" itself: the technologically unemployed, the unorganized white collar men and women, the migrants and farm workers, the unprotected Negroes, the poor, all of whom are isolated now from the power structure of the economy, but who are the potential base for a broader and more forceful unionism.

HORIZON

In summary: a more reformed, more human capitalism, functioning at three-fourths capacity while one-third of America and two-thirds of the world goes needy, domination of politics and the economy by fantastically rich elites, accommodation and limited effectiveness by the labor movement, hard-core poverty and unemployment, automation confirming the dark ascension of machine over man instead of shared abundance, technological change being introduced into the economy by the criteria of profitability—this has been our inheritance. However inadequate, it has instilled quiescence in liberal hearts—partly reflecting the extent to which misery has been overcome, but also the eclipse of social ideals. Though many of us are "affluent," poverty, waste, elitism, manipulation are too manifest to go unnoticed, too clearly unnecessary to go accepted. To change the Cold War status quo and other social evils, concern with the challenges to the American economic machine must expand. Now, as a truly better social state becomes visible, a new poverty impends: a poverty of vision, and a poverty of political action to make that vision reality. Without new vision, the failure to achieve our potentialities will spell the inability of our society to endure in a world of obvious, crying needs and rapid change. . . .

TOWARDS AMERICAN DEMOCRACY

Every effort to end the Cold War and expand the process of world industrialization is an effort hostile to people and institutions whose interests lie in perpetuation of the East-West military threat and the postponement of change in the "have not" nations of the world. Every such effort, too, is bound to establish greater democracy in America. The major goals of a domestic effort would be:

1 *America must abolish its political party stalemate.*

Two genuine parties, centered around issues and essential values, demanding allegiance to party principles shall supplant the current system of organized stalemate which is seriously inadequate to a world in flux. . . . What is desirable is sufficient party disagreement to drama- tize major issues, yet sufficient party overlap to guarantee stable transi- tions from administration to administration.

Every time the President criticizes a recalcitrant Congress, we must ask that he no longer tolerate the Southern conservatives in the Demo- cratic Party. Every time a liberal representative complains that "we can't expect everything at once" we must ask if we received much of anything from Congress in the last generation. Every time he refers to "circumstances beyond control" we must ask why he fraternizes with racist scoundrels. Every time he speaks of the "unpleasantness of personal and party fighting" we should insist that pleasantry with Dixiecrats is inexcusable when the dark peoples of the world call for American support.

2 *Mechanisms of voluntary association must be created through which political information can be imparted and political participation encouraged.*

Political parties, even if realigned, would not provide adequate out- lets for popular involvement. Institutions should be created that engage people with issues and express political preference, not as now with huge business lobbies which exercise undemocratic *power* but which carry political *influence* (appropriate to private, rather than public, group- ings) in national decision-making enterprise. Private in nature, these should be organized around single issues (medical care, transportation systems reform, etc.), concrete interest (labor and minority group organizations); multiple issues or general issues. These do not exist in America in quantity today. If they did exist, they would be a significant politicizing and educative force bringing people into touch with public life and affording them means of expression and action. Today, giant lobby representatives of business interests are dominant, but not educative. The Federal government itself should counter the latter forces whose intent is often public deceit for private gain, by subsidizing the preparation and decentralized distribution of objective materials on all public issues facing government.

3 *Institutions and practices which stifle dissent should be abolished, and the promotion of peaceful dissent should be actively promoted.*

The First Amendment freedoms of speech, assembly, thought, religion and press should be seen as guarantees, not threats, to national security. While society has the right to prevent active subversion of its laws and institutions, it has the duty as well to promote open discussion of all issues—otherwise it will be in fact promoting real subversion as the only means of implementing ideas. To eliminate the fears and apathy from national life it is necessary that the institutions bred by fear and apathy be rooted out: the House Un-American Activities Committee, the Senate Internal Security Committee, the loyalty oaths on Federal loans, the Attorney General's list of subversive organizations, the Smith and McCarran Acts. The process of eliminating the blighting institutions is the process of restoring democratic participation. Their existence is a sign of the decomposition and atrophy of participation.

4 *Corporations must be made publicly responsible.*

It is not possible to believe that true democracy can exist where a minority utterly controls enormous wealth and power. The influence of corporate elites on foreign policy is neither reliable nor democratic; a way must be found to subordinate private American foreign investment to a democratically-constructed foreign policy. . . .

Labor and government as presently constituted are not sufficient to "regulate" corporations. A new re-ordering, a new calling of responsibility is necessary: more than changing "work rules" we must consider changes in the rules of society by challenging the unchallenged politics of American corporations. Before the government can really begin to control business in a "public interest," the public must gain more substantial control of government: this demands a movement for political as well as economic realignments. We are aware that simple government "regulation," if achieved, would be inadequate without increased worker participation in management decision-making, strengthened and independent regulatory power, balances of partial and/or complete public ownership, various means of humanizing the conditions and types of work itself, sweeping welfare programs and regional *public* development authorities. These are examples of measures to re-balance the economy toward public—and individual—control.

5 *The allocation of resources must be based on social needs. A truly "public sector" must be established, and its nature debated and planned.*

At present the majority of America's "public sector," the largest part of our public spending, is for the military. When great social needs are so pressing, our concept of "government spending" is wrapped up in the "permanent war economy." . . .

The main *private* forces of economic expansion cannot guarantee a steady rate of growth, nor acceptable recovery from recession—especially in a demilitarizing world. Government participation will inevitably expand enormously, because the stable growth of the economy demands increasing "public" investments yearly. Our present outpour of more than $500 billion might double in a generation, irreversibly involving government solutions. And in future recessions, the compensatory fiscal action by the government will be the only means of avoiding the twin disasters of greater unemployment and a slackening rate of growth. Furthermore, a close relationship with the European Common Market will involve competition with numerous planned economies and may aggravate American unemployment unless the economy here is expanding swiftly enough to create new jobs.

All these tendencies suggest that not only solutions to our present social needs but our future expansion rests upon our willingness to enlarge the "public sector" greatly. Unless we choose war as an economic solvent, future public spending will be of non-military nature— a major intervention into civilian production by the government. . . .

6 *America should concentrate on its genuine social priorities: abolish squalor, terminate neglect, and establish an environment for people to live in with dignity and creativeness.*

A. A program against *poverty* must be just as sweeping as the nature of poverty itself. It must not be just palliative, but directed to the abolition of the structural circumstances of poverty. At a bare minimum it should include a *housing* act far larger than the one supported by the Kennedy Administration, but one that is geared more to low- and middle-income needs than to the windfall aspirations of small and large private entrepreneurs, one that is more sympathetic to the quality of communal life than to the efficiency of city-split highways. Second, *medical care* must become recognized as a lifetime human right just as vital as food, shelter and clothing—the Federal government should guarantee health insurance as a basic social service turning medical treatment into a social habit, not just an occasion of crisis, fighting sickness among the aged, not just by making medical care financially feasible but by reducing sickness among children and younger people. Third, existing institutions should be expanded so the Welfare State cares for *everyone's* welfare according to need. *Social Security* payments should be extended to everyone and should be proportionately greater for the poorest. A *minimum wage* of at least $1.50 should be extended to all workers (including the 16 million currently not covered at all). Programs for equal *educational opportunity* are as important a part of the battle against poverty.

B. A full-scale public initiative for civil rights should be undertaken despite the clamor among conservatives (and liberals) about gradualism, property rights, and law and order. The executive and legislative branches of the Federal government should work by enforcement *and* enactment against any form of exploitation of minority groups. No Federal cooperation with racism is tolerable—from financing of schools, to the development of Federally-supported industry, to the social gatherings of the President. Laws hastening school desegregation, voting rights, and economic protection for Negroes are needed right now. The moral force of the Executive Office should be exerted against the Dixiecrats specifically, and the national complacency about the race question generally. Especially in the North, where one-half of the country's Negro people now live, civil rights is not a problem to be solved in isolation from other problems. The fight against poverty, against slums, against the stalemated Congress, against McCarthyism, are all fights against the discrimination that is nearly endemic to all areas of American life.

C. The promise and problems of long-range *Federal economic development* should be studied more constructively. It is an embarrassing paradox that the Tennessee Valley Authority is a wonder to most foreign visitors but a "radical" and barely influential project to most Americans. The Kennedy decision to permit private facilities to transmit power from the $1 billion Colorado River Storage Project is a disastrous one, interposing privately-owned transmitters between publicly-owned generators and their publicly (and cooperatively) owned distributors. The contrary trend, to public ownership of power, should be generated in an experimental way.

The Area Redevelopment Act of 1961 is a first step in recognizing the underdeveloped areas of the United States. It is only a drop in the bucket financially and is not keyed to public planning and public works on a broad scale. It consists only of a few loan programs to lure industries and some grants to improve public facilities to lure these industries. The current public works bill in Congress is needed—and a more sweeping, higher-priced program of regional development with a proliferation of "TVAs" in such areas as the Appalachian region are needed desperately. However, it has been rejected already by Mississippi because the improvement it bodes for the unskilled Negro worker. This program should be enlarged, given teeth, and pursued rigorously by Federal authorities.

D. We must meet the growing complex of "city" problems; over 90 percent of Americans will live in urban areas within two decades. Juvenile delinquency, untended mental illness, crime increase, slums, urban tenantry and non-rent controlled housing, the isolation of the individual in the city—all are problems of the city and are major symptoms of the present system of economic priorities and lack of public planning. Private property control (the real estate lobby and a few selfish landowners and businesses) is as devastating in the cities as corporations are on the national level. But there is no comprehensive way to deal with these problems now amidst competing units of government, dwindling tax resources, suburban escapism (saprophitic to the sick central cities), high infrastructure costs and no one to pay them.

The only solutions are national and regional. "Federalism" has thus far failed here because states are rural-dominated; the Federal government has had to operate by bootlegging and trickle-down measures dominated by private interests, with their appendages through annexation or federation. A new external challenge is needed, not just a Department of Urban Affairs but a thorough national *program* to help the cities. The *model* city must be projected—more community decision-making and participation, true integration of classes, races, vocations—provision for beauty, access to nature and the benefits of the central city as well, privacy without privatism, decentralized "units" spread horizontally with central, regional democratic control—provision for the basic facility-needs, for everyone, with units of planned *regions* and thus public, democratic control over the growth of the civic community and the allocation of resources.

E. *Mental health institutions* are in dire need; there were fewer mental hospital beds in relation to the numbers of mentally-ill in 1959 than there were in 1948. Public hospitals, too, are seriously wanting; existing structures alone need an estimated $1 billion for rehabilitation. Tremendous staff and faculty needs exist as well, and there are not enough medical students enrolled today to meet the anticipated needs of the future.

F. Our *prisons* are too often the enforcers of misery. They must be either re-oriented to rehabilitative work through public supervision or be abolished for their dehumanizing social effects. Funds are needed, too, to make possible a decent prison environment.

G. *Education* is too vital a public problem to be completely entrusted to the province of the various states and local units. In fact, there is no good reason why America should not progress now toward internationalizing rather than localizing, its education system—children and young adults studying everywhere in the world, through a United Nations program, would go far to create mutual understanding. In the meantime, the need for teachers and classrooms in America is fantastic. This is an area where "minimal" requirements should hardly be considered as a goal—there always are improvements to be made in the education system, e.g., smaller classes and many more teachers for them, programs to subsidize the education for the poor but bright, etc.

H. America should eliminate *agricultural policies* based on scarcity and pent-up surplus. In America and foreign countries there exist tremendous needs for more food and balanced diets. The Federal government should finance small farmers' cooperatives, strengthen programs of rural electrification, and expand policies for the distribution of agricultural surpluses throughout the world (by Food-for-Peace and related

UN programming). Marginal farmers must be helped to either become productive enough to survive "industrialized agriculture" or given help in making the transition out of agriculture—the current Rural Area Development program must be better coordinated with a massive national "area redevelopment" program.

I. *Science* should be employed to constructively transform the conditions of life throughout the United States and the world. Yet at the present time the Department of Health, Education, and Welfare and the National Science Foundation together spend only $300 million annually for scientific purposes in contrast to the $6 billion spent by the Defense Department and the Atomic Energy Commission. One-half of all research and development in America is directly devoted to military purposes. Two imbalances must be corrected—that of military over non-military investigation, and that of biological-natural-physical science over the sciences of human behavior. Our political system must then include planning for the human use of science: by anticipating the political consequences of scientific innovation, by directing the discovery and exploration of space, by adapting science to improved production of food, to international communications systems, to technical problems of disarmament, and so on. For the newly-developing nations, American science should focus on the study of cheap sources of power, housing and building materials, mass educational techniques, etc. Further, science and scholarship should be seen less as an apparatus of conflicting power blocs, but as a bridge toward supra-national community: the International Geophysical Year is a model for continuous further cooperation between the science communities of all nations.

The Civil Rights Movement

ROBERT D. MARCUS

The decade of the 1960s was a great age for dreams, for a sense of the possibilities of life. Rarely has the American belief in progress been so converted to an almost tangible presence—something to touch and feel, to grasp at and possess. At the core of this sense of progress was a millennial vision arising from deep within American religious history: the belief in the achievement of a holy commonwealth, a Kingdom of God on earth, in the United States, and—especially—here and now.

In the 1950s and 1960s no other man in public life so clearly enunciated this millennial vision as did Martin Luther King, Jr., in the civil rights movement. His famous speech "I Have a Dream," delivered at the Lincoln Memorial in August 1963 before a crowd of over a quarter of a million people, announced the theme that was to provoke more and more of these vast, peaceful meetings in imitation of this first great, stately gathering. This vision foresaw a suddenly achieved community of love. The march with its amiable mixing of races, its peacefulness, its grandeur, and its noble spirit momentarily symbolized the world that mundane activities in meeting rooms, on dusty roads, or in voter registration lines are supposed to achieve. Here was integration, the just society, a momentary glimpse of the Kingdom. Later gatherings—whether of flower children, veterans against the war, or supporters of the Nixon administration—seemed to seek the same symbolic grace and the same assembly of communicants, although they rarely achieved King's perfection in expressing these emotions.

The movement for Negro civil rights in the year spanning the Montgomery bus boycott of 1955 and the passage of civil rights legislation in 1964–1966 meshed with the flourishing of two main traditions in American culture: secular liberalism and religious activism. The movement provided an object for liberal solicitude, a moral edge to liberal emotions, and a justification for liberal power that fitted the traditional image of moral custodianship, free from the many ambivalences that would come to torment liberalism later in the decade. The movement under Martin Luther King, Jr., and his young followers was exactly fitted to command the imagination of liberalism. It was formal in a curious and gracious way, waging revolution in the cause of the law, and executing with restraint and precision its limited acts of civil disobedience. In its abjurations of hatred it seemed almost obsessively watchful over the quality of its feelings. And it was, so it appeared at instants, a community of grace, with powerful appeal to the central tendency of American religious history, the search for the Kingdom of God on earth. It renewed the liberal tendencies in American religion, providing the first important social content to the churches after their great numerical expansion in the preceding years.

The civil rights movement was both powerful and fragile. It had behind it the force of law and the potential power of the federal government. Beyond that it had peculiar moral strength resting on a rare combination of circumstances. Part of this force came from its unique opportunity at once to violate local ordinance and to uphold the national law. There is a special Christian symbolism in peaceful disobedience, though it is a symbolism in precarious antinomian relation to Christian orthodoxy. It can mean not only martyrdom, but also the witness of love against statute, of the New Testament against the rules of the Pharisees. And since, on the other hand, the laws against which civil disobedience was directed had been declared or were presumed to be unconstitutional, and some of the private discriminatory practices were outlawed by federal statute, the activists were nearly free of the moral ambivalence inherent in the conscientious violation of law. The goals that civil disobedience pursued, moreover, had a dual appeal. They were simple and understandable: it was easy to identify with the desire for a meal at a lunch counter, a seat on a bus, a swim at a pool, the use of a library. Rarely in modern times has the ordinary had such dignity conferred upon it. And the goals were capable of instantaneous accomplishment. In a moment a lunch counter can be integrated, or a Negro seated at the front of a bus. The activists could do more than compel this kind of integration—in a very simple act of entering or sitting down, they could make it a fact. By its immediacy and clarity, integration of this sort implied the Christian drama of conversion; King urged that a man could throw off, in an instant, his racist past. A society at work training its poor for jobs, arranging for a better distribution of its people, or mixing and improving its schools—all goals of the movement—is engaging in the lengthy plodding tasks of moral common sense; but in the small gesture of stepping across an invisible line, a society might give outward sign of its regeneration.

For decades white liberals had provided money and personnel for civil rights organizations—the National Association for the Advancement of Colored People, founded in 1909, and later the Urban League and the Congress of Racial Equality (CORE). Integration would provide exactly the kind of social circumstances liberals could believe in, for it was their own: good education and an entrance into the salariat, the professions, and the government. White lawyers had fought alongside black in a series of court contests over segregation that culminated in the great Supreme Court decision of 1954 in *Brown* v. *Board of Education,* which declared segregated public schooling to be unconstitutional. The direct actionist movement that gained its first national attention with the Montgomery bus boycott of 1955 therefore compelled a response from liberalism.

The relation of liberalism to the movement was to be ambivalent. The young liberals who directly participated, and in their participation passed to the left of conventional politics, were perhaps clearest among the white youths as to what they were doing; their main confusion would come with the arrival of black nationalism. But as the incidence of disorder increased, there were others who looked on hopefully and wistfully, who worried over the excesses and mistakes. Their cautious regard for procedures and their fears over political consequences strained the patience of the activists. Or the estrangement came indirectly: rights workers simply entered upon a new experience and acquired a style that was outside the terms in which other Americans lived.

In February 1960 the movement turned into a major revolt when four black students from the North Carolina Agricultural and Technical College in Greensboro sat in at the local Woolworth's segregated lunch counter. The men who began the "second American Revolution" were even younger than the youthful revolutionaries of 1773. Ezell Blair, Jr., David Richmond, Franklin McCain, and Joseph McNeill were all freshmen, seventeen- and eighteen-year-olds, when they requested their cups of coffee on the afternoon of February 1. Their return the next day with sixteen fellow students brought national wire service attention. On the third day, they were fifty strong and they had been joined by a few white girls, students from the Women's College. On Friday the movement started to spread, to other stores and then to other cities.

The effect was electric. In an estimated 130 localities, whites, mostly students, demonstrated in support. Such major figures of the civil rights movement as Bob Moses, Julian Bond, James Forman, and John Lewis suddenly discovered their vocation in that exciting February; many other young people abandoned the passivity of the 1950s for a purposeful existence. The Congress of Racial Equality, organized and until 1961 led by whites, leapt into the movement, offering years of experience with nonviolent techniques of direct action, which the students readily took up.

The older civil rights groups and liberal forces rapidly followed, some enthusiastically, some with hesitancy over the tactic of direct action. The NAACP Legal Defense Fund proved to be the mainstay of the student movement, clearing at enormous expense and exertion the legal problems that the tactics were designed to create. In fact, the NAACP, later ritually denounced by the militants as an Uncle Tom organization, engaged extensively in direct action itself while continuing its more traditional work in litigation and lobbying. The Urban League, long the most conservative of the major civil rights organizations, became far more outspoken and powerful under its new leader, Whitney Young, Jr. And Martin Luther King, Jr., who could claim authorship of the student movement, rose to preeminence in the civil rights revolution. His Southern Christian Leadership Conference (SCLC) flourished, and he presided at the forming of the Student Nonviolent Coordinating Committee (SNCC), destined to be the strong left arm of the revolution for the next several years. Outside the movement, white liberal politicians as well as the directors of major foundations hastened to catch up with the advance guard.

None of this ought to be surprising. The students had set off a

competition for leadership and for credits that is entirely understandable. In such circumstances, militancy itself is an advantage,
just as in quieter ages consistency and patience are the assets. As
expectations grow, whatever promises the most immediate results wins
support. And the sit-ins did gain immediate results. These few years
bubbled with illusion, but won massive accomplishment as well. Moral
power did seem capable of overcoming evil. Genuine social progress did
result, and the sense of identity among all the groups engaged in the
struggle was strengthened in positive ways, for the blacks most of all,
but also for their student allies, the liberal wing of the Democratic
party, and the white churches.

What made these times so heady, so prolific of dangers and opportunities, was that this was one of the unusual moments when
initiative could actually come upwards, from the ranks to the established leadership. "We don't need the adults," one of the youths at
the NAACP convention in 1961 announced, "but they need us." The
older leaders had talked courageously about integration and made
firm beginnings for it, but they were Black Moses, pointing across
the river at the promised land. They had fed their flock in the cruelest
desert for more than the biblical forty years, but the mass integration
for which they labored had never yet been seen. A nervous black man
in a somber suit at a liberal party, or Jackie Robinson finally able to
show his temper on a baseball field, was not the realization of a dream
deferred. King had already shown that behind the careful legal strategies
and the astute lobbying lay a millennial impulse demanding something
more than modest gains and an end to the grossest indignities.

The young people of the civil rights revolution in those brief
years crossed the river into the promised land. In retrospect they may
appear to have walked on the water, so difficult does it seem now. The
common cause and the common danger seemed capable of transforming
old attitudes exactly as Martin Luther King said they should. For a
white youth of a northern city to learn from a summer in Mississippi
that white people were to be feared and black ones trusted was to un-
learn his whole life's history, genuinely to solve the personal "Negro
problem" that Norman Podhoretz has attributed to every white American. It was not the integrationist objectives of the movement that mattered most (when he was finally served at the lunch counter, Dick
Gregory used to say, he discovered that the food was terrible), and
some crucial ones were never realized; rather, the movement *was* integration. It kindled, briefly, a vision of a communal brotherhood that casts
into shadow much in the nation's history. The possibilities those years
raised that white and black might live together (or die together, like
Andrew Goodman, James Chaney, and Michael Schwerner in Mississippi
in 1964) will haunt the American psyche. But so too will the cracking
of that fragile coalition.

"Movement" and "direct action" are crucial terms denoting the
psychology that the Negro revolution released upon the decade. They
were not clichés—not then. The revolution needed pace, an incessant
sequence of confrontations and victories that would capture men and

women of good will and impress the opposition with the resistlessness of the movement. The coverage given by the media sustained the impression. While all groups in American society were becoming more and more open to the medium of television as an instrument of persuasion and power, the young people had a particularly close if not always efficacious sense of it. Doubtlessly they were less deliberate in their use of it than many of their elders, but their methods suited it perfectly. Dramas of immediacy, the act or threat of violence from the opposition, the clear posing of moral issues in physical confrontations, all fitted the visual form in which the news was conveyed. Still, it would be inaccurate to attribute all the power of the demonstrations to the media: people must be responsive to the moral content of an incident or it will soon be forgotten. A century before, John Brown's raid had become known and felt almost as quickly, with as much emotion, as the acts of the civil rights workers.

The momentum continued into 1961 with the Freedom Rides. The Congress of Racial Equality, with the longest history of direct action, moved into the forefront with the appointment of James Farmer as its national director. Within three months after his appointment, he had organized and sent out groups to test racial discrimination in interstate travel. The riders, despite the rigid nonviolent discipline they maintained, left behind them a long trail of violence, especially the burning of a bus by white segregationists in Anniston, Alabama. The major effect of the rides was to force the federal government into action. The Kennedy administration sent federal marshals into Alabama to protect the riders, and the Attorney General, Robert F. Kennedy, requested the Interstate Commerce Commission to ban segregation in interstate bus terminals. By November 1, the prohibition was in effect. It achieved immediate compliance in many places, and it was the beginning of a long process that within the decade would end virtually all discriminatory practice in public transportation.

The direct actionists by now were forcing the pace not only of the older civil rights leadership, but of the national government as well. The federal marshals of 1961 were followed by federal troops in 1962 at the University of Mississippi, where the governor of the state attempted to prevent James Meredith from enrolling as the first Negro student and then reneged on agreements with Washington to keep order with state troopers. In 1963 the federal government was forced to move from executive action to the support of new civil rights legislation, while the demonstrators were turning to larger and more dangerous targets in the deep South and now even in the North. The year 1963 was rich in symbolic fulfillments and practical frustrations for the civil rights movement and the nation. It marked an important turning point between a time of élan and the subsequent years of power and confusion for the movement that were to reach their climax in 1968.

The last field to which the activists rushed and the leadership followed was Birmingham, Alabama. What appeared to be a decision by Martin Luther King and the SCLC was in fact, by King's testimony, the product of the Reverend Fred Shuttlesworth's seven-year-old

Birmingham organization, student boycotts in 1962, and rumors that the SCLC would enter the battle if agreements white businessmen had made with Shuttlesworth were not kept. With the local organization in danger and SCLC's credibility inadvertently involved in its success, King and his associates, in his words, "reached the conclusion that we had no alternative but to go through with our proposed . . . campaign."

The campaign faced difficulties from every side. The city was a bastion of segregation and the state governor, George Wallace, was moving into leadership of the segregation forces in the country. The black community of Birmingham was itself hesitant to engage in any radical action, fearing divisions in its own midst and lacking confidence in the ability of its leaders to control the black poor. And the state of the movement by 1963 had called forth increasing militancy. A few arrests no longer made an impression: the scale of activities would have to be massive, with all the dangers that suggested, especially since there seemed so little grounds for optimism over the possibility of achieving the local goals around which the movement would revolve.

What happened in Birmingham is vividly remembered: the fire hoses and the police dogs, the rioting and the bombings, the thousands in jail, and the dead children. Out of it occurred events that changed irrevocably the nature of the movement. The demonstration touched the black community far beyond the reach of the civil rights leadership. Peaceful demonstration was met, as so often, with white violence, but now in response to white violence black crowds rose under no man's control. One thing that became apparent for the first time was the extent to which the success of the middle-class aims the revolution pursued had rested on the passivity of the ghetto blacks, who could not afford a meal in an integrated restaurant, who had no money to travel, and who thought too little about politics to be concerned about their right to vote. The period of urban rioting began in Birmingham. Not all Americans understood this, for they could still blame what happened on conditions peculiar to the South, but the President was prophetic. Proclaiming that demonstrations could no longer be conducted with order and safety, Kennedy raised the alarm on the "fires of frustration and discord . . . burning in every city, North and South," and called for a civil rights bill to end segregation in most "places of public accommodation." He had finally thrown the mantle of the national administration, the Democratic party, and the liberal community over the civil rights movement. Henceforth the generals would lead the troops. The time had arrived for practical activity in place of direct demonstration.

The result was a major effort to slow the direct actionists or to turn them in another direction, an effort that gradually met with substantial though never total success. The prospect of civil rights legislation was a motive for restraint, as were the threat from the Right in 1961 and the whole range of Great Society programs. The solid historic gains of the era came in these years. There were also reasons internal to the movement, bringing it, if not to a halt, at least to a fragmentation of its energies.

Techniques of direct action had largely reached their limits by 1963. They made sense only for the kinds of discrimination that could be ended immediately, and even these changes had proved possible only in localities where the Negro also constituted a political threat. In the deep South—in Orangeburg, in Baton Rouge, and in Jackson—the demonstrations had been failures. Even the Birmingham trouble, which had led to federal legislation, resulted at the time in only partial success for the local demands of the civil rights forces. Without voting strength such as the larger urban ghettos provided, there was no future in direct action, and some of the radicals, especially Bob Moses of SNCC in Mississippi, rapidly realized this. Yet the radicals who turned to voter registration (encouraged in many cases by support from white liberal foundations urged on by the administration) were, after all, doing little more than strengthening the Democratic party. Whatever they did, they directly served the cause of the national government, which was asking them to replace their demonstrations by orthodox political activity. Now the radicals were in the service of the moderates, applying pressure for them to use or even adding to their voting strength.

The urban North was also bounded in its possibilities. The year 1963 was the time when the demonstrations spread northward in force. They met with less direct resistance, but also less accomplishment. Demonstrations against discriminatory building trades unions and de facto segregation were fruitless. The ritual was inadequate: no instant capitulation was possible when the demands were complicated and the objectives gradual. The northern demonstrations, in fact, had a double handicap. Not only did they not succeed either practically or in cathartic satisfactions; they also threatened the liberal coalition that had now become the primary hope for ending segregation. The motives, from within and without, for at least a lull in the movement were overwhelming.

On the other hand, a movement cannot easily slow down of its own volition; it is too dependent on a mood of militancy. Followers fall away while leaders become confused by the need to press a rhetoric that ceases to conform to the realities. After Birmingham, as King was beginning to teach his followers to wait, he wrote a book entitled Why We Can't Wait. Since civil rights bills were before Congress, the movement could remain credible for a while longer, but it was in danger.

Out of these tensions came the extraordinary March on Washington of August 28, 1963, the symbolic culmination of the freedom marches, and the model for many demonstrations in other causes during the succeeding years. This strategically brilliant and psychologically perfect event exactly suited the needs of the situation. The idea had been that of Bayard Rustin, long an important radical activist for civil rights and socialism; the call came from A. Philip Randolph, dean of black labor leaders and originator of the March on Washington movement of 1941, which had persuaded Franklin Roosevelt to issue an order banning discrimination in war industries.

But the march, originally designed to press for federal action on jobs, was quickly transformed by moderate white leaders, especially the clergy, into a demonstration in support of the civil rights bill pending in Congress. White liberals were in control; radical proposals by the more militant actionists were softened. Several liberal congressmen and senators joined the march as did a few labor leaders, headed by Walter Reuther of the United Auto Workers. The AFL-CIO national council declined to endorse it; here was a hint that the estrangement between labor and the civil rights movement, which had revealed itself in the early sixties, was becoming a serious split. Promoted by liberals, who insisted on limits to the tactics of the marchers—keeping them from Capitol Hill, discouraging acts of civil disobedience, and toning down the most radical speakers—the march received presidential endorsement.

The demonstration was a precious moment in American history. The gentle army of over two hundred thousand, mostly black but with many whites, assembled under Daniel Chester French's great statue of Lincoln to hear a medley of speeches and performers that caught the moods of the day and the moral direction of the times. Randolph saw the realization of a hope over twenty years old. Roy Wilkins eulogized W. E. B. DuBois, who as much as any other individual had created the forces in triumph on that August day—and who, by some miracle of historical fitness, had died the night before at the age of 95, disillusioned, expatriated, and totally alienated from the nation that only now was showing its willingness to meet the challenge he had posed. Martin Luther King articulated the dream of black history: the dream that came to Frederick Douglass and DuBois and Booker T. Washington of black men in America "Free at last." But a speech by John Lewis, SNCC chairman, which he had tempered when white religious leaders threatened not to attend if he spoke according to his original intentions, still unmistakably suggested that a revolutionary change in American institutions would be necessary before blacks could achieve equality. The march was indeed, as the President noted, something of which "the nation [could] properly be proud."

The "movement" phase of the revolution did not end at the Lincoln Memorial on that August Wednesday. The moral authority of the leaders had been based on the courage of the demonstrators, and men like King had gone to jail many times. Even the NAACP had committed itself to direct action at its 1963 convention. But the main attention had clearly passed to legislative and political activity: lobbying for the civil rights bills, registering voters, and trying to thwart the white backlash that emerged in municipal elections in Philadelphia and Chicago that year, and that the leaders rightly feared had a long future. This unquestionably meant holding demonstrations to a minimum and keeping down the more extreme forms of protest. Liberal allies such as the President and the liberal newspapers vigorously supported the leadership in these endeavors. Men like King found themselves caught between the dynamics of their organizations and the needs of the national movement for moderation and patience.

The radicals responded in most cases with even more confusion. The new demands brought great internal conflict in groups, such as SNCC and CORE, that had been both radical and a part of the cooperative strategy. The millennial impulse had little place to turn but inward in many cases, to a radical assessment of motivations and a painful testing of allies. The instabilities of the union between white and black youths emerged under the strategy of cooperation with dominant liberal institutions. The black youths had stressed their militancy, young whites their lack of racism and their radicalism. The rhetorical emphasis on black militancy increased as outlets were denied or became less satisfactory; the white civil rights workers could now find within the movement tests of their freedom from racism. The white workers were on the average far better trained to do the tasks of negotiating and administration, and their expertise had often given them special positions within the movement; black radicals therefore turned upon the predominantly white infrastructure, and their white allies had to accept, with whatever bitterness, the logic of the attack. The psychology of both groups called for the Negroes to drive out the whites. The white activists ended in the same position as the client-centered liberals with whom events had yoked them: suffering an ingratitude that had to be accepted because it was an indication of the health and progress they had originally sought for their clients.

While some radicals of both races retreated into a wasting spiritual and psychological crisis, others were turning to the intricacies of American political institutions. The voter registration drive, which could be among the most daring possible acts in some places, took much energy. The trial of its import for the radicals came in 1964 with the Mississippi Freedom Democratic Party. At the Democratic Convention of 1964 this SNCC-sponsored group, a product of heroic voter registration work that cost several lives, challenged the credentials of the regular delegation from Mississippi. The ultimate issue would be the sincerity of the Democratic party; in its interests the major party spokesmen were urging a cool summer in the ghettos.

Party leaders showed how far they would go by offering to seat a portion of the Freedom Democratic delegation and by pledging that they would exact racial standards from all delegations at the next convention. Important figures such as King urged the young radicals to accept the proposal. They refused, retaining the independence of their party rather than entering into the normal process of political compromises. The tiny party, which two years later metamorphosed into the Black Panthers, was to have a phoenixlike existence in the netherworld of the urban ghettos, far from its origins in Mississippi. After the 1964 convention, groups like SNCC and then the Black Panthers took on the mystique of black nationalism; a few people, principally Martin Luther King, searched for a course that would work through piecemeal gains to the millennial dream they had glimpsed in the early sixties. The mid-sixties was a time of accomplishment in civil rights, a harvest season of the earlier planting, but the civil rights movement that had given the decade its flavor—flamed its radicalisms and made its liberalism meaningful—was dead, a sacrificial offering for the achievements and an atonement for the failures of the decade.

. . .

Even the bill President Kennedy sent to Congress in June 1963 provided for only partial desegregating of public accommodations. There was still the fear on Kennedy's part that the stronger his position on civil rights the less he would accomplish elsewhere. But even before his death it had become apparent that powerful forces were converging in favor of a meaningful civil rights act. Peaceful demonstrations, as well as violence in Birmingham during May 1963, had an indirect effect on federal legislators by forcing some exemplary laws through on the local and state level. Then for the first time the nation's churches—so effective in promoting the prohibition movement more than a generation earlier—entered the civil rights movement in force. They would have a special influence in the Senate, which held the threat of a filibuster, for they could influence church-oriented members whose support was needed to shut off debate. Senator Everett Dirksen, minority leader and head of his party's uncommitted moderates, was besieged by churchmen, as well as by liberal Republicans and the new President who, a White House assistant remarked, "never let him alone for thirty minutes." The vote to end the southern filibuster in June 1964, taken after ample time had been allowed for a full expression of views, was 71 to 29, and then the bill itself passed by a slightly greater margin. The minority tallies included only five Republicans from outside the South, notably Barry Goldwater, and even fewer nonsouthern Democrats. It was the first time the Senate had ever invoked cloture on civil rights. The bill outlawed racial discrimination in all public places and in federally aided programs, as well as by employers and unions. Enforcement provisions were stronger than any that had existed previously. Subsequently, it became fashionable to employ blacks; banks, law firms, and industries concerned with their public image offered them managerial positions.

. . .

By 1966 the Johnson coalition was in process of breaking up. The first specific issue to threaten it was, of course, that of civil rights and civil disorder. Johnson was obliged to ask for passage of the 1964 Civil Rights Act; he could not simply assume any of the Democratic coalition's northern constituency—and especially the Negro, who might be pushed beyond the point of coalition politics. But the sincerity of his devotion to the cause became clear in the next two years. Johnson was willing to risk loss of ethnic support; the long-promised "backlash" of the white working class, resentful of special treatment for blacks, was beginning to materialize. In 1965 he asked the Justice Department what else could be done before the reform impulse weakened. The department suggested that voting rights needed strengthening. An occasion to press for new legislation came in the spring of 1965 when Negro freedom marchers were repelled at Selma, Alabama, by police using clubs, whips, and ropes. Speaking in person before both Houses of

Congress, the President presented a new tactic for voter registration in seven southern states, and the result was the Civil Rights Act of 1965. According to the new law, most voter registration would be accomplished henceforth not by "tedious" lawsuits but immediately by federal examiners.

In January 1966 Johnson offered still another major civil rights request in his State of the Union message. He took a radical step by recommending laws prohibiting discrimination in the sale or rental of all housing. Johnson also asked that a federal crime be made of interference with the rights of others in voting, education, housing, employment, jury service, and travel. Both bills passed, but the weakened housing measure ran against emotions in the North. Before and after the bill was passed, realtors and homeowners deluged Congress and the President with protest. When Martin Luther King led a group of blacks into a white residential area in Chicago, the act enraged a white mob. "I have never seen such hatred—not in Mississippi or Alabama," said King. By 1966 the Negro was no longer pictured in the public mind as a praying, nonviolent victim of southern "justice"; three summers of urban riots had discharged that image, replacing it with that of black power and the Molotov cocktail.

On Revolution

MALCOLM X

Malcolm X emerged as one of the first to attack the civil rights movement from the left. As a member of the Black Muslims (Nation of Islam), a black nationalist group, Malcolm X rejected the Christian millennialism of Martin Luther King, Jr., the belief in nonviolence, and the notion that whites could be converted to racial integration. This speech delivered in November 1963, three months after King's "I Have a Dream" speech, strikes the themes that dominated black power movements in the ensuing years: solidarity with African nationalism, emphasis on revolution with the attendant threat of violence, and insistence on black separatism rather than integration with whites.

During the years after Malcolm X left the Muslims, he moderated some of his rhetoric. But overall he remains important as one of the first major black voices in the 1960's to speak from the city streets rather than from the rural southern base that King represented. Of course, the principal successes in the drive against segregation and discrimination did come in the South; the issues Malcolm X raised—what future lies beyond civil rights for black Americans—remain to be resolved.

. . .

Of all our studies, history is best qualified to reward our research. And when you see that you've got problems, all you have to do is examine the historic method used all over the world by others who have problems similar to yours. Once you see how they got theirs straight, then you know how you can get yours straight. There's been a revolution, a black revolution, going on in Africa. In Kenya, the Mau Mau were revolutionary; they were the ones who brought the word "Uhuru" to the fore. The Mau Mau, they were revolutionary, they believed in scorched earth, they knocked everything aside that got in their way, and their revolution also was based on land, a desire for land. In Algeria, the northern part of Africa, a revolution took place. The Algerians were revolutionists, they wanted land. France offered to let them be integrated into France. They told France, to hell with France, they wanted some land, not some France. And they engaged in a bloody battle.

So I cite these various revolutions, brothers and sisters, to show you that you don't have a peaceful revolution. You don't have a turn-the-other-cheek revolution. There's no such thing as a nonviolent revolution. The only kind of revolution that is nonviolent is the Negro revolution. The only revolution in which the goal is loving your enemy is the Negro revolution. It's the only revolution in which the goal is a desegregated lunch counter, a desegregated theater, a desegregated park, and a desegregated public toilet; you can sit down next to white folks—on the toilet. That's no revolution. Revolution is based on land.

Land is the basis for all independence. Land is the basis for freedom, justice, and equality.

The white man knows what a revolution is. He knows that the black revolution is world-wide in scope and in nature. The black revolution is sweeping Asia, is sweeping Africa, is rearing its head in Latin America. The Cuban Revolution—that's a revolution. They overturned the system. Revolution is in Asia, revolution is in Africa, and the white man is screaming because he sees revolution in Latin America. How do you think he'll react to you when you learn what a real revolution is? You don't know what a revolution is. If you did, you wouldn't use that word.

Revolution is bloody, revolution is hostile, revolution knows no compromise, revolution overturns and destroys everything that gets in its way. And you, sitting around here like a knot on the wall, saying, "I'm going to love these folks no matter how much they hate me." No, you need a revolution. Whoever heard of a revolution where they lock arms . . . singing "We Shall Overcome?" You don't do that in a revolution. You don't do any singing, you're too busy swinging. It's based on land. A revolutionary wants land so he can set up his own nation, an independent nation. These Negroes aren't asking for any nation—they're trying to crawl back on the plantation.

When you want a nation, that's called nationalism. When the white man became involved in a revolution in this country against England, what was it for? He wanted this land so he could set up another white nation. That's white nationalism. The American Revolution was white nationalism. The French Revolution was white nationalism. The Russian Revolution too—yes, it was—white nationalism. You don't think so? Why do you think Khrushchev and Mao can't get their heads together? White nationalism. All the revolutions that are going on in Asia and Africa today are based on what?—black nationalism. A revolutionary is a black nationalist. He wants a nation. . . . If you're afraid of black nationalism, you're afraid of revolution. And if you love revolution, you love black nationalism.

To understand this, you have to go back to what the young brother here referred to as the house Negro and the field Negro back during slavery. There were two kinds of slaves, the house Negro and the field Negro. The house Negroes—they lived in the house with the master, they dressed pretty good, they ate good because they ate his food—what he left. They lived in the attic or the basement, but still they lived near the master; and they loved the master more than the master loved himself. They would give their life to save the master's house—quicker than the master would. If the master said, "We got a good house here," the house Negro would say, "Yeah, we got a good house here." Whenever the master said "we," he said "we." That's how you tell a house Negro.

If the master's house caught on fire, the house Negro would fight harder to put the blaze out than the master would. If the master got sick, the house Negro would say "What's the matter, boss, *we* sick?" *We* sick! He identified himself with his master, more than his master identified with himself. And if you came to the house Negro and said, "Let's run away, let's escape, let's separate," the house Negro would look at you and say, "Man, you crazy. What you mean, separate? Where is there a better house than this? Where can I wear better clothes than this? Where can I eat better food than this?" That was that house Negro. In those days he was called a "house nigger." And that's what we call them today, because we've still got some house niggers running around here.

This modern house Negro loves his master. He wants to live near him. He'll pay three times as much as the house is worth just to live near his master, and then brag about "I'm the only Negro out here." "I'm the only one on my job." "I'm the only one in this school." You're nothing but a house Negro. And if someone comes to you right now and says, "Let's separate," you say the same thing that the house Negro said on the plantation. "What you mean, separate? From America, this good white man? Where you going to get a better job than you get here?" I mean, this is what you say. "I ain't left nothing in Africa," that's what you say. Why, you left your mind in Africa.

On that same plantation, there was the field Negro. The field Negroes—those were the masses. There were always more Negroes in the field than there were Negroes in the house. The Negro in the field caught hell. He ate leftovers. In the house they ate high on the hog. The Negro in the field didn't get anything but what was left of the insides of the hog. They call it "chitt'lings" nowadays. In those days they called them what they were—guts. That's what you were—gut-eaters. And some of you are still gut-eaters.

The field Negro was beaten from morning to night; he lived in a shack, in a hut; he wore old, castoff clothes. He hated his master. I say he hated his master. He was intelligent. That house Negro loved his master, but that field Negro—remember, they were in the majority, and they hated the master. When the house caught on fire, he didn't try to put it out; that field Negro prayed for a wind, for a breeze. When the master got sick, the field Negro prayed that he'd die. If someone came to the field Negro and said, "Let's separate, let's run," he didn't say "Where we going?" He'd say, "Any place is better than here." You've got field Negroes in America today. I'm a field Negro. The masses are the field Negroes. When they see this man's house on fire, you don't hear the little Negroes talking about *our* government is in trouble." They say, *"The* government is in trouble." Imagine a Negro: *"Our* government!" I even heard one say *"our* astronauts." They won't even let him near the plant—and *"our* astronauts!" *"Our* Navy"—that's a Negro that is out of his mind, a Negro that is out of his mind.

Just as the slavemaster of that day used Tom, the house Negro, to keep the field Negroes in check, the same old slavemaster today has Negroes who are nothing but modern Uncle Toms, twentieth-century Uncle Toms, to keep you and me in check, to keep us under control, keep us passive and peaceful and nonviolent. That's Tom making you nonviolent. It's like when you go to the dentist, and the man's going to take your tooth. You're going to fight him when he starts pulling.

So he squirts some stuff in your jaw called novocaine, to make you think they're not going to do anything to you. So you sit there and because you've got all of that novocaine in your jaw, you suffer—peacefully. Blood running all down your jaw, and you don't know what's happening. Because someone has taught you to suffer—peacefully.

The white man does the same thing to you in the street, when he wants to put knots on your head and take advantage of you and not have to be afraid of your fighting back. To keep you from fighting back, he gets these old religious Uncle Toms to teach you and me, just like novocaine, to suffer peacefully. Don't stop suffering—just suffer peacefully. As Rev. Cleage pointed out, they say you should let your blood flow in the streets. This is a shame. You know he's a Christian preacher. If it's a shame to him, you know what it is to me.

There is nothing in our book, the Koran, that teaches us to suffer peacefully. Our religion teaches us to be intelligent. Be peaceful, be courteous, obey the law, respect everyone; but if someone puts his hand on you, send him to the cemetery. That's a good religion. In fact, that's that old-time religion. That's the one that Ma and Pa used to talk about: an eye for an eye, and a tooth for a tooth, and a head for a head, and a life for a life. That's a good religion. And nobody resents that kind of religion being taught but a wolf, who intends to make you his meal.

This is the way it is with the white man in America. He's a wolf—and you're sheep. Any time a shepherd, a pastor, teaches you and me not to run from the white man and, at the same time, teaches us not to fight the white man, he's a traitor to you and me. Don't lay down a life all by itself. No, preserve your life, it's the best thing you've got. And if you've got to give it up, let it be even-steven.

· · ·

The Great Society

LYNDON B. JOHNSON

Lyndon Johnson announced his Great Society program in a speech delivered at the University of Michigan in 1964. This, in effect, was his "I Have a Dream" speech, and Johnson was indeed a man of large dreams and grandiose vision. He promised to tackle the full range of social problems that American society faced in the mid-1960's: racial injustice, poverty, a decaying environment, as well as the need to improve the quality of life by applying American economic advances in the twentieth century to the resolution of these problems.

In this speech Johnson spoke of leading the nation's intelligentsia toward formulation of social polices to solve the problems he identified. This dream was the source of the Great Society legislation of the mid- and late 1960's. The implementation of this far-reaching social program became sadly tangled with the parallel pursuit of elusive victory in the Vietnam War. The outcome of these noble dreams has had a mixed reception. To some extent, a fair assessment of Johnson's programs is still premature. The Great Society was clearly a major effort in the history of American reform. Much of our opinion of the reform tradition in American politics will be colored by the eventual assessment that American historians reach of the programs that Lyndon Johnson created in a few frenetic years.

I have come today from the turmoil of your capital to the tranquility of your campus to speak about the future of your country.

The purpose of protecting the life of our nation and preserving the liberty of our citizens is to pursue the happiness of our people. Our success in that pursuit is the test of our success as a nation.

For a century we labored to settle and to subdue a continent. For half a century we called upon unbounded invention and untiring industry to create an order of plenty for all of our people.

The challenge of the next half century is whether we have the wisdom to use that wealth to enrich and elevate our national life, and to advance the quality of our American civilization.

Your imagination, your initiative, and your indignation will determine whether we build a society where progress is the servant of our needs, or a society where old values and new visions are buried under unbridled growth. For in your time we have the opportunity to move

Speech at Ann Arbor, Mich., May 22, 1964. *Public Papers of the Presidents of the United States: Lyndon B. Johnson,* Government Printing Office (Washington, D.C., 1965), I (1963-1964), 704-707.

not only toward the rich society and the powerful society, but upward to the Great Society.

The Great Society rests on abundance and liberty for all. It demands an end to poverty and racial injustice, to which we are totally committed in our time. But that is just the beginning.

The Great Society is a place where every child can find knowledge to enrich his mind and to enlarge his talents. It is a place where leisure is a welcome chance to build and reflect, not a feared cause of boredom and restlessness. It is a place where the city of man serves not only the needs of the body and the demands of commerce but the desire for beauty and the hunger for community.

It is a place where man can renew contact with nature. It is a place which honors creation for its own sake and for what it adds to the understanding of the race. It is a place where men are more concerned with the quality of their goals than the quantity of their goods.

But most of all, the Great Society is not a safe harbor, a resting place, a final objective, a finished work. It is a challenge constantly renewed, beckoning us toward a destiny where the meaning of our lives matches the marvelous products of our labor.

So I want to talk to you today about three places where we begin to build the Great Society—in our cities, in our countryside, and in our classrooms.

Many of you will live to see the day perhaps fifty years from now, when there will be 400 million Americans—four-fifths of them in urban areas. In the remainder of this century urban population will double, city land will double, and we will have to build homes, highways, and facilities equal to all those built since this country was first settled. So in the next forty years we must rebuild the entire urban United States.

Aristotle said: "Men come together in cities in order to live, but they remain together in order to live the good life." It is harder and harder to live the good life in American cities today.

The catalogue of ills is long: there is the decay of the centers and the despoiling of the suburbs. There is not enough housing for our people or transportation for our traffic. Open land is vanishing and old landmarks are violated.

Worst of all expansion is eroding the precious and time-honored values of community with neighbors and communion with nature. The loss of these values breeds loneliness and boredom and indifference.

Our society will never be great until our cities are great. Today the frontier of imagination and innovation is inside those cities and not beyond their borders. . . .

A second place where we begin to build the Great Society is in our countryside. We have always prided ourselves on being not only America the strong and America the free, but America the beautiful. Today that beauty is in danger. The water we drink, the food we eat, the very air that we breathe, are threatened with pollution. Our parks are overcrowded, our seashores overburdened. Green fields and dense forests are disappearing.

A few years ago we were greatly concerned about the "Ugly American." Today we must act to prevent an ugly America.

For once the battle is lost, once our natural splendor is destroyed, it can never be recaptured. And once man can no longer walk with beauty or wonder at nature his spirit will wither and his sustenance be wasted.

A third place to build the Great Society is in the classrooms of America. There your children's lives will be shaped. Our society will not be great until every young mind is set free to scan the farthest reaches of thought and imagination. We are still far from that goal. . . .

Each year more than 100,000 high school graduates, with proved ability, do not enter college because they cannot afford it. And if we cannot educate today's youth, what will we do in 1970 when elementary school enrollment will be 5 million greater than 1960? And high school enrollment will rise by 5 million. College enrollment will increase by more than 3 million.

In many places, classrooms are overcrowded and curricula are outdated. Most of our qualified teachers are underpaid, and many of our paid teachers are unqualified. So we must give every child a place to sit and a teacher to learn from. Poverty must not be a bar to learning, and learning must offer an escape from poverty.

But more classrooms and more teachers are not enough. We must seek an educational system which grows in excellence as it grows in size. This means better training for our teachers. It means preparing youth to enjoy their hours of leisure as well as their hours of labor. It means exploring new techniques of teaching, to find new ways to stimulate the love of learning and the capacity for creation.

These are three of the central issues of the Great Society. While our government has many programs directed at those issues, I do not pretend that we have the full answer to those problems. . . .

But I do promise this: We are going to assemble the best thought and the broadest knowledge from all over the world to find those answers for America. I intend to establish working groups to prepare a series of White House conferences and meetings—on the cities, on natural beauty, on the quality of education, and on other emerging challenges. And from these meetings and from this inspiration and from these studies we will begin to set our course toward the Great Society.

The solution to these problems does not rest on a massive program in Washington, nor can it rely solely on the strained resources of local authority. They require us to create new concepts of cooperation, a creative federalism, between the national capital and the leaders of local communities.

Within your lifetime powerful forces, already loosed, will take us toward a way of life beyond the realm of our experience, almost beyond the bounds of our imagination.

For better or for worse, your generation has been appointed by history to deal with those problems and to lead America toward a new age. You have the chance never before afforded to any people in any age. You can help build a society where the demands of morality, and the needs of the spirit, can be realized in the life of the nation.

So, will you join in the battle to give every citizen the full equality which God enjoins and the law requires, whatever his belief, or race, or the color of his skin?

Will you join in the battle to give every citizen an escape from the crushing weight of poverty?

Will you join in the battle to make it possible for all nations to live in enduring peace—as neighbors and not as mortal enemies?

Will you join in the battle to build the Great Society, to prove that our material progress is only the foundation on which we will build a richer life of mind and spirit?

There are those timid souls who say this battle cannot be won; that we are condemned to a soulless wealth. I do not agree. We have the power to shape the civilization that we want. But we need your will, your labor, your hearts, if we are to build that kind of society.

Those who came to this land sought to build more than just a new country. They sought a new world. So I have come here today to your campus to say that you can make their vision our reality. So let us from this moment begin our work so that in the future men will look back and say: It was then, after a long and weary way, that man turned the exploits of his genius to the full enrichment of his life.

The Welfare Explosion

FRANCES FOX PIVEN and RICHARD A. CLOWARD

One view of the growth of social welfare programs is that of a progressive liberalization as "rugged individualism" has given way to "welfarism." More and more forms of social welfare—relief for the poor, old age and unemployment insurance, free medical services for the aged and the indigent—have become increasingly available in an industrial economy that could afford such benefits and had less use for the labor of old people, mothers and children, and unskilled workers. According to this view, the growth of the welfare roles in the 1960's— as well as the rising opposition to this development in the 1970's—is easy to understand as liberal thrust and conservative reaction, Democratic initiative and Republican consolidation, Johnson's New Society versus Nixon's New American (Counter) Revolution.

Frances Fox Piven and Richard A. Cloward contest this consensus notion of welfare history. They argue that the timing of growth in welfare rolls does not support such a view. They point out how welfare roles "exploded" in the mid-1960's as well as in other eras extending back at least to Elizabethan England. In effect, Piven and Cloward argue, the welfare system responds to political, rather than to social or economic, stimuli; it feeds on fear, not on generosity. Thus when social fears diminish, so does the number of welfare "cases."

The authors raise important questions about the so-called Moynihan thesis that attributes a large part of the welfare rise of the 1960's to the presumed disintegration of the black family under the impact of migration from country to city. Yet the reader must consider whether social welfare benefits can be separated from the other developments in social legislation that seem to show a more steady progress throughout the twentieth century. These include unemployment insurance; federal Social Security; disability and workmen's compensation systems; and growth of social services, clinics, and government-financed medicine. Is the function of social welfare programs markedly different from that of these other social services? Or do these services show some of the same flaws as the relief-giving system? The welfare issue remains a subject of live controversy that has taken an increasingly bitter tone during the 1970's.

During the 1950's the welfare rolls rose by only 110,000 families or 17 per cent. But from December 1960 to February 1969, some 800,000 families were added to the rolls, an increase of 107 per cent in just eight years and two months. In the course of the 1960's, then, the nation experienced a "welfare explosion"; for all practical purposes, traditional restrictions collapsed and the relief money poured out. As costs rose, the relief system once again became a major public issue, a

source of political controversy and conflict, and thus an object of proposals for "reorganization" and "reform." The remainder of this essay
will deal with the economic and political sources of this relief explosion.

SOME DIMENSIONS OF THE WELFARE RISE

The relief rise was pervasive: even the rural counties of the South
showed an increase of 34 per cent (see Table 1). However (and this is
important), the rises in some places were much greater than in others.
By region, the rolls almost tripled in the Northeast and in the West,
while the rolls rose by 78 per cent in the North-Central area and by
54 per cent in the South as a whole.

TABLE I

AFDC Caseload Increase By Area

	% Change 1950–1960	*% Change 1960–1969*	*% of 1960–1969 Change Occurring After 1964*
National Total	17%	107%	71%
Regions			
Northeast	26	180	69
North Central	27	78	59
West	38	161	72
South	0	54	86
Deep South	7	57	98
Other South	−3	52	81
121 Major Urban Counties	35	165	71
5 Most Populous	26	217	75
116 Remaining	41	135	68
78 Northern	41	175	70
43 Southern	13	121	80
All Less Urban Rural Counties	6	60	71
Northern	17	87	62
Southern	−3	34	93

Among urban counties, the steepest increase (217 per cent) occurred in the 5 most populous ones—New York, Philadelphia, Cook County (Chicago), Wayne County (Detroit), and Los Angeles. A smaller upsurge took place in the 116 remaining urban centers (135 per cent). The rise was larger in Northern urban centers (175 per cent) than in Southern ones (121 per cent).

The nation's rural counties—many of which, especially in the South, experienced considerable outmigration of their poor—nevertheless had a rise of 60 per cent. The Northern rural rolls almost doubled (87 per cent), and Southern rolls moved up more modestly (34 per cent).

Another way to describe these increases is to ask: How many of the 800,000 additional families on the rolls in February 1969 were located in one region or another, in urban areas or in rural ones? Table 2 [not shown] shows that many families in all parts of the country got on the rolls, although there were great variations by region. The Northeast and West accounted for most of the national increase (39 per cent and 26 per cent respectively). Seventeen per cent of the increase occurred in the North Central region. Finally, the South contributed 18 per cent to the national increase; this fact deserves special note, for the Southern rolls had not changed at all during the 1950's. It also deserves note because the welfare explosion is popularly believed to be a wholly Northern phenomenon.

Urban areas as a whole accounted for the overwhelming share of the national AFDC increases (70 per cent), but it was the "big five" urban centers that experienced the most dramatic rise. During the 1950's, these countries accounted for only 23 per cent of the national increase, while the remaining 116 urban counties accounted for two and a half times as much (57 per cent). In the 1960's, however, the "big five" counties contributed as much to the national increase as all the remaining urban counties in the nation combined (34 and 36 per cent, respectively).

Finally, rural counties contributed 30 per cent to the increase, although the contribution by Northern rural counties (22 per cent) was much greater than by Southern ones (9 per cent). (Still, it is worth remembering that the Southern rural rolls had fallen during the 1950's.)

We come now to the most striking feature of the welfare rise. To speak only of its magnitude and where it took place is to overlook an extraordinary fact: *that the rolls went up all at once*—by 31 per cent in the first four years of the decade, but by 58 per cent in the next four years. Stated another way, fully 71 per cent of the huge welfare increase during the 1960's took place in the four years *after* 1964 (Table 1). It was truly an explosion.

Among the regions, all but the North Central area experienced at least two thirds of their increases after 1964. Indeed, 86 per cent of the total Southern increase and an astonishing 98 per cent of the Deep South increase occurred after 1964!

Urban and rural areas show the same pattern (with the exception of Northern rural counties, where only 62 per cent of the increase took place after 1964). The rural South had an especially abrupt increase— 93 per cent of the rise occurred after 1964. Any explanation of the welfare rise in the 1960's must account for this extraordinary precipitousness.

In summary, the welfare explosion occurred in all regions, and in both urban and rural counties. But the explosion was far greater in urban areas; and among those urban areas it was a handful of the most populous Northern cities that showed the largest rises. Finally, most of the increase occurred all at once, in just a brief period after 1964.

SOME EXPLANATIONS OF THE WELFARE RISE

Of the explanations that have been advanced to account for the welfare explosion, three deserve mention here. One points to continued migration of the black poor from the South. Another attributes the increase to rising formal benefit levels. And the third fixes responsibility on the presumed deterioration of "the Negro family."

We believe that these explanations share a common defect that makes them at best incomplete. All are based on the extremely doubtful premise that *the relief rolls automatically grow when the pool of people eligible for relief grows.* Each of these explanations does, to be sure, point to a factor that increased the pool: the more poor people who migrate from Southern states with restrictive welfare systems to Northern states with more liberal ones, the larger the pool; the higher the formal benefit levels, the larger the pool of eligible families; and the more families without male heads, the larger the pool. But relief-giving does not increase simply because economic deprivation spreads; nor did it increase for this reason in the 1960's. The families who got on the rolls after 1964 were, on the whole, just as much in need of aid before 1964. A pool of eligible people had always been there; and although it grew for the reasons given above, it had also been growing for some time.

If these theories were valid, welfare increases should have occurred where the pool of eligible people was growing. In principle, for example, poor black families in Southern states with low payment levels and severe eligibility restrictions improved their chances of obtaining relief if they migrated to Northern states with higher formal benefit levels and fewer restrictions; some families may even have migrated for that reason. But the principle hardly worked out in practice during the 1950's. Indeed, the number of black families moving northward in the 1950's was greater than in the 1960's, yet the Northern regional increases were from three to seven times larger in the 1960's (Table 1). In the Northeast, for example, the rolls rose by 26 per cent in the 1950's, but by 180 per cent in the 1960's. New York and Los Angeles experienced great in-migration during the 1950's, not only by Southern blacks but by Spanish-speaking families as well; nevertheless, the rolls in these counties went up by only 16 and 14 per cent, respectively.

During the 1960's, however, *the rolls in both counties quadrupled* (300 per cent and 293 per cent respectively), despite the fact that in-migration by blacks had slackened.

Not all of the Southern black poor were dislodged from agriculture in recent decades went North; many migrated to Southern cities. Although such migration might thus account for the decline in Southern rural rolls in the 1950's, it surely would lead us to expect an increase of more than 13 per cent in the Southern cities. The situation in the 1960's is even more puzzling: the rolls in the Southern cities jumped by 121 per cent, and that could be said to be a delayed response to in-migration; but such a speculation is made dubious by the fact that the Southern rural rolls also jumped, and this despite continued out-migration.

The upgrading of benefit levels obviously expands the pool of people who are eligible for assistance. However, even the most cursory examination of the relationship between this factor and changes in the welfare rolls reveals the inadequacy of this explanation. In the 1950's, the national average level of payment per recipient rose almost by half, thus greatly enlarging the pool; but in fact the rolls rose a mere 17 per cent. In the South, furthermore, average payments went up by half but the rolls remained absolutely unchanged. During the 1960's, these patterns were reversed: a national increase of only one-third in average payment was accompanied by more than a doubling of the rolls. In short, neither decade provides evidence to support the rising-payment-level thesis.

The record of individual states also casts serious doubt on this explanation. Between 1960 and early 1969, California increased its average monthly payment per recipient from $43 to $48—a change of 11 per cent. During the same period, California's rolls increased by 219 per cent. In Georgia, the average payment rose by 4 per cent, and the rolls rose 138 per cent. North Carolina raised its average payment by 45 per cent, yet the rolls went up only 4 per cent.

Nor does the evidence from many individual cities bear out the thesis. The quadrupling of New York City's rolls could be explained by a series of substantial payment-level changes enacted by the state beginning in 1960; however, the rolls in Los Angeles also quadrupled although there was no significant upgrading of payment levels in California during the same period.

Before we examine the adequacy of the family-deterioration thesis, it might be well to say a bit more about the thesis itself. This view of the welfare rise was put forward by Daniel P. Moynihan in a much-publicized report on "The Negro Family." Having noted that the number of individuals on the AFDC rolls trebled between 1940 and 1963, and that a disproportionate share of the increase was attributable to black families, he asserted that "the steady expansion of . . . [the AFDC] program, as of public assistance programs in general, can be taken as a measure of the steady disintegration of the Negro family structure over the past generation in the United States."

We find this explanation of the relief rise inadequate, but not because we dismiss the evidence showing that the black family has been weakened by uprooting, urban resettlement, and chronically high rates of urban unemployment. These forces have taken their toll, as they did of other dislocated groups in earlier periods of our history. (Indeed, we will return to the evidence on the erosion of the black family, . . . for we believe it does help to explain the welfare rise, albeit very circuitously. From our perspective, the weakening of the family signified a weakening of social control, especially over the young, and it was the young who were the most prominent in the disorders of the 1960's. Disorder, in turn, was a critical force in producing more liberal relief practices, or so we shall argue.) But Moynihan leaps to the conclusion that AFDC rolls rose simply because the changing structure of the black family increased the pool of families *presumably eligible* for relief; the rolls rose, in other words, as an automatic result of a growing pool of eligibles. But that conclusion does not accord with the facts.

Until 1948, blacks did not appear on the AFDC rolls in significant proportions. Whatever their family structure, they were severely discriminated against prior to that time, especially in the South. Two changes then combined to increase their proportion on the rolls in the years immediately after 1948, neither of which had anything to do with family structure. One was pressure by the federal government on Southern states to relax discriminatory practices, a circumstance that produced a sharp increase in the number of blacks who received aid in the South, especially between 1948 and 1952. . . . The second factor was the steady migration of blacks to more liberal Northern cities, where they were less likely to be disqualified for assistance. These factors (or any other factors, for that matter) did not appreciably increase the *magnitude* of the national AFDC rolls between 1948 and 1960, a remarkable phenomenon on which we have already commented; however, they did significantly alter their *composition,* for the proportion of blacks increased from 31 to 40 per cent.

However worrisome the gradual AFDC rise in the 1950's, the rapid rise beginning in 1960 was a special source of alarm to Moynihan, for he thought he detected in this trend the basis for concluding that the black family had become so disorganized that "the present tangle of pathology is capable of perpetuating itself without assistance from the white world." To arrive at this conclusion, Moynihan compared the trends in black male unemployment rates with trends in the total number of AFDC cases opened. From 1953 to 1958, he shows, the black male unemployment rate rose and the total number of new AFDC cases also rose, as if caused by the rising trend in unemployment. After 1958, the unemployment level slowly moved downward, but the total number of new AFDC cases inexplicably continued to climb. It was this failure of the relief rolls to decline in response to ostensibly improved economic conditions in the late 1950's and early 1960's that led Moynihan to say that the pathology of the black family had become so serious that it "may indeed have begun to feed on itself."

The obvious question to which this conclusion leads is whether the absolute increase in female-headed families was as large as the absolute rise in AFDC cases. In a detailed examination of this question, Lurie found that even if all of the new female-headed families in the period between 1959 and 1966 had received AFDC assistance, only about 10 per cent of the AFDC increase would have been accounted for: "It is clear, then, that the rise in the number of families receiving AFDC cannot be explained by the rise in the number of poor families headed by females."

Furthermore, how is one to reconcile recent AFDC increases in the rural South with an "urbanization leads to family deterioration" thesis? Even the urban data yield little support. The nation's 121 urban counties accounted for most of the recent increase, and at first glance this fact might seem to support the explanation, except that a major shift occurred among the urban communities that contributed to the welfare rise in the 1950's, as contrasted with the 1960's. In the 1950's, as we noted earlier, the "big five" counties accounted for only 23 per cent of the national increase; in the 1960's, however, they represented 34 per cent, or as much as the remaining 116 urban counties combined. A family-deterioration argument would have to explain why, during the 1950's, families were more likely to deteriorate in cities of less than one million persons, whereas in the 1960's the vulnerable families had shifted to cities of over one million persons. What such an explanation would be is not readily apparent.

Finally, and of great importance, none of these explanations, including the family-breakdown thesis, helps to account for the striking fact that 71 per cent of the welfare rise in the 1960's took place after 1964. The extraordinary precipitousness of the Southern rise is clearly incompatible with all three of these theories, for the Southern rolls rose by just half, but virtually all of that increase (86 per cent) took place after 1964.

And so the puzzle remains, for if neither the rate of migration nor formal benefit levels skyrocketed after 1964, the rolls clearly did, and if family life among blacks did not suddenly collapse in those few years, many of the restrictive practices of the relief system clearly did. What must be explained, in short, is not why the pool of eligible families grew, although the existence of a pool of unemployed poor is one precondition for a welfare explosion; what must be explained is why so many of the families in that pool were finally able to get on the rolls.

. . .

The contemporary relief explosion was a response to the civil disorder by rapid economic change—in this case, the modernization of Southern agriculture. The impact of modernization on blacks was much greater than on whites: it was they who were the chief victims of the convulsion in Southern agriculture, and it was they who were more likely to encounter barriers to employment once relocated in the cities, a combination of circumstances which led to a substantial weakening of social controls and widespread outbreaks of disorder. For if unemployment and forced migration altered the geography of black poverty, it also created a measure of black power. In the 1960's, the growing mass of black poor in the cities emerged as a political force for the first time, both in the voting booths and in the streets. And the relief system was, we believe, one of the main local institutions to respond to that force, even though the reaction was greatly delayed.

The relationship between increasing black power and the expanding welfare rolls is not altogether obvious. Great masses of poor blacks did not rise up in anger against a welfare system that denied them sustenance (although some did). Nor did the increased flow of public aid result from demands made by black political leaders; quite to the contrary, the expanding welfare rolls have often been as much a source of dismay to black elites as to white elites. Finally, there is a puzzling absence of liberalizing legislation. Legislative enactments in the years between 1960 and 1969 were intended not to put more families on the rolls, but to get them off via rehabilitation services (the passage of AFDC-UP is an exception). Indeed, the puzzle deepens because some legislative enactments—particularly the congressional amendments of 1967—actually made the relief system more restrictive. Still, the rolls more than doubled. The policies of the welfare rise, in short, are anything but self-evident.

In our previous analysis of why relief restrictions collapsed in the Great Depression, we found that the critical factor was the growing volatility of those dislodged from the occupational order. Mass unemployment alone did not lead to the expansion of relief arrangements —not, that is, until unemployment had generated so much unrest as to threaten political stability. In other words, economic convulsions which also produce mass turbulence—whether riots in the streets or upheavals in electoral alignments—are likely to lead to the temporary liberalization of relief provisions.

Although unemployment during the Great Depression rapidly produced a political crisis and impelled the expansion of public aid, two decades passed before the unemployment resulting from modernization and migration after World War II produced mass disorder, and so the relief rolls did not rise appreciably until after 1964. Agricultural modernization and migration to the cities brought blacks within the sphere of electoral politics, to be sure, but larger voting numbers alone did not produce concessions. It was not until this mass of unintegrated people finally became turbulent that both local government and the federal government began to register and react to their presence.

The welfare explosion occurred during several years of the greatest domestic disorder since the 1930's—perhaps the greatest in our history. It was concurrent with the turmoil produced by the civil rights struggle, with widespread and destructive rioting in the cities, and with the formation of a militant grass-roots movement of the poor dedicated to the combatting welfare restrictions. Not least, the welfare rise was also concurrent with the enactment of a series of ghetto-placating federal programs (such as the antipoverty program) which, among other things, hired thousands of poor people, social workers, and lawyers who, it subsequently turned out, greatly stimulated people to apply for relief and helped them to obtain it. And the welfare explosion, although an urban phenomenon generally, was greatest in just that handful of large metropolitan counties where the political turmoil of the middle and late 1960's was the most acute.

In other words, we shall argue that the expansion of the welfare rolls was a political response to political disorder. If many of the welfare restrictions were not legislated out of existence in the 1960's, *their implementation in many localities (especially in the cities) almost completely broke down.* And that was very much a matter of politics. Moreover, it was a matte of black politics, or so we shall argue . . .

Lyndon Johnson and Vietnam: 1968

TOWNSEND HOOPES

Americans have historically liked their wars simple. War should pit "democratic" peoples against "aggressors," it should call for "unconditional surrender," and it should be fought "all out." If the Korean war brought such narrow assumptions into question, Vietnam destroyed them completely. Here was a twilight conflict—undeclared and misunderstood at home, an enigma to our friends and allies abroad—fought in limited ways against an enemy who could not always be identified. The war clearly could not end all wars, and few believed that it could even make the nation in which it was fought safe for democracy. Bitterest note of all, there was no possibility of victory. American policy, reversing General MacArthur's arrogant dictum "there is no substitute for victory," became a search for a substitute for defeat.

The Limits of Intervention by Townsend Hoopes is one of the first insider's accounts of the American decision to cease escalating the American military presence and to seek some means of withdrawing from our untenable position in Southeast Asia. The turning point came with the Tet offensive of early 1968. This event destroyed most remaining illusions about what a campaign of firepower from the air and "search and destroy" missions on the ground might accomplish toward defeating the Viet Cong and their northern allies. The new Secretary of Defense Clark Clifford and President Truman's Secretary of State Dean Acheson argued against deeper involvement in March 1968. Tet, perhaps combined with political pressures at home, produced the great decision to begin the agonizing and protracted movement toward acknowledging the failure of American policy in Vietnam. Whatever his critics might say, Johnson had at least taken the first step.

ARVN—The Army of the Republic of [South] Vietnam
GVN—The Government of [South] Vietnam
JCS—Joint Chiefs of Staff

On January 31 [1968] in a surprise offensive that burst with the suddenness of a giant bombshell all over South Vietnam, the enemy launched a wide range of powerful, simultaneous attacks against dozens of key cities and towns. A commando unit of nineteen Viet Cong infiltrated the compound of the U.S. Embassy, made their way into several buildings, but were unable to get into the Embassy itself. After six hours of fighting with Embassy guards and reinforcements, including thirty-six U.S. paratroopers landed by helicopter on the Embassy roof, the entire Viet Cong unit was wiped out.

But the Embassy raid was only the political spearhead of a massive political–military assault on the entire U.S.-GVN structure. Saigon was attacked and partially occupied by several thousand enemy troops who had arrived in civilian disguise on bicycles and public buses. There were 1,000 enemy soldiers in Hue, 2,500 in Ben Tre. NVN forces seized large sections of Kontum in the central highlands, and of Mytho, Cantho, and Soc Trang in the Mekong Delta. In Washington the first reports were confused and fragmentary, but even these gave unmistakable shape to the truth that South Vietnam was experiencing a spreading disaster.

[General] Westmoreland [the commander of allied troops] was quick to conclude that "the enemy's well laid plans went afoul." He and his spokesmen dismissed the enemy's tactics as suicidal, and pressed the suggestion that we were witnessing a "last desperate push," a final NVN effort to redress a military balance that had been moving inexorably against Hanoi by reason of the great weight of the U.S. effort. . . . In fact, [such] words were premature and optimistic in the extreme, for even the first phase of the Tet offensive swept on for another two weeks with mounting casualties, destruction, and irreversible political consequences for the allied war effort.

The enemy was carrying out a carefully calculated three-pronged drive—one prong directed against Saigon and the major cities and a second against U.S. forces at Khesanh and other outlying posts; the third was designed to fill the vacuum left in the countryside by government troops who were drawn back to defend the cities. By occupying large rural sections abandoned by the government, the NVN-VC not only dealt the whole pacification program a grievous blow, but threatened to strangle the towns by cutting them off from normal sources of supply. Three to four weeks later, a number of towns were still surrounded and dependent on airlift. Very heavy fighting continued in Saigon and its suburbs through February 20, with action centering in the Cholon district. An estimated 11,000 U.S. and ARVN forces were committed to battle against 1,000 Viet Cong. In an effort to dislodge the enemy, artillery and air strikes were repeatedly used against densely populated areas of the city, causing heavy civilian casualties. An additional 4,000 U.S. troops were brought in on February 9, part of them being helicoptered to the Pho Tho racetrack where a large Viet Cong force was entrenched. On February 11, two ARVN battalions were locked in battle with 400 VC near an ammo dump along the Ben Cat River.

Everywhere, the U.S.-ARVN forces mounted counterattacks of great severity. In the delta region below Saigon, half of the city of Mytho, with a population of 70,000, was destroyed by artillery and air strikes in an effort to eject a strong VC force. In Ben Tre on February 7, at least 1,000 civilians were killed and 1,500 wounded in an effort to dislodge 2,500 VC.

The effort to recapture Hue, the cultural and religious center of Vietnam, met fierce resistance from the 1,000 NVN troops who had captured it on January 31. After ten days of bitter street fighting, U.S.

Marines finally penetrated the inner city, an area of two square miles known as the Citadel, to which the enemy force had withdrawn. On that same day, the Mayor of Hue found the bodies of three hundred local officials and prominent citizens in a common grave several miles from the city, slain en masse by the enemy. The fierce house-to-house fighting gradually exhausted the small contingent of Marines, and reinforcements were called for on February 21 "because the steam has gone out." Not until February 24 did U.S. forces achieve reoccupation of the city as a whole and ARVN forces capture the Imperial Palace. The enemy had gradually been driven to the southern part of the Citadel. There he did not put up a last-ditch resistance, but slipped away one night to the southwest, with a sizable part of his men and equipment. The guns fell silent on a devastated and prostrate city. Eighty percent of the buildings had been reduced to rubble, and in the smashed ruins lay 2,000 dead civilians (apparently more civilians died than soldiers). Three-quarters of the city's people were rendered homeless and looting was widespread, members of the ARVN being the worst offenders.

David Douglas Duncan, a famous combat photographer who had covered all of the world's major battlefronts since World War II, including Korea, Algeria, and the French struggle to keep Vietnam, was appalled by the U.S.-ARVN method of freeing Hue. He said, "The Americans pounded the Citadel and surrounding city almost to dust with air strikes, napalm runs, artillery and naval gunfire, and the direct cannon fire from tanks and recoilless rifles—a total effort to root out and kill every enemy soldier. The mind reels at the carnage, cost, and ruthlessness of it all. Wouldn't a siege-blockade have been a more effective and less wasteful military tactic?" He contrasted this response with Henry Stimson's intervention in World War II to save Kyoto, the religious heart of Japan, which had been marked for destruction by allied airforces, and with John J. McCloy's similar rescue of classic Rothenburg in Germany. "Poor Hue, it had no friends or protectors. Now it is gone." . . .

One thing was clear to us all: the Tet offensive was the eloquent counterpoint to the effusive optimism [that had held sway the previous November]. It showed conclusively that the U.S. did not in fact control the situation, that it was not in fact winning, that the enemy retained enormous strength and vitality—certainly enough to extinguish the notion of a clear-cut allied victory in the minds of all objective men. Nor could we take seriously the view that the Vietnamese were stepping up their operations out of despair, out of a certain knowledge that time worked against them. On the contrary, the Tet offensive seemed to proceed from an NVN assessment that the situation presented a number of ripe opportunities: the garrison at Khesanh was surrounded and under increasing pressure; another sizable portion of U.S. combat forces in northern I Corps was pinned down by heavy Communist artillery fire from across the DMZ; the cities were vulnerable to attack and the surrounding countryside to recapture. In general, the doctrine of search-and-destroy had resulted in scattering U.S. combat forces all over uninhabited border lands; the Tet offensive had made blindingly clear the fatuousness of Westmoreland's ground strategy. What seemed imperative now was a shift that would deemphasize search-and-destroy, concentrate on the protection of population centers, and curtail American casualties; otherwise, I thought, domestic support for any form of long-continued effort could not be assured. Even the staunch and conservative *Wall Street Journal* was saying in mid-February, "We think the American people should be getting ready to accept, if they haven't already, the prospect that the whole Vietnam effort may be doomed, that it may be falling apart beneath our feet."

But modifications of strategy ran counter to Westmoreland's every instinct, and there was no will in Washington to bell that particular cat. It is quite possible that the idea of a strategy change never occurred to the President; that is, that either he never understood the incompatibility of Westmoreland's ground strategy with his own stated political objective, i.e., to gain the political allegiance of the people of South Vietnam—or that he regarded the political aim as mere words and the need for military victory as the only governing reality. McNamara, though he complained privately of the error and waste inherent in search-and-destroy operations, could not get his hands on the levers without explicit presidential support; and the Joint Chiefs of Staff, although some of them were disquieted by the attrition strategy, were unwilling to *direct* changes. In the particular circumstances, continued JCS deference to Westmoreland seemed an extreme form of professional courtesy, but it was a cold fact that in February 1968 the men and the means did not exist in Washington to change our military strategy in Vietnam.

The President's basic reaction to the Tet offensive was to convince himself anew that the war was a test of wills between parties of equal interest. While pressure rose on every side for a reexamination of America's prospects and strategy, he and his closest advisers gave the unmistakable impression that all the big questions had been long since resolved—and that the answer was to plunge onward. He spent much time in February visiting U.S. military bases. He announced to the world he was in no mood to compromise. He defended Westmoreland. He urged total firmness on the war. . . .

The chances of producing any dramatic change of policy seemed remote in mid-February. Control of the war effort remained tightly held by the inner group, and they were, with the exception of McNamara, united both in their conviction about the rightness of present policy and in the fact that all were implicated in the major decisions since 1964. Worse still, as it seemed, McNamara's designated successor [as Secretary of Defense] was not only a close friend of LBJ, but an eloquent hawk with no doubts about the war. In all respects, Clark Clifford seemed to fit the President's temperamental requirement for harmony within the inner group. *Newsweek* called him "loyal, well-seasoned and, more important, determined to hold the line in Vetnam." Still, I was not without hope. . . .

I had known Clifford over a number of years, particularly during the Truman period when he was at the White House, and had been impressed, then and later, by the steely independence beneath the velvet charm. He was, I thought, above all his own man. Moreover, he was too intelligent, too much the trained lawyer, with too firm a sense of proportion and too strong a passion for reasoned answers, not to grasp the galloping distortions that now dominated the conduct of Vietnam policy. I did not foresee the full measure of his courage and tenacity that the ensuing months would reveal, but I was encouraged. In any event, Clifford was the only remaining hope for restoring some sense of proportion to our national position at home and abroad. . . .

The reappraisal of Vietnam policy began on February 26 with the arrival of a cable from General Wheeler sent from Saigon. He had been dispatched by the President about February 20 "to find out what else Westmoreland might need." For three days he conferred with Westmoreland and inspected the battle areas. Then he sent a cable for McNamara, Rusk, Rostow, and Helms setting forth his assessment of the situation and of the additional "force requirements" that he and Westmoreland considered necessary or at least very desirable. . . .

Since his Senate confirmation in January, Clifford had of course been preparing himself for his new responsibilities by conferring frequently with McNamara, Nitze, and the Joint Chiefs of Staff. On February 28, two days before the swearing-in ceremony, the President named [an] *Ad Hoc* Task Force on Vietnam with Clifford as chairman. Its purpose was to examine the Wheeler-Westmoreland request for more forces and to determine the domestic implications. As the principals understood it, the assignment from the President was a fairly narrow one—how to give Westmoreland what he said he needed, with acceptable domestic consequences.

Clifford moved immediately to broaden the inquiry's frame of reference by stating that, to him, the basic question was whether the U.S. should continue to follow the same course in Vietnam. What was likely to happen if we put in another 200,000 men? Would that bring us any closer to our objectives? Perhaps Westmoreland did need 200,000 additional troops under his present strategic concept, but was that a sensible concept? McNamara said Westmoreland's forces had been asked to carry more of the burden of achieving U.S. political objectives in Vietnam than could be borne by military power; we could not, he said, "by limited military means" force North Vietnam to quit, but neither could they drive us out of South Vietnam; the time had therefore come to recognize the necessity for negotiations and a compromise political settlement. Nitze argued the need to reexamine the involvement in Vietnam in the wider context of U.S. interests and commitments elsewhere in the world; he said that, whatever the result in Vietnam itself, we would have failed in our purposes if the war should spread to the point of direct military confrontation with China or Russia, or to the point where our resources were so heavily committed in Vietnam as to put our other commitments in serious doubt. He thought a less ambitious strategy should be devised, in order to buy time for strengthening ARVN and for getting out. Habib, who was William Bundy's deputy and a specialist on Vietnamese affairs, thought any alternative course would be preferable to sending more U.S. troops, because that would simply take the pressure off the GVN and ARVN to stand on their own feet.

Rostow, Wheeler, and Taylor expounded the hard line, arguing that the Tet offensive was in reality a new and unexpected opportunity. The guerrilla enemy, so long elusive and unwilling to give battle under conditions that favored America's superior firepower, had suddenly exposed himself all over the country. He had come into the open in large numbers, in a desperate attempt to seize cities and promote popular uprisings. This dramatic shift of strategy indicated he could no longer stand the relentless pressure of U.S. military power in a protracted war. Therefore, the prompt and substantial reinforcing of Westmoreland could open the way to victories that would decimate the enemy force and bring Hanoi, much more quickly than otherwise, to the conference table under conditions favorable to our side. Speaking for the JCS, Wheeler said the full 206,000 men were needed, and that to provide less would be taken by Westmoreland as a vote of no confidence. Taylor doubted whether sending even the full 206,000 would enable Westmoreland "to do what he is trying to do."

Nitze and Warnke, supported by Katzenbach, sought to counter these arguments. There was, they argued, no very convincing evidence that the enemy's attack was motivated by desperation or that his immediate aims were as ambitious as a popular uprising against the GVN and the wholesale desertion of ARVN. It seemed more likely, they argued, that the enemy had decided the time was ripe for a major effort to achieve several very important, but still limited, purposes: to capture one or more major cities, to cause large-scale panic in the ARVN, to recapture large parts of the countryside in order to destroy the pacification program and gain access to new recruits; above all, to show public opinion in America that, contrary to the optimistic projections of November, the U.S. was not winning the war and in fact could not seriously attempt to win it without undermining its domestic and global interests. . . .

These various countermovements notwithstanding, the Task Force ended its seven-day effort by drafting a set of recommendations which in all essential respects confirmed existing policy. In a short, unsigned memorandum for the President, it recommended an immediate deployment of about 20,000 additional troops and the prompt approval of reserve call-ups, larger draft calls, and lengthened duty tours in Vietnam sufficient both to provide the remaining 186,000 men requested by Westmoreland and to restore a strategic reserve force adequate to meet contingencies that might arise elsewhere in the world. There was to be a reiteration of the San Antonio formula, but no new initiative toward negotiations or peace. There was also to be a step-up in the bombing, with Wheeler, Taylor, and Rostow advocating measures beyond those acceptable to the other members of the Task Force, i.e., to expand the targets around Hanoi and Haiphong, and to mine Haiphong harbor. These were the central recommendations. . . .

Clifford, although he passed along the report, was uneasy about it, for the Task Force deliberations had deepened his doubts as to the wisdom and practicality of existing policy. Moreover, in separate meetings with the Joint Chiefs of Staff, he had probed for their professional assessment of the battlefield effect of adding 206,000 troops, but had received only "vague and unsatisfactory" answers. They could not promise victory; at most, they could say that more troops would add to the cumulative weight of our pressure on the enemy. . . .

But by far the most serious deficiency of the Task Force report was its failure to gauge the horrendous political implications of its basic recommendation that the military manpower request be met. For this involved a reserve mobilization on the order of 250,000 men as well as increased draft calls. Together, these measures would add 450,000 men to U.S. active duty forces, bringing the total strength to about 8.9 million. With his sensitive journalistic antennae quivering, Goulding hastily dictated an appendix which Clifford circulated within the Task Force, but which did not go forward to the President. Goulding's appendix noted that there had been absolutely no preparation of public opinion for such a large-scale mobilization. The official line had stressed our ability to fight in Vietnam and at the same time to meet commitments elsewhere without undue strain; it had held that we were winning the war and, specifically, that we had emerged victorious from the Tet offensive; it insisted that ARVN was improving every day. Now suddenly 250,000 American reservists were to be separated from their families and careers and another 200,000 men drafted—all in the absence of any new or palpable national crisis.

Goulding argued that the shock wave would run through the entire American body politic. The doves would say the President was destroying the country by pouring its finest men and resources into a bottomless pit. The hawks would cry that the Administration had no moral right to disrupt the lives of all these young men and still insist on waging a war of limited objectives, limited geographical boundaries, and limited weapons. They would demand, Goulding wrote, that the Administration "unleash . . . hit the sanctuaries . . . if necessary invade." The antiwar demonstrations and resistance to the draft would rise to new crescendos, reinforced by civil rights groups who would feel the President had once again revealed his inner conviction that the war in Vietnam was more important than the war on poverty. It would be quite unavailing for the Administration to say that only 20,000 more men were being committed to Vietnam. That might or might not prove to be true; in the larger sense the claim would be irrelevant for, in the context of steady escalation over the past three years, it simply would not be believed. Moreover, the major political damage would be done by the increased mobilization itself, for it was this that would bring the defense budget to rise by $2.5 billion in 1968 and by $10 billion in 1969. The actual deployment of the other 186,000 to Vietnam would be, as the saying went, a "secondary explosion."

Goulding's appendix made clear that the Administration had trapped itself in repeated expressions of overblown optimism and could thus carry into effect the recommendations of the Task Force only if it were ready to accept the gravest domestic political risks. Clifford was deeply impressed by its unanswerable logic; others were equally taken aback. Fowler, who had concluded that a formal war mobilization was the only sure way to obtain the higher taxes and controls that he felt were necessary for a successful defense of the dollar, was apparently chastened by the chilling implications of the Goulding analysis.

The Task Force recommendations were sent to the President on March 7. The following day, Clifford went to the White House to discuss the proposed actions and their implications, and also to lay before the President some of the fundamental questions which had formed in his own thinking about Vietnam. The recommendations, he explained, were responsive to instructions and represented actions that the President could take "if that is the way you wish to go."

He felt obliged to add, however, that, while not yet agreeing or disagreeing with the thrust of the Task Force report, he had developed "doubts" about the efficacy of the ground strategy, the effectiveness of the bombing campaign, and what could really be accomplished by a further large infusion of American troops. He acknowledged that his doubts did not appear to be shared by the other principals on the Task Force, namely, Rusk, Rostow, Wheeler, Taylor, and Fowler. . . .

The session on March 3 ended with Clifford emphasizing the tentative nature of his own judgments and expressing the hope that there would be time for further study. Wheeler and the JCS were anxious to move ahead on the Task Force recommendations, but Rusk and Rostow were prepared to have the issues studied further, in part because the domestic implications, political and economic, seemed to grow more ominous with each passing day. Some reasonable delay appeared to meet the President's preferences. . . .

March 12 was the day of the Democratic primary in New Hampshire. While President Johnson won as a write-in candidate with 49.4 percent of the vote, Senator Eugene McCarthy polled 42.2 percent. The shock to Johnson and his supporters was very real, for the voting proved beyond denial that the reports of deep divisiveness in the country were more than newspaper talk. One Democratic politician, reflecting on New Hampshire and watching the storm clouds gather over Wisconsin, where the primary voting would take place on April 2, said "The Democratic Party is on the edge of rebellion."

On Saturday, March 16, Robert Kennedy announced for the Presidency and embarked immediately on a whirlwind campaign beginning with two speeches that produced the largest political crowds in the history of Kansas—15,000 at Kansas State University, and 17,000 at the University of Kansas. Clifford was uncertain whether Kennedy would have stayed out of the race even if the President had accepted the essential elements of his proposal, but he regarded the President's reasons for refusal as entirely cogent. He also drew the inference from this episode that the President definitely intended to run for reelection. . . .

Despite strident declarations which reflected the visceral Johnson, the President was privately troubled and uneasy during February and early March. Whatever his strong instinctive preferences, he could not responsibly ignore the hard realities of the human and financial cost of the war, the fading support for it in the country, the malaise in the foreign-military bureaucracy, and the galloping deterioration of the Democratic party. However unpalatable, these were facts that could not be wished away.

In late Febraury he had consulted Dean Acheson whom he held in the highest regard as a brilliant mind, a courageous and distinguished former Secretary of State, and the toughest of Cold Warriors. When the President asked him his opinion of the current situation in Vietnam, Acheson replied he wasn't sure he had a useful view because he was finding it impossible, on the basis of occasional official briefings given him, to discover what was really happening. He had lost faith in the objectivity of the briefers: "With all due respect, Mr. President, the Joint Chiefs of Staff don't know what they're talking about." The President said that was a shocking statement. Acheson replied that, if such it was, then perhaps the President ought to be shocked. The President said he wanted Acheson's considered judgment; Acheson replied he could give this only if he were free to make his own inquiry into the facts so that he would not be dependent on "canned briefings" from the JCS, Rostow, and the CIA. The President agreed he should have the necessary resources for an independent study.

Acheson thereupon assembled a small group of knowledgeable people at the second and third levels and worked with them over a two-week period, holding meetings at his home where he cross-examined them at length. The group included Philip Habib of State, George Carver of CIA, and Major General William DuPuy of the Joint Chiefs of Staff organization. On March 15, Acheson gave the President his findings, at a luncheon where the two men were completely alone. Acheson told the President he was being led down a garden path by the JCS, that what Westmoreland was attempting in Vietnam was simply not possible—without the application of totally unlimited resources "and maybe five years." He told the President that his recent speeches were quite unrealistic and believed by no one, either at home or abroad. He added the judgment that the country was no longer supporting the war. This was tough, unvarnished advice in the Acheson manner, though served with the customary polish and elegance. The President obviously did not like it, but he greatly respected the purveyor.

The luncheon with Acheson took place just three days after the New Hampshire primary, on the same day that Ambassador Goldberg's bombing memorandum arrived from New York, and one day before Robert Kennedy entered the presidential race. In the face of these unpalatable new pressures and of unwanted but unignorable advice, Lyndon Johnson began to feel "crowded"; his immediate reaction was to lash out in a kind of emotional tantrum. On March 17, he flew to the Middle West to deliver two thoroughly truculent speeches—to the National Alliance of Businessmen and the National Farmers Union—in the drafting of which Rostow and Fortas had a major hand. . . .

By March 20, the President appeared to have passed through his first explosive reaction to the mounting pressures and to have recovered a measure of calm. . . . Two days later, on March 22, he announced that Westmoreland would be relieved of his command and come home to be Army Chief of Staff. No successor was immediately named and no date fixed for the return. In light of his major decisions several days later, it seemed that by these acts President Johnson was tentatively clearing away the accumulated underbrush and preparing the site for the construction of a possibly different policy. Neither act was conclusive, or committed him to substantive change. Those who knew him very well thought in retrospect that the process was largely subconscious, but it did seem that, in a mysterious way peculiar to the U.S. Presidency, something was stirring and changing. Clifford continued to see hope in the mere fact that the debate went on, that the President remained willing to hear him out, rather than turning him off "which he was perfectly capable of doing." . . .

The Senior Advisory Group on Vietnam met in the White House on March 25 and 26. Those present were: Dean Acheson, Secretary of State under President Truman; George Ball, Under Secretary of State in the Kennedy-Johnson period; McGeorge Bundy, Special Assistant to Presidents Kennedy and Johnson; Douglas Dillon, Ambassador to France under President Eisenhower and Secretary of the Treasury under President Kennedy; Cyrus Vance, Deputy Secretary of Defense under McNamara and a diplomatic troubleshooter for President Johnson; Arthur Dean, chief Korean War negotiator; John J. McCloy, High Commissioner to West Germany under President Truman and Assistant Secretary of War during World War II; General Omar Bradley, World War II Commander and the first JCS Chairman; General Matthew Ridgway, Korean War Commander and later NATO Commander; General Maxwell Taylor, JCS Chairman under President Kennedy and later Ambassador to Saigon; Robert Murphy, a senior career Ambassador of the Truman-Eisenhower period; Henry Cabot Lodge, former U.S. Senator and twice Ambassador to Saigon; Abe Fortas, a sitting Associate Justice of the Supreme Court and a personal adviser to President Johnson; and Arthur Goldberg, Ambassador to the United Nations and a former Secretary of Labor and Supreme Court Justice.

They assembled in the afternoon to read a number of background papers, and then went on to dinner with the principal cabinet officers plus Rostow, Harriman, and William Bundy whom they questioned at length. After dinner, the entire group heard briefings from Habib of the State Department, Carver of the CIA, and Major General DuPuy. The discussion continued late into the evening and resumed at a session the next morning preparatory to luncheon with the President. It was apparent at an early stage that the unanimity of October had evaporated and that a majority was now deeply troubled. . . .

Two days later, on March 28, Clifford met in Rusk's office together with Rostow, William Bundy, and McPherson. He was unaccompanied by anyone from the Pentagon. The announced purpose of the meeting was to "polish the draft" of the speech the President was now scheduled to make just three days later. . . . It was still essentially a defiant, bellicose speech written to be delivered between clenched teeth. . . .

After reading the draft, Clifford said, "The President cannot give that speech! It would be a disaster! What seems not to be understood is that major elements of the national constituency—the business community, the press, the churches, professional groups, college presidents, students, and most of the intellectual community—have turned against this war. What the President needs is not a war speech, but a peace speech." This opening comment seemed to place his main argument on the grounds of domestic considerations, but in the course of a comprehensive presentation he dealt fully with the military situation in Vietnam and elsewhere in the world. For the first hour or so, Clifford still appeared to be alone, meeting only silent patience from Rusk and Rostow, and with Bundy and McPherson "not taking substantive positions, but simply sitting in as aides." But significantly Rusk did not attempt to cut him off, as he might have, with the comment, "I know your views, but let's get on with the reading." As he talked on, Clifford began to feel he was making progress with Rusk who was "troubled and sincerely anxious to find some way to the negotiating table." The Clifford manner is deliberate, sonorous, eloquent, and quite uninterruptable. It gathers momentum as it proceeds, and soon achieves a certain mesmerizing effect; the perfection of the grammar is uncanny. During the course of several hours, speaking slowly, his fingertips pressed together, and glancing occasionally at an envelope on which he had scribbled a series of points, Clifford mustered every available argument in the powerful arsenal of reasons why it was not in the United States' interest to go on pouring military resources into South Vietnam; he drew heavily on the earlier analyses provided by Nitze, Warnke, Goulding, and myself. When the meeting finally broke up at 5 P.M., the group had inadvertently reviewed not only the speech draft, but the whole of Vietnam policy. Moreover, Rusk had agreed that McPherson should prepare an alternative draft, in order that the President might have two speeches to consider and thus the benefit of a clear-cut choice. Rusk did not object to giving the President a choice. Clifford thought Rostow refrained from making a fuss because he considered the President had already made up his mind not to stop the bombing—which was now the central point at issue.

The occasion had a major impact on McPherson, who was deeply impressed by Clifford's "brilliant and utterly courageous performance" and who from that point forward became not merely a semi-covert dove, but an aroused and powerful ally. Working all through that night, McPherson wrote the first draft of the "peace speech," containing an unconditional bombing cut-off at the 20th parallel and a promise of total cessation if Hanoi provided assurances that it would respect the DMZ and refrain from attacking the cities. He sent this draft to the President early on Friday, March 29, with a note saying that it seemed to reflect the views of "your leading advisers." Later in the day, the President telephoned to ask about a passage "on page 3." McPherson had to compare the two texts in his own office before he discovered to his relief that the President was now working from the alternative draft, the peace speech. From then until the late afternoon of Sunday, March 31, the President worked with McPherson, Clifford, and a number of others to polish the new speech.

At 9 o'clock on Sunday evening, speaking from his office in the White House, the President said "Good evening, my fellow Americans. Tonight I want to talk to you of peace in Vietnam and Southeast Asia." He reviewed his Administration's efforts "to find a basis for peace talks," especially the San Antonio formula of the preceding September, and asserted that there was "no need to delay the talks that could bring an end to this long and this bloody war." He then moved to the principal conclusion of the reappraisal and the pivotal element of the new approach to Hanoi. He said "So, tonight . . . I am taking the first step to de-escalate the conflict. We are reducing—substantially reducing—the present level of hostilities . . . unilaterally and at once. Tonight, I have ordered our aircraft and our naval vessels to make no attacks on North Vietnam, except in the area north of the Demilitarized Zone where the continuing enemy buildup directly threatens allied forward positions. . . ." This meant stopping the bombing, he said, in areas inhabited by "almost 90 percent"of North Vietnam's population. "I call upon President Ho Chi Minh to respond positively, and favorably, to this new step toward peace."

He referred to the emergency deployment in mid-February of 10,500 Marine and airborne troops, and argued that to enable these forces to reach maximum combat effectiveness "we should prepare to send—during the next five months—support troops totaling approximately 13,500 men." He announced that President Thieu had, in the previous week, ordered the mobilization of 135,000 additional South Vietnamese, which would bring the total strength of ARVN to more than 800,000, and he pledged an effort to "accelerate the re-equipment of South Vietnam's armed forces" which "will enable them progressively to undertake a larger share of combat operations against the Communist invaders." The tentative estimate of these additional U.S. and ARVN costs was, he said, $2.5 billion in 1968 and $2.6 billion the following year. He then made a strong pitch for a ten percent surtax, saying "The passage of a tax bill now, together with expenditure control that the Congress may desire and dictate, is absolutely necessary to protect this nation's security, to continue our prosperity, and to meet the needs of our people."

Turning to "an estimate of the chances for peace," the President said, "As Hanoi considers its course, it should be in no doubt of our intentions. . . . We have no intention of widening this war. But the United States will never accept a fake solution to this long and arduous struggle and call it peace. . . . Peace will come because Asians were willing to work for it—and to sacrifice for it—and to die by the thousands for it. But let it never be forgotten: Peace will come also because America lent her sons to help secure it."

Finally, and somewhat surreptitiously, he came to his surprise withdrawal from the presidential race. Asserting that the country's "ultimate strength" lies in "the unity of our people," he acknowledged that "There is division in the American house now. There is divisiveness among us all tonight. And holding the trust that is mine, as President of all the people, I cannot disregard the peril to the progress of the American people and the hope and prospect of peace for all people. . . . With America's sons in the fields faraway, with America's future under challenge right here at home . . . I do not believe that I should devote an hour or a day of my time to any personal partisan causes. . . . Accordingly, I shall not seek, and I will not accept, the nomination of my party for another term as your President." . . .

How did the President come to these decisions? No one can be sure. He seemed finally to have grasped the seismic shift in public opinion and the absolute political temperature of yielding to it, at least temporarily. This shift was borne in upon him by the New Hampshire primary, Robert Kennedy's entrance into the presidential race, the solid congressional opposition to mobilizing larger reserves, and the almost unanimous hostility of the press. The intractable nature of the new environment was made personal by the sharply changed outlook of Acheson, McGeorge Bundy, Vance, and Dillon. Without question, Clifford played a pre-eminent—and I believe the decisive—role. He was the single most powerful and effective catalyst of change, bringing each day to the stale air of the inner circle a fresh perception of the national interest, unfettered by connection with the fateful decisions of 1965. He rallied and gave authoritative voice to the informed and restless opposition within the government, pressing the case for change with intellectual daring, high moral courage, inspired ingenuity, and sheer stubborn persistence. It was one of the great individual performances in recent American history, and achieved in the remarkably taut time span of thirty days. Moreover, it retained its luster and its central effectiveness amid all the backsliding and ambiguity of the Administration's final ten months in office. If, as later events showed, these prodigious efforts did not really change President Johnson's mind about the Vietnam war, at least they compelled him to decide—in favor of reason, restraint, and a new approach. And such decisions by the incumbent of perhaps the most powerful office on earth created a new situation that virtually precluded a return to the old.

Clifford's own view of the March 31 decisions was both modest and mystical: "Presidents have difficult decisions to make and go about making them in mysterious ways. I know only that this decision, when finally made, was the right one."

PART FOUR

The 1970's

The 1970's did not begin with the sharp assertiveness of the previous decade, when John F. Kennedy announced in his inaugural the coming into power of "a new generation." Rather, the nation was ruled by a man long familiar to the electorate—the man who "got" Alger Hiss in the 1940's, who had given his "Checkers" speech two decades before. The war in Vietnam, already the longest in the history of the United States, dragged on. Gone were the young leaders who gave the early 1960's its special flavor; and the even younger radicals who had colored the rest of the decade grew older and shed their flamboyance. As Eisenhower had done in the 1950's, Nixon could settle a war he had not made, thereby easing world tension generally and in the process calming a nation too long distracted by political agitation.

Yet the history of the 1950's and 1960's was not repeated. The Vietnam War stretched into Nixon's second administration. The young people's demonstrations ceased, with several of the young shot to death on college campuses. Instead of an expected tranquillity following the resolution of the war came the resignation of a president in the aftermath of the Watergate scandals, and this created a new period of political excitement. Revelations of sinister doings by hitherto respected institutions—the Oval Office, the CIA, the FBI, and the Justice Department of the United States—came as a shock to the public.

Even before the war in Vietnam ended, the economy sagged just short of depression, buffeted by major shifts in world economic relations. People who had once worried about—or boasted of—the overweening power of the United States in the world economy now fretted over the irresponsibility of multinational corporations. Earlier concern for developing the poorer nations turned to fears of economic blackmail by the oil-producing nations. And midway through the decade came the country's bicentennial celebration. Its unexpected symbol—the event that captured the nation's imagination most fully—was a parade of "tall ships," reminders of an American economic excellence of more than a century before, the swift and beautiful clipper ships of the 1850's that had so rapidly become obsolete. Most of the tall ships sailing up New York harbor in that city's year of greatest trial since the Revolutionary era were foreign, just as most American goods shipped by sea went on ships of foreign registry. The nautical parade was at once a suitable celebration both of our old independence and our new interdependence—an indication of the mood of quiet realism that marked the era. And a new Democratic administration led by President Jimmy Carter was moving with apparent confidence into the post–Watergate era.

Friendly Fire

C. D. B. BRYAN

Vietnam was the war that no one understood. The leaders of the United States could never quite convince the public why they were fighting in a distant corner of Asia. Young people in large numbers saw no reason to risk their lives there. The poor and less sophisticated who entered military service, or those like Michael Mullen who carelessly drifted into the war, frequently became disillusioned with the effort once they were in "Nam." Drugs, alcohol, and refusals to go into combat became problems of a sort that were wholly new to the United States armed forces. Even now it remains uncertain in strategic terms what the nation won or lost in Vietnam. In human terms, however, the answer is all too clear. C. D. B. Bryan, a journalist focusing on a single family trying to learn how their boy died by "friendly fire," reveals with astonishing clarity the dimensions of that price in lives needlessly lost, in the erosion of trust in American institutions, in the disruption of American communities.

On his last night of leave, Wednesday, September 3, 1969, Michael Eugene Mullen worked until ten o'clock on his family's farm—a hundred-and-twenty-acre tract five miles northwest of La Porte City, in Black Hawk County, Iowa. He stayed down in the lower eighty acres on his father's old plum-red Farm-all H-series tractor, ripping out brush and dead trees, bulldozing the trash into the dry streambed of Miller Creek, clearing and filling in the land so it could be used as pasture again. Shortly after midnight, when his father, Oscar Eugene Mullen, who is called Gene, had returned from working the second shift at the huge John Deere tractor plant in Waterloo, Michael had almost finished packing and was talking to his younger brother, John, behind the closed door of the bedroom they shared. Peg Mullen, Michael's mother, and Mary and Patricia, his two younger sisters, were asleep, so Gene made himself a cup of instant coffee and sat down alone at the kitchen table. From where he sat, Gene could see Michael's Vietnam orders resting on a little corner table, where they had been all through his son's twenty-three-day advance leave. When he had finished his coffee, he got up and knocked on his son's bedroom door. Michael opened it, and at the far side of the room Gene could see the closed barracks bags, the Army uniform, and the shined black shoes set out for the morning.

"Would you like anything from the kitchen, Michael? A beer?" Gene asked.

Michael finished locking up his metal tackle box. It held his arrowhead collection, some special letters, some snapshots, the corporal's stripes he'd earned at Fort Benning, addresses, insurance papers.

"No, thanks, Dad," Michael said. He slid the tackle box onto the top shelf of his closet.

Gene, still standing in the doorway, could not look away from Michael's uniform hanging on the back of the closet door. "Mikey?"

"Yes?"

"Be careful?"

Michael smiled at his father and said, "I will, Dad. I will."

The next morning was warm and sunny. John got up early and caught the bus to school. Michael was all packed and in his uniform. Breakfast was over, the dishes done. Gene kept looking at the electric clock over the wall-oven door. "What time did you say your plane left?" he asked.

"Ten," Michael said. "I have to check in by nine-thirty." Michael looked at his wristwatch, and Gene again looked at the electric clock. (Over a period of years, I had countless talks with the Mullens, and, as accurately as they could, they recalled for me the important scenes and conversations in the family's history. I have taken the liberty of changing the names of some of the minor participants.)

Peg Mullen was moving back and forth across the kitchen, dabbing at counters with a sponge. "Would anyone like some more coffee?" she asked.

"No, thanks," Gene said.

"You, Michael?" she asked.

"No thanks, Mom," Michael said, and he looked at his watch again.

"What time is it?" Patricia asked him.

Before Michael could tell her, he had to look at his watch once more. "Eight-fifteen," he said.

The Mullens decided to leave for the Waterloo Municipal Airport early. Gene drove, with Michael sitting up front next to him; Peg, Patricia, and Mary sat in the back. During the drive, the family hardly spoke.

The center of Waterloo is about twelve miles northwest of the Mullens' farm, and the airport is another few miles beyond that. The Mullens drove past a big new shopping center on Highway 218, with the Hy-Vee Market and the Sears and J. C. Penney stores. Gene said something about how fast all that area was changing, and Michael agreed. They passed the Robo Car Wash and Burger King, Donutland and the Cadillac Bowling Lanes, and then they were in Waterloo, caught up in the traffic until they cleared the city. Beyond were the flatlands and railroad tracks they had to cross to reach the airport.

The Mullens entered the terminal building a little after nine. Michael wouldn't let his father help him with the barracks bags, insisting that it would be easier for him to carry both of them himself. The family took seats in the near-empty waiting room and stared out the large window at the vacant airfield.

Michael kept wiping the palms of his hands on his knees.

"Do you need a magazine?" Peg asked. "Something to read?"

Michael stood up abruptly. "Maybe I can check in," he said.

"It's still early yet," his father said.

"I know," Michael said. "But maybe I can check in anyway."

"I'll go with you," Mary said.

"No," Michael said. He smiled at her. "I'll be right back."

Peg followed him with her eyes.

"He looks scared," Patricia said.

"He's fine," Gene said.

A few minutes later, Michael returned, waving his tickets. "I'm all checked in," he said.

"Did you get a magazine?" his mother asked.

"I'll read something on the plane," he said.

"Do you have everything?" she asked.

"I'm fine, Mom. *Really.*"

Peg looked away from her son and out the window.

When Michael's plane came in, he stood up, and his family rose with him.

"Look," Michael told them. "Don't stick around for the plane to leave. You don't have to wait."

"We'll wait," his mother said firmly.

"No, please," Michael said. "I'll be all right." He went to Mary and Patricia and told them that they shouldn't wait around, and that they should tell John there'd be a lot more work now that he was going. And each sister had a moment to herself with Michael, a chance to tell him to take care of himself, to be careful, that she would pray for him, miss him, that she loved him and would write letters all the time and would send him things—anything; all he had to do was say what he needed. Michael gave them each a kiss, and then they moved away, because it was their parents' turn.

Gene fingered a bronze medallion the size of a twenty-five-cent piece which hung from a chain around his neck. The medal, depicting the Virgin Mary, had been given to Gene more than thirty-five years earlier by a Chinese student he had befriended when they were undergraduates together at Marquette University, in Milwaukee. Gene had worn it ever since. He lifted its chain from around his neck and handed it to his son, saying, "Mikey, I've tried to give you everything—" His voice broke, and he took a deep breath and began again. "Tried to do everything a father—"

Michael was looking down at the medallion, now chestnut-colored with age.

"I wore this medal through the Second World War," Gene was saying. "I give you this—I give you—" he could say no more. Gene just looked at his son, half in pride, half in agony.

"I'll wear it," Michael said.

He loosened his black Army tie and unbuttoned the collar of his khaki-colored shirt. He draped the medal and chain around his neck, carefully centered it with the dog tags on his chest, and buttoned his shirt. Then Michael turned to his mother and hugged her. It was an awkward embrace, shorter in duration than either of them wished. He put his hand out to comfort her, and Peg took it. When she looked up at him, she, too, was unable to speak.

"Mom?" Michael said. "Don't worry yourself now, O.K.? O.K.? Come on, now, Mom, please? It'll all be over March 1st."

He gently pulled his hand from hers, picked up his barracks bags, and turned away. Peg watched her son walk past the cafeteria toward the doors that led to his plane. Michael stopped in the narrow passageway, dropped his barracks bags, and turned back for one last look at his family, but as they started to move towards him he quickly lifted his bags and hurried out.

Mary and Patricia cried quietly on the drive back to the farm. Peg could see that Gene was gripping the steering wheel so tightly that his knuckles were white. When they were once again on the other side of Waterloo, back on Highway 218, past the Burger King and Robo Car Wash and heading toward their farm, Peg resolved to cheer them all up by telling them what Michael had said to her just before boarding the plane—that the war would be over by March 1st.

"Why March 1st?" Gene asked her.

"I don't know," Peg said. "He just told me not to worry. That it would all be over then."

On March 1, 1970, Michael Eugene Mullen, aged twenty-five, was returned to the Waterloo Airport in a United States Army-issue twenty-gauge-steel casket.

. . .

Michael had the same love for the land that his father did. When Gene Mullen walks his fields, he will sometimes pause and wonder whether his great-grandfather might have walked that same section, or his grandfather. This sense of continuity was a strong link between Gene and Michael. Gene never felt that Michael was to fall heir to acres only. He was to inherit all those generations of Mullens and Dobshires, who would walk beside him each time he turned the soil. Mary and Patricia would presumably marry young men met in college and move away with them. John, younger than Michael by seven years, didn't seem to have the same feeling for the land that Michael did. So there was never any question about which of the children would succeed to the farm. There certainly wasn't any question in Michael's mind; he spent his life preparing for it.

In 1944, the year Michael was born, fifty-five bushels an acre was considered a high yield for an Iowa cornfield. Twenty-five years later, it was necessary to harvest a hundred bushels an acre just to break even. And, as Michael knew, even higher yields would be required if there was to be any profit when it became time for him to inherit the land. Therefore, he was determined to educate himself, to learn as much about the land and farming as he could. He showed his first 4-H project, a Berkshire sow, when he was ten. At fourteen, he had his first winner—a Hereford steer that was Black Hawk County Reserve Champion. A photograph of Michael at twelve shows a wiry, fiercely determined black-haired boy, perhaps a bit small for his age, standing with one cowboy-booted foot braced against the side of a barn; he is grimly tugging at a balky steer's halter, pitting all his weight and strength against the steer's unwillingness to move. The photograph, taken by a Waterloo *Courier* photographer at a county 4-H tour, appeared in wire-service newspapers across the country captioned "Something's Got to Give." It is unlikely that Michael was amused. He took his farming seriously. It had never occurred to him not to.

Everybody liked Michael—especially older people. However, he was so *straight* that at times he made people his own age feel a bit uneasy. He didn't smoke. He didn't swear. He rarely drank anything stronger than a beer. He served as an altar boy at La Porte City's Sacred Heart Catholic Church. He kept his grades near the top of his class at Don Bosco High School, in Gilbertville. He worked his way through Rockhurst, a small, quiet, conservative Jesuit college in Kansas City, Missouri, majoring in chemistry. He never learned how to dance. He had no serious girl friends. Perhaps, with his solemn, steady gray eyes, black hair prematurely flecked with white, and his earnest, brisk demeanor, he seemed far older than his years.

. . .

All the Mullen children were well liked. They stayed out of trouble, got good grades, were popular with their classmates. Peg and Gene Mullen are innately generous, decent people, and they brought up their children to believe in the same basic values with which they themselves had been brought up. When the Mullens spoke of themselves in the mid-sixties, they described themselves as being "average" or "typical" or "good solid citizens," from a background in no way different from that of their "silent majority" contemporaries in neighboring communities.

. . .

In the early years of the war in Vietnam, Michael Mullen and his family accepted the notion that the United States was in Southeast Asia to defend it. They accepted the equation of our presence in Vietnam with our presence in Korea and our participation in the Second World War. Nevertheless, after Michael reached draft age, Peg and Gene were concerned, and they hoped that the war would soon end. They read about the war and discussed it with friends, and by the mid-sixties they were beginning to doubt that the United States had a legitimate stake in the outcome. In February of 1965, President Lyndon Johnson ordered the commencement of Operation Rolling Thunder, the sustained air bombardment of North Vietnam. Michael, who had urged his parents to pay attention to Barry Goldwater in the 1964 Presidential election, called his mother from college. "You remember kidding me about Goldwater?" he asked. "Well, who's trigger-happy now?" The heavy bombing shocked the Mullens—Peg especially. She had voted for Johnson in the belief that he would bring peace; now she felt betrayed. Operation Rolling Thunder convinced Peg that the President had never had any intention of ending the war. When, in July of 1965, President Johnson announced the increase of United States forces in Vietnam from seventy-five thousand men to a hundred and twenty-five thousand men, the Mullens' doubts about the war increased. By the time of the 1968 Presidential election, they had turned completely against the war. They still had not protested, but there didn't seem to be any way to do that in Black Hawk County. Added to their political and moral objections to the war was, of course, their growing fear that it would not end before their son's college deferment elapsed.

In 1967, Michael received a graduate research assistantship at the University of Missouri, in Columbia, where he started working toward an M.A. in biochemistry. Early in the summer of 1968, when he came back to the farm for a short vacation, he brought Caroline Roby, a diminutive, pretty, happy auburn-haired girl, with him. Caroline, about four years Michael's junior, was an undergraduate student in the same laboratory in which Michael was doing research. Michael was clearly in love with her. Caroline stayed a week, then went South to spend the rest of the summer with her mother, who was divorced. Michael mooned about a bit, but he didn't let his dejection interfere with his farm work. Besides, he had other things to worry about.

After Michael's graduation from Rockhurst, he had applied for, and received, a twelve-month extension of his student deferment from the draft. His deferment had now elapsed. Shortly after Michael returned to the University of Missouri for the 1968 summer session, he received his draft notice, ordering him to report in September for induction into the United States Army. Michael left school and reported to the Des Moines draft board, as instructed. On the day of his induction, Michael was to have been placed on a military flight to Fort Polk, Louisiana, where he would begin basic infantry training. But no flight was available, so he was given a job for a day in the draft-board office filing case histories of young men who opposed the war and had found ways of having their induction orders changed, revoked, or ignored. He spent the day reading about young men who had themselves certified physically or psychologically unfit for the military, who had declared themselves to be homosexuals, who claimed to be conscientious objectors, who had fled the country rather than serve. He read about young men who did not for one instant believe that it was their patriotic duty—or any of their country's business—to fight a war halfway around the world, who had burned their draft cards, been arrested in campus demonstrations, gone to jail, done everything in their power to escape the draft and show their opposition to the war. He filed paper after paper on young men who had not been pulled away from their studies, who had never even attended college, much less a graduate school, but who had still found ways to beat the draft.

At first, Michael was angry, and resentful of the other young men, and then furious with himself, and, finally, inevitably, just depressed. That night, he telephoned his mother back at the farm and told her, "The whole setup is corrupt. I don't need to *be* here!" Over and over again, as if in disbelief, he repeated, "I don't need to *be* here! I don't need to *be* here! I simply didn't *need* to be drafted!"

The next morning, Michael was flown to Fort Polk, and began basic training. While there, he applied for Noncommissioned Officers'

School, hoping to forestall being sent immediately to Vietnam. His application was accepted and he was sent to the N.C.O. School at Fort Benning, Georgia. He made sergeant (E-5) at Benning and was sent next to Fort McClellan, Alabama, for advanced infantry training. It was at McClellan, on July 31st, that he received his orders for Vietnam. His hope that the war would wind down before he completed his training had failed to materialize. He applied for and was granted twenty-three days' advance leave prior to reporting to Fort Lewis, Washington, for transshipment to Vietnam. He decided to spend his entire leave at home, and he arrived at the farm on the tenth of August, 1969.

Peg Mullen had expected Caroline to visit for at least a part of Michael's leave. She had written to the girl inviting her to the farm, but Michael wasn't saying whether she was coming or not. Finally, after four days of not knowing, Peg couldn't remain silent any longer, and asked Michael, "Isn't Caroline coming?"

"No," he said. "She's out West this summer with her father." And that's all he would say. However, Peg could not help noticing that Michael spent two whole afternoons writing to Caroline, and that he never received an answer.

There were then more than five hundred thousand United States troops in Vietnam, fighting a war that had lasted for nearly a decade and had already cost the lives of more than thirty-eight thousand American men. During that first week of leave, while Michael was out fixing fences, clearing brush, painting, and doing general cleanup work around the family farm, two hundred and forty-four United States soldiers were killed and one thousand four hundred and nine were wounded.

Michael left Iowa on September 4th; he was processed at Fort Lewis, Washington; and on September 11th, his twenty-fifth birthday, he arrived in Vietnam. That same month, Peg, searching for some way to express her anguish about the war, wrote to the Another Mother for Peace organization asking what she could do, but she did not receive a reply. She also began writing to President Nixon, urging him to end the war. Then on October 15th, the first Moratorium Day, Peg, like hundreds of thousands of other Americans across the nation, wore a black armband to signify her opposition to the war. That morning, an outraged American Legionnaire, seeing the armband, backed Peg up against the post-office wall and called her "a disgrace to the country." Peg shoved him aside, saying, "You better get with it, you son of a bitch!"

On the morning of Saturday, the twenty-first of February, 1970, about five months after Michael's departure, the sun finally broke through the flat, pearl-gray overcast that had been brooding over the Mullens' farm. Although the temperature hovered near freezing, the week-long Arctic winds had ceased and at last it felt warm enough again to be outside.

Gene Mullen walked back from the mailbox to the house. As he came into the kitchen, he called out, "Letter from Mikey!" He dropped the bills, the Des Moines *Register,* and the second-class mail on the kitchen table and tore open the envelope. Peg wiped her hands on a dish towel and put a kettle of water on to boil.

"What's he say?" she asked. "When did he write it?"

Gene glanced at the top of the letter. "Dated the thirteenth," he said. "Let's see, now. 'Dear Mom and Dad: Went down off the hill to get a haircut and clean up, but ended up hitching a ride to Chu Lai. Went to Mars [Military Affiliate Radio System] station by chance—they were open and not busy—so got a chance to call. Suppose it was midnight at home and guess you were surprised—' "

"Oh," Peg said. "He must have written this the same day he called."

Gene had not been home eight days earlier when Michael telephoned from Vietnam. Peg had written "Mike called" on an envelope and left it on the kitchen table for Gene to see when he came home from work. It was twelve-thirty by the time Gene returned to the farm, and after reading the note he woke Peg up. She told him that she had spoken with Michael for only about a minute and a half, and that just before hanging up Michael had said, "Mom, it's so sticky over here—goodbye." Peg had been depressed, and consequently hadn't felt like waiting up to tell Gene when he came home; that was why she had simply left him a note.

Now Peg mixed Gene a mug of instant coffee, took it to him at the kitchen table, and sat down. "What else does he say?"

"He says. Let's see. He says, 'Guess you were surprised . . .' Now, here: 'Will be on the bunker line about two more days, then back out into the field.' "

"Ugh!" Peg groaned. "That means more 'search and destroy.' "

"No, it doesn't," Gene said. "He's been doing 'company sweeps,' like he wrote in the other letter."

"Same thing," Peg said.

"No, it isn't," Gene insisted. "A 'company sweep' is—"

Peg waved her hand impatiently. "Go on with the letter."

"All right, all right. Let's see. He says, 'Glad that all is well—weather here been rather good. . . . Have decided not to take an R. and R. if I can get a drop. So, til later, hang loose.' " Gene looked at the letter more closely. " 'Hang loose'?"

"Hang loose. You know," Peg said. "Take it easy."

Gene shrugged, " 'So, til later, hang loose. Love, Michael.' "

"That's it?"

"That's it," Gene said.

By getting a "drop," Michael meant that he hoped to qualify for an early discharge under a program that allowed a soldier who had been accepted at an accredited college or university to leave the service as much as ninety days early. In a previous letter, Michael had written that he felt his chances were very good. The only part of his current letter that bothered his parents was that he would again be going into the field, away from the relative safety of the fire-base bunker line. Still, in one of his first letters, Michael had written that he was in "probably one of the better places over here"—a comparatively quiet part of Vietnam. The Mullens were grateful for that.

"So he might be coming home in June," Gene said.

"Looks that way," Peg said. "Knock wood."

Gene finished his coffee and stood up. "Well, Mother," he said, "I guess I might as well try to fix the television antenna for you."

The television antenna was attached to a post near the east side of the house. Gene was just coming around that east corner, blowing hot breath on his fingertips and trying to remember where he had last put the light wrench he would need, when, out of the corner of his eye, he noticed two automobiles turning into his driveway. He thought he recognized the first car as that of their parish priest, Father Otto Shimon, but that second car . . . Gene was now close enough to read black letters painted on the door of the olive-drab Chevrolet: "U.S. Army—For Official Use Only." Gene felt his chest tighten, and he stood still while the priest and an Army sergeant stepped out of their cars and slammed the doors shut.

Gene watched them walking toward him as if in slow motion. He tried to see beyond the thin, stooped late-middle-aged country priest's black-metal-framed glasses to what might show in his eyes. But Father Shimon's downcast lenses reflected only the snow. Not until the priest forced himself to look up did Gene recognize the fright, the despair, the agony in his eyes, and then, very quietly, he asked, "Is my boy dead?"

Father Shimon halted so abruptly that the Army sergeant, who was following, bumped into him from behind. "Gene," the priest said, "this is Sergeant Fitzgerald. He's from Fifth Army Headquarters. He . . ." Shimon was silent.

Gene looked beyond Father Shimon to the Sergeant and asked again, "Is my boy *dead?*"

"Let's go into the house, Gene," Father Shimon said. "I want to talk to you there."

"No!" Gene said, not moving. "I want to *know!* Tell me, *is my boy dead?*"

"I can't tell you here" Father Shimon said, his hand moving toward Gene's shoulder. "Come into the house with us. Please?"

Gene spun away before the priest's fingers could touch him.

Peg Mullen heard the back door open, heard Gene rush into the kitchen, heard him shout *"It's Mikey! It's Mikey!"*—his voice half a sob, half a scream.

Peg was in her sewing room, and she hurried out in time to glimpse the Army uniform entering the kitchen. Gene was standing with his back to the sink, clutching the counter behind him, and the Sergeant had halted just to the side of the doorway. Father Shimon, between them, had removed his glasses to wipe away the steam. Peg started to move toward her husband but had to turn away. Never had she seen such devastation in his face. She looked next at the Sergeant, who avoided her eyes by glancing at the priest, whose job it was to tell them. But Father Shimon would not stop wiping his glasses, and

Peg, wanting to scream, to kick over a chair, to do anything rather than endure this awful silence, asked the Sergeant, "Did Michael die on Thursday?"

Thursday morning, upon waking up, Peg had burst into tears for no apparent reason, and had cried off and on that entire day.

"Why do you ask me when he died?" Sergeant Fitzgerald said. "I haven't told you your son is dead."

Peg glared at him with contempt. "You know the Army doesn't come to tell parents that their sons are *wounded!*" she said. "You know the Army comes only when they're *dead!*"

The Sergeant again turned to the priest, but Father Shimon was incapable of talking. He couldn't tell the Mullens; he simply didn't have the courage to be the one.

Then, very slowly, almost threateningly, Gene pushed himself away from the sink and moved toward the two men. "Now, I want to know the *truth!*" he told hem. "Is my boy *dead?*"

Sergeant Fitzgerald looked at the priest, then back at Gene, and said, "Yes."

And "Yesss," Father Shimon said, too, as if he had been holding his breath all this time. "Yes, Gene. Yes, Peg. I'm sorry. Yesss."

Gene sagged as if he had been hit. He looked at Peg and she at him. Gene stumbled backward until he was against the sink. He was shaking his head like a groggy fighter trying to clear his brain. He began to cry.

Peg had moved to the kitchen table and stood now gripping the wooden rung of a chair back. She remained there until she felt herself under enough control to speak. Then she asked the Sergeant how Michael had been killed.

Sergeant Fitzgerald sorted through some papers in a file folder and pulled one out. "I only know the official casualty message given me by Fifth Army Headquarters this morning over the phone."

"Read it," Peg said.

The Sergeant lifted the paper to the light. "It states that 'Sergeant (E-5) Michael Eugene Mullen, US 54 93'—so on—'died while at a night defensive position when artillery fire from friendly forces landed in the area.'" Sergeant Fitzgerald's hand dropped. "I'm sorry. I really am very sorry, Mr. and Mrs. Mullen." He put the paper away and began buttoning up his trenchcoat as if to leave. "Generally, at this time," he said, "families of casualties prefer to be alone with their priests—"

"Sit down," Peg said.

"Perhaps," Sergeant Fitzgerald was saying, "tomorrow would be a better time to—"

"*Sit down!*" Peg repeated. "We're going to talk about this message, this official casualty report."

"Mrs. Mullen, I only—" the Sergeant began.

"Sergeant," Gene ordered, "sit down and read that thing again."

Fitzgerald cleared his throat. "'Sergeant (E-5) Michael Eugene Mullen, US 54 93 22 54, died while at a night defensive position when artillery fire from friendly forces landed in the area,'" he read. He looked up from the paper. "That's all it says. Really."

"Listen," Gene said. "I was a master sergeant in the United States Army myself during World War Two, and I . . .." He stopped, no longer certain what the point was that he had wished to make.

"We're going to talk about this message," Peg said. "I want you to explain it to me. This word 'friendly'—what do you mean by 'friendly'?"

"It merely means that it wasn't enemy artillery," the Sergeant said. "Your son was killed by friendly fire."

"Friendly fire? *Friendly* fire?" Peg repeatedly incredulously.

Sergeant Fitzgerald shrugged lamely. "It means any artillery from forces not the enemy."

"*Not* the enemy! *God damn you!*" Peg cried, beating the chair back with her fists in frustration. "You couldn't even give him the—the *decency* of being killed by the enemy!" She glared at the Sergeant. "These, these 'forces not the enemy'—how come the word 'American' isn't used?"

The back door opened, and Michael's brother John, finished with his chores, came into the kitchen. He peered curiously at the Army sergeant first and next at the priest, then at his mother and father, before quietly taking a place by the door.

"Why wasn't the word 'American' used?" Peg repeated.

"Because it wasn't 'American,'" the Sergeant said.

"And why wasn't the word 'accidental' there?"

"Because, Mrs. Mullen, it wasn't an accident."

"Wait a minute," Peg warned ominously.

Sergeant Fitzgerald began talking about a shelling at the Bien Hoa airbase by South Vietnamese artillery which had resulted in the death of three Americans and the wounding of twenty. Peg had seen the report on the television news a few days earlier, had read about it in the following morning's Des Moines *Register*.

"We know all about Bien Hoa," Peg snapped.

"Well," Sergeant Fitzgerald said, "this is how and where your son was killed."

There was a sudden moan, and before Peg could reach John his knees buckled and he collapsed onto the floor. Gene rushed over and, with Peg, eased their son into a chair. "Oh, poor John," Peg said. "Are you all right?"

"Take it easy, Son," Gene said.

"Michael's dead?" John asked.

"What were you thinking?" Peg asked him. "I thought you knew. I thought seeing the Army car—"

"No, I never thought of Michael," John said. "I thought they were after *me*. That I'd done something wrong."

John had registered for the draft only five days before.

"What happened to Michael?" he asked.

"This sergeant is telling us," Peg said.

"But is he—Is Michael—"

"Yes, Son," Gene said. "Mikey's gone."

"And now," Peg said, whirling on the Sergeant, "we want to know how. And we want to know why!"

"Well," Sergeant Fitzgerald said. "You said you heard about Bien Hoa—"

"*Bien Hoa?*" Peg said. "You don't know very much. Michael wasn't anywhere *near* Bien Hoa. My son was three, four hundred miles from there."

"Good God," Sergeant Fitzgerald said. "It might have happened all over Vietnam that night." He sat down at the kitchen table. "You understand, then, how it could have happened," he said. "The Vietcong infiltrated these South Vietnamese artillery units, got onto their radio channels, and called in the wrong artillery coördinates, so that when the ARVN artillery fired they hit Americans." Sergeant Fitzgerald apologized for not having any more information than was contained in the official casualty message, and added that he did not want to say positively that this was what had happened to Michael. He said only that the Vietcong had infiltrated ARVN radio channels in the past and this was what might have happened to their son's unit.

Sergeant Fitzgerald then explained that the Mullens had the right to request a Special Escort to accompany Michael's body back from Vietnam, and that if they had some special friend of Michael's in mind, someone whom they would like to have return with Michael's remains, they should let him know.

"Well, it's so soon, so sudden," Peg said. "Michael had so many friends. I really don't know . . ."

"There's no need to decide now," Sergeant Fitzgerald said. "Either myself or another Survivor's Assistance Officer will call you tomorrow. Now, what funeral home do you want your son's body delivered to?"

Peg and Gene looked at each other speechlessly.

"Well, we don't know," Peg said. "We really don't know yet."

"How soon will it be before Michael— Michael's body returns?" Gene asked.

"Just as soon as they have a planeful," Sergeant Fitzgerald said.

"Well," Peg said, "I know it won't be long, then."

"One more thing, Sergeant," Gene asked. "How long do we have before Michael's death is announced on the news?"

"As soon as I notify Fort Leonard Wood that I've seen you, they'll release it. That should be about two hours from now."

"Two hours!" Peg protested. "You can't! You've got to give us time to tell our other children. Our daughters are away at college, and we can't let them just hear about it on the radio. You've got to tell them to hold back the news."

"Can't you call them?" Sergeant Fitzgerald asked. "You'll have at least two hours."

"They'll be in classes," Peg said. "I won't be able to reach them until tonight. Can't you wait?"

"I'm sorry, Mrs. Mullen. I'm only a sergeant. I can't tell the Army what to do."

"Well, I can!" Peg said angrily. "I'm not afraid of the Army or the Pentagon. If you won't do anything about it, then I'll—I'll call our senator, Harold Hughes, in Washington. He'll help."

"Look, Mrs. Mullen," Sergeant Fitzgerald said. "You don't have to do that. I'll tell Fifth Army you want them to wait. They won't release the news until you give them the go-ahead."

"Gene, I can't just tell Mary and Patricia over the phone. They'd . . ." She shook her head helplessly.

"What about your sister?" Gene asked.

"Louise?" Peg thought for a moment. "She could maybe drive to Kansas City and pick up Mary . . ."

"Well, if there's nothing else," Sergeant Fitzgerald said.

"I'll walk you out," Gene said.

"That's not necessary," Sergeant Fitzgerald said. "Oh, and Father Shimon? You'll stay a little longer, won't you?"

"Of course, Sergeant. Of course," the priest said.

Peg just looked at Father Shimon and shrugged. Back in November, after a Sunday Mass, she had stopped on the way out of church to ask Father Shimon to say some special prayers for Michael. "You've got to pray for him, Father," she had said. "He hasn't got a chance."

"Oh, I know, I know," Father Shimon had replied, taking Peg by the arm to move her out of the path of his other parishioners. "I do pray for him. I'm praying for him every day. We pray for all our servicemen."

Peg telephoned a friend in La Porte to tell her that Michael was dead and to ask if she would be good enough to drive the seventy-five miles to Iowa City to inform Patricia, who was a senior at the University of Iowa there. Peg next called her sister, Louise Petersen, in Des Moines, and asked her to pick up Mary, who was a freshman at Rockhurst College, Michael's alma mater, in Kansas City. And then she called her brothers—William Goodyear, in Lake City, Iowa, and Howard Goodyear, in Pittsburgh. She did not cry. She kept the calls short; she remained in control of herself. She informed them only of what she had been told so far—that Michael had been killed by artillery fire from friendly forces, possibly South Vietnamese. Her brothers told her that they would arrive at the farm as soon as possible. When she finished, she saw that Sergeant Fitzgerald had left and that Gene was waiting to use the phone.

Gene telephoned the local newspapers and television stations and gave them what few details he knew, and asked them not to release the news until he and his wife had been able to inform their daughters. While Gene was doing that, Peg began drawing up a list of people they would need to get in touch with.

"Now, Peg," Father Shimon said, joining Peg at the table. "Ahh, I didn't know Michael very well and I'm sure you'll want, ahh, someone else to say the Mass."

"Well, yes," Peg said. "As a matter of fact, we'll want Father Hemesath to say the Mass." Father Gregory Hemesath, of St. Peter's Church, in New Haven, a small town in Mitchell County, in northern Iowa, was an old friend of the Mullens'.

"That's just fine," Father Shimon said. "You just write down whoever you want and I'll ask them. I'll bow out and won't have any part in the, ahh, funeral Mass."

"We'll want music, too," Gene said, pausing in mid-phone call. "Michael always liked good music."

"We would like Sister Mary Richard and the Don Bosco Chorus," Peg said.

"Oh, well," Father Shimon said. "That's fine. That's just fine."

"And I'd like Father Hirsch to say a few words," Peg said. Father Robert Hirsch was the principal of Don Bosco, where all the Mullen children had gone. "And I want a white funeral." (The "black funeral," or Requiem Mass, the traditional Catholic funeral Mass, is one of mourning. The "white funeral," or Mass of Resurrection, introduced in 1969, is a celebration of rebirth and of entrance into eternal life.)

"I can't, Peg," the priest said, shaking his head. "I can't have one."

"And why not?"

"Because when the permission order came to change the service, each priest had to request permission from the archdiocese. I didn't want the change, so I ignored it."

"That doesn't matter," Peg said. "All you've got to do is just have it now. We had one only two months ago, a few miles from here, when that boy from Jesup died in Vietnam."

"Nope. Nope. Nope," Father Shimon said. "I can't do it."

Peg regarded him coldly, then lowered her head and went back to work on her list.

After a moment, the priest stood up. "Well," Father Shimon said, "I, ahh, probably should be going."

"Fine, Father," Peg said.

A few minutes later, the Mullens heard the priest's car drive away. Gene, off the telephone, came over to the kitchen table. There was nothing they could do while they were waiting for the rest of the family to arrive but make a list of those friends who would want and need to know that which they themselves were still scarcely willing or able to accept: their son Michael was dead.

The Mullens' friends and neighbors, stunned by word of Michael's death, began arriving at the farm shortly after Father Shimon left. The men, some wearing faded coveralls, ankle-high work boots, and Day-Glo-orange earflapped vinyl caps, and some wearing their Sunday suits, approached Gene hesitantly; they touched him on the shoulder, placed their calloused hands almost tenderly on his back. Their wives, in woollen slacks and heavy hand-knit cardigans, brought stews and casseroles, baskets of food, and pots of coffee that they set to simmer at the rear of the Mullen's stove. And then they moved back to take Peg's hands in their own, hugged her, kissed her lightly on the cheek, begged her to give them something to do, wanting to help.

The women gathered around the kitchen table with Peg, and the men sat in the living room with John and Gene. Over and over, the men tried to express their sorrow, tried to say something comforting about Michael's service to his country. And suddenly, astonishingly, one of the men, and then another, would begin to cry, and would wipe at his face with a big, billowing pocket bandanna.

What could the Mullens say to these friends, these well-meaning neighbors who had driven out to see them? Peg and Gene could not help thinking how none of these people's sons had had to go. How Michael was the only boy from any of the farms around who had put himself through graduate school, how he had shown the most potential for being successful at farming. What was more, the Mullens sensed that the general attitude among their son's contemporaries was not that Michael had been a patriot but, rather, that he had been a poor, unfortunate scapegoat who hadn't had enough sense or enough pull not to get caught. "I don't need to *be* here! I don't need to *be* here!" Michael had protested that night he telephoned from Des Moines. "I simply didn't *need* to be drafted!"

.　.　.

There is no telegraph office in La Porte City. Telegrams are transmitted by telephone from the Waterloo Western Union office to the La Porte city hall, and it is old Peter Dobkin's job to deliver the telegrams in person. Dobkin, a tall, thin, grandfatherly-looking First World War veteran in his early seventies, knocked on the Mullens' door on Sunday morning, Washington's Birthday.

Gene Mullen ushered Dobkin into the kitchen, which was crowded again with the Mullen family and friends.

"Hello, Peter," Peg said. "Would you care for a cup of coffee?"

"No. No, thank you, Mrs. Mullen," he said. "I've come on official business. I've got a telegram for you."

"Oh? Well, fine, then." Peg started to reach for the telegram, but Dobkin didn't pass it to her.

"I'm supposed to read it to you," he said. He looked at his wristwatch, and then, as the voices hushed about him, began to read: "Time: 11:17 A.M. To: 'Mr. and Mrs. Oscar E. Mullen. Report. Deliver. Don't phone.'" Dobkin paused to clear his throat, then continued: "'The Secretary of the Army has asked me to express his deep regret that your son, Sergeant Michael E. Mullen, died in Vietnam on 18 February 1970. He was at a night defensive position when artillery fire from friendly forces landed in the area. Please accept my deepest sympathy. This confirms personal notification made by a representative of the Secretary of the Army.' It is signed 'Kenneth G. Wickham, Major General, United States Army, C-052-189, the Adjutant General, Department of the Army, Washington, D.C.'"

There was an awkward moment of silence while Dobkin stood there in a pose somewhat suggesting the position of attention, and then Peg said, "Well, thank you, Peter."

Dobkin nodded, handed her the telegram, and left.

Sunday afternoon, Peter Dobkin returned with a second telegram. "Time: 3:05 P.M. To: 'Oscar Mullen. Report. Deliver. Don't phone. . . .'" The telegram contained information on the return of Michael's body, and on how much money would be allowed for the burial, and cautioned the Mullens not to set a date for the funeral until the Army told them when Michael's body would arrive in La Porte. It also listed Michael's rank as private first class, not sergeant. The error was routine administrative carelessness, but as an indication of the bureaucratic impersonality with which the Army treated the death of their son it infuriated the Mullens. Dobkin handed the telegram to Peg, and then, because he was also a representative of the local Veterans of Foreign Wars chapter, he began talking about the military funeral he expected the Mullens to hold. "We can provide an Honor Guard and a bugler at the grave," Dobkin was saying. "Oh, the Honor Guard will be in uniform, white helmets, and ties, with regulation Army rifles. We will fire a salute if you wish—"

"I *don't* wish!" Peg said.

"Pardon?"

"We don't want a military funeral, Peter," Peg said. "Michael was a biochemistry student, not a professional soldier."

"Well, yes," Dobkin said, "but he's entitled—"

"I don't care," Peg said.

"O.K., but if you should change your mind—"

"We won't!" Gene said, with such certainty that Peg looked at him with surprise.

"You don't want one, either?" she asked.

Gene Mullen had been on one of the first Honor Guard firing squads in Iowa during the Second World War. The body of a young soldier had been brought back to Des Moines for a military funeral, and his grave was no more than twenty-five feet from one of the main roads into Des Moines. As Gene and the rest of the Honor Guard had stood at attention with their rifles at Present Arms, car after car had passed by. Not one driver had slowed or paid the least bit of attention. Gene didn't want that sort of thing to happen to his boy. And, too, he knew who would make up Dobkin's Honor Guard firing squad. Later, when Peg asked him why he hadn't wanted a military funeral, he answered, "Because I just don't want those 'U.S.O. soldiers' firing over our son's grave."

Several of the Mullens' friends called that afternoon to ask them to release the news of Michael's death, since there were many people in La Porte who still thought it was only a rumor. Peg called the local radio and television stations and newspapers and told them that it was all right to release the information that Gene had given them the day before.

A little after ten o'clock on Monday morning, an Army captain arrived at the farm and introduced himself as Ralph T. Pringle, a Survivors' Asistance Officer. He had come to the farm to pick up their request for the Special Escort and Alternate Special Escort. The Mullens named Thomas Hurley and John Salvato, two boys who had been in college with Michael and who were now in Vietnam. Captain

Pringle said he would send their request to the Pentagon immediately, since time was short.

"Now, Mr. and Mrs. Mullen," Captain Pringle went on, "you can plan on a delay of about ten days between the time of your son's death and his body's arrival. That would mean he should arrive in Waterloo on or about the— Let's see, the twenty-eighth."

"He'll be here Saturday?" Gene asked.

"We can't state that for certain," Captain Pringle said. "The time of his arrival depends entirely on the number of deaths in Vietnam during the week he died."

"We know that," Peg said. "Sergeant Fitzgerald told us the body is returned when they have enough to make a planeful. I also know Michael will be home soon. I'm sure the losses are greater than we're being told. I'm positive of that."

. . .

[News came that Michael's body] would arrive at the Waterloo Airport at seven-forty-five the following evening, February 25th, "escorted by Sergeant First Class Ronald Fallon."

"*Fallon?*" Peg asked. "We didn't ask for any Sergeant Fallon! Hold on a minute, will you?" She cupped the mouthpiece and called to Gene, "It's the funeral home. They say Michael's body will be here tomorrow night—escorted by a Sergeant Ronald Fallon."

"Who's he?" Gene asked.

"Hello?" Peg said into the telephone. "We don't know any Sergeant Fallon. We've never heard of him. He isn't the escort we asked for." As soon as she could, Peg called Captain Pringle. He explained that he had telegraphed their request for the Special Escort to the Memorial Division at the Pentagon the day before, but that either it had arrived too late in the day for anyone to act on it or it had been ignored because Monday was an official holiday, Washington's Birthday having fallen on a Sunday.

"Captain Pringle," Peg said (and as she went on talking she began to come down hard on her "r"s). "Captain Pringle, may I remind you that our son tramped through the mud and jungles of Vietnam for five months regardless of holidays, and we still want the escort we chose, not this Sergeant Fallon, who nobody's heard of. Now, we were told that to have a deceased soldier's body returned accompanied by a Special Escort chosen by the next of kin was our right. A right accorded the families of *all* war victims. Isn't that so?"

"Yes, but—"

"Then that's what we'll have," Peg said. "That's who we want. We don't want this Fallon, who Michael never met. We want either John Salvato or Tom Hurley—those are the boys we want. Now, don't you tell me that the Pentagon can't even honor the dead by providing the services they need, just because it's a holiday."

"All right, Mrs. Mullen," Pringle said. "I'll call the Pentagon and see what I can do."

About twenty minutes later, Captain Pringle called back. "Mrs. Mullen," he said, "I'll give it to you straight. A man in the Pentagon in the office of Special Escorts, when I told him you still wanted your escort, he said, 'Tell that lady in La Porte City that she can have her escort in—take it or leave it—ten to fifteen more days.'"

"Fifteen more days!" Peg said. "Captain Pringle, you can tell that son of a bitch in the Pentagon that I'll wait fifteen *years* for my son to come back! My son's *dead!* We could put off having him come back in a casket *forever!* We don't care when he gets back. He's *dead!"*

Captain Pringle tried to explain why there would be such a long delay: that it would take a couple of days to cut the orders in Washington, another couple of days to get them to Vietnam, another couple of days to locate their escort, another day to get him on a plane, and so on.

Peg listened impatiently, then said, "I don't believe you. My boy was killed in the jungles of Vietnam, airlifted out of there, rammed through a mortuary in Saigon, put on a plane, and was in Oakland in less than five days! So don't you tell me that you can't get a *live* boy out of there in less than two days!"

Captain Pringle apparently thought for a moment. Then he said, "I'll tell you what, Mrs. Mullen. I think you'd be better off if you called the Pentagon yourself and told them that. Talk to a man named Murtaugh—he's in charge of Special Escorts, and he's the one to talk to." He gave her the telephone number.

"Well, I don't see why we have to make that call," Peg said. "You're the man who's supposed to assist us."

"I'm trying to, Mrs. Mullen," Captain Pringle said. "But I think you should be aware that your insistence on the Special Escort will definitely be a delaying factor. A great many people prefer to cancel the Special Escort requests so that they can more quickly complete their funeral plans, but if you insist . . . I feel certain you'll have more success if you call Mr. Murtaugh at the Pentagon yourself."

As soon as Captain Pringle hung up, Peg called Senator Harold Hughes' office in Washington. Hughes was on the Senate floor at the time, but he later returned Peg's call. Through her activities with the County Democratic Party, she had met Hughes years earlier, when he was the governor of Iowa. Peg relayed Captain Pringle's remarks about Mr. Murtaugh at the Pentagon, and said she felt that the Senator was the only one she could turn to for help.

Senator Hughes hesitated. "Peg, I can't cure all the ills in the world."

"But can't you do something?" Peg pleaded. "My family is upset."

"All right, Peg, we'll try."

Apparently, Senator Hughes did intervene in the Mullens' behalf. Between seven and eight that evening, Peter Dobkin delivered a fourth telegram—this time over the telephone. The telegram, from the Oakland Army Terminal Mortuary, informed the Mullens that they should disregard all previous messages—that Michael's body would be held pending arrival of his Special Escort. An hour later, the Memorial Division duty officer at the Pentagon telephoned the Mullens to say that their request for a Special Escort would be honored after all.

And then Father Shimon called.

"Peg," he said, "I've been thinking about what you want. This white funeral, this Don Bosco Chorus, Father This and Father That, and, ahh, I think it's time to call a halt to the production you're talking about for Michael's funeral. I can't go along with you, Peg. We're not going to have a production."

"Well, Father Shimon," Peg replied, "if you consider perfection a production, then that's what we'll have. Because Michael's life was sort of perfect. He did things well. He didn't leave many jobs undone. If doing things right for him means having a production, we'll just have a production."

Father Shimon said, "Nope. Nope. Nope."

Peg hung up on him.

Peter Dobkin telephoned the Mullens early Wednesday morning with a fifth telegram. It was sent by the Memorial Division, and it confirmed that either Tom Hurley or John Salvato would be returned from Vietnam to serve as Michael Mullen's Special Escort.

The morning mail contained a nine-by-twelve-inch manila envelope from the White House. Inside, on a half-size White House letterhead, was a message signed by a minor aide stating that President Nixon wished her to know that he was truly sorry that her son had died. The note was paper-clipped to a collection of President Nixon's Vietnamization speeches. Peg was so offended that she showed the contents of the envelop to no one, resealed it, and mailed it back to the White House with the notation, printed in large red letters in the upper left-hand corner, "RETURN TO SENDER. NOT INTERESTED."

Added to the Mullens' anguish over the continuing wait was their uncertainty over what condition Michael's body would be in. A close friend had told them that her sister-in-law law's brother, a mortician in Oakland, had called to tell her he had worked on Michael's body. He said that three plainloads of bodies had arrived in Oakland—one, on Monday, of "viewable" bodies and two, on Tuesday, of "non-viewable" bodies. Peg and Gene were unable to believe that Michael could be "viewable." If Michael had been killed by ARVN artillery, would he not have been blown to pieces?

During the six days since the Mullens had learned of their son's death, their farmhouse had been filled with family and friends waiting for Michael's body to arrive. The people in town knew only that for some reason or other the Mullens had refused to permit the corpse to be returned. A great many La Porte people couldn't understand the Mullens' behavior, and thought it vaguely unAmerican, somehow unpatriotic.

Thursday morning, Father Shimon telephoned and asked Peg if she knew yet when the funeral would be held.

"I hope to know by noon today, Father," Peg said. "If Michael comes today, we'll hold the funeral on Saturday."

"*Saturday?*" the priest said. "You know we can't have the funeral on Saturday!"

"Why not?" Peg asked. "Why can't we?"

"We have catechism on Saturday, Peg. And I'm, ahh, I'm not going to interrupt my catechism program."

"Well, O.K., Father," Peg said. "Then we'll have our funeral service in our front yard if we have to. But we'll have it on Saturday if this is what we want."

She hung up the telephone and looked first at her husband and then at her houseful of family and friends, the classmates of their children, neighbors who had come to their farmhouse. She told Gene she thought it might be a good idea to get out of the house for a while.

Four more boys from northern Iowa had died in Vietnam that week, and one was missing in action. Sergeant Fitzgerald had confided to the Mullens that it was only a matter of time before he would have to tell the missing boy's mother that her son was dead. The young man had apparently been trapped and incinerated in his tank; but because no identifiable remains existed, the Army was, for the time being, categorizing him as missing in action. The woman was a widow, and he had been her only son. Peg thought that they should visit her to see whether there was anything they might do.

. . .

It was now the morning of Friday, February 27th, the seventh day since the Mullens had learned of their son's death and the third day since Captain Pringle had told Peg Mullen to call the Pentagon herself. The Mullens had not heard from the Captain since, so they still did not know who would be escorting Michael's body, nor did they know when it would arrive. Several members of the Mullen family were anxious, tired of waiting, and beginning to grow impatient with Peg.

By four o'clock that afternoon, when the Captain had still not called, Peg decided to telephone his office. She was told that Captain Pringle was not in, that he was not expected back, and that she might try him later at his home.

When Pig did try Captain Pringle's home, there was no answer, so she tried his office again. This time, the phone was busy. For the next hour, Peg tried both phones. The office continued busy and there was no answer at the house. When the office phone remained busy for several hours into the evening, Peg called a friend who worked for the Northwestern Bell Telephone Company in Waterloo to ask whether there might be something wrong with the Captain's phone. Peg continued trying to reach Captain Pringle until eleven o'clock that night before finally giving up.

Peg's friend who worked for the Telephone Company called early Saturday morning to say that Captain Pringle's office phone had in fact been off its hook. The Mullens decided that they would have to help themselves. They first got in touch with Ozark Air Lines, one of the airlines serving their part of the Midwest, and explained that it had been a week since they received notification of their son's death, and that they were finding it almost unbearable to wait until Monday before hearing from the Army again. Might Ozark Air Lines have any advance booking that would indicate when their son's body would be returned?

Within minutes, an Ozark employee was able to tell the Mullens that Michael's body was scheduled to arrive at the Waterloo Airport on the airline's 7:45 P.M. Sunday flight.

At about ten o'clock Saturday morning, Sergeant Fitzgerald checked in. He said that the Captain had gone off without notifying him that he was to act in the Captain's stead. Peg told him that they had been able to learn when Michael was to reach Waterloo, but could the Sergeant find out for them which of the two boys they had requested as the escort would be the one to accompany him? Sergeant Fitzgerald explained that there was no way for him to find out; he knew only that the body would be escorted.

Gene called Ozark Air Lines again, and the same employee who had helped them before was able to check the passenger manifest within minutes and tell them that it was Tom Hurley, Michael's friend from Rockhurst, who would be coming. The Mullens telephoned Hurley's parents, in Sedalia, Missouri, and informed them that their son would be arriving in Waterloo the next night. His parents could barely conceal their surprise and delight, although they were quick to add that they were terribly sorry for the circumstances that had permitted him to return. The Mullens understood.

At 7:45 P.M. on Sunday, the Ozark Air Lines flight carrying Michael's casket touched down at the far end of the Waterloo Airport runway. Peg was not there to see it. She simply could not make herself drive out to the airport where six months earlier Michael had kissed her goodbye and told her not to worry, saying that it would all be over March 1st. It was March 1st and it was all over. Patricia remained behind to keep Peg company, and John and Mary went with Gene and Sergant Fitzgerald to meet the plane.

Tom Hurley was the last passenger to leave the plane. His parents, who were inside the terminal, moved up to the window to watch. Hurley walked down the boarding steps and stood next to the freight bay, watching while Michael's casket, covered by an American flag, was slid onto a baggage conveyor. The conveyor then backed away from the plane, turned, and gently lowered and guided Michael's casket into a hearse. Only when the back doors of the hearse were closed did Hurley enter the terminal to embrace his family.

The Hurleys departed together, and the Mullens and Sergeant Fitzgerald followed the hearse to Waterloo. Michael's casket was taken to the Loomis Funeral Home. Inside, Tom Loomis, the director, asked the Mullens to wait out in the vestibule while the casket was opened. Sergeant Fitzgerald followed Loomis, and Gene, Mary, and John stayed behind. They sat silently, patiently, in the vestibule, wondering whether they could be certain it was Michael, worried that his body would have been so shattered by the artillery shell's explosion that they might never be able to know. After about twenty minutes, Tom Loomis returned and told Gene that he could now view the body. Gene rose and glanced, stricken, at his children.

"We'll be all right, Dad. You go ahead," John said.

Gene nodded and slowly turned away. He took a few steps and

paused in the dorway of the funeral parlor's viewing room. The casket, its cover raised, was in the center of the room. Feeling apprehensive and ill, Gene made himself walk forward until he could see a uniformed body inside.

It was Michael, his son. There was no question about it.

Gene made himself move close enough to touch the cold hands so carefully folded across his son's body. Gene examined the military tunic, the strangeness of its brass buttons, the uniform jacket's lapels with the brass infantry and United States insignia, the black Army tie, the starched shirt collar, the throat, the lower jaw, the still, blue lips, the mustache—the *mustache?* Michael had a mustache! When had he grown a mustache? But it wasn't the mustache that bothered Gene. There was something else. He wasn't sure what; he just sensed that there was something wrong. Suddenly, he realized that there wasn't a mark on his son.

Gene looked up at the funeral director in bewilderment, then back down. He noticed that Michael's face was a little puffy, that his neck seemed swollen, but if it weren't for the uniform there would be no sign that he'd been in a war at all. In exasperation and puzzlement, Gene removed his glasses and wiped his hands across his eyes.

"Something wrong, Gene?" the funeral direceter asked.

"But, Tom, he was supposed to have been killed by *artillery!*"

"Well, Gene, when we lifted the body up out of the casket— We had to, because it had settled into it a little. When we lifted the body, I couldn't feel any broken bones."

"Do you think he could have been killed by the concussion?"

"I couldn't say," Loomis said. "I just don't know." The funeral director leaned forward and traced his finger beneath Michael's shirt collar. "There's some tape along here," he said. "But that's where they embalmed him."

Gene looked again at his son. For some reason, Michael's coal-black hair, which when he had left was already thickly flecked with white, had become a strange and alien brown. He noticed, too, that his son's complexion, which had always been dark, almost mahogany-colored, seemed gray, chalky, a pallor foreign even to death. But Michael's hair and complexion were the only things that seemed strange, and Gene kept asking himself how Michael could have been killed by an artillery burst, an explosion of burning, jagged chunks of shrapnel, and still be perfectly whole. And the more he tried to understand it, the more agitated and suspicious he became, until finally he asked the funeral director where Sergeant Fitzgerald had gone.

"I'm right here, Mr. Mullen," Fitzgerald said. The Sergeant had been standing out of the way at the back of the room, and now he came forward.

Gene scowled at the Sergeant, "Now, I want to know *how* my son died! I want a death certificate. I want a death certificate stating how my son was killed."

Sergeant Fitzgerald opened an accordion-pleated manila file folder. He fiddled through the papers and finally pulled a sheet from the file.

It was the paper from which he had read the official casualty message to the Mullens. Fitzgerald simply began to read it again: ". . . died while at a night defensive position when artillery fire from friendly forces—"

"That's not it! You know that isn't it!" Gene interrupted indignantly. "Look at him! *Look* at his body! There isn't a mark on him. Now, let's get down to the bottom of that stack of papers and find out. I want to *know*. I want a death certificate. I want this confirmed before I bury that boy or I'm going to have that body held."

The Sergeant began leafing through the folder again. "I don't have a death certificate, Mr. Mullen," he said. "All I have is the original message I read to you—that and the note I made when I received the information over the phone. That's this, here." Sergeant Fitzgerald resignedly handed Gene a piece of white typing paper on which he'd handwritten the note. It said, "Sgt. Michael E. Mullen, son of Oscar and Margaret Mullen, RFD #3, La Porte City, Iowa. Killed 18 Feb 70 near the village of Chu Lai. Non-battle."

Gene studied the page for several moments, and then asked, "What does this mean—'Non-battle'?"

"It means a casualty not the result of action by hostile forces," Sergeant Fitzgerald replied.

When Gene Mullen returned to the farm that night after viewing Michael's body, Peg asked him, "Is it Michael?"

"Yes," Gene said, dashing the one desperate remaining hope she had been nurturing all along.

.   .   .

A few days after Michael's funeral, a letter arrived at the Mullens' farm:

DEPARTMENT OF THE ARMY
HEADQUARTERS, 1ST BATTALION,
6TH INFANTRY
198TH INFANTRY BRIGADE,
AMERICAL DIVISION
APO SAN FRANCISCO 96219

2 Mar 1970

MR. AND MRS. OSCAR E. MULLEN
RURAL ROUTE 3,
LA PORTE CITY, IOWA 50651
DEAR MR. AND MRS. MULLEN:

It is with deepest sorrow that I extend to you the sympathy of the men of the 1st Battalion, 6th Infantry, for the loss of your son, Michael.

On the early morning of February 18, 1970, Michael's unit was located in their night defensive position near the village of Tu Chanh, approximately 13 miles south of Tam Ky City, in Quang Tin Province, Republic of Vietnam. At 2:50 A.M., the unit was adjusting artillery to provide a predetermined range of fire in the event of enemy contact. During the testing, Michael received a fatal missile wound when an artillery round fell short of its intended target and detonated near his position. May you gain some consolation in knowing that Michael was not subjected to any prolonged suffering.

I sincerely hope that the knowledge that Michael was an exemplary soldier who gave his life assisting his fellowman and in the service of his country will comfort you in this hour of great sorrow.

A memorial service was conducted for your son. Michael's comrades joined me in rendering military honors and final tribute to him. You were in our thoughts and prayers at that time also.

The sincere sympathy of this unit is extended to you in your bereavement.

Sincerely yours,
s/
H. NORMAN SCHWARZKOPF
LTC, Infantry
Commanding

The second paragraph was the only one that interested Peg. She picked up a ballpoint pen and carefully underlined "Tu Chanh," "13," "Tam Ky," "Quang Tin," and then, after a pause, she underlined "prolonged."

What did that mean? It could mean that Michael had suffered for anywhere from a few seconds to fifteen minutes or more. But he had certainly suffered.

"Near the village of Tu Chanh, approximately 13 miles south of Tam Ky City . . ." Peg's Hammond map of "Vietnam and Neighboring Countries" showed Tam Ky about twenty miles northwest of Chu Lai. Chu Lai was where he had been when he telephoned his mother. His final words had been "Mom, it is so sticky over here—goodbye."

"Michael's unit was located in their night defensive position," the letter stated. "At 2:50 A.M., the unit was adjusting artillery to provide a predetermined range of fire in the event of enemy contact." Peg read those two lines again: "Michael's unit was located . . . The unit was adjusting artillery . . ." It could mean only that Michael's unit was adjusting the artillery. In other words, someone in Michael's own outfit had called in the artillery that had killed her son. Why? And why at two-fifty—nearly three o'clock in the morning? It didn't make sense unless they were under attack. And yet the Mullens had been told that Michael was a non-battle casualty. The letter clearly implied that the unit hadn't been under attack, that the artillery had been called for "in the event of enemy contact"—*in case of* enemy contact. There was nothing in the letter about Vietcong infiltrating radio channels, no mention that the artillery was from a South Vietnamese unit. In fact, as Peg studied that paragraph, she became more and more suspicious.

Why had Michael's unit, which apparently was not under attack, asked for artillery to be fired over its position at three o'clock in the morning?

How could the one shell have "detonated near his position"—have exploded next to Michael—and left him virtually unmarked except for a small hole in his back the size of a pen top—or a bullet?

Why, if Michael's unit had called in the artillery, hadn't he been in a foxhole? Why hadn't he been wearing his flak jacket?

Why had the shell fallen short?

Why had the only letter that the Mullens received from anyone even remotely connected with their son been from the battalion commander? Why had they not heard from his company commander? His platoon leader? Why had she not heard from anyone in Michael's unit? He had been dead for two weeks. Hadn't Michael had any friends?

Had no one else been hurt?

There had not been any newspaper accounts of an accidental shelling—nothing on the evening news. The casualty list released the week Michael died listed only eighty-eight deaths, and yet three planeloads—planes supposedly carrying seventy-five bodies each—had flown into California in just two days.

What had *really* happened to her son?

. . .

What about how he died? Why was the artillery fired at three o'clock in the morning? Who called in that round? How come nothing was ever in the paper about this? Why wasn't there an investigation? Don't you understand?" She looked sharply at Gene. "Schwarzkopf's letter doesn't tell us *any*thing! The Army doesn't believe people should really know how their sons died. That people really want to know."

"We'll find out," Gene said.

"But how?" Peg asked. "Who can we write? You know the Army won't tell us anything."

"The *official* Army won't," Gene said. "But we could write one of Mikey's friends."

"*Who?* We don't know any of his friends. The Army won't give us any names. Michael never told us any—No, wait! Wait a minute! There *was* somebody." Peg went to the box containing Michael's letters and began sifting through them. "He mentioned one boy. Someone from Waterloo . . . In one of his last letters . . . Here! Here it is: 'Ran into a boy from Waterloo by name of Culpepper.' "

Gene walked over to the Waterloo-Cedar Falls Telephone Directory and riffled through the pages. "There are four Culpeppers in the book."

"Call them," Peg said. "See if one of them has a son in Vietnam."

Gene looked up at the clock over the wall oven. "Peg, it's after midnight."

. . .

The following week's mail brought letters of consolation from the commanding general of Michael's Americal Division, Lloyd B. Ramsey, and from Stanley R. Resor, the Secretary of the Army. Major General Ramsey wrote, "We sincerely hope that your burden may be lightened by the knowledge that Michael was a model soldier, whose actions and conduct brought credit to himself, the Division, and the United States Army. Michael was an exemplary soldier whose ability, spirit, and dedication to the service earned for him the respèct of his associates and superiors alike. . . . We share your burden and we pray that you will find consolation in the sympathy of your friends, your family, and your faith." (Peg later sent Major General Ramsey copies of Michael's letters, "so that you can see what one of your model, exemplary soldiers thought of you and your war.") The Secretary of the Army wrote,

"We are proud of his military accomplishments and grateful to him for his contribution to our Nation's strength."

The kitchen table was now covered with piles of mail, and Peg tossed both of these letters onto the pile she reserved for "official mail." The letters landed in such a way that General Ramsey's overlapped Colonel Schwarzkopf's just enough to display the date "2 Mar 1970" stamped on both. The rubber stamp infuriated her; it was as if some anonymous Army bureaucrat had simply decided, "O.K., on March 2nd send all these letters out." Suddenly she noticed something even more disturbing: the "1970" on the two letters was stamped just a hair lower than the "2 Mar" and both "Mar"'s seemed to tilt slightly to the left. Of course, Peg realized that the Army bought rubber date stamps by the thousand, but was it mere coincidence that the battalion's rubber stamp and the division's contained identical flaws? The more likely explanation, she thought, was that the two letters had originated in the same office. And she felt certain that the correspondence could have been coordinated for only one reason: the Army had something to hide.

Peg had cause to be skeptical. During the week Michael was killed, seven other Iowans died in the same part of Vietnam. If these eight deaths were about average for the total losses from each of the fifty states, it would indicate that some four hundred Americans must have died that week in Vietnam. Peg already knew that during the week Michael's body arrived, one planeload of bodies had landed in Oakland, California, on Monday and two on Tuesday. The planes carried seventy-five bodies each. And yet the official casualty figure for the week of Michael's death listed only eighty-eight Americans killed in Vietnam.

On Wednesday, March 11th, the Waterloo *Courier* published a letter from a local woman appealing to her fellow-citizens "to fly the American flag . . . in recognition of veterans and our men in Vietnam." The woman accused her fellow-citizens of lacking patriotism. Peg wrote a furious reply, which appeared on Sunday, March 15th:

Please get down and pray for the boys in Vietnam and for the boys and girls who are not waving the flag in defiance to this cruel and immoral war.

Our boy was buried on March 3 in a beautiful, Christian, "non-military" funeral. We have been criticized because we did not have a military funeral and our decision was made on the fact that the Army took our boy (who was a chemist and not a soldier), trained him to kill, sent him to Vietnam and on February 21 they tell us he was killed by friendly forces—accidentally, we will never believe.

Do you realize how many thousands of American boys have been lost in this manner—denied the decency of being killed by the enemy? These boys' deaths are listed as "non-battle"—are they included in casualty lists? Do we know how many bodies come back to Oakland each week—does the number of dead tie in with the casualty list? Think about this. Please . . . "think"— "read"—"study"—"evaluate" this war.

Publication of this letter marked the opening of an overt anti-war campaign by the Mullens—an effort that was to require a deeper and more consuming commitment than either of them then realized. After Michael was sent to Vietnam, in September of 1969, Peg had begun writing to President Nixon, pleading with him to end the war, and in October she had worn a black Moratorium armband into Washburn, a small town just north of the Mullens' farm. Whenever the Des Moines *Register* carried an account of an Iowa soldier's death, she would send the clipping to Iowa's hawkish Republican senator, Jack Miller, with the note "Put another notch in your gun, Jack." She had joined a national organization called Another Mother for Peace. But, Peg had to admit, her anti-war protests had been limited and ineffective. And private. From now on, she would make her opposition known.

On Thursday, March 19th, Peg returned from the mailbox with a letter from Martin Culpepper, in Vietnam. Culpepper's letter, which was written in response to hers, was the first that the Mullens had received from anyone who had served in Michael's company—C (Charlie) Company, 1st Battalion, 6th Infantry, 198th Infantry Brigade of the American Division, headquartered at Chu Lai. Michael had been dead a month, and they still had not heard from any members of his platoon or from an R.O.T.C. lieutenant he had mentioned in one letter or from his company commander. Peg had written to the Pentagon complaining, "It's just too damned bad that we cannot find out who lived and died with our son. There's simply no communication, and I firmly believe my son had at least *one* friend in Vietnam."

From Culpepper's letter, which was handwritten and was three pages long, Peg discovered that six or seven other soldiers in Charlie Company had been wounded on the night of Michael's death, and one other had been killed. The account began:

It was an air burst, it hit in between your son's bunker and another bunker. The round burst in the air when it hit a tree in between the fox holes. . . . This was about 2:15 A.M. on Feb. 18 before daylight. It was a short round that killed him. Meaning the round didn't travel the distant it was suppose to travel. He was not killed by enemy forces, but an accident.

Culpepper went on to say that Michael had been killed by a "D.T." round, and he explained that D.T.s were defensive targets—targets selected by a unit commander and his forward observer to provide a predetermined range of fire on the routes an enemy was most likely to use in approaching the unit's defensive perimeter. A minimum of two test rounds was fired for each D.T. The first, a white-phosphorus (W.P.) marking round, was set to explode fifty feet above the selected target. If this round detonated at the desired spot, and no corrections were needed, a second round, a high-explosive (H.E.) shell, was then fired to impact on the target. The aiming data necessary to bring the D.T. under fire could then be read off the gun and retained for future use. One line of Culpepper's letter particularly interested Peg: "They normal shot about 200 to 300 meters away from you, they use to do this almost every night until that accident." They *used* to, they stopped. Two killed, six or seven wounded, never anything in the newspapers about it, no investigation, no communication with anyone but Culpepper—who Peg had discovered only by chance. The obvious reason, Peg believed, was that what had happened was so wrong, so inexcusable, that the Army didn't want anybody to find out about it. That was why no one had written to her, why the newspaper stories apparently had been blacked out, and why the letters from the battalion and division commanders had been coordinated. She was certain that at least half the casualties in Vietnam were due to mysterious circumstances—"accidents"—because maps were wrong, because someone high on drugs was shooting off his gun, because men were being killed by their own artillery. In a postscript, Culpepper had added, "If the army's story is different please let me know." Clearly, Culpepper would not be surprised to learn that the Army had lied.

Because the circumstances of Michael's death seemed mysterious to the Mullens, and because his body had been virtually unmarked, they had demanded that the Army send them a death certificate. It arrived on Tuesday, March 17th. The document, a Department of the Army Form 10-249, forwarded from the U.S. Army Mortuary at Danang, was dated February 18, 1970, and below the statement "I have viewed the remains of the deceased and death occurred at the time indicated and from the causes as stated above" was the signature of John S. Schrechter, identified as "MD, CPT., Co D. 23D Medical Bn." The certificate incorrectly listed Michael's parents as Mr. and Mrs. Oscar *T.* Mullen instead of Oscar E. Mullen, the mode of death as "accident," the interval between onset and death as "unknown," and the cause of death ("Enter only one cause per line") as "missile wound of chest." A space reserved for "circumstances surrounding death due to external causes" was blank, and so was a space for indicating whether or not an autopsy had been performed. Although the date and hour of death, "0250 18 February 1970," and the map coordinates for the place of death, "BT 366 015" (a hillside overlooking the village of Tu Chanh), confirmed the information given them in Colonel Schwarzkopf's letter, the death certificate did nothing to allay the Mullens' suspicions. Why was the space reserved for "circumstances surrounding death" blank? Michael, the Mullens had been told, was killed when an artillery round fell short. If, as Colonel Schwarzkopf had said, Michael had not been "subjected to any prolonged suffering," why was the "interval between onset and death" unknown? Most disturbing of all was the question why—since according to Tom Loomis, the funeral director, Michael's only wound had been a small puncture above his right kidney—Captain Schechter had listed Michael's cause of death as a "missile wound of chest." The Mullens wrote back requesting a "complete" medical report on their son's death.

. . .

Peg mailed to the Des Moines *Register* copies of letters from Michael in which he said that President Nixon's Vietnamization program would fail and, referring to anti-war protests, that most of the troops were hoping that things would "get wilder at home." The editors decided to run the letters in the Easter Sunday edition. On March

27th, Good Friday, an editorial quoted excerpts from Michael's letters and concluded:

He was in a night defensive position when artillery fire from friendly forces landed in the area and killed him.

Why? and for what? his parents still ask.

So far some 41,000 Americans and 102,000 "friendlies" have been. killed in this futile war. These are not statistics, they are individual human beings—sons and husbands and brothers.

The *Register* planned to run an article about Peg on the same day it published Michael's letters, so a *Register* reporter, Nick Lamberto, telephoned Peg for an interview. He called at a bad time. Earlier that day, Peg had written to the Memorial Division of the United States Army about Michael's headstone. The Army insisted that if the Mullens accepted the free headstone offered to them, the words "U.S. Army" and "Sergeant" would have to be on it. Peg was so disgusted that she made up her mind to buy a headstone on her own. She went to a memorial carver in Waterloo and recounted her quarrel with the military; the stone carver, a man in his mid-sixties, replied, "God damn the Army! Good for you, Peg. I'll give it to you at cost."

Peg had the stone engraved:

> MICHAEL E. MULLEN
> Born Sept. 11, 1944
> Killed Feb. 18, 1970
> Son of Gene & Peg
> "He dared to ripple my pond"

The quotation was from a letter to the Mullens written by Caroline Roby after Michael's death. Peg was worried that the phrase might seem mawkish, but she considered it the most appropriate sentiment they had received. It described Michael. He never left anything undone. "If someone needed their pond rippled, Michael did it," Peg said. Far more indicative of Peg's mood at this time, however, was the word "Killed." Michael had not died in the war; he had been *killed*.

Lamberto's call came shortly after Peg returned from the stone carver, and she was still furious. Peg complained that "the military-industrial complex in this country has for the past five years systematically drained this great United States of thousands of our future leaders."

Lamberto's piece about Peg began, "A distraught mother, bitter over the death of her son in South Vietnam, has vowed to use his insurance money 'to save the boys still over there.' "

. . .

For close to a week now, the gratuity check for $2,014.20 had been lying on the kitchen table. Gene and Peg were determined to use the Army money to buy space in the Des Moines *Register,* and although they had not yet decided what to say, they knew it was essential to make themselves heard. After the publication of Michael's letters and

Lamberto's interview in the *Register,* the Mullens had received numerous letters and phone calls, and this response had convinced them that they were not alone—that all over Iowa there were families like them, wanting to "cry out." The silent majority's unwillingness to speak out was, the Mullens believed, more than anything else the reason that the war had been allowed to drag on. Each night Gene and Peg stayed up late trying to figure out how to make their neighbors care enough to get involved. The Mullens were obsessed with the war; they were unable to think or talk about anything else. Gene had started looking into the Black Hawk County draft calls, and as he began learning who had received deferments and how, it seemed to him that the Iowa fatalities were coming predominantly from small towns and farm communities, where the boys had "nobody to fight for them." Peg was unable to forget the phone call that Michael made to her and Gene from the Des Moines draft headquarters, where, after his induction, he had spent a day filing case histories of young men who had managed to avoid being drafted. "I simply didn't *need* to be drafted!" he had said, and he had also said that the whole draft setup was corrupt. And so each night Peg and Gene would sit late at the kitchen table talking about the draft and the war. If anyone came to the house, the conversation would turn to the war. Every morning, Gene would tune his transoceanic radio to a Sydney, Australia, station that carried the Vietnam news. At night, the first thing he did when he returned from John Deere was listen to the local news; he read the *Register* and the *Courier* daily. Peg, during the day, would cull what she could from the mail, telephone contacts, and the television news. John, their only child still living at home, was finding it increasingly difficult to be around his parents. No longer able to bear hearing them talk about the war twenty-four hours a day, he would think up one excuse after another for getting out of the house.

One night during the first week of April, Gene was sitting at the kitchen table making little marks on a yellow pad. He and Peg had been discussing their advertisement again. "How many Iowa deaths have there been now?" he asked.

"Altogether? Since the beginning of the war?" Peg thought for a moment. "I suppose somewhere around seven hundred by now. At least that many, don't you think?"

Gene did not answer. He continued to doodle on the pad. Suddenly, he said, "*Crosses!*"

"What?"

"A page full of crosses!" Gene said excitedly. "Think of it! Just crosses. A cross for every boy who died in Vietnam. A page full, a half page—whatever we can afford."

"Of just crosses?"

"Well, we'd need to explain what they mean," Gene said. "Something like 'Each cross represents an Iowa boy who has died—' No, 'who gave his life in Vietnam.' I don't know. You know what to say, Peg. You always put things better than I do."

Peg considered the suggestion for a while. "Just a page full of crosses." She reached over and patted Gene's hand. "You know? I think that's a real good idea."

"Why, thank you, Mother," Gene said, and smiled.

The Mullens' half-page Des Moines *Register* advertisement appeared April 12, 1970, and exploded habitually taciturn Sunday-breakfast tables into conversation throughout the state.

There was a half-inch-high banner headline:

A SILENT MESSAGE TO FATHERS AND MOTHERS OF IOWA:

And below that, in slightly smaller type, were the words:

We have been dying for nine, long, miserable years in Vietnam in an undeclared war . . . how many more lives do you wish to sacrifice because of your SILENCE?

Two inches to the right of the last word were a small black cross and, beneath it, the epitaph *"Sgt. Michael E. Mullen—killed by friendly fire."*

Then came the crosses. Row upon row of crosses. Fourteen rows of forty-nine crosses each, a fifteenth row of twenty-seven, with space left open for more. Their ranks, so starkly aligned and black against the bleak, white page, suggested a photographic negative of some well-kept battlefield cemetery viewed from afar. The crosses blurred, vibrated, played optical tricks. There were too many for the eye to take in. One could only grasp blocks with white space in between. But as the eye moved across the page ranks appeared to open up, re-form themselves into ghostly platoons, companies, battalions on parade.

At the bottom of the page, a legend explained:

These 714 crosses represent the 714 Iowans who have died in Vietnam.

Near the bottom left-hand corner was printed:

In memory of Vietnam War Dead whom our son joined on February 18, 1970 . . . and to those awaiting the acceptable sacrifice in 1970. . . .

On the opposite side appeared the credit:

Sponsored by Mr. and Mrs. Gene Mullen, La Porte City, Iowa.

The Mullens' telephone began ringing at eight o'clock, and it didn't let up for the rest of the day. United Press International interviewed the Mullens at nine. At ten, a news announcer for a Des Moines television station complained to Peg that he had been trying to reach them for several hours but there had been so many incoming calls about their advertisement that he hadn't been able to get an outside line. "Everybody wants to know what you meant by your ad," he said.

Peg explained that the Army had drafted their son, a biochemistry student in graduate school, and sent him to Vietnam; that Michael was on a combat mission when he was killed by his own artillery but was considered a "non-battle casualty" and therefore "wasn't counted." She told the news announcer she was now convinced that the American deaths in Vietnam were much greater than the people at home were being told—that the public didn't realize "how many thousands of American boys have been lost in this manner." Peg said that there was a discrepancy between the actual number of Iowa deaths and the Pentagon's "official casualty lists" and that the death of their son had convinced them that "the time had come for us to speak out." Peg went on, "Our advertisement was our way of telling the world what we feel about the draft, the war, and the loss of life in Vietnam."

One by one, broadcasting stations throughout Iowa telephoned, but the majority of the callers were people who simply wished to express their sympathy and their agreement with the Mullens' views. They were people from Iowa and neighboring states, and were of all ages, and nearly all of them said they were sure that the Mullens would be receiving a lot of "crank calls" (or "outraged calls" or "negative calls"), that the Mullens would be accused of being "un-American" (or "Communists," or "deranged"), but that they had telephoned because "we just wanted to say, 'Good for you!' " Peg replied each time that they hadn't received any calls from people who didn't agree, that *everyone* who had called was sick of the war, too. The person on the other end of the phone would pause, surprised, and then say something like "Well, I'll be darned!"

. . .

The only objection that the Mullens did receive arrived in an envelope bearing the return address of Mr. and Mrs. P. J. Schultz, 2113 Clinton Street, Iowa City. It consisted of a tearsheet of the Mullens' advertisement with a message printed in red ink across the bottom:

MY SON BELIEVED IN WHAT HE WAS FIGHTING FOR IN VIETNAM, FREEDOM from the communists; HE believed that they are taking over country after country like Lenin and Krushev said they would, and he believed it best to stop them in VIETNAM, rather than in the streets of U.S. If your son did not believe this, he was a fool to go, but *don't* drag the rest of our sons down to your son's level.

Peg wrote to the family, but her letter was returned. No one named Schultz lived at that address, and there was no P. J. Schultz in the Iowa City Telephone Directory.

. . .

Peg learned from Martin Culpepper that the publication of Michael's letters and the Lamberto interview in the *Register* had reached Vietnam. "I've just come from Bayonet [the 1st Battalion's base camp] to the field," Culpepper wrote Peg. "In the rear they told me about your articles in the Des Moines *Register*. I'm glad to see that your son told how it was and you had it published so the public can see what goes on over here. . . . I'm glad that you stand up for us boys in Vietnam." Culpepper also told Peg that if anyone asked where she was getting her information, she should "tell them about me," adding, "They can't do anything to me. It might get me out of the field."

Peg was enormously gratified by Culpepper's letter. He had provided vindication for the antagonism that her outspokenness had generated among her neighbors. She was proud to be able to "stand up for us boys in Vietnam." She was even more encouraged when she learned later that soldiers who had seen the advertisement were writing back for fifty copies at a time. The Mullens heard that their anti-war protest was being tacked up on orderly-room walls all over South Vietnam.

Late in April, a letter arrived from Major General Kenneth G. Wickham, the Army Adjutant General, in Washington:

I have the honor to inform you that your son has been awarded posthumously the Bronze Star Medal and the Good Conduct Medal.

Prior to death, Michael had been awarded the National Defense Service Medal, Vietnam Service Medal, Vietnam Campaign Medal, Combat Infantryman Badge, and the Marksman Badge with rifle, automatic rifle, and machine gun bars.

Arrangements are being made to have these awards presented to you in the near future by a representative of the Commanding General, Fifth United States Army.

"What do you think of the Army suddenly offering us medals?" Peg asked Gene. "That Good Conduct Medal—I mean, really!"

"It's only a piece of ribbon." Gene shrugged. "We used to laugh about getting them during the war."

" 'Posthumously'?" Why would they award Michael a Good Conduct Medal after he was dead? It's as though they were giving it to him for not—for not complaining about what they did to him!"

Gene reread the list of medals, "Well, these others—the National Defense Medal, the Vietnam medals—he got those for just being in the Army, for being in Vietnam. But the Bronze Star . . ." Gene brushed his hand through his white hair. "That's supposed to be for bravery."

"That doesn't make sense, either," Peg said. "Mikey said he'd only ever seen the enemy—what? Three times? I'll tell you why I think they gave him the Bronze Star. It's because he *died!* I'm sure of it."

The Mullens refused their son's medals.

.   .   .

Peg had castigated Iowa's Senator Jack Miller for letting ten weeks pass since Michael's death without any expression of sympathy. "You always find time to vote in the Senate in favor of those issues which condemned our sons to death in Vietnam," Peg had written. "How is it you are unable to find time to write these dead soldiers' grieving parents?" Senator Miller's reply arrived one week after the Army Finance Center's letter about the deduction of nine days from Michael's final pay period:

UNITED STATES SENATE
COMMITTEE ON AGRICULTURE AND FORESTRY
WASHINGTON, D. C. 20510
MAY 18, 1970

Mrs. Gene Mullen
La Porte City, Iowa

DEAR MRS. MULLEN:

Replying to your letter of May 5th, I naturally extend my deepest sympathy to you over the loss of your son. I have written a good many letters of sympathy—not only to people like you, but to parents and wives of our prisoners of war. Also you should know that many Members of Congress have shared some tragedies and concerns of people like you. Our son-in-law flew over 120 combat missions in Vietnam, and fortunately returned.

It has been my observation that, with few exceptions, the persons bearing the real burden of this war—the men who have been doing the fighting, the wounded, their wives and parents—have been the least complaining of anyone over this tragic war.

I regret that you are one of the exceptions.

Very truly yours,
s/
JACK MILLER

Senator Miller's letter reached Peg on the day that a hundred thousand hardhats and other blue-collar workers carrying thousands of American flags marched in New York City in support of President Nixon's war policy. That morning's mail also contained Senator Fulbright's reply to Peg's request for the total casualty list for the week Michael had died. The Senator wrote that he had not yet been able to acquire that information, but he did enclose the Defense Department's response to his inquiry about how nonbattle casualties as a result of artillery fire were arrived at. The communication read, in part:

One cannot assume that all such casualties [of friendly artillery fire] are included in the category of "U.S. Casualties Not the Result of Action by Hostile Forces." If it is determined that such casualties occurred during an action with enemy forces, the casualty is placed in the category of "U.S. Casualties Killed as a Result of Action by Hostile Forces."

This meant that if, for example, American troops were surrounded and in danger of being overrun and they called in artillery over their own position, those Americans who were killed by their defensive artillery barrage would be considered "Killed as a Result of Action by Hostile Forces," or battle casualties. This would also hold true if American troops were advancing behind their own artillery screen and a round fell short, killing a few. Both of these actions are more common than one would wish to believe; such casualties are, however, taken for granted as an ugly facet of war. At any rate, the major point was that just because a man was killed by his own artillery he need not necessarily be considered a non-battle casualty.

The letter from the Defense Department continued:

All Vietnam deaths, hostile and nonhostile, are reported on the daily casualty lists which are available to the press. Only when the next-of-kin specifically object to the publication of the name of the deceased is that name withheld. The casualty is also included in the weekly statistical summary of casualties.

I am informed that each instance where Americans have been killed by friendly artillery fire is investigated. These are included in a category designated by the Military Assistance Command Vietnam (M.A.C.V.) ·as "Misadventure," and are not tabulated separately.

The Mullens were so outraged to discover that the Army, with a cosmic inappropriateness that seemed to amount almost to levity, referred to the manner in which their son had been killed as a "Misadventure" that they almost missed the information that an investigation had been conducted. If they were able to read the results of that investigation, they would know exactly how their son had died. The Defense Department had neglected to mention, however, that such investigations were classified "For Official Use Only" and were not available for public scrutiny. All that the Mullens now knew was that their son had been killed by "friendly fire" and was, therefore, a "nonhostile" casualty as a result of an artillery incident officially referred to as a "Misadventure" in a war that had never been declared.

·   ·   ·

The Multinational Corporations

RICHARD J. BARNET and RONALD E. MULLER

*The interrelationship between foreign policy and economic develop-
ment is one of the classic themes of twentieth-century historical
thought. A whole school of historians has argued that the search for
markets has dominated American foreign policy, producing periodic
wars and creating the sources for repressive government at home. Students of this struggle for world markets have recently introduced a new
perspective in which international corporations—not national policies—
are the main movers and shakers of the earth. According to Barnet our
conception of foreign relations as transactions and conflicts among
nation states has become outmoded, as global corporations with trans-
national interests have seemingly achieved independence of individual
national bases and gained the ability to manipulate governments and
whole societies for their own narrow ends.*

*Some implications of this new perspective are clear. Economic de-
velopment, according to this model, is unlikely to be a straight-line
advance dividing the world into "developed" and "underdeveloped"
(Third World) countries. Rather, economic development is more likely
to take place in a setting of constant fluctuation as multinational corporations find new pools of cheap labor to form "export platforms,"
to be abandoned as prices and wages begin to rise. Other issues are less
clear-cut. To what extent do these corporations really conflict with
national governments? What means do national governments possess to
manipulate the corporate structures in the interests of maintaining social stability? What counterthrusts are available to multinational corporations? Is this a passing stage of industrialization, the product of
uneven economic development among countries? Or is it a new "stage"
of world capitalism? What (as Marxists would ask) are its "contra-
dictions?" The understanding of these new institutions, whether an evo-
lutionary stage or simply an aberration of international political
economy, is a major item for study on the agenda of the social sciences in this generation.*

The men who run the global corporations are the first in history
with the organization, technology, money, and ideology to make a
credible try at managing the world as an integrated unit. The global
visionary of earlier days was either a self-deceiver or a mystic. When
Alexander the Great wept by the riverbank because there were no more
worlds to conquer, his distress rested on nothing more substantial than
the ignorance of his mapmaker. As the boundaries of the known world
expanded, a succession of kings, generals, and assorted strong men tried

298

to establish empires of ever more colossal scale, but none succeeded in making a lasting public reality out of private fantasies. The Napoleonic system, Hitler's Thousand Year Reich, the British Empire, and the Pax Americana left their traces, but none managed to create anything approaching a global organization for administering the planet that could last even a generation. The world, it seems, cannot be run by military occupation, though the dream persists.

The managers of the world's corporate giants proclaim their faith that where conquest has failed, business can succeed. "In the forties Wendell Willkie spoke about 'One World,' says IBM's Jacques G. Maisonrouge. "In the seventies we are inexorably pushed toward it." Aurelio Peccei, a director of Fiat and organizer of the Club of Rome, states flatly that the global corporation "is the most powerful agent for the internationalization of human society." "Working through great corporations that straddle the earth," says George Ball, former Under Secretary of State and chairman of Lehman Brothers International, "men are able for the first time to utilize world resources with an efficiency dictated by the objective logic of profit." The global corporation is ushering in a genuine world economy, or what business consultant Peter Drucker calls a "global shopping center," and it is accomplishing this, according to Jacques Maisonrouge, "simply by doing its 'thing,' by doing what came naturally in the pursuit of its legitimate business objectives."

The global corporation is the first institution in human history dedicated to centralized planning on a world scale. Because its primary purpose is to organize and to integrate economic activity around the world in such a way as to maximize global profit, the global corporation is an organic structure in which each part is expected to serve the whole. Thus in the end it measures its successes and its failures not by the balance sheet of an individual subsidiary, or the suitability of particular products, or its social impact in a particular country, but by the growth in global profits and global market shares. Its fundamental assumption is that the growth of the whole enhances the welfare of all the parts. Its fundamental claim is efficiency.

Under the threat of intercontinental rocketry and the global ecological crisis that hangs over all air-breathing creatures, the logic of global planning has become irresistible. Our generation, the first to discover that the resources of the planet may not last forever, has a particular reverence for efficiency. The global corporations, as Maisonrouge puts it, make possible the "use of world resources with a maximum of efficiency and a minimum of waste . . . on a global scale." Rising out of the post-World War II technological explosion which has transformed man's view of time, space, and scale, global corporations are making a bid for political acceptance beyond anything ever before accorded a business organization. The first enterpreneurial class with the practical potential to operate a planetary enterprise now aspires to become global managers.

"For business purposes," says the president of the IBM World Trade Corporation, "the boundaries that separate one nation from another are no more real than the equator. They are merely convenient demarcations of ethnic, linguistic, and cultural entities. They do not define business requirements or consumer trends. Once management understands and accepts this world economy, its view of the market-place—and its planning—necessarily expand. The world outside the home country is no longer viewed as series of disconnected customers and prospects for its products, but as an extension of a single market."

The rise of the planetary enterprise is producing an organizational revolution as profound in its implications for modern man as the Industrial Revolution and the rise of the nation-state itself. The growth rate of global corporations in recent years is so spectacular that it is now easy to assemble an array of dazzling statistics. If we compare the annual sales of corporations with the gross national product of countries for 1973, we discover that GM is bigger than Switzerland, Pakistan, and South Africa; that Royal Dutch Shell is bigger than Iran, Venezuela, and Turkey; and that Goodyear Tire is bigger than Saudi Arabia. The average growth rate of the most successful global corporations is two to three times that of most advanced industrial countries, including the United States. It is estimated that global corporations already have more than $200 billion in physical assets under their control. But size is only one component of power. In international affairs Mao's dictum that political power grows out of the barrel of a gun shocks no one. To those who question their power, corporate statesmen like to point out that, like the Pope, they have no divisions at their command. The sources of their extraordinary power are to be found elsewhere—the power to transform the world political economy and in so doing transform the historic role of the nation-state. This power comes not from the barrel of a gun but from control of the means of creating wealth on a worldwide scale. In the process of developing a new world, the managers of firms like GM, IBM, Pepsico, GE, Pfizer, Shell, Volkswagen, Exxon, and a few hundred others are making daily business decisions which have more impact than those of most sovereign governments on where people live; what work, if any, they will do; what they will eat, drink, and wear; what sorts of knowledge schools and universities will encourage; and what kind of society their children will inherit.

Indeed, the most revolutionary aspect of the planetary enterprise is not its size but its worldview. The managers of the global corporations are seeking to put into practice a theory of human organization that will profoundly alter the nation-state system around which society has been organized for over 400 years. What they are demanding in essence is the right to transcend the nation-state, and in the process, to transform it. "I have long dreamed of buying an island owned by no nation," says Carl A. Gerstacker, chairman of the Dow Chemical Company, "and of establishing the World Headquarters of the Dow company on the truly neutral ground of such an island, beholden to no nation or society. If we were located on such truly neutral ground we could then really operate in the United States as U.S. citizens, in Japan as Japanese citizens and in Brazil as Brazilians rather than being governed in prime by the laws of the United States. . . . We could even pay any natives handsomely to move elsewhere."

A company spokesman for a principal competitor of Dow, Union Carbide, agrees: "It is not proper for an international corporation to put the welfare of any country in which it does business above that of any other." As Charles P. Kindleberger, one of the leading U.S. authorities on international economics, puts it, "The international corporation has no country to which it owes more loyalty than any other, nor any country where it feels completely at home." The global interests of the world company are, as the British financial writer and Member of Parliament Christopher Tugendhat has pointed out, separate and distinct from the interests of every government, including its own government of origin. Although, in terms of management and ownership, all global corporations are either American, British, Dutch, German, French, Swiss, Italian, Canadian, Swedish, or Japanese (most, of course, are American), in outlook and loyalty they are becoming companies without a country.

It is not hard to understand, however, why American corporate giants, even those whose presidents must still make do with an office in a Park Avenue skyscraper instead of a Pacific island, feel that they have outgrown the American Dream. The top 298 U.S.-based global corporations studied by the Department of Commerce earn 40 percent of their entire net profits outside the United States. A 1972 study by Business International Corporation, a service organization for global corporations, shows that 122 of the top U.S.-based multinational corporations had a higher rate of profits from abroad than from domestic operations. In the office-equipment field, for example, the overseas profit for 1971 was 25.6 percent, compared with domestic profits of 9.2 percent. The average reported profit of the pharmaceutical industry from foreign operations was 22.4 percent as against 15.5 percent from operations in the United States. The food industry reported profits from overseas of 16.7 percent as compared with U.S. profits of 11.5 percent. (Extraordinarily high profit on relatively low overseas investment is not uncommon. In 1972, for example, United Brands reported a 72.1 percent return on net assets, Parker Pen 51.2 percent, Exxon 52.5 percent.) By 1973, America's seven largest banks were obtaining 40 percent of their total profits from abroad, up from 23 percent in 1971.

Department of Commerce surveys show that dependence of the leading U.S.-based corporations on foreign profits has been growing at an accelerating rate since 1964. In the last ten years it has been substantially easier to make profits abroad than in the U.S. economy. The result has been that U.S. corporations have been shifting more and more of their total assets abroad: about one-third of the total assets of the chemical industry, about 40 percent of the total assets of the consumer-goods industry, about 75 percent of those of the electrical industry, about one-third of the assets of the pharmaceutical industry are now located outside the United States. Of the more than $100 billion invested worldwide by the U.S. petroleum industry, roughly half is to be found beyond American shores. Over 30 percent of U.S. imports and exports are bought and sold by 187 U.S.-based multinational corporations through their foreign subsidiaries. It is estimated by the British financial analyst Hugh Stephenson that by the mid-1970's, 90 percent of overseas sales of U.S.-based corporations "will be manufactured abroad by American-owned and controlled subsidiaries." "Investment abroad is investment in America" is the new slogan of the global corporations.

The popular term for the planetary enterprise is "multinational corporation." It suggests a degree of internationalization of management, to say nothing of stock ownership, which is not accurate. A study of the 1,851 top managers of the leading U.S. companies with large overseas payrolls and foreign sales conducted a few years ago by Kenneth Simmonds reveals that only 1.6 percent of these high-level executives were non-Americans. It is well known that non-Americans hold no more than insignificant amounts of the stock of these enterprises.

More important, the term is inadequate because it fails to capture that aspect of the contemporary world business which is most revolutionary. Businessmen have been venturing abroad a long time—at least since the Phoenicians started selling glass to their Mediterranean neighbors. Some of the great trading companies like the sixteenth-century British Company of Merchants Adventurers antedated the modern nation-state. Each of the great nineteenth-century empires—the British, the French, the Dutch, and even the Danish—served as a protector for private trading organizations which roamed the earth looking for the markets and raw-material sources on which the unprecedented comforts of the Victorian Age depended. Nor could it be said that doing business abroad is a new departure for Americans. At the turn of the century, American firms, such as the Singer Sewing Machine Company, were already playing such an important role in the British economy that the book *The American Invaders* was assured an apoplectic reception in the city when a London publisher brought it out in 1902. Ford has had an assembly plant in Europe since 1911, and the great oil companies have been operating on a near-global scale since the early days of the century.

What makes the global corporation unique is that unlike corporations of even a few years ago, it no longer views overseas factories and markets as adjuncts to its home operations. Instead, as Maisonrouge puts it, the global corporation views the world as "one economic unit." Basic to this view, he points out, "is a need to plan, organize, and manage on a global scale." It is this holistic vision of the earth, in comparison with which "internationalism" seems parochial indeed, that sets the men who have designed the planetary corporation apart from the generations of traders and international entrepreneurs who preceded them.

. . .

The managers of the global corporations keep telling one another that there can be no integrated world economy without radical transformations in the "obsolete" nation-state; but however progressive a notion this may be, those who depend on the old-fashioned structures for their careers, livelihood, or inspiration are not easily convinced. The executives who run the global corporations have persuaded themselves that they are far ahead of politicians in global planning because political managers are prisoners of geography. As much as the mayor of Minneapolis or Milan or São Paulo may aspire to a planetary vision, his career depends upon what happens within his territorial domain. Rulers of nations exhibit a similar parochialism for the same reasons. They are jealous of their sovereign prerogatives and do not wish to share, much less abdicate, decision-making power over what happens within their territory.

The new globalists are well aware of the problem. "Corporations that buy, sell, and produce abroad," says George Ball, "do have the power to affect the lives of people and nations in a manner that necessarily challenges the prerogatives and responsibilities of political authority. How can a national government make an economic plan with any confidence if a board of directors meeting 5,000 miles away can by altering its pattern of purchasing and production affect in a major way the country's economic life?" But the World Manager's answer to the charge of being a political usurper is not to deny the extraordinary power he seeks to exercise in human affairs but to rationalize it.

David Rockefeller has called for a "crusade for understanding" to explain why global corporations should have freer rein to move goods, capital, and technology around the world without the interference of nation-states; but such a crusade calls for the public relations campaign of the century. Perhaps the logic of One World has never been so apparent to so many, yet the twentieth century is above all the age of nationalism. There has been no idea in history for which greater numbers of human beings have died, and most of the corpses have been added to the heap in this century. The continuing struggle for national identity is the unifying political theme of our time. The imperial architects of Germany, Italy, and Japan; the guerrilla leaders of liberation movements, Tito, Ho, Castro; and those who are still fighting to free Africa from colonial rule have all been sustained by the power of nationalism. "The nation-state will not wither away," the chairman of Unilever, one of the earliest and largest world corporations, predicts. A "positive role" will have to be found for it.

· · ·

The World Managers, sensitive to such criticism as UAW President Leonard Woodcock's charge that the companies don't care that they are causing unemployment in the United States, like to minimize their interest in coolie labor. (Woodcock is fond of quoting Thomas Jefferson's observation about merchants without a country: "The mere spot they stand on does not constitute so strong an attachment as that from which they draw their gain.") Their sudden interest in Taiwan, global managers argue, has nothing to do with either their treasure or their heart being there. They want merely to be better able to make use of supply markets. It is not usually considered good taste to talk about 14-cents-an-hour help, but occasionally an entrepreneur breaks loose from the public relations department and gives an honest answer. "In South Korea, Taiwan, and Indonesia," says Henry Ford II, "we see promising markets and we see an attractive supply of cheap labor." William Sheskey told the House Ways and Means Committee how he purchased a modern U.S. shoe factory, shut it down, and shipped the lasts, dies, patterns, management, and much of the leather to Europe:

I am making the same shoes under the same brand name, selling them to the same customers with the same management, with the same equipment, for one reason. The labor where I am now making the shoes is 50 cents an hour as compared to the $3 I was paying. Here is a perfect example of where I took everything American except the labor and that is exactly why I bought it.

Relocating production in Mexico, Taiwan, Brazil, or the Philippines is an even more irresistible way to cut costs. In the office-macinery field, a company must pay its U.S. workers about ten times what it pays its Taiwanese and Korean workers and about six times what it pays its Mexican workers. In the last few years more than 50,000 jobs have been created along the Mexican border, and exports from the area back to the United States have climbed from $7 million in 1966 to $350 million in 1972. During the latter year, imports from Taiwan to the U.S. market amounted to $1.3 billion. No amount of statistical magic can obscure the commonsense conclusion that servicing the U.S. market from Taiwanese and Mexican factories rather than U.S. factories deprives American workers in the affected industries of their jobs.

However, the continuing exodus to the export platforms of the underdeveloped world is creating problems for the American labor movement in addition to structural unemployment. Corporate organization on a global scale is a highly effective weapon for undercutting the power of organized labor everywhere. Capital, technology, and marketplace ideology, the bases of corporate power, are mobile; workers, by and large, are not. The ability of corporations to open and close plants rapidly and to shift their investment from one country to another erodes the basis of organized labor's bargaining leverage, the strike. While it may be true to argue, as IBM's Arthur Watson does, that when a plant is closed in the United States and opened in Korea "we have not lost jobs; one can trade jobs internationally," the trading process does not benefit the worker who has lost his job and cannot afford to sit home until the uncertain day when his town feels the beneficial effects of industrial expansion overseas. Even when World Managers defend their labor policies, they unwittingly attest to their great bargaining edge over organized labor.

The power of corporations to neutralize the strike weapon is not merely theoretical. It is used. Perhaps the most celebrated example is the strike at Ford's British operation in 1970. After a summit conference with the Prime Minister, Henry Ford II delivered a stiff note to the British people. "We have got hundreds of millions of pounds invested in Great Britain and we can't recommend any new capital investment in a country constantly dogged with labor problems. There is nothing wrong with Ford of Britain but with the country." Shortly thereafter he shifted back to Ohio a proposed £30-million operation for building Pinto engines. The following year he pointedly announced that Ford's major new plant would be put in Spain, a country that offered "social peace."

Management finds that its power to close an entire operation in a community and to transfer everything but the workers out of the country produces a marvelously obliging labor force. The threat, real or imagined, of retaliatory plant closings has caused unions in both Europe and the United States to moderate their demands and in a number of cases to give "no-strike" pledges. There have been enough cases in which global corporations have used their superior mobility to defeat unions to make the threat credible. Dunlop Pirelli, to give one example, closed its Milan-area plant and moved it across the Swiss border, where it proceeded to rehire Italian workers as low-wage migrant labor. (The savings in pensions and accumulated seniority rights accomplished by this thrifty maneuver were, one would hope, passed on to the purchasers of rubber tires around the world, but there is no evidence of this.)

There are also less drastic alternatives available to management which further weaken labor's bargaining power. One is the layoff. A Burroughs subsidiary making computers in France suddenly laid off one-third of its workers on orders from its headquarters in New York. (The case is a good illustration of how the interests of subsidiaries are subordinated to the corporation's global strategy, for the plant in question was operating at near capacity and was making good profits. Evidently some company consideration having nothing to do with the French operation itself dictated the layoff.) Neither the French Government nor the outraged local manager could do a thing about it. A global corporation can also protect itself from a strike by establishing what is called "multiple sourcing"—i.e., different plants in different countries producing the same component. It is a strategy by which the corporation can make itself independent of the labor force in any one plant. Chrysler, British Leyland, Goodyear, Michelin, and Volkswagen are among the many firms which use this technique for managing their labor problems. When Ford in Britain was faced with a strike at the plant that was its sole supplier for a crucial component, the company reclaimed the die used in the manufacture from the struck plant and had it flown within five days to a German plant. As *The Times* observed in 1970, "In some cases Ford has beaten strikes by 'pulling' tools and dies in time to start alternative production before employees in the original firm have stopped work." Unions are attempting to organize a campaign to counteract plant juggling as a strike-breaking strategy and are beginning to achieve some successes.

The confrontation of capital and labor, a battle scarcely more than 100 years old, has now moved to the global stage. Because it is easier to write a check than to move a worker and his family, the owners and managers of capital, as we have seen, enjoy certain advantages over labor. Paul Ramadier's studies confirm that strikes in global companies are on the average of shorter duration than strikes in domestic firms in Europe. He attributes this fact to the superior bargaining power of the global companies. (IBM's Jacques Maisonrouge, on the other hand, prefers to explain the fact that his French workers stayed at their jobs during the massive strikes of 1968 as evidence of their international outlook.)

A number of lesser advantages also inure to the global corporation because of its very structure. Because lines of authority are kept deliberately murky in many global enterprises, the local union does not know with whom it should deal. Many union leaders in Europe complain of "buck-passing" in negotiations. They are unable to get a decision out of the local manager and are never sure what issues he has the authority to settle. Labor unions up to this point lack anything comparable to the sophisticated communications system of the corporations. Thus they have difficulty finding out what the corporation may have paid in other countries or whether there are precedents for the concessions they are demanding. Corporations surmount differences in language, customs, and outlook by spending money for translators, language schools, and cram courses on local culture which unions do not have. The airborne executive corps can develop a properly statesmanlike international consciousness as its members dart in and out of the capitals of the world, but for the union organizer in Liège or Milan, without anything equivalent to the global intelligence system of the corporation, the mysteries of the outside world continue to loom large. These mysteries represent a management asset.

The most crucial mysteries concern the company's books. The complexity of intracorporate balance sheets, further obfuscated by the miracles of modern accounting, makes it exceedingly difficult for unions to find out how much money the employer is making or, indeed, if he is really losing money, as he frequently claims. Transfer pricing and other mysterious intracorporate transactions, hidden behind the veil of consolidated balance sheets, are formidable obstacles for union negotiators trying to get an accurate picture of what the local subsidiary of the global company can and should be paying in wages. (Of course, companies seek to maximize or minimize income depending upon whether they are talking to shareholders, tax collectors, or workers. In ITT's frenetic growth campaign, the company bookkeeper has on occasion employed rather unusual accounting methods to demonstrate "record earnings." In 1968, ITT's consolidated balance sheet showed $56 million in "miscellaneous and nonoperating income," of which, a diligent analyst discovered, $11 million was attributable to its having sold off properties and investments in Europe.)

A global company often bargains with several unions representing different parts of its conglomerate empire. Because of the way unions are typically organized, what impact they have is limited to that phase of the global operation in which the labor dispute is taking place. They have little leverage to affect other aspects of the global operation, although, as we shall see, they are trying to develop that leverage. Most unions are nationalistic and cannot afford to risk jobs to support workers in other countries.

Moreover, unions lack a tightly organized structure for dealing with the global corporate hierarchy. Thus they not only are at a disadvantage because they know less about the company than the company knows about them but also lack the common purpose that unites the worldwide operation of a global corporation—i.e., global profit maximization. In Europe the ideological splits of the Cold War that divided Communist and non-Communist unions still persist, though they are growing weaker. Moreover, there are sharp differences between "pragmatic" labor leaders looking for a bigger paycheck and more job security and "ideological" union functionaries who, in Charles Levinson's words, want not merely a bigger piece of the pie but a voice in baking it. In general, European unions are more radical than U.S. unions in demands for a share in management decisions about the workplace, but they are are less well organized and, with few exceptions, appear to have even less comprehension of the nature of the challenge which the global corporation poses to workers. Moreover, legislation hampers organizing efforts in many parts of the world. Like the United States, both Germany and Holland have laws against sympathy strikes and secondary boycotts. Countries such as Greece, Ireland, Singapore, Malaysia, and Indonesia advertise their repressive labor legislation.

Nonetheless, the exploitation of wage differentials in different parts of the world by the global corporations is causing unions to dust off the classic phrase "international worker solidarity" and to try to make it relevant to "bread and butter" bargaining. But even as U.S. union leaders begin to realize that the army, 34,000 strong, of 30-cents-an-hour child laborers in Hong Kong is not only a sin to be deplored at the annual convention but a real and growing economic threat to American workers, they are confused about what to demand. Should the wages in Hong Kong and Detroit be the same? Not even powerful unions in Europe are making demands for parity with U.S. workers. Despite the logic in paying the same wage for the same work for the same company irrespective of race, creed, color, or national origin, the practical union organizer is reluctant to ask for it. Given the risk that the company may decide to pull out altogether, he is happy if he can get a few more francs or marks a day. The only case of an American union's successfully negotiating international wage parity is the United Auto Workers contract covering Canadian automobile workers. But this was a special case because of a long history of governmental and union efforts to harmonize labor policy. International solidarity has yet to extend to Brazil or Singapore, where, of course, there are no local unions. However, the boldness with which such governments are competing with one another in offering their docile labor force to global corporations is posing a challenge to the American union movement which it knows it can no longer ignore.

. . .

The global corporation is the most powerful human organization yet devised for colonizing the future. By scanning the entire planet for opportunities, by shifting its resources from industry to industry and country to country, and by keeping its overriding goal simple—world-wide profit maximization—it has become an institution of unique power. The World Managers are the first to have developed a plausible model of the future that is global. They exploit the advantages of mobility while workers and governments are still tied to particular territories. For this reason, the corporate visionaries are far ahead of the rest of the world in making claims on the future. In making business decisions today they are creating a politics for the next generation.

We have shown that because of their size, mobility, and strategy, the global corporations are constantly accelerating their control over the world productive system and are helping to bring about a profound change in the way wealth is produced, distributed, and defended. There are a number of elements in this extraordinary transformation, but the global corporation is the most dynamic agent of change in a new stage in world capitalism.

In assessing the role the global corporation is playing and ought to play in this sweeping process, the issue is not whether the World Managers wish the global corporation to be a force for peace, stability, and development, but whether it can be. We would put the question this way: Given its drive to maximize world profits, the pressures of global oligopolistic competition, and its enormous bargaining power, can the global corporation modify its behavior in ways that will significantly aid the bottom 60 percent of the world's population—in the rich nations as well as in the poor?

. . .

There has never been a time since the Great Depression when there has been more economic uncertainty around the world. But the corporate prospect of a world without borders offers something more distressing than uncertainty. It is a vision without ultimate hope for a majority of mankind. Our criterion for determining whether a social force is progressive is whether it is likely to benefit the bottom 60 percent of the population. Present and projected strategies of global corporations offer little hope for the problems of mass starvation, mass unemployment, and gross inequality. Indeed, the global corporation aggravates all these problems, because the social system it is helping to create violates three fundamental human needs: social balance, ecological balance, and psychological balance. These imbalances have always been present in our modern social system; concentration of economic power, antisocial uses of that power, and alienation have been tendencies of advanced capitalism. But the process of globalization, interacting with and reinforcing the process of accelerating concentration, has brought us to a new stage.

The role of the global corporation in aggravating social imbalance is perhaps the most obvious. As owner, producer, and distributor of an ever greater share of the world's goods, the global corporation is an instrument for accelerating concentration of wealth. As a global distributor, it diverts resources from where they are most needed (poor countries and poor regions of rich countries) to where they are least needed (rich countries and rich regions).

Driven by the ideology of infinite growth, a religion rooted in the existential terrors of oligopolistic competition, global corporations act as if they must grow or die, and in the process they have made thrift into a liability and waste into a virtue. The rapid growth of the global corporate economy requires ever-increasing consumption of energy. The corporate vision depends upon converting ever-greater portions of the earth into throwaway societies: ever-greater quantities of unusable waste produced with each ton of increasingly scarce mineral resources; ever-greater consumption of nondisposable and nonreturnable packaging; ever-greater consumption of energy to produce a unit of energy; and ever more heat in our water and our air—in short, ever more ecological imbalance.

The processes that lead to psychological imbalance are more difficult to analyze than the processes of social or ecological imbalance. But the World Managers have based their strategy on the principles of global mobility, division of labor, and hierarchical organization—all of which may be efficient, in the short run, for producing profits but not for satisfying human beings. The very size of the global corporation invites hierarchy. The search for economic efficiency appears to require ever more division of labor and to challenge traditional loyalties to family, town, and nation. Another name for mobility is rootlessness. There is nothing to suggest that loyalty to a global balance sheet is more satisfying for an individual than loyalty to a piece of earth, and there is a good deal of evidence that being a "footloose" and airborne executive is not the best way to achieve psychological health—for either the managers themselves or their families. By marketing the myth that the pleasures of consumption can be the basis of community, the global corporation helps to destroy the possibilities of real community—the reaching out of one human being to another. The decline of political community and the rise of consuming communities are related. Each TV viewer sits in front of his own box isolated from his neighbor but symbolically related through simultaneous programmed activity and shared fantasy. How much the pervasive sense of meaninglessness in modern life can be attributed to the organizational strategies and values of the huge corporation we are only beginning to understand, but for the longer run the psychological crises associated with the emerging socioeconomic system are potentially the most serious of all, for they undermine the spirit needed to reform that system.

If we are right that the strategies of growth of the global corporation are incompatible with social, ecological, and psychological balance, why will such growth be permitted to continue? Is the earth—or indeed, the corporation itself—so lacking in self-correcting mechanisms that we are doomed to be diverted with upbeat balance sheets while we and our descendants wait for the air to give out? Stephen Hymer argues that high noon for the global corporation has already come and gone. The highly centralized hierarchical model of organization is simply too much at odds with the aspirations of too many of the 4 billion inhabitants of the planet for greater control over their own lives and greater political participation. (There is instability in every major hierarchical organization, including the Catholic Church, universities, the American and German armed forces, and authoritarian states like the Soviet Union.) Why should the global corporation be successful in establishing its political legitimacy to gather more and more public decisions into private hands at a time of worldwide political awakening?

Public anticorporate criticism is growing. Monkey-wrench politics also threatens the symmetry of the corporate global model (oil boycotts, kidnapping, extortion, bomb threats, trucker stall-ins). The worldwide resource scarcity jeopardizes global planning, which was based on the assumption that transportation costs could be kept low and that ships, trucks, and planes would always be available. Winging components and managers around the world to take advantage of differentials in labor costs, tax rates, and tariffs may no longer be the key to higher profits. If the Global Factory, with its worldwide division of labor, no longer represents the ultimate in economic efficiency, much of the rationale for the global corporation is gone. Is it possible that resource limitations are forcing an alternative model of a world economy in which *decentralization* is the hallmark? Perhaps the wave of the future is not the "Cosmocorp" but the backyard steel factory?

Whether global corporations will continue to increase their power will depend upon how successfully they can adapt to rapid change. They are more adaptable than government, because their goals are simpler, their bureaucracies are often more authoritarian, their planning cycle is shorter, and fewer conflicting interests need be heard. The dependence of advanced capitalist societies on privately controlled sources of power for maintaining employment, transferring money, and distributing technology and services is so great that government as a practical matter can no longer control them. The very advantages the global corporation enjoys over government—principally mobility and control of information—are creating a structural lag. Government is operating under a set of economic assumptions and legal theories which treat the corporation as if it were a private and national institution when it is in fact a social institution of global dimension. While the structural lag makes it possible for the corporation to accumulate more and more power, this lag renders increasingly ineffective the traditional tools of government for trying to achieve social stability. Thus in its continual quest for its own stability the global corporation is helping to create instability for society as a whole. As social, ecological, and psychological imbalances become more pronounced, the temptation increases to maintain the appearance of stability with repressive measures. For example, the gospel of growth requires a tolerant attitude toward inflation, but the management of inflation demands tough governmental controls. "There is little doubt," says Storey-Boekh Associates, bank-credit analysts not given to bleeding-heart rhetoric or to casual predictions of fascism, "that we could correct a lot of problems with a large dose of authoritarianism, at least for a while, but the chances of operating a successful inflationary economy like Brazil within the confines of democracy are just about nil."

The prospect, then, is not the death of the nation-state in a world without borders, but the transformation of the nation-state. The increasing impotence of the nation-state to solve its domestic affairs with traditional economic policies will probably drive it to seek survival by more direct and more violent means. The breakdown in the consensus among the industrialized nations on the international ground rules governing economic activity and the growing struggle over scarce resources signal a return to protectionism and economic nationalism. As oligopolistic competition among U.S., Japanese, and European firms intensifies, they will increasingly call upon their governments to back their efforts. The fading of the Cold War is making modern replays of World War I-type geopolitics more plausible. Despite their laudable vision of world peace through world trade, global corporations are more likely to act as instruments of competitive economic and geopolitical rivalry. In sum, if global corporations do not undergo profound changes in their goals and strategies, or are not effectively controlled, they will continue to act as disturbers of the peace on a global scale.

Women's Role in Contemporary Society

The hearings on "Women's Role in Contemporary Society" held by the New York City Commission on Human Rights, September 21–25, 1970, presented a striking and historically important documentation of the problems of women in a male-dominated society. The hearings were oriented to presenting explicit examples of discrimination in practical matters such as jobs. The then mayor of New York, John V. Lindsay, summed up the findings of the commission: "Women are victims of discrimination in employment at all levels, in housing, in mortgage lending and credit practices, in health care and social services, in higher education, in civil and criminal statues of many kinds, in literature, and the mass media, and, not least of all, politics" (pp. 17–18). As an outcome of the hearings, the commission made a wide-ranging series of recommendations, many of which have subsequently entered into law.

In the ensuing years, the women's movement, or at least branches of it, moved beyond this workaday practicality to more cultural and ideological questions and entered the realm of sexual identity that probes more deeply the status of women and the discriminations against them. But the kinds of inquiry and recommendation represented here probably still symbolize for most Americans the main thrust of the women's movement. And all too many goals announced here have yet to be achieved.

A STRATEGY FOR CHANGE

ELEANOR HOLMES NORTON

[*Chairman, New York City Commission on Human Rights*]

If these hearings are important for their attempt to be a comprehensive governmental inquiry into a subject not yet taken fully seriously by the public, they are nevertheless no occasion for either government or women to indulge in self-congratulation. The blame for the status of women has been laid almost everywhere in society—on government, on education, on employees, on men, indeed on women themselves. But in my view, the blame laid has been far too unspecific and rhetorical to insure the kind of critique necessary to produce a strategy for change.

Women have done an unprecedented job in rapidly raising the issue of women's rights to that of a major issue of our time. It may be too much to expect that so indispensable and brilliant a job of consciousness-raising should be accompanied by organized, rather than a hit-and-miss, strategy for change. But if change is to come, it must be pursued not in general but in its hard specifics and with the clarity of strategies that is all-required when a group seeks profound change.

As a city official most specifically charged with eliminating bias, and indeed as a woman participating in the women's struggle, I feel something of a duty to leave off celebrating the rise of this newly discovered issue today. Instead, I would like to use this occasion to offer a few suggested trial balloons regarding the critique and strategy I believe are missing from the women's rights issue.

If we are to fully appreciate the need for a clear strategy, we must attempt to discern the tenacity of the problem. To underestimate its depth, to assume its evils have a self-evident quality, as I believe some of us have, is to lay the way for devastating failure.

No change in society has ever been seen or envisioned as deeply as the prospect of equality of the sexes. None of the great revolutions has altered the most fundamental relationship of all, that between man and woman—not the abolition of classes envisioned by the great political and economic revolutionaries; not the spread of the great religions of the world; not the eradication of racial prejudice, for which we still toil. To alter the economic and political order, to be sure, is to change society very profoundly indeed. To raise the blight of racial bigotry is to rediscover the principles of both humanism and Judeo-Christian ethics. But basic as would be the changes, they would change society, not civilization, as sexual equality would. For the inequality of the sexes is the oldest inequality of all, preceding both class and racial discrimination and tapping us at our most vulnerable sources.

Thus, if we demand rapid changes in the status of women—and we most certainly do demand—we must nevertheless not misjudge the difficulty, thereby failing to develop real and lasting cures. Yet I believe we have already shown that we are new and tentative to the uses and ways of power. We have, to be sure, demonstrated the potential for awesome strength, as witnessed in the way we engendered the 350 to 50 votes in the House [in 1970] in favor of the Women's Rights Amendment.

. . .

I believe we must forge a women's political coalition equal in its competence, professionalism and drive to any lobby the Congress has ever seen. We must replace the American Medical Association, the National Rifle Association and other dubious spokesmen, who are the strongest lobbyists in Washington today. The difference between a women's political coalition and our present lobbying efforts is simple. Such a coalition would signal the inauguration of a unified strategy for achieving women's announced goals. It is unfair to leave the achievement of these goals to a few valiant sisters who labor at hard political tasks while the rest of us rap away at consciousness-raising sessions. Rap sessions are critical, and they must continue if we are to undo thousand of years of damage to ourselves. But it is too late to neatly divide our thrust into compartments—so many years to raise our collective consciousness, so many years to pursue our goals. If women do not demand concrete results simultaneously with ideological conversion, they will be the first exploited group I know to be so patient or so foolish.

. . .

I can but challange women to come forward just as blacks and Puerto Ricans have come forward, identify yourselves as a discriminated-against group and pursue your rights with vigor. Yet I call for the women's political coalition because much of the law I administer will be incapable of vigorous enforcement if women do not achieve other political gains unrelated to the city's Human Rights Law.

For example, women must be freed from constant child care if the law against discrimination based on sex is to be a truly effective instrument of equality. We have sought to dramatize this point by opening a drop-in child care center here during this week of hearings, with the certain knowledge that many women would be unable to come to learn of their role in contemporary American society without such a facility available, just as millions cannot work for lack of such facilities. Only a women's political coalition will be able to marshal the effort to convince a skeptical public that women are a uniquely exploited group in this and so many other ways.

It is time we left off decrying the ignorant myths that surround our status and organize to defeat them. Eight million women heads of families need to join the struggle for women's rights, to take to task that large segment of the public who believe women work for pin money; so do the 84 percent of mothers who, though living with their husbands, must work to supplement low male wages; so do the one-third of working mothers who go to work, though they have children under six years of age and no adequate child care facilities.

Working and union women who have won millions of dollars in back pay for unequal wages received for doing the same work as men need to tell it and join the women's struggle to banish wage inequality. And trade union sisters who have sued to nullify weight lifting and overtime laws aimed at women need to challenge the unions to represent them equally with men. The union movement I was taught to revere—the movement of Debs, Reuther, of Randolph—is surely ashamed that so many unions have been joined as defendants with employers who denied women equal advancement opportunities.

Another deadly myth that traps us, or sometimes fulfills its own prophecy, is that job turnover of women's work is greater than men's. A recent study revealed that sex and job turnover are not related; rather, the correlation is between low status and turnover. Compared by job level, women leave their jobs less frequently than men. And I am sure it will astound many women to learn that women have fewer absences than men, even counting absences for pregnancies and absences to take care of children. Only by organizing women can we break the hold of these old myths.

There is one myth that troubles me personally as much as all the rest, and that is the myth that somehow black women are not a part of the struggle for women's rights but belong exclusively to the move-

ment for black liberation. That cannot be. For black women are pre-
eminently working women who have borne double oppression. Without day care facilities, almost half of all black mothers with preschool
children work, compared with 28 percent of white mothers with preschool children. And once their children go to school, nearly 70 percent
of black mothers go to work. Theirs are the lowest of wages. Fully 64
percent of women reporting their jobs as day workers or hourly workers
—maids and laundresses—are black. These women need to join the
struggle for women's rights and demand that part of our efforts go to
making women's work a dignified and well-paid work.

I heard a white sister demand that white women stop employing
black household workers on the theory that such work is per se exploitative. But no work is exploitative if well paid, if devices such as
carfare and hand-me-down clothes are not employed to pay wages.

Wouldn't it be fine if no one had to do housework for pay? But
what the white woman does not know is that black women do not
have the prospect of going back to school, for many are too old or
have passed the time in their lives when they can build a new life.
The alternative to unemployment for millions of black workers is
housework and other low-paid work. But good wages would do much
to take away the image and psychology that bothers many white women
in the women's movement.

I do not mean to be critical of the white sister who made the facile
point that black household workers are exploited and should not be
employed. For we who are black have failed to develop our own issues
in this struggle. Black sisters need to stop criticizing the white woman's
struggle for being white, for it will only take on color if we who are
black join it. It is hypocritical for us who are black to insist upon
speaking for ourselves but to blame white women for articulating their
needs, not ours.

Finally, black women need to spurn the rhetoric of those who
would divide blacks from women, and who talk about whose cause
has priority. No person's oppression has priority over another's. And
I believe this to be the case, although it is clearly true that America
reserved for black people a special form of oppression she kept from
others. Slavery and its attendant racial prejudice is too awful a state of
oppression to afford comparison. Yet, those who insist upon meaningless talk of priorities of oppression are caught in a philosophical dilemma deeper than they appear to understand.

For example, using the logic of a comparative oppression, would
they have black people compare their oppression in this country with
the American Indians' to see who comes out first?—or last, whichever
you prefer. How do you compare slavery with genocide? If we are to
debate blacks versus women, perhaps we should also debate blacks
versus Puerto Ricans, with Puerto Ricans citing their worse statistics
as to unemployment and education, and blacks citing their history as
slaves. What an antihuman debate! How foreign to the humanism,
mutual respect and decency that must undergird every movement for
justice.

I am confident that black women will never forget their special task in the fight for black liberation and their special role in helping the black male to regain what was taken from him in greater proportion than from black women by slavery and racism. For we who are black men and women have worked side by side out of necessity and out of love. Our men, who have known strong mothers and sisters and wives, also know that it is such women to whom they have often owed their survival. I do not for a moment believe that black men will insist that black women continue in or accept an inferior status, because I believe the experience of blacks has prepared them for sexual equality better than other Americans.

Finally, I would like to emphasize some facts critical to the formation of a women's political coalition.

Women are losing ground. In 1945, 45 percent of all professional and technical workers were women, but today only 39 percent are women. In 1955, women's full-time median wages were 64 percent of men's; today they have plummeted to 58 percent. These distressing percentages are there despite a significant rise in the proportion of working women. Working women have doubled their numbers since World War II, and there are eight times as many working mothers as then. Yet the most alarming rate of unemployment recently has been found among women. The 1969 average was 4.7 unemployed women as compared with 2.8 unemployed men.

I realize that a broad and well-coordinated political coalition is not the answer to all women's problems. But surely it is a beginning. Women have raised profound, complex issues by striving to change women's status. We have thus made inevitable the necessity to work on every front, for no major area of life has remained untouched by sexual stereotypes.

If there is reason for blacks to join with women, there is reason for men to join as well. Our roles are no more rigid than yours; oppressive female stereotypes have their correlative in previous male stereotypes. We are none of us free.

· · ·

PUBLIC TESTIMONY

JEROLYN LYLE, PH.D.

I am from the U.S. Equal Employment Opportunities Commission.

The gap in earnings between men and women is widening in New York City just as it is in the national economy. Arresting this trend requires many courses of action at the present time, the least of which is better occupational placement of the female work force. Until women receive average earnings commensurate with men in average occupations, and until women participate at high rates in high-paying occupations, the gap will not begin to close.

New York City has the special problem in terms of increasing female participation in high-paying occupations. Its largest companies are failing to exercise meaningful leadership toward this end.

The United States Equal Opportunities Commission's interview data for last year reveals a disappointing fact. New York City's ten largest corporations, rather than leading city-wide averages, fall far short of city-wide figures in terms of participation of women in high-paying managerial, professional, technical and sales jobs.

Last year women represented only five percent of all managers in the ten largest corporations in the city, compared to 14 percent in the 5,800 establishments surveyed throughout the city. Employing over 92,000 persons, these ten companies accounted for nearly 24,000 jobs held by women. The women's share of professional employment was only 9 percent in the big ten, but 22 percent in the city as a whole. The disparity in technical fields was even greater. Women held a mere 4 percent of all technical jobs in the top ten companies, compared to 23 percent in the entire city. The familiar concentration of women in clerical jobs in these ten companies was evident, since 63 percent of the female workers were clericals.

No evidence of consistent leadership among major employers in the city's financial community exists, despite the fact that women constitute over half of that sector's work force. The city's ten largest banks and insurance companies utilize women in the managerial and technical field at rates about equal to the city, but the five largest brokerage houses, also in the financial sector, fall far short of city-wide rates in both of these occupational categories.

However, some signs of progress appeared in the financial sector. Staff papers given during our 1968 hearings on discrimination in white-collar employment in New York point out that in 1966 only the banking segment of New York City's financial community employed women in the professions at a rate exceeding the city's average. Three years later both the five largest insurance companies and the five largest banks exceeded the city average in the employment of professional women. Women held 28 percent of all professional jobs in these insurance companies and 27 percent in these banks. The city-wide average was only 22 percent last year.

Careless analysts might call the city's five largest publishing houses labor market leaders in utilizing women in responsible positions. In these companies, for example, women held 21 percent of all managerial positions and 40 percent of all professional jobs last year. These rates exceed the city and national averages by wide margins. Yet these companies fall below the city rate of 23 percent in technical employment since they give only 19 percent of all technical jobs to women. Furthermore, evidence presented at these hearings suggests that women in publishing are denied advancement within the profession, remaining researchers rather than moving into writing jobs. Opportunity to be hired is only the first need. Upper mobility within high-paying occupations is desperately needed.

Many groups of large companies in New York City display mixed employment patterns, with better than average utilization of women in some occupations, but worse than average in others. The city's five largest advertising agencies are a case in point. Weak in managerial and sales occupations, these companies employ women in only 8 percent of all managerial positions, and 14 percent of all sales jobs. The city rates for these occupations are 14 and 34 percent respectively. Yet these agencies are strong utilizers of women in professional and technical fields. Women represent 29 percent of all professionals and 32 percent of all technicians. The city rates are many percentage points lower, 22 and 23 percent respectively.

Thus, on behalf of the U.S. Equal Employment Opportunities Commission, I urge this city's major employers to exert every effort to recruit, hire and promote women so as to improve their opportunities for job in managerial, professional, technical and sales fields.

· · ·

MARY DAVIS

I have before me a draft made out by women who work for Bell Telephone Company and I would like to read it to you:

Women are hired under false pretenses by the New York Telephone Company which advertises congenial working conditions and equal opportunities for employment. This is an outright lie.

Let us take a look at the congenial working conditions at New York Telephone. For example, the company requires that when a woman is stricken on the job, she is required to turn on her light and remain at her post until a supervisor acknowledges her. There are hundreds of cases on record where the supervisor did not believe that the operator's illness was valid, and as a result these women have suffered major illnesses, including death, as a result of this treatment.

There is a case on record where a woman employed by Bell Telephone for 18 years was denied her sick benefits for six months. She stated that each time she complained to her so-called union, TTU, which is known as the Telephone Traffic Union, she was sold out. Not to mention the harassment such as the threat of loss of employment if you do not return in a hurry, regardless of your physical ability.

There is a great similarity between the management of Ma Bell and the campaign of Adolph Hitler. Hitler was obsessed with the dream of controlling the world and Ma Bell is obsessed with controlling employees in the same manner which Hitler tried to enslave the world. It is a known fact that she controls our so-called union, TTU.

It is outrageous that our so-called union permits Bell Telephone to use a weapon called "final warning" to harass us. An employee at West 50th Street was absent twice since January 1970 and was told her attendance was atrocious. A month ago she was told if she was absent once in the next nine months she would be placed on final warning. Final warning in the telephone company is just like being on parole. When you are on final warning one mistake, no matter how minor, can result in dismissal. Final warning can last anywhere from one week until forever.

To cite other incidents, an operator employed for 17 years with two and a half more years to work to receive retirement benefits dared to stand up for her rights as a human being against Bell Telephone and TTU. She was forced to quit because of harassment and abuse by supervisors and management.

As far as equal opportunities go, an operator would have to "prostitute" herself for advancement, thereby forefeiting her self-respect and dignity.

I want to read a list of our grievances. Number one, we need a living wage corresponding to cost of living in New York City for 1970. Two, leaves of absence without loss of seniority. Straight five day work week instead of being scattered. Complete medical coverage. Uniformity —eliminate double standards. Double time and a half for all emergency work. Time and a half for all Saturdays. Double time for every Sunday. Time and a half after 35 hours. Qualified personnel for competent training in all training programs. Abolishment of absentee control policy. Monthly union meetings. Elimination of TTU which is known, again, as the Telephone Traffic Union. More improved equipment. Ethnic representation in executive capacities. Job classifications. Grievance machinery to handle cases of alleged discrimination. Better promotion opportunities. Opportunity to train for all jobs regardless of sex. Improved planning of training periods.

COMMISSIONER BECKER: In what position are you employed by the Telephone Company?

MS. DAVIS: I am employed as an operator in the Traffic Department.

COMMISSIONER BECKER: What do you think the company is going to say when they hear about your statement today? I am wondering whether they will take any steps? I admire you for your statement, but I am wondering whether they will take any steps.

MS. DAVIS: I might be put out on final warning or I might be harassed to the point of resigning or all of these things can happen.

COMMISSIONER BECKER: If that happens will you please come back to our Commission?

MS. DAVIS: Yes.

HELEN A. STANTON

In 1945 I was hired as a hostess with Trans-World Airlines. That same year TWA hired pursers to fly on their overseas routes.

My job is essentially the same as the purser with the exceptions that the purser had to be male, was in charge of cabin service and made approximately 40 percent more salary than I. At that time I was qualified to be a purser except for the fact that I was female.

Some 23 years later in 1968 after trying very hard to become a purser—incidentally they changed the qualifications for a purser several times and one qualification that they required was the knowledge of two languages; I already spoke another language and I learned a second so that I would qualify—so that in 1968 finally through pressure from the government and a contract between my union which is the Airline Steward and Stewardess Association, and TWA, I was finally allowed to become a purser in March of 1968.

At that time 12 other girls from the hostess ranks were allowed to become pursers. We lost all our hostess seniority even though we are governed by the same contract and we are all considered cabin attendants. And incidentally, other airlines such as Northwest and Pan American have all their cabin attendants under one seniority list. TWA has a separate list.

Now, all our bidding for flight time, time off, vacations and overtime are based on our seniority as pursers, so being at the bottom of the list I was forced to take what was left.

Incidentally, they hired some 60 pursers from the street after I became a purser. After six months, in October, when traditionally airlines cut their service, it was found that they had too many pursers. So rather than furlough any of the new men that they had hired, they decided they would put the 13 girl pursers back to hostess rank at a considerable loss in salary.

I promptly filed a complaint against TWA with the New York State Division of Human Rights, EEOC and the Department of Defense Contract Compliance Division, saying they were discriminating against my sex. In all cases except for the EEOC, which takes a little time, I was awarded the case. As a result of this we were never taken off purser status.

Incidentally, you might like to know that a purser gets a raise in salary every six months and reaches top salary at the end of five years; a hostess gets a raise in salary every year and reaches her top salary in eight years.

As a result of my complaint, as I said, I was never taken off the purser list. I am still a purser, but I am still trying to get my seniority as a cabin attendant. The reason I was not given my seniority right away was because our union contract was about to expire at the time I made my initial complaints so it was agreed by TWA and the Department of Defense that this was a contractual item and would be corrected with the signing of the new contract. Our contract has not been signed for two years. As a matter of fact, we just broke off mediation and a strike vote is being taken.

In the meantime, it is over three years that I have suffered with no seniority simply because I am a woman. Also TWA has, as far as I know, no women above the managerial level and I am hoping that through meetings and discussions such as these, I will have my rightful place on the seniority list and TWA will give women their rightful place in the organization.

.   .   .

Watergate

JONATHAN SCHELL

The Watergate crisis with its bizarre, abrupt rhythm of mysterious events following one upon another, each out of beat with the one before—trivial burglaries, odd dealings with reclusive billionaires, Saturday night massacres during which no blood was shed, statements that the President of the United States is not a "crook," unseemly hassles with reporters, the impeachment and resignation of a president—was perhaps the greatest piece of political theatrics in American history. The story dominated not just the news but the national imagination for many months. Since its dramatic conclusion, theories about its meaning, even about its cause, flourish like weeds in a horticulturist's nightmare. Impeachment is such a drastic measure that a president must experience almost every kind of failure to fall under its threat. He must find his political support hopelessly collapsed, his morality highly suspect, his associates seriously tainted, his policies in disarray. But even then he must be unlucky as well. It is almost impossible for a president to be forced to resign. But this happened to Richard M. Nixon.

Jonathan Schell offers one of the more persuasive and even-tempered views of the spectacle. Schell emphasizes the problems of conducting foreign policy in secret as well as Nixon's personality as contributing influences leading to the Watergate scandals. Other writers, however, have with equal plausibility emphasized entirely other explanations. The journalists J. Anthony Lucas and Norman Mailer have viewed Nixon's involvements with the eccentric billionaire Howard Hughes as a key element in the coverup. Other arguments emphasize different issues: new Nixon men undermining old party arrangements, new Texas and California money threatening the East. In many ways, we must understand the whole history of the Cold War, the intelligence apparatus it spawned, and the domestic political and economic arrangements that it influenced before a full assessment of this catastrophe will become apparent.

In mid-1972, as President Nixon returned to the United States from his trip to Russia—where he had signed the first Soviet-American agreements on the limitation of nuclear arms—and as his reëlection campaign got under way, the systemic crisis that had been threatening the survival of Constitutional government in the United States ever since he took office was deepening. The crisis had apparently had its beginnings in the war in Vietnam. Certainly the lines connecting the crisis to the war were numerous and direct. The war had been the principal issue in the struggle between the President and his political opposition—a struggle that had provoked what he called the Presidential Offensive, which was aimed at destroying independent centers of authority in the nation. In more specific ways, too, the evolution of the Administration's usurpations of authority had been bound up with the war. Almost as soon as the President took office, he had ordered a secret bombing campaign against Cambodia (theretofore neutral). When details of the campaign leaked out, he had placed warrantless wiretaps on the phones of newsmen and White House aides. And when J. Edgar Hoover, the Director of the Federal Bureau of Investigation, seemed to be on the verge of getting hold of summaries of those tapped conversations, the President, in his efforts to prevent this, had entered into a venomous hidden struggle with the Director, and the Nixon White House had tried to damage the Director's reputation in the press. In another incident growing out of the war, the White House had hired undercover operatives to "nail" Daniel Ellsberg (as their employers expressed it) after Ellsberg gave the Pentagon Papers to the press; and then some of these operatives had been transferred to the Committee for the Re-Election of the President, where they went on to plan and execute criminal acts against the Democrats.

The evolution of the warrantless-wiretap incident and of the Pentagon Papers incident illustrated one of the ways in which the crisis of the Constitutional system was deepening. Large quantities of secret information were building up in the White House, first in connection with the war policy and then in connection with the President's plans to insure his reëlection. Every day, as the White House operatives went on committing their crimes, the reservoir of secrets grew. And the very presence of so many secrets compelled still more improper maneuverings, and thus the creation of still more secrets, for to prevent any hint of all that information from reaching the public was an arduous business. There had to be ever-spreading programs of surveillance and incrasing efforts to control government agencies. Only agencies that unquestioningly obeyed White House orders could be relied upon to protect the White House secrets, and since in normal times it was the specific obligation of some of the agencies to uncover wrongdoing, wherever it might occur, and bring the wrongdoers to justice, some agencies had to be disabled completely. In effect, investigative agencies such as the F.B.I. and the Central Intelligence Agency had to be enlisted in the obstruction of justice.

At some point back at the beginning of the Vietnam war, long before Richard Nixon became President, American history had split into two streams. One flowed aboveground, the other underground. At first, the underground stream was only a trickle of events. But during the nineteen-sixties—the period mainly described in the Pentagon Papers—the trickle grew to a torrent, and a significant part of the record of foreign affairs disappeared from public view. In the Nixon years, the torrent flowing underground began to include events in the domestic sphere, and soon a large part of the domestic record, too, had plunged out of sight. By 1972, an elaborate preëlection strategy—the Administration strategy of dividing the Democrats—was unfolding in deep secrecy. And this strategy of dividing the Democrats governed not only a program of secret sabotage and espionage but the formation of

Administration policy on the most important issues facing the nation. Indeed, hidden strategies for consolidating Presidential authority had been governing expanding areas of Administration policy since 1969, when it first occurred to the President to frame policy not to solve what one aide called "real problems" but to satisfy the needs of public relations. As more and more events occurred out of sight, the aboveground, public record of the period became impoverished and misleading. It became a carefully smoothed surface beneath which many of the most significant events of the period were being concealed. In fact, the split between the Administration's real actions and policies was largely responsible for the new form of government that had arisen in the Nixon White House—a form in which images consistently took precedence over substance, and affairs of state were ruled by what the occupants of the White House called scenarios. The methods of secrecy and the techniques of public relations were necessary to one another, for the people, lacking access to the truth, had to be told something, and it was the public-relations experts who decided what that something would be.

When the President made his trip to Russia, some students of government who had been worried about the crisis of the American Constitutional system allowed themselves to hope that the relaxation of tensions in the international sphere would spread to the domestic sphere. Since the tensions at home had grown out of events in the international sphere in the first place, it seemed reasonable to assume that an improvement in the mood abroad would give some relief in the United States, too. These hopes were soon disappointed. In fact, the President's drive to expand his authority at home was accelerated; although the nation didn't know it, this was the period in which White House operatives advanced from crimes whose purpose was the discovery of national-security leaks to crimes against the domestic political opposition. The Presidential Offensive had not been called off; it had merely been routed underground. The President spoke incessantly of peace, and had arranged for his public-relations men to portray him as a man of peace, but there was to be no peace—not in Indo-China, and not with a constantly growing list of people he saw as his domestic "enemies." Détente, far from relaxing tensions at home, was seen in the White House as one more justification for its campaign to crush the opposition and seize absolute power.

On Sunday, June 18, 1972, readers of the front page of the *Times* learned, among other things, that heavy American air strikes were continuing over North Vietnam, that the chairman of President Nixon's Council of Economic Advisers, Herbert Stein, had attacked the economic proposals of Senator George McGovern, who in less than a month was to become the Presidential nominee of the Democratic Party, and that the musical "Fiddler on the Roof" had just had its three-thousand-two-hundred-and-twenty-fifth performance on Broadway. Readers of page 30 learned, in a story not listed in the "News Summary and Index," that five men had been arrested in the headquarters of the Democratic National Committee, in the Watergate office building, with burglary tools, cameras, and equipment for electronic surveillance in their possession. In rooms that the men had rented, under aliases, in the adjacent Watergate Hotel, thirty-two hundred-dollar bills were found, along with a notebook containing the notation "E. Hunt" (for E. Howard Hunt, as it turned out) and, next to that, the notation "W. H." (for the White House). The men were members of the Gemstone team, a White House undercover group, which had been attempting to install bugging devices in the telephones of Democrats.

Most of the high command of the Nixon Administration and the Nixon reëlection committee were out of town when the arrests were made. The President and his chief of staff, H. R. Halderman, were on the President's estate in Key Biscayne, Florida. The President's counsel, John Dean, was in Manila, giving a lecture on drug abuse. John Mitchell, the former Attorney General, who was then director of the Comimttee for the Re-Election of the President, and Jeb Magruder, a former White House aide, who had become the committee's assistant director, were in California. In the hours and days immediately following the arrests, there was a flurry of activity at the headquarters of the committee, in a Washington office building; in California; and at the White House. Magruder called his assistant in Washington and had him remove certain papers—what later came to be publicly known as Gemstone materials—from his files. Gordon Liddy, by then the chief counsel of the Finance Committee to Re-Elect the President, went into the headquarters himself, removed from his files other materials having to do with the break-in, including other hundred-dollar bills, and shredded them. At the White House, Gordon Strachan, an aide to Haldeman, shredded a number of papers having to do with the setting up of the reëlection committee's undercover operation, of which the break-in at the headquarters of the Democratic National Committee was an important part. Liddy, having destroyed all the evidence in his possession, offered up another piece of potential evidence for destruction: himself. He informed Dean that if the White House wished to have him assassinated he would stand at a given street corner at an appointed time to make things easy. E. Howard Hunt went to his office in the Executive Office Building, took from a safe ten thousand dollars in cash he had there for emergencies, and used it to hire an attorney for the burglars. In the days following, Hunt's name was expunged from the White House telephone directory. On orders from John Ehrlichman, the President's chief domestic-affairs adviser, his safe was opened and his papers were removed. At one point, Dean—also said to have been acting under instructions from Ehrlichman—gave an order for Hunt to leave the country, but then the order was rescinded. Hunt's payment to an attorney for the burglars was the first of many. The President's personal attorney, Herbert Kalmbach, was instructed by Dean and, later, by Ehrlichman, Haldeman, and Mitchell to keep on making payments, and he, in turn, delegated the task to Anthony Ulasewicz, a retired New York City policeman who had been hired to conduct covert political investigations for the White House. Theirs was a hastily improvised operation. Kalmbach and Ulasewicz spoke to each other from phone booths. (Phone booths apparently had a strong attraction for Ulasewicz. He attached a change-maker to his belt to be sure to have enough coins for his calls, and he chose to make several of his "drops" of the payoff money in them.) He and Kalmbach used aliases and code language in their conversations. Kalmbach became Mr. Novak and Ulasewicz became Mr. Rivers—names that seem to have been chosen for no specific reason. Hunt, who had some forty mystery stories published, was referred to as "the writer," and Haldeman, who wore a crewcut, as "the brush." The payoff money became "the laundry," because when Ulasewicz arrived at Kalmbach's hotel room to pick up the first installment he put it in a laundry bag. The burglars were "the players," and the payoff scheme was "the script." Apparently, the reason the White House conspirators spoke to one another from phone booths was that they thought the Democrats might be wiretapping them, just as they had wiretapped the Democrats. In late June, the President himself said to Haldeman, of the Democrats, "When they start bugging us, which they have, our little boys will not know how to handle it. I hope they will, though." Considerations like these led Kalmbach, Ulasewicz, and others working for the White House to spend many unnecessary hours in phone booths that summer.

All these actions were of the sort that any powerful group of conspirators might take upon the arrest of some of their number. Soon, however, the White House was taking actions that were possible only because the conspirator occupied high positions in the government, including the highest position of all—the Presidency. For almost four years, the President had been "reorganizing" the executive branch of the government with a view to getting the Cabinet departments and the agencies under his personal control, and now he undertook to use several of these agencies to cover up crimes committed by his subordinates. In the early stages of the coverup, his efforts were directed toward removing a single evidentiary link: the fact that the Watergate burglars had been paid with funds from his campaign committee. There was a vast amount of other information that needed to be concealed—information concerning not just the Watergate break-in but the whole four-year record of the improper and illegal activities of the White House undercover operators, which stretched from mid-1969, when the warrantless wiretaps were placed, to the months in 1972 when the secret program for dividing the Democrats was being carried out—but if this one fact could somehow be suppressed, then the chain of evidence would be broken, and the rest of it might go undetected. On June 23rd, the President met with Haldeman and ordered him to have the C.I.A. request that the F.B.I. halt its investigation into the origin of the Watergate burglars' funds, on the pretext that C.I.A. secrets might come to light if the investigation went forward The problem, Haldeman told the President, was that "the F.B.I. is not under control, because Gray doesn't exactly know how to control it." Patrick Gray was Acting Director of the F.B.I. "The way to handle this now," he went on, "is for us to have Walters call Pat Gray and just say, 'Stay to hell out of this.' " The reference was to Vernon Walters, Deputy

Director of the C.I.A. A moment later, Haldeman asked the President, concerning the F.B.I., "And you seem to think the thing to do is get them to stop?" "Right, fine," the President answered. But he wanted Haldeman to issue the instructions. "I'm not going to get that involved," he said. About two hours later, Haldeman and Ehrlichman met with C.I.A. Director Richard Helms and Deputy Director Walters, and issued the order.

The maneuver gave the White House only a temporary advantage. Six days later, on June 29th, Gray did cancel interviews with two people who could shed light on the origin of the burglars' funds. (On the twenty-eighth, Ehrlichman and Dean had handed him all the materials taken from Hunt's safe, and Dean had told him that they were never to "see the light of day." Gray had taken them home, and later he burned them.) But soon a small rebellion broke out among officials of the F.B.I. and the C.I.A. Meetings were held, and at one point Gray and Walters told each other they would rather resign than submit to the White House pressure and compromise their agencies. Several weeks after the request was made, the F.B.I. held the interviews after all. The rebellion in the ranks of the federal bureaucracy was not the first to break out against the Nixon White House. As early as 1969, some members of the Justice Department had fought Administration attempts to thwart the civil-rights laws. In 1970, members of the State Department and members of the Office of Education, in the Department of Health, Education, and Welfare, had protested the invasion of Cambodia. In 1970, too, J. Edgar Hoover had refused to go along with a White House scheme devised by a young lawyer named Tom Huston for illegal intelligence-gathering. The executive bureaucracy was one source of the President's great power, but it was also acting as a check on his power. In some ways, it served this function more effectively than the checks provided by the Constitution, for, unlike the other institutions of government, it at least had some idea of what was going on. But ultimately it was no replacement for the Constitutional checks. A President who hired and fired enough people could in time bring the bureaucracy to heel. And although a Gray, a Walters, or a Helms might offer some resistance to becoming deeply involved in White House crimes, they would do nothing to expose the crimes. Moreover, the bureaucracy had no public voice, and was therefore powerless to sway public opinion. Politicians of all persuasions could—and did—heap abuse on "faceless," "briefcase-toting" bureaucrats and their "red tape," and the bureaucracy had no way to reply to this abuse. It had only its silent rebellions, waged with the passive weapons of obfuscation, concealment, and general foot-dragging. Decisive opposition, if there was to be any, had to come from without.

With respect to the prosecutorial arm of the Justice Department, the White House had aims that were less ambitious than its aims with respect to the F.B.I. and the C.I.A., but it was more successful in achieving them. Here, on the whole, the White House men wished merely to keep abreast of developments in the grand-jury room of the U.S. District Court, where officials of the Committee for the Re-Election of the President were testifying on Watergate, and this they accomplished through the obliging coöperation of Henry Petersen, the chief of the Criminal Division, who reported regularly to John Dean and later to the President himself. Dean subsequently described the coöperation to the President by saying, "Petersen is a soldier. He played —he kept me informed. He told me when we had problems, where we had problems, and the like. Uh, he believes in, in, in you. He believes in this Administration. This Administration had made him." What happened in the grand-jury room was further controlled by the coördinating of perjured testimony from White House aides and men working for the campaign committee. As for the prosecutors, a sort of dim-wittedness—a failure to draw obvious conclusions, a failure to follow up leads, a seeming willingness to construe the Watergate case narrowly—appeared to be enough to keep them from running afoul of the White House.

While all these moves were being made, the public was treated to a steady stream of categorical denials that the White House or the President's campaign committee had had anything to do with the break-in or with efforts to cover up the origins of the crime. The day after the break-in, Mitchell, in California, described James McCord, one of the burlars, as "the proprietor of a private security agency who was employed by our Committee months ago to assist with the installation of our security system." Actually, McCord was the committee's chief of security at the moment when he was arrested. Mitchell added, "We want to emphasize that this man and the other people involved were not operating either in our behalf or with our consent. . . . There is no place in our campaign or in the electoral process for this type of activity, and we will not permit nor condone it." On June 19th, two days after the break-in, Ronald Ziegler, the President's press secretary, contemptuously dismissed press reports of White House involvement. "I'm not going to comment from the White House on a third-rate burglary attempt," he said. On June 20th, when Lawrence O'Brien, the chairman of the Democratic Party, revealed that the Party had brought a one-million-dollar civil-damages suit against the Committee for the Re-Election of the President and the five burglary suspects, charging invasion of privacy and violation of the civil rights of the Democrats, Mitchell stated that the action represented "another example of sheer demagoguery on the part of Mr. O'Brien." Mitchell said, "I reiterate that this committee did not authorize and does not condone the alleged actions of the five men apprehended there."

Among the nation's major newspapers, only one, the Washington Post, consistently gave the Watergate story prominent headlines on the front page. Most papers, when they dealt with the story at all, tended to treat it as something of a joke. All in all, the tone of the coverage was not unlike the coverage of the Clifford Irving affair the previous winter, and the volume of the coverage was, if anything, less. "Caper" was the word that most of the press settled upon to describe the incident. A week after the break-in, for instance, the Times headlined its Watergate story "WATERGATE CAPER." When another week had passed, and Howard Hunt's connection with the break-in had been made known, *Time* stated that the story was "fast stretching into the most provocative caper of 1972, an extraordinary bit of bungling of great potential advantage to the Democrats and damage to the Republicans in this election year." In early August, the *Times* was still running headlines like "THE PLOT THICKENS IN WATERGATE WHODUNIT" over accounts of the repercussions of the burglary. "Above all, the purpose of the break-in seemed obscure," the *Times* said. "But these details are never explained until the last chapter." The President held a news conference six weeks after the break-in, and by then the story was of such small interest to newsmen that not one question was asked concerning it.

Disavowals such as those made by Mitchell and Ziegler carried great weight in the absence of incontrovertible evidence refuting them. The public had grown accustomed to deception and evasion in high places, but not yet to repeated, consistent, barefaced lying at all levels. The very boldness of the lies raised the cost of contradicting them, for to do so would be to call high officials outright liars. Another effective White House technique was to induce semi-informed or wholly uninformed spokesmen to deny charges. One of these spokesmen was Clark MacGregor, a former member of Congress from Minnesota, who became reëlection-campaign director early in July, when John Mitchell resigned, pleading family difficulties. A few weeks later, when Senator McGovern described the break-ins as "the kind of thing you expect under a person like Hitler," MacGregor called McGovern's remark "character assassination." The practice of using as spokesmen officials who were more or less innocent of the facts was one more refinement of the technique of dissociating "what we say" from "what we do." In this manner, honest men could be made to lend the weight of their integrity to untruths. They spoke words without knowing whether the words were true or false. Such spokesmen lent their vocal cords to the campaign but left their brains behind, and confused the public with words spoken by nobody.

On Septembter 15th, the five men who had been caught in the Democratic National Committee headquarters were indicted—together with E. Howard Hunt and G. Gordon Liddy, who were elsewhere in the Watergate complex at the time of the break-in—for the felonies of burglary, conspiracy, and wiretapping. A few days later, the seven defendants pleaded not guilty. As the case stood at that moment, their crimes were officially motiveless. The prosecutors had not been able to suggest who might have asked employees of the Committee for the Re-Election of the President to wiretap the Democratic headquarters, or why a check belonging to that committee should have found its way into the bank account of Bernard Barker. That afternoon, the President met with Haldeman and Dean, and congratulated Dean on his work, "Well," he said, "the whole thing is a can of worms. . . . But the, but the way you, you've handled it, it seems to me, has been very skillful, because you— putting your fingers in the dikes every time that leaks have sprung here and sprung there." Representative Wright Patman, the chairman of the House Banking and Currency Committee, was planning to hold hearings on the Watergate break-in, and the President, Dean, and Haldeman went on to discuss ways of "turning that off," as Dean put it. Dean reported to the two others that he was studying the possibility of blackmailing members of the Patman committee with damaging information about their own campaigns, and then the President suggested that Gerald Ford, the minority leader of the House, would be the man to pressure Patman into dropping the hearings. Ford should be told that "he's got to get at this and screw this thing up while he can," the President said. Two and a half weeks later, a majority of the members of the committee voted to deny Patman the power to subpoena witnesses. But Patman made the gesture of carrying on anyway for a while, and asked questions of an empty chair.

At the end of September—more than a month before the election—the Washington *Post* reported that John Mitchell had had control of a secret fund for spying on the Democrats. Throughout October, denials continued to pour out from the Administration. As before, some were outright lies by men who knew the facts, and others were untruths spoken by men who were simply repeating what they had been told. On October 2nd, Acting Director Gray of the F.B.I. said that it was unreasonable to believe that the President had deceived the nation about Watergate. "Even if some of us [in federal law enforcement agencies] are crooked, there aren't that many that are. I don't believe everyone is a Sir Galahad, but there's not been one single bit of pressure put on me or any of my special agents." In reality, of course, Gray had once considered resigning because the pressure from the White House to help with the coverup had been so intense, and even as he spoke he was keeping the contents of E. Howard Hunt's safe in a drawer of a dresser at his home in Connecticut. Gray went on to say, "It strains the credulity that the President of the United States—if he had a mind to—could have done a con job on the whole American people." Gray added, "He would have to control the United States."

In the months since the election, the issue of Watergate had faded, and the papers had devoted their front pages to other news. Shortly after the trial began, however, the front-page news was that all the defendants but two had pleaded guilty. In the courtroom, Judge John Sirica, who presided, found himself dissatisfied with the questioning of witnesses by the government prosecutors. The prosecutors now had a suggestion as to the burglars' motive. They suggested that it might be blackmail. They did not say of whom or over what. At the trial, the key prosecution witness, the former F.B.I. agent Alfred Baldwin, related that on one occasion he had taken the logs of the Watergate wiretaps to the headquarters of the Committee for the Re-Election of the President. But this suggested nothing to the Justice Department, one of whose spokesmen had maintained when the indictment was handed up in September that there was "no evidence" showing that anyone except the defendants was involved. Sirica demurred. "I want to know where the money comes from," he said to the defendant Bernard Barker.

"There were hundred-dollar bills floating around like coupons." When Barker replied that he had simply received the money in the mail in a blank envelope and had no idea who might have sent it, Sirica commented, "I'm sorry, but I don't believe you." When the defense lawyers protested Sirica's questioning, he said, "I don't think we should sit up here like nincompoops. The function of a trial is to search for the truth."

All the Watergate defendants but one were following the White House scenario to the letter. The exception was James McCord. He was seething with scenarios of his own. He hoped to have the charges against him dismissed, and, besides, he had been angered by what he understood as a suggestion from one of his lawyers that the blame for the Watergate break-in be assigned to the C.I.A., his old outfit, to which he retained an intense loyalty. There was some irony in the fact that McCord's anger had been aroused by an Administration plan to involve the C.I.A. in its crimes. McCord believed that Nixon's removal of C.I.A. director Richard Helms, in December of 1972—at the very time that McCord himself was being urged to lay the blame for Watergate at the door of the C.I.A.—was designed to pave the way for an attempt by the Administration itself to blame the break-in on the agency and for a takeover of the agency by the White House. He had worked for the White House, but he did not see the reorganizational wars from the White House point of view. He saw them from the bureaucrats' point of view; in his opinion, President Nixon was attempting to take over the C.I.A. in a manner reminiscent of attempts by Hitler to take control of German intelligence agencies before the Second World War. The White House, that is, belatedly discovered that it had a disgruntled "holdover" on its hands. And this particular holdover really was prepared to perform sabotage; he was prepared, indeed, to sabotage not just the President's policies but the President himself, and, what was more, he had the means to do it. McCord was putting together a scenario that could destroy the Nixon Administration. In a letter delivered to his White House contact, the undercover operative John Caulfield, McCord pronounced a dread warning: If the White House continued to try to have the C.I.A. take responsibility for the Watergate burglary, "every tree in the forest will fall," and "it will be a scorched desert." Piling on yet another metaphor of catastrophe, he wrote, "Pass the message that if they want it to blow, they are on exactly the right course. I am sorry that you will get hurt in the fallout." McCord was the first person in the Watergate conspiracy to put in writing exactly what the magnitude of the Watergate scandal was. Many observers had been amazed at the extreme hard line that the President had taken since his landslide reëlection—the firings in the bureaucracies, the incomprehensible continuation of the attacks on Senator McGovern, the renewed attacks on the press, the attacks on Congress's power of the purse, the bombing of Hanoi. They could not know that at the exact moment when President Nixon was wreaking devastation on North Vietnam, James McCord was threatening to wreak devastation on him.

On February 7th, the Senate, by a vote of seventy-seven to none, established a Select Committee on Presidential Campaign Activities, to look into abuses in the Presidential campaign of 1972, including the Watergate break-in; and the Democratic leadership appointed Senator Sam Ervin, of North Carolina, the author of the resolution to establish the Select Committee, to be its chairman. Three days later, the Administration secretly convened a Watergate committee of its own, in California—at the La Costa Resort Hotel and Spa, not far from the President's estate in San Clemente, with John Dean, H. R. Haldeman, John Ehrlichman, and Richard Moore, a White House aide, in attendance. The meeting lasted for two days. Its work was to devise ways of hampering, discrediting, and ultimately blocking the Ervin committee's investigation.

The President's drive to take over the federal government was going well. By the end of March those legislators who were worried about the possibility of a collapse of the Constitutional system were in a state of near-hopelessness. It seemed that the President would have his will, and Congress could not stop him; as for the public, it was uninterested in Constitutional matters. Senator Muskie had now joined Senator McGovern in warning against the dangers of "one-man rule," and he said that the Administration's proposal for preventing the release of "classified" information, no matter how arbitrarily the "classified" designation had been applied, could impose "the silence of democracy's graveyard." Senator William Fulbright, of Arkansas, had expressed fear that the United States might "pass on, as most of the world has passed on, to a totalitarian system." In the press, a new feeling seemed to be crystallizing that Congress had had its day as an institution of American life. Commentators of all political persuasions were talking about Congress as though it were moribund. Kevin Phillips, a political writer who had played an important role in formulating "the Southern strategy," and who had once worked in John Mitchell's Justice Department, wrote, in an article in *Newsweek* called "Our Obsolete System," that "Congress's separate power is an obstacle to modern policy-making." He proposed a "fusion of powers" to replace the Constitution's separation of powers. "In sum," he wrote, "we may have reached a point where separation of powers is doing more harm than good by distorting the logical evolution of technology-era government." In *The New Republic,* the columnist TRB, who, like Senator McGovern and Senator Muskie, was worried that "one-man rule" was in prospect, wrote, "President Nixon treats Congress with contempt which, it has to be admitted, is richly deserved. We have a lot of problems—the economy, inflation, the unfinished war, Watergate —but in the long run the biggest problem is whether Congress can be salvaged, because if it can't, our peculiar 18th-century form of government, with separation of powers, can't be salvaged," And he wrote, "A vacuum has to be filled. The authority of Congress has decayed till it is overripe and rotten. Mr. Nixon has merely proclaimed it." At the Justice Department, Donald Santarelli, who was shortly to become head of the Law Enforcement Assistance Administration, told a reporter, "Today, the whole Constitution is up for grabs." These observers took the undeniable fact that the Congress was impotent as a sign that the Congress was obsolete. And the executive branch, having helped reduce the Congress to helplessness, could now point to that helplessness as proof that the Congress was of no value.

The coverup and the takeover had merged into a single project. For four years, the President's anger at his "enemies" had been growing. As his anger had grown, so had that clandestine repressive apparatus in the White House whose purpose was to punish and destroy his enemies. And as this apparatus had grown, so had the need to control the Cabinet departments and the agencies; and the other branches of government, because they might find out about it—until, finally, the coverup had come to exceed in importance every other matter facing the Administration. For almost a year now, the coverup had been the motor of American politics. It had safeguarded the President's reëlection, and it had determined the substance and the mood of the Administration's second term so far. In 1969, when President Nixon launched his Presidential Offensive, he had probably not foreseen that the tools he was developing then would one day serve him in a mortal struggle between his Administration and the other powers of the Republic; but now his assault on the press, the television networks, the Congress, the federal bureaucracy, and the courts had coalesced into a single, coordinated assault on the American Constitutional democracy. Either the Nixon Administration would survive in power and the democracy would die or the Administration would be driven from power and the democracy would have another chance to live. If the newly reëlected President should be able to thwart investigations by the news media, the agencies of federal law enforcement, the courts, and Congress, he would be clear of all accountabiilty, and would be above the law; on the other hand, if the rival institutions of the Republic should succeed in laying bare the crimes of his Administration and in bringing the criminals to justice, the Administration would be destroyed.

In the latter part of March, the pace of events in this area of the coverup quickened. Under the pressure of the pending sentences, two of the conspirators were breaking ranks: James McCord and Howard Hunt. McCord, who had been threatening the White House with exposure since December, now wrote a letter to Judge Sirica telling what he knew of the coverup. Hunt, for his part, was angry because he and the other defendants and their lawyers had not been paid as much money as they wanted in return for their silence. In November, 1972, he called Charles Colson to remind him that the continuation of the coverup was a "two-way street," and shortly after the middle of March he told Paul O'Brien, an attorney for the reëlection committee, that if more funds weren't forthcoming immediately he might reveal some of the "many things" he had done for John Haldeman—an apparent reference to the break-in at the office of Daniel Ellsberg's psychiatrist. Shortly thereafter, O'Brien informed Dean of Hunt's demand. These events on one edge of the coverup had an immediate influence on the chemistry of the whole enterprise. On March 21st, John Dean, convinced now that the coverup could not be maintained, met with the President and told him the story of it as he knew it from beginning to end. The President's response was to recommend that the blackmail money be paid to Hunt. "I think you should handle that one pretty fast," he said. And later he said, "But at the moment don't you agree that you'd better get the Hunt thing? I mean, that's worth it, at the moment." And he said, "That's why, John, for your immediate thing you've got no choice with Hunt but the hundred and twenty or whatever it is. Right?" The President was willing to consider plans for limited disclosure, and the meeting ended with a suggestion from Haldeman, who had joined the two other men: "We've got to figure out where to turn it off at the lowest cost we can, but at whatever cost it takes."

The defection of Hunt and McCord had upset the delicate balance of roles demanded by the coverup. Information that had to be kept secret began to flow in a wide loop through the coverup's various departments. Not only Hunt and McCord but Dean and Magruder began to tell their stories to the prosecutors. The prosecutors, in turn, relayed the information to Attorney General Kleindienst and Assistant Attorney General Petersen, who then relayed it to the President, who then relayed it to Haldeman and Ehrlichman, who in this period were desperately attempting to avoid prosecution, and were therefore eager to know what was happening in the Grand Jury room. Any defections placed the remaining conspirators in an awkward position. In order to get clear of the collapsing coverup, they had to become public inquisitors of their former subordinates and collaborators. Such a transformation, however, was not likely to sit well with the defectors, who were far from eager to shoulder the blame for the crimes of others, and who, furthermore, were in possession of damaging information with which to retaliate.

Notwithstanding these new tensions, the President sought to continue the coverup. In the weeks following his meeting with Dean on March 21st, his consistent strategy was what might be called the hors d'oeuvre strategy. The President described the strategy to Haldeman and Ehrlichman after a conversation with Dean on April 14th by saying, "Give 'em an hors d'oeuvre and maybe they won't come back for the main course." His hope was that by making certain public revelations and by offering a certain number of victims to the prosecutors he could satisfy the public's appetite, so that it would seek no more revelations and no more victims. (This technique, which Ehrlichman, on another occasion, called a "modified limited hang-out," was also what Haldeman had had in mind when he suggested that they should "turn it off at the lowest cost" they could.) Hors d'oeuvres of many kinds came under consideration. Some were in the form of scapegoats to be turned over to the prosecutors, and others were in the form of incomplete or false reports to be issued to the public. By now, the country's appetite for revelations was well developed, and in the White House it was decided that no less a man than Mitchell was needed to satisfy it. As Ehrlichman explained the new plan to the President, Mitchell would be induced to make a statement saying, "I am both morally and legally responsible."

"How does it redound to our advantage?" the President asked.

"That you have a report from me based on three weeks' work," Ehrlichman replied, "that when you got it, you immediately acted to call Mitchell in as the provable wrongdoer, and you say, 'My God, I've got a report here. And it's clear from this report that you are guilty as hell. Now John . . . go on in there and do what you should.'"

That way, the President could pose as the man who had cracked the conspiracy.

Shortly thereafter, Mitchell was called down to the White House, and Ehrlichman proposed the plan. Mitchell did not care for it. He not only maintained his innocence but suggested that the guilt lay elsewhere; namely, in the White House. Ehrlichman told the President when Mitchell had left that Mitchell had "lobbed, uh, mud balls at the White House at every opportunity." Faced with Mitchell's refusal to play the scapegoat, the President, Haldeman, and Ehrlichman next invited Dean to step into the role. Soon after Ehrlichman's unsatisfactory experience with Mitchell, the President met with Dean and attempted to induce him to sign a letter of resignation because of his implication in the scandal.

The President approached the subject in an offhand manner. "You know, I was thinking we ought to get the odds and ends, uh . . . we talked, and, uh, it was confirmed that—you remember we talked about resignations and so forth," he said.

"Uh huh," Dean replied.

"But I should have in hand something, or otherwise they'll say, 'What the hell did you—after Mr. Dean told you all of this, what did you do?'" the President went on.

Again Dean answered "Uh huh."

The President then related that even Henry Petersen had been concerned about "this situation on Dean," and Dean once more answered with an "uh huh."

"See what I mean?" the President asked the uncommunicative Dean.

"Are we talking Dean, or are we talking Dean, Ehrlichman, and Haldeman?" Dean finally asked.

"Well, I'm talking Dean," the President answered.

But Dean, like Mitchell before him, was talking Ehrlichman and Haldeman, too, and would not resign unless they also resigned. He did not want to be an hors d'oeuvre any more than Mitchell did. And since Dean was in possession of highly detailed information that implicated not only Haldeman and Ehrlichman but the President as well, the President was unable to "bite the Dean bullet," as he put it, until he also was willing to let Haldeman and Ehrlichman go. Their turn came quickly. By now the President was under intense pressure to act soon. If he did not, he could hardly pose as the man who had cracked the case. On April 17th, the day after the unproductive conversation with Dean, the President said to Haldeman and Ehrlichman, "Let me say this. . . . It's a hell of a lot different [from] John Dean. I know that as far as you're concerned, you'll go out and throw yourselves on a damned sword. I'm aware of that. . . . The problem we got here is this. I do not want to be in a position where the damned public clamor makes, as it did with Eisenhower, with Adams, makes it necessary or calls—to have Bob come in one day and say, 'Well, Mr. President, the public—blah, blah, blah—I'm going to leave.' " But Ehrlichman was not willing to throw himself on a sword. The person he was willing to throw on a sword was Dean. "Let me make a suggestion," he responded. It was that the President give Dean a leave of absence and then defer any decision on Ehrlichman and Haldeman until the case had developed further. However, the President pursued the point, seeming at times to favor Haldeman's and Ehrlichman's resignation, and finally Ehrlichman did what McCord, Hunt, Mitchell, and Dean had done before him. He lobbed mud balls at the White House—which in this case meant the President.

If he and Haldeman should resign, Ehrlichman observed, "we are put in a position of defending ourselves." And he went on, "The things that I am going to have to say about Dean are: basically that Dean was the sole proprietor of this project, that he reported to the President, he reported to me only incidentally."

" 'Reported to the President'?" the President inquired.

A moment later, speaking in his own defense, the President said, "You see the problem you've got there is that Dean does have a point there which you've got to realize. He didn't see me when he came out to California. He didn't see me until the day you said, 'I think you ought to talk to John Dean.' "

At this point, Ehrlichman retreated into ambiguity, and said, "But you see I get into a very funny defensive position then vis-à-vis you and vis-à-vis him, and it's very damned awkward. And I haven't thought it clear through. I don't know where we come out."

On April 17th, the President made a short statement saying simply that there had been "major developments in the case concerning which it would be improper to be more specific now." He was unable to offer any diversionary reports or propitiatory victims to deflect the public's wrath at the forthcoming disclosures. He and his aides had talked over countless schemes, but all of them had foundered on the unwillingness of any of the aides to sacrifice themselves for him—or for "the Presidency," as he had asked them to do. The coverup was all one piece, and it cohered in exposure just as it had cohered in concealment.

The President had become adept at recollecting whatever was needed at a particular moment. By April of 1973, he and his aides were spending most of their time making up history out of whole cloth to suit the needs of each moment. Unfortunately for them, the history they were making up was self-serving history, and by April their individual interests had grown apart. Each of them had begun to "recollect" things to his own advantage and to the detriment of the others. As their community of interests dissolved under the pressure of the investigation, each of them was retreating into his own private, self-interested reality. The capacity for deception which had once divided them from the country but united them with one another now divided them from one another as well.

In the White House, the fabric of reality had disintegrated altogether. What had got the President into trouble from the start had been his remarkable capacity for fantasy. He had begun by imagining a host of domestic foes. In retaliating against them, he had broken the law. Then he had compounded his lawbreaking by concealing it. And, finally, in the same way that he had broken the law although breaking it was against his best interests, he was bringing himself to justice even as he thought he was evading justice. For, as though in anticipation of the deterioration of his memory, he had installed another memory in the Oval Office, which was more nearly perfect than his own, or anyone else's merely human equipment: he had installed the taping system. The Watergate coverup had cast him in the double role of conspirator and investigator. Though the conspirator in him worked hard to escape the law, it was the investigator in him that gained the upper hand in the end. While he was attempting to evade the truth, his machines were preserving it forever.

At the moment when the President announced "major developments" in the Watergate case, the national process that was the investigation overwhelmed the national process that was the coverup. The events that followed were all the more astounding to the nation because, at just the moment when the coverup began to explode, the President, in the view of many observers, had been on the point of strangling the "obsolete" Constitutional system and replacing it with a Presidential dictatorship. One moment, he was triumphant and his power was apparently irresistible; the next moment, he was at bay. For in the instant the President made his announcement, the coverup cracked—not just the Watergate coverup but the broader coverup, which concealed the underground history of the last five years—and the nation suffered an inundation of news. The newspaper headlines now came faster and thicker than ever before in American history. The stories ran backward in time, and each day's newspaper told of some event a little further in the past as reporters traced the underground history to the early days of the Administration, and even into the terms of former Administrations. With the history of half a decade pouring out all at once, the papers were stuffed with more news than even the most diligent reader could absorb. Moreover, along with the facts, non-facts proliferated as the desperate men in the White House put out one false or distorted statement after another, so that each true fragment of the story was all but lost in a maze of deceptions, and each event, true or false, came up dozens of times, in dozens of versions, until the reader's mind was swamped. And, as if what was in the newspapers were not already too much, television soon started up, and, in coverage that was itself a full-time job to watch, presented first the proceedings of the Ervin committee and then the proceedings of the House Judiciary Committee, when it began to weigh the impeachment of the President. And, finally, in a burst of disclosure without anything close to a precedent in history, the tapes were revealed—and not just once but twice. The first set of transcripts was released by the White House and was doctored, and only the second set, which was released by the Judiciary Committee, gave an accurate account of the President's conversations.

As the flood of information flowed into the public realm, overturning the accepted history of recent years, the present scene was also transformed. The Vice-President was swept from office when his bribe-taking became known, but so rapid was the pace of events that his departure was hardly noticed. Each of the institutions of the democracy that had been menaced by the President—and all had been menaced—was galvanized into action in its turn: the press, the television networks, the Senate, the House of Representatives, and, finally, in a dispute over release of the tapes, the Supreme Court. The public, too, was at last awakened, when the President fired the Special Proscutor whom he had appointed to look into the White House crimes. In an outpouring of public sentiment that, like so much else that happened at the time, had no precedent in the nation's history, millions of letters and telegrams poured in to Congress protesting the President's action. The time of letters sent by the President to himself was over, and the time of real letters from real people had come. No one of the democracy's institutions was powerful enough by itself to remove the President; the efforts of all were required—and only when those efforts were combined was he forced from office.

Report on the Central Intelligence Agency

SENATOR FRANK CHURCH

Formed in 1949 to centralize all intelligence activities of the United States, the Central Intelligence Agency (CIA) was in some respects a copy of a similar Soviet agency. The CIA was born in secrecy. No one knew how much funding it received. And since its members often assumed a "cover" identity, no one could be sure who, in or out of government, belonged to the CIA. An unhealthy situation, charged its critics; essential to our security, argued its proponents. Whatever its merits, the new agency enjoyed great popularity during the high drama of the Cold War. Yet it was probably destined for trouble in an era of less international tension. There is a strong American tradition that abhors secrecy. And as Watergate reminded a later generation, power corrupts. Eventually a widespread demand among citizens arose for the federal bureaucracy, as well as national leaders, to come into the open. Senator Frank Church's Senate committee report, sections of which are presented here, tells part of the CIA story.

The Senate Select Committee on Intelligence Activities has conducted a 15-month long inquiry, the first major inquiry into intelligence since World War II. The inquiry arose out of allegations of substantial, even massive wrongdoing within the "national intelligence" system. This final report provides a history of the evolution of intelligence, an evaluation of the intelligence system of the United States, a critique of its problems, recommendations for legislative action and recommendations to the executive branch. The committee believes that its recommendations will provide a sound framework for conducting the vital intelligence activities of the United States in a manner which meets the nation's intelligence requirements and protects the liberties of American citizens and the freedoms which our Constitution guarantees.

The shortcomings of the intelligence system, the adverse effects of secrecy and the failure of Congressional oversight to assure adequate accountability for executive branch decisions concerning intelligence activities were major subjects of the committee's inquiry. Equally important to the obligation to investigate allegations of abuse was the duty to review systematically the intelligence community's overall activities since 1915, and to evaluate its present structure and performance.

An extensive national intelligence system has been a vital part of the United States Government since 1944. Intelligence information has had an important influence on the direction and development of American foreign policy and has been essential to the maintenance of our national security. The committee is convinced that the United States requires an intelligence system which will provide policy-makers with accurate intelligence and analysis. We must have an early warning system to monitor potential military threats by countries hostile to United States interests. We need a strong intelligence system to verify that treaties concerning arms limitation are being honored. Information derived from the intelligence agencies is a necessary ingredient in making national defense and foreign policy decisions. Such information is also necessary in countering the efforts of hostile intelligence services and in halting terrorists, international drug traffickers and other international criminal activities. Within this country certain carefully controlled intelligence activities are essential for effective law enforcement.

The United States has devoted enormous resources to the creation of a national intelligence system, and today there is an awareness on the part of many citizens that a national intelligence system is a permanent and necessary component of our Government. The system's value to the country has been proven, and it will be needed for the foreseeable future. But a major conclusion of this inquiry is that Congressional oversight is necessary to assure that in the future our intelligence community functions effectively, within the framework of the Constitution.

The committee is of the view that many of the unlawful actions taken by officials of the intelligence agencies were rationalized as their public duty. It was necessary for the committee to understand how the pursuit of the public good could have the opposite effect. As Justice Brandeis observed:

"Experience should teach us to be most on our guard to protect liberty when the Government's purposes are beneficent. Men born to freedom are naturally alert to repel invasion of their liberty by evil-minded rulers. The greatest dangers to liberty lurk in insidious encroachment by men of zeal, well-meaning but without understanding."
Olmstead v. *United States*, 277 U.S. 438, 479 (1928)

. . .

THE DILEMMA OF SECRECY AND OPEN CONSTITUTIONAL GOVERNMENT

Since World War II, with steadily escalating consequences, many decisions of national importance have been made in secrecy, often by the executive branch alone. These decisions are frequently based on information obtained by clandestine means and available only to the executive branch.

Recent Presidents have justified this secrecy on the basis of "national security," "the requirements of national defense" or "the confidentiality required by sensitive, ongoing negotiations or operations." These justifications were generally accepted at face value. The Bay of Pigs fiasco, the secret war in Laos, the secret bombing of Cambodia, the anti-Allende activities in Chile, the Watergate affair, were all instances of the use of power cloaked in secrecy which when revealed provoked widespread popular disapproval. This series of events has ended, for the time being at least, passive and uncritical acceptance by the Congress of executive decisions in the areas of foreign policy, national security and intelligence activities. If Congress had met its oversight responsibilities some of these activities might have been averted.

An examination of the scope of secret intelligence activities undertaken in the last three decades reveals that they ranged from war to conventional espionage. It appears that some United States intelligence activities may have violated treaty and covenant obligations, but more importantly the rights of United States citizens have been infringed upon. Despite citizen and Congressional concern about these programs, no processes or procedures have been developed by either the Congress or the executive branch which would assure Congress of access to secret information which it must have to carry out its constitutional responsibilities in authorizing and giving its advice and consent. The hindsight of history suggests that many secret operations were ill-advised or might have been more beneficial to United States interests had they been conducted openly, rather than secretly.

The committee stresses that these questions remain to be decided by the Congress and the executive jointly:

What should be regarded as a national secret?

Who determines what is to be kept secret?

How can decisions made in secret or programs secretly approved be reviewed?

Two great problems have confronted the committee in carrying out its charge to address these issues.

The first is how our open democratic society, which has endured and flourished for 200 years, can be adapted to overcome the threats to liberty posed by the continuation of secret Government activities. The leaders of the United States must devise ways to meet their respective intelligence responsibilities, including informed and effective Congressional oversight, in a manner which brings secrecy and the power that secrecy affords within constitutional bounds.

For the executive branch, the specific problem concerns instituting effective control and accountability systems and improving efficiency. Many aspects of these two problem areas which have been examined during the committee's inquiry of intelligence agencies are addressed in the recommendations. It is our hope that intelligence oversight committees working with the executive branch will develop legislation to remedy the problems exposed by our inquiry and described in this report. The committee has already recommended the creation of an oversight committee with the necessary powers to exercise legislative authority over the intelligence activities of the United States.

It is clear that the Congress must exert its will and devise procedures that will enable it to play its full constitutional role in making policy decisions concerning intelligence activities. Failure to do so would permit further erosion of constitutional government.

In a meeting with President Ford at the outset of our inquiry in

February 1975, the committee agreed not to disclose any classified information provided by the executive branch without first consulting the appropriate agencies, offices and departments. In the case of objections, the committee agreed to carefully consider the executive's reasons for maintaining secrecy, but the committee determined that final decisions on any disclosure would be up to the committee.

The select committee has scrupulously adhered to this agreement. The Interim Report on Alleged Assassination Plots Involving Foreign Leaders, the report on C.I.A. activities in Chile, the report on illegal N.S.A. surveillance, and the disclosures of illegal activities on the part of F.B.I. Cointelpro, the F.B.I. harassment of Dr. Martin Luther King, Jr. and other matters revealed in the committee's public hearings, were all carefully considered by the committee and the executive branch working together to determine what information could be declassified and revealed without damaging national security. In those reports and hearings, virtually all differences between the committee and the executive were resolved. The only significant exception concerned the release to the public of the Assassination Report, which the executive branch believed would harm national security. The committee decided otherwise.

Some criteria for defining a valid national secret have been agreed to over the last year. Both the committee and the executive branch now agree that the names of intelligence sources and the details of sensitive methods used by the intelligence services should remain secret. Wherever possible, the right of privacy of individuals and groups should also be preserved. It was agreed, however, that the details of illegal acts should be disclosed and that the broad scope of United States intelligence activities should be sufficiently described to give public reassurance that the intelligence agencies are operating consistent with the law and declared national policy.

· · ·

RECOMMENDATIONS

1. The National Security Act should be recast by omnibus legislation which would set forth the basic purposes of national intelligence activities, and define the relationship between the Congress and the intelligence agencies of the executive branch. This revision should be given the highest priority by the intelligence oversight committee of Congress, acting in consultation with the executive branch.

2. The new legislation should define the charter of the organizations and entities in the United States intelligence community. It should establish charters for the National Security Council, the Director of Central Intelligence, the Central Intelligence Agency, the national intelligence components of the Department of Defense, including the National Security Agency and the Defense Intelligence Agency, and all other elements of the intelligence community, including joint organizations of two or more agencies.

3. This legislation should set forth the general structure and procedures of the intelligence community and the roles and responsibilities of the agencies which comprise it.

4. The legislation should contain specific and clearly defined prohibitions or limitations on various activities carried out by the respective components of the intelligence community.

THE NATIONAL SECURITY COUNCIL AND THE OFFICE OF THE PRESIDENT

The National Security Council is an instrument of the President and not a corporate entity with authority of its own. The committee found that in general the President has had, through the National Security Council, effective means for exerting broad policy control over at least two major clandestine activities—covert action and sensitive technical collection. The covert American involvement in Angola and the operations of the Glomar Explorer are examples of that control in quite different circumstances, whatever conclusions one draws about the merits of the activities. The Central Intelligence Agency, in broad terms, is not "out of control."

The committee found, however, that there were significant limits to this control.

CLANDESTINE ACTIVITIES

¶The degree of control and accountability regarding covert action and sensitive collection has been a function of each particular President's willingness to use these techniques.

¶The principal N.S.C. vehicle for dealing with clandestine activities, the 40 Committee and its predecessors, was the mechanism for reviewing and making recommendations regarding the approval of major covert action projects. However, this body also served generally to insulate the President from official involvement and accountability in the approval process until 1974.

¶As high-level Government officials, 40 Committee members have had neither time nor inclination to adequately review and pass judgment on all of the literally hundreds of covert action projects. Indeed, only a small fraction of such projects (those which the C.I.A. regards as major or sensitive) are so approved and/or reviewed. This problem is aggravated by the fact that the 40 Committee has had virtually no staff, with only a single officer from the clandestine services acting as executive secretary.

¶The process of review and approval has been, at times, only general in nature. It sometimes has become *pro forma* conducted over the telephone by subordinates.

¶The President, without consulting any N.S.C. mechanism, can exercise personal direction of clandestine activities as he did in the case of Chile in 1970.

¶There is no systematic White House-level review of either sensitive foreign espionage or counterintelligence activities. Yet these operations may also have a potential for embarrassing the United States and sometimes may be difficult to distinguish from covert action operations. For example, a proposal to recruit a high foreign government official as an intelligence "asset" would not necessarily be previewed outside the Central Intelligence Agency, at the N.S.C. level, despite the implications that recruitment might pose in conducting American foreign relations. Similarly, foreign counterintelligence operations might be conducted without any prior review at the highest Government levels. The committee found instances in the case of Chile when counterintelligence operations were related to, and even hard to distinguish from, the program of covert action.

¶The President's proposals to upgrade the 40 Committee into the Operations Advisory Group and to give explicit recognition to its role in advising the President on covert activities are desirable. That upgrading, however, will strain further the Group's ability to conduct a systematic review of sensitive clandestine operations. Under the new structure, the Group members are cabinet officers who have even less time than their principal deputies, who previously conducted the 40 Committee's work. The Group's procedures must be carefully structured, so that the perspective of Cabinet officers can in fact be brought to bear.

COUNTERINTELLIGENCE

There is no N.S.C.-level mechanism for coordinating, reviewing or approving counterintelligence activities in the United States, even those directed at United States citizens, despite the demonstrated potential for abuse.

COORDINATION AND RESOURCE ALLOCATION

The Director of Central Intelligence has been assigned the function of coordinating the activities of the intelligence community, ensuring its responsiveness to the requirements for national intelligence and for assembling a consolidated national intelligence budget. Until the recent establishment of the Committee on Foreign Intelligence, there was no effective N.S.C.-level mechanism for any of these purposes.

EXECUTIVE OVERSIGHT

The committee finds that Presidents have not established specific instruments of oversight to prevent abuses by the intelligence community. In essence, Presidents have not exercised effective oversight.

RECOMMENDATIONS

5. By statute, the National Security Council should be explicitly empowered to direct and provide policy guidance for the intelligence

activities of the United States, including intelligence collection, counter-intelligence, and the conduct of covert action.

6. By statute, the Attorney General should be made an adviser to the National Security Council in order to facilitate discharging his responsibility to insure that actions taken to protect American national security in the field of intelligence are also consistent with the constitution and the laws of the United States.

7. By statute, the existing power of the Director of Central Intelligence to coordinate the activities of the intelligence community should be reaffirmed. At the same time, the N.S.C. should establish an appropriate committee, such as the new Committee on Foreign intelligence, with responsibility for allocating intelligence resources to insure efficient and effective operation of the national intelligence community. This committee should be chaired by the D.C.I. and should include representatives of the Secretary of State, the Secretary of Defense, and the Assistant to the President for National Security Affairs.

8. By statute, an N.S.C. committee (like the Operations Advisory Group) should be established to advise the President on covert action. It would also be empowered, at the President's discretion, to approve all types of sensitive intelligence collection activities. If an O.A.G. member dissented from an approval, the particular collection activity would be referred to the President for decision. The group should consist of the Secretary of State, the Secretary of Defense, the Assistant to the President for National Security Affairs, the Director of Central Intelligence, the Attorney General, the Chairman of the Joint Chiefs of Staff and the Director of O.M.B., as an observer. The President would designate a chairman from among the group's members.

9. The chairman of the group would be confirmed by the Senate for that position, if he were an official not already subject to confirmation.

In the execution of covert action and sensitive intelligence collection activities specifically approved by the President, the chairman would enter the chain of command below the President.

10. The group should be provided with adequate staff to assist in conducting thorough reviews of covert action and sensitive collection projects. That staff should not be drawn exclusively from the Clandestine Service of the C.I.A.

11. Each covert action project should be reviewed and passed on by the group. In addition, the group would review all ongoing projects at least once a year.

12. By statute, the Secretary of State should be designated as the principal Administration spokesman to the Congress on the policy and purpose underlying covert action projects.

13. By statute, the Director of Central Intelligence should be required to fully inform the intelligence oversight committee(s) of Congress of each covert action prior to its initiation. No funds should be expended on any covert action unless and until the President certifies and provides to the Congressional intelligence oversight committee(s) the reasons that a covert action is required by extraordinary circum-

stances to deal with grave threats to the national security of the United States. The Congressional intelligence oversight committee(s) should be kept fully and currently informed on all covert action projects, and the D.C.I. should submit a semiannual report on all such projects to the committee(s).

14. The committee recommends that when the Senate establishes an intelligence oversight committee with authority to authorize the national intelligence budget, the Hughes-Ryan Amendment (22 U.S.C., 2422) should be amended so that the foregoing notifications and Presidential certifications to the Senate are provided only to that committee.

15. By statute, a new N.S.C. counterintelligence committee should be established, consisting of the Attorney General as chairman, the Deputy Secretary of Defense, the Director of Central Intelligence, the Director of the F.B.I. and the Assistant to the President for National Security Affairs. Its purpose would be to coordinate and review foreign counterintelligence activities conducted within the United States and the clandestine collection of foreign intelligence within the United States, by both the F.B.I. and the C.I.A. The goal would be to insure strict conformity with statutory and constitutional requirements and to enhance coordination between the C.I.A. and F.B.I. This committee should review the standards and guidelines for all recruitments of agents within the United States for either counterintelligence or positive foreign intelligence purposes, as well as for the recruitment of U.S. citizens abroad. This committee would consider differences between the agencies concerning the recruitment of agents, the handing of foreign assets that come to the United States, and the establishment of the bona fides of defectors: It should also treat any other foreign intelligence or counterintelligence activity of the F.B.I. and C.I.A. which either agency brings to the forum for Presidential level consideration.

THE DIRECTOR OF CENTRAL INTELLIGENCE

The 1947 National Security Act gave the D.C.I. responsibility for "coordinating the intelligence activities of the several Government departments and agencies in the interest of national security." In addition, the D.C.I. as the President's principal foreign intelligence adviser was given responsibility for coordinating and producing national intelligence for senior policymakers. However, the committee found that these D.C.I. responsibilities have often conflicted with the particular interests and prerogatives of the other intelligence community departments and agencies. They have not given up control over their own intelligence operations, and in particular the Department of Defense and the military services, which allocate 80 percent of the direct costs for national intelligence, have insisted that they must exercise direct control over peacetime intelligence activities to prepare for war. Thus, while the D.C.I. was given responsibility under the 1947 act for intelligence community activities, he was not authorized to centrally coordinate or manage the overall operations of the community.

Because the D.C.I. only provides guidance for intelligence collection and production and does not establish requirements, he is not in a position to command the intelligence community to respond to the intelligence needs of national policymakers. Where the D.C.I. has been able to define priorities, he has lacked authority to allocate intelligence resources—either among different systems of intelligence collection or among intelligence collection, analysis and finished intelligence production.

In the area of providing finished intelligence, the committee discovered that the D.C.I. in his role as intelligence adviser, has faced obstacles in insuring that his national intelligence judgments are objective and independent of department and agency biases. The committee has been particularly concerned with pressures from both the White House and the Defense Department on the D.C.I. to alter his intelligence judgments. One example of such pressure investigated by the committee occurred in the fall of 1969, when the D.C.I. modified his judgment on the capability of the Soviet SS-9 system when it conflicted with the public position of Secretary of Defense Laird. After a meeting with Staff of the Office of the Secretary of Defense, Director Helms deleted a paragraph from the draft of the National Intelligence Estimate on Soviet strategic forces which stated that within the next five years it was "highly unlikely" that the Soviet would attempt to achieve "a first strike capability, i.e., a capability to launch a surprise attack against the United States with assurance that the U.S.S.R. would not itself receive damage it would regard as unacceptable."

The committee believes that over the past five years the D.C.I.'s ability to produce objective national intelligence and resist outside pressure has been reduced with the dissolution of the independent Board of National Estimates and the subsequent delegation of its staff to the departments with responsibility for drafting D.C.I.'s national intelligence judgments.

The committee believes that the Congress, in carrying out its responsibilities in the area of national security policy, should have access to the full range of intelligence produced by the United States intelligence community. The committee further believes that it should be possible to work out a means of insuring that the D.C.I.'s national intelligence judgments are available to the appropriate Congressional committee on a regular basis without compromising the D.C.I.s' role as personal adviser to the President.

Finally, the committee has found concern that the function of the D.C.I. in his role as intelligence community leader and principal intelligence adviser to the President is inconsistent with his responsibility to manage one of the intelligence community agencies—the C.I.A. Potential problems exist in a number of areas. Because the D.C.I. as head of the C.I.A. is responsible for human clandestine collection overseas, interception of signals communication overseas, the development and interception of technical collection systems, there is concern that the D.C.I. as community leader is in "a conflict of interest" situation when ruling on the activities of the over-all intelligence community.

The committee is also concerned that the D.C.I.'s new span of control—both the entire intelligence community and the entire C.I.A.—may be too great for him to exercise effective detailed supervision of clandestine activities.

RECOMMENDATIONS

16. By statute, the D.C.I. should be established as the President's principal foreign intelligence adviser, with exclusive responsibility for producing national intelligence for the President and the Congress. For this purpose, the D.C.I. should be empowered to establish a staff directly responsible to him to help prepare his national intelligence judgments and to coordinate the views of the other members of the intelligence community. The committee recommends that the director establish a board to include senior outside advisers to review intelligence products as necessary, thus helping to insulate the D.C.I. from pressures to alter or modify his national intelligence judgments. To advise and assist the D.C.I. in producing national intelligence, the D.C.I. would also be empowered to draw on other elements of the intelligence community.

17. By statute, the D.C.I. should be given responsibility and authority for establishing national intelligence requirements, preparing the national intelligence budget and providing guidance for United States national intelligence program operations. In this capacity he should be designated as chairman of the appropriate N.S.C. committee, such as the C.F.I. and should have the following powers and responsibilities.

a. The D.C.I. should establish national intelligence requirements for the entire intelligence community. He should be empowered to draw on intelligence community representatives and others whom he may designate to assist him in establishing national intelligence requirements and determining the success of the various agencies in fulfilling them. The D.C.I. should provide general guidance to the various intelligence agency directors for the management of intelligence operations.

b. The D.C.I. should have responsibility for preparing the national intelligence program budget for presentation to the President and the Congress. The definition of what is to be included within that national intelligence program should be established by Congress in consultation with the executive. In this capacity, the Director of Central Intelligence should be involved early in the budget cycle in preparing the budgets of the respective intelligence community agencies. The director should have specific responsibility for choosing among the programs of the different collection and production agencies and departments and to insure against waste and unnecessary duplication. The D.C.I. should also have responsibility for issuing fiscal guidance for the allocation of all national intelligence resources. The authority of the D.C.I. to reprogram funds within the intelligence budget should be defined by statute.

c. In order to carry out his national intelligence responsibilities the D.C.I. should have the authority to review all foreign and military intelligence activities and intelligence resource allocations, including tactical military intelligence which is the responsibility of the armed forces.

d. The D.C.I. should be authorized to establish an intelligence community staff to support him in carrying out his managerial responsibilities. This staff should be drawn from the best available talent within and outside the intelligence community.

e. In addition to these provisions concerning D.C.I. control over national intelligence operations in peacetime, the statute should require establishment of a procedure to insure that in time of war the relevant national intelligence operations come under the control of the Secretary of Defense.

18. By statute, the position of Deputy Director of Central Intelligence for the intelligence community should be established as recommended in Executive Order No. 11905. This Deputy Director should be subject to Senate confirmation and would assume the DCI's intelligence community functions in the D.C.I.'s absence. Current provisions regarding the status of the D.C.I. and his single deputy should be extended to cover the D.C.I. and both deputies. Civilian control of the nation's intelligence is important; only one of the three could be a career military officers, active or retired.

19. The committee recommends that the intelligence oversight committee(s) of Congress consider whether the Congress should appropriate the funds for the national intelligence budget to the D.C.I., rather than to the directors of the various intelligence agencies and departments.

20. By statute, the Director of Central Intelligence should serve at the pleasure of the President but for no more than 10 years.

21. The committee also recommends consideration of separating the D.C.I. from direct responsibility over the C.I.A.

. . .

FOREIGN INTELLIGENCE COLLECTION IN THE UNITED STATES

The C.I.A. engages in both overt and clandestine activity within the United States for the purpose of foreign intelligence collection. The agency's Domestic Collection Division is responsible primarily for overt collection, while the Foreign Resources Division manages clandestine collection of foreign intelligence. Both divisions are currently within the Directorate of Operations. Formerly run and staffed by the Directorate of Intelligence, the D.C.D. was moved to Operations in 1973 and now has many clandestine services officers assigned to it.

The Domestic Collection Division openly collects foreign intelligence information from American citizens on a wide variety of subjects, primarily of an economic and technological nature. The Domestic Collection Division currently maintains contact with tens of thousands of American citizens who, on a confidential basis, volunteer information of intelligence value to the United States. The committee notes that the Central Intelligence Agency is overtly in contact with many members of the American academic community to consult with them on the subjects of their expertise. On occasion, at the request of the academic concerned, these contacts are confidential.

The committee believes there are significant benefits to both the Government and the universities in such contacts and that they should not be discouraged. The committee sees no danger to the integrity of American academic institutions in continuing such overt contacts.

The Domestic Collection Division operates from 38 offices around the United States and lists itself in local telephone directors, although it conducts its business as discreetly as possible.

The committee notes that due to the recent revelations about C.I.A. activities, some foreign intelligence sources are shying away from cooperation with the Domestic Collection Division, thus impeding this division's most important function, namely, the overt collection of foreign intelligence.

The committee also questions the recruiting, for foreign espionage purposes, of immigrants desiring American citizenship because it might be construed as coercive.

FOREIGN COUNTERINTELLIGENCE

Counterintelligence is defined quite broadly by the C.I.A. It includes the knowledge needed for the protection and preservation of the military, economic, and productive strength of the United States, as well as the Government's security in domestic and foreign affairs, against or from espionage, sabotage and subversion designed to weaken or destroy the United States.

Counterintelligence is a special form of intelligence activity, aimed at discovering hostile foreign intelligence operations and destroying their effectiveness. It involves protecting the United States Government against infiltration by foreign agents, as well as controlling and manipulating adversary intelligence operations. An effort is made to discern the plans and intentions of enemy intelligence services and to deceive them about our own.

The committee finds that the threat from hostile intelligence services is real. In the United States alone, well over a thousand Soviet officials are on permanent assignment. Among these, over 40 percent have been identified as members of the KGB or GRU, the Soviet civilian and military intelligence units, respectively. Estimates for the number of unidentified Soviet intelligence officers raise this figure to over 88 percent and some defector sources have estimated that 70 percent to 80 percent of Soviet officials in the United States have some intelligence connection.

Furthermore, the number of Soviets with access to the United States has tripled since 1960, and is still increasing. In 1974, for example, over 200 Soviet ships with a total crew complement of 13,000 officers and men visited this country. Some 4,000 Soviets entered the United States as commercial or exchange visitors in 1974. In 1972-1973, for example, approximately one-third of the Soviet exchange students here for the academic year under the East-West Student Exchange Program were cooperating with the KGB, according to the Central Intelligence Agency.

Other areas of counterintelligence concern include the sharp increase in the number of Soviet immigrants to the United States (4,000 in 1974 compared to fewer than 500 in 1972): the rise in East-West commercial exchange visitors (from 641 in 1972 to 1,500 in 1974); and the growing number of officials in this country from other Communist block nations (from 416 in 1960 to 798 in 1975).

Coordination between C.I.A. and F.B.I. counterintelligence units is especially critical. The history of C.I.A.-F.B.I. liaison has been turbulent, though a strong undercurrent of cooperation has usually existed at the staff level since 1952 when the bureau began sending a liaison person to the C.I.A. on a regular basis. The sources of friction between the C.I.A. and F.B.I. in the early days revolved around such matters as the frequent unwillingness of the bureau to collect positive intelligence for the C.I.A. within the United States or to help recruit foreign officials in this country.

The committee believes that counterintelligence requires the direct attention of Congress and the executive for three reasons: (1) two distinct and partly incompatible approaches to counterintelligence have emerged and demand reconciliation; (2) recent evidence suggests that F.B.I. counterespionage results have been less than satisfactory; and (3) counterintelligence has infringed on the rights and liberties of Americans.

RECOMMENDATIONS

22. By statute, a charter should be established for the Central Intelligence Agency which makes clear that its activities must be related to foreign intelligence. The agency should be given the following missions:

¶The collection of denied or protected foreign intelligence information.

¶The conduct of foreign counterintelligence.

¶The conduct of foreign covert action operations.

¶The production of finished national intelligence.

23. The C.I.A., in carrying out foreign intelligence mission I, would be permitted to engage in relevant activities within the United States so long as these activities do not violate the Constitution nor any Federal, state or local laws within the United States. The committee has set forth in its domestic recommendations proposed restrictions on such activities to supplement restrictions already contained in the 1947 National Security Act. In addition, the committee recommends that by statute the intelligence oversight committee(s) of Congress and the proposed counterintelligence committee of the National Security Council be required to review, at least annually, C.I.A. foreign intelligence activities conducted within the United States.

24. By statute, the Attorney General should be required to report

to the President and to the intelligence oversight committee(s) of Congress any intelligence activities which, in his opinion, violate the constitutional rights of American citizens or any other provision of law and the actions he has taken in response. Pursuant to the committee's domestic recommendations, the Attorney General should be made responsible for ensuring that intelligence activities do not violate the Constitution or any other provision of law.

25. The committee recommends the establishment of a special committee of the Committee on Foreign Intelligence to review all foreign human intelligence collection activities. It would make recommendations to the C.F.I. with regard to the scope, policies, and priorities of U.S. clandestine human collection operations and choices between overt and clandestine human collection. This committee would be composed of a representative of the Secretary of State as chairman, the other statutory members of the C.F.I., and others whom the President may designate.

26. The intelligence oversight committee(s) of Congress should carefully examine intelligence collection activities of the Clandestine Service to assure that clandestine means are used only when the information is sufficiently important and when such means are necessary to obtain such information.

27. The intelligence oversight committee(s) should consider whether:

¶the Domestic Collection Division (overt collection operations) should be removed from the Directorate of Operations (the Clandestine Service), and returned to the Directorate of Intelligence,

¶the C.I.A.'s regulations should require that the D.C.D.'s overt contacts be informed when they are to be used for operational support of clandestine activities,

¶the C.I.A.'s regulations should prohibit recruiting as agents immigrants who have applied for American citizenship.

28. The President of the United States, in consultation with the intelligence oversight committee(s) of Congress, should undertake a classified review of current issues regarding counterintelligence. This review should form the basis for a classified Presidential statement on national counterintelligence policy and objectives, and should closely examine the following issues: compartmentation, operations, security, internal review, deception, liaison and coordination, and manpower.

• • •

COVERT ACTION AND PARAMILITARY OPERATIONS

Covert action is the attempt to influence the internal affairs of other nations in support of United States foreign policy in a manner that conceals the participation of the United States Government. Covert action includes political and economic action, propaganda and paramilitary activities.

The basic unit of covert action is the project. Covert action "project" can range from single assets, such as a journalist placing propaganda, through a network of assets working in the media, to major covert and military intervention such as in Laos. The agency also maintains what it terms an "operational infrastructure of "standby" assets (agents of influence or media assets) who can be used in major operations—such as in Chile. These "standby" assets are part of ongoing, most often routine, projects. There are no inactive assets.

COVERT ACTION

The committee has found that the C.I.A. has conducted some 900 major or sensitive covert action projects since 1961. The need to maintain secrecy shields covert action projects from the rigorous public scrutiny and debate necessary to determine their compatibility with established American foreign policy goals. Recently, a large-scale covert paramilitary operation in Angola was initiated without any effort on the part of the executive branch to articulate and win public support for its overall policy in Africa. Only public disclosure has allowed the nation to apply its standards of success or failure to covert action projects and then only in retrospect, often without the benefit of the details prompting the original choice of covert rather than overt action.

The secrecy covert action requires means that the public cannot determine whether such actions are consistent with established foreign policy goals. This secrecy also has allowed covert actions to take place which are inconsistent with our basic traditions and values.

Some covert operations have passed retrospect public judgments, such as the support given Western European democratic parties facing strong Communist opposition in the late 1940's and 1950's. Others have not. In the view of the committee, the covert harassment of the democratically elected government of Salvador Allende in Chile did not command U.S. public approval.

PARAMILITARY OPERATIONS

Covert paramilitary operations are a special, extreme form of covert action. These operations most often consist of covert military assistance and training, but occasionally have involved actual combat activities by American advisers.

Because military assistance involves foreign policy commitments, it is, with one exception, authorized by the Congress. That exception is covert military assistance which is channeled through the C.I.A. without being authorized or approved by the Congress as a whole.

Covert U.S. paramilitary combat operations frequently amount to making war, but do not come under the War Powers Act since they usually do not involve uniformed U.S. military officers. American military officers engaged in C.I.A.-sponsored paramilitary operations are "sheep-dipped" for paramilitary duty—that is, they appear to resign from the military yet preserve their place for reactivation once their tour as civilians in paramilitary operations has ended.

The committee finds that major paramilitary operations have often failed to achieve their intended objective. Most have eventually been exposed. Operations, as in Angola, recently, and Indonesia in the late 1950's are examples of such paramilitary failures. Others, such as Laos, are judged successes by the C.I.A. and officials within the executive branch. The "success" in Laos, however, must be seen against the larger American involvement in Indochina which failed.

Paramilitary operations often have evolved into large-scale programs with a high risk of exposure (and thus embarrassment and/or failure) in some cases, the C.I.A. has been used to undertake paramilitary operations simply because the agency is less accountable to the public for highly visible "secret" military operations. In all cases considered by the committee, command and control within the executive branch was rigorous. However, all such operations have been conducted without direct Congressional authority or public debate. In recent years, some have been continued in the face of strong Congressional disapproval.

Recently, however—apart from Angola—United States paramilitary activities have been at a very low level. The capability for these actions, residing jointly in the C.I.A. and the Department of Defense, consists of a cadre of trained officers, stockpiles of military equipment, logistic networks and small collections of air and maritime assets.

RECOMMENDATIONS

35. The legislation establishing the charter for the Central Intelligence Agency should specify that the C.I.A. is the only U.S. Government agency authorized to conduct covert actions. The purpose of covert actions should be to deal with grave threats to American security. Covert actions should be consistent with publicly defined United States foreign policy goals, and should be reserved for extraordinary circumstances when no other means will suffice. The legislation governing covert action should require executive branch procedures which will insure careful and thorough consideration of both the general policies governing covert action and particular covert action projects; such procedures should require the participation and accountability of highest level policymakers.

36. The committee has already recommended, following its investigation of alleged assassination attempts directed at foreign leaders, a statute to forbid such activities. The committee reaffirms its support for such a statute and further recommends prohibiting the following covert activities by statute:

¶All political assassinations.

¶Efforts to subvert democratic governments.

¶Support for police or other internal security forces which engage in the systematic violation of human rights.

37. By statute, the appropriate N.S.C. committee (e.g., the Operations Advisory Group) should review every covert action proposal.

The Committee recommends that the Operations Advisory Group review include:

¶A careful and systematic analysis of the political premises underlying the recommended actions, as well as the nature, extent, purpose, risks, likelihood of success and costs of the operation. Reasons explaining why the objective can not be achieved by overt means should also be considered.

¶Each covert action project should be formally considered at a meeting of the OAG, and if approved, forwarded to the President for final decision. The views and positions of the participants would be fully recorded. For the purpose of OAG, Presidential and Congressional considerations, all so-called non-sensitive projects should be aggregated according to the extraordinary circumstances or contingency against which the project is directed.

38. By statute, the intelligence oversight committee(s) of Congress should require that the annual budget submission for covert action programs be specified and detailed as to the activity recommended. Unforeseen covert action projects should be funded from the Contingency Reserve Fund which could be replenished only after the concurrence of the oversight and any other appropriate congressional committees. The Congressional Intelligence Oversight Committee should be notified prior to any withdrawal from the Contingency Reserve Fund.

39. By statute, any covert use by the U.S. Government of American citizens as combatants should be preceded by the notification required for all covert actions. The statute should provide that within 60 days of such notification such use shall be terminated unless the Congress has specifically authorized such use. The Congress should be empowered to terminate such use at any time.

40. By statute, the executive branch should be prevented from conducting any covert military assistance program (including the indirect or direct provision of military material, military or logistics advice and training, and funds for mercenaries) without the explicit prior consent of the intelligence oversight committee(s) of Congress.

. . .

RELATIONS WITH UNITED STATES INSTITUTIONS AND PRIVATE CITIZENS

In the immediate postwar period, as the Communists pressed to influence and to control international organizations and movements, mass communications, and cultural institutions, the United States responded by involving American private institutions and individuals in the secret struggle over minds, institutions, and ideals. In the process, the C.I.A. subsidized, and even helped develop "private" or nongovernment organizations that were designed to compete with Communists around the world. The C.I.A. supported not only foreign organizations, but also the international activities of United States student, labor, cultural, and philanthropic organizations.

These covert relationships have attracted public concern and this committee's attention because of the importance that Americans attach to the independence of these institutions.

The committee found that in the past the scale and diversity of these covert actions has been extensive. For operational purposes, the C.I.A. has:

¶Funded a special program of a major American business association.

¶Collaborated with an American trade union federation.

¶Helped to establish a research center at a major United States university.

¶Supported an international exchange program sponsored by a group of United States universities.

¶Made widespread use of philanthropic organizations to fund such covert action programs.

1. COVERT USE OF THE U.S. ACADEMIC COMMUNITY

The Central Intelligence Agency is now using several hundred American academies, who in addition to providing leads and, sometimes making introductions for intelligence purposes, occasionally write books and other material to be used for propaganda purposes abroad. Beyond these, an additional few score are used in an unwitting manner for minor activities.

These academies are located in over 100 American colleges, universities and related institutes. At the majority of institutions, no one other than the individual academic concerned is aware of the C.I.A. link. At the others, at least one university official is aware of the operational use made of academies on his campus. In addition, there are several American academies abroad who serve operational purposes, primarily the collection of intelligence.

The C.I.A. gives a high priority to obtaining leads on potential foreign intelligence sources especially those from Communist countries. This agency's emphasis reflects the fact that many foreign nationals in the United States are in this category. The committee notes that American academies provide valuable assistance in this activity.

The committee is concerned, however, that American academies involved in such activities may undermine public confidence that those that train our youth are upholding the ideals, independence and integrity of American universities.

GOVERNMENT GRANTEES

C.I.A. regulations adopted in 1967 prohibit the "operational" use of certain narrow categories of individuals. The C.I.A. is prohibited from receiving grants from the Board of Foreign Fellowships under the Fulbright-Hayes Act. There is no prohibition on the use of individuals participating in any other federally funded exchange programs. For example, the C.I.A. may use those grantees—artists, specialists, athletes, leaders, etc.—who do not receive their grants from the Board of Foreign Scholarships. The Committee is concerned that there is no prohibition against exploiting such open Federal programs for clandestine purposes.

2. THE COVERT USE OF BOOKS AND PUBLISHING HOUSES

The committee has found that the Central Intelligence Agency attaches a particular importance to book publishing activities as a form of covert propaganda. A former officer in the Clandestine Service stated that books are "the most important weapon of strategic (long-range) propaganda." Prior to 1967, the Central Intelligence Agency sponsored, subsidized or produced over 1,000 books: approximately 25 percent of them in English. In 1967 alone, the C.I.A. published or subsidized over 200 books, ranging from books on African safaris and wildlife to translations of Machiavelli's "The Prince" into Swahili and works of T. S. Eliot into Russian, to a competitor to Mao's little red book, which was entitled "Quotations from Chairman Liu."

The committee found that an important number of the books actually produced by the Central Intelligence Agency were reviewed and marketed in the United States.

3. DOMESTIC "FALLOUT"

The committee finds that covert media operations can result in manipulating or incidentally misleading the American public. Despite efforts to minimize it, C.I.A. employees, past and present, have conceded that there is no way to shield the American public completely from "fallout" in the United States from agency propaganda or placements overseas. Indeed, following the Katzenbach inquiry, the Deputy Director for Operations issued a directive stating: "Fallout in the United States from a foreign publication which we support is inevitable and consequently permissible."

The domestic fallout of covert propaganda comes from many sources: books intended primarily for an English-speaking foreign audience, C.I.A. press placements that are picked up by an international wire service, and publications resulting from direct C.I.A. funding of foreign institutes. For example, a book written for an English-speaking foreign audience by one C.I.A. operative was reviewed by another C.I.A. agent in *The New York Times.*

4. COVERT USE OF AMERICAN RELIGIOUS PERSONNEL

The committee has found that over the years the C.I.A. has used very few religious personnel for operational purposes. The C.I.A. informed the committee that only 21 such individuals have ever participated in either covert action projects or the clandestine collection of intelligence. On Feb. 10, 1976, the C.I.A. announced: "C.I.A. has no secret paid or contractual relationships with any American clergyman or missionary. This practice will be continued as a matter of policy."

The committee welcomes this policy with the understanding that the prohibition against all "paid or contractual relationships" is in fact a prohibition against any operational use, of all Americans following a religious vocation.

RECOMMENDATIONS

In its consideration of the recommendations that follow, the committee noted the Central Intelligence Agency's concern that further restriction on the use of Americans for operational purposes will constrain current operating programs. The committee recognizes that there may be at least some short-term operational losses if the committee's recommendations are effected. At the same time, the committee believes that there are certain American institutions whose integrity is critical to the maintenance of a free society and which should therefore be free of any unwitting role in the clandestine service of the United States Government.

42. The committee is concerned about the integrity of American academic instructions and the use of individuals affiliated with such institutions for clandestine purposes. Accordingly, the committee recommends that the C.I.A. amend its internal directives to require that individual academics used for operational purposes by the C.I.A., together with the President or equivalent official of the relevant academic institutions, be informed of the clandestine C.I.A. relationship.

43. The committee further recommends that, as soon as possible, the permanent intelligence oversight committee(s) of Congress examine whether further steps are needed to insure the integrity of American academic institutions.

44. By statute, the C.I.A. should be prohibited from the operational use of grantees who are receiving funds through educational and/or cultural programs which are sponsored by the United States Government.

45. By statute, the C.I.A. should be prohibited from subsidizing the writing, or production for distribution within the United States or its territories, of any book, magazine, article, publication, film, or video or audio tape unless publicly attributed to the C.I.A. Nor should the C.I.A. be permitted to undertake any activity to accomplish indirectly such distribution within the United States or its territories.

46. The committee supports the recently adopted C.I.A. prohibitions against any paid or contractual relationship between the agency and U.S. and foreign journalists accredited to U.S. media organizations. The C.I.A. prohibitions should, however, be established in law.

47. The committee recommends that the C.I.A. prohibitions be extended by law to include the operational use of any person who regularly contributes material to, or is regularly involved directly or indirectly in the editing of material, or regularly acts to set policy or provide direction to the activities of U.S. media organizations.

48. The committee recommends that the agency's recent prohibition on covert paid or contractual relationship between the agency and any American clergyman or missionary should be established by law.

PROPRIETARIES AND COVER

PROPRIETARY ORGANIZATIONS

C.I.A. proprietaries are business entities wholly owned by the agency which do business, or only appear to do business, under comboth internally and externally. Generally, those auditing the C.I.A. Clandestine Services. They have been used for espionage as well as covert action. Most of the larger proprietaries have been used for paramilitary purposes. The committee finds that too often large proprietaries have created unwarranted risks of unfair competition with private business and of compromising their cover as clandestine operations. For example, Air America, which at one time had as many as 8,000 employees, ran into both difficulties.

While internal C.I.A. financial controls have been regular and systematic, the committee found a need for even greater accountability both internally and externally. Generally, those auditing the C.I.A. have been denied access to operational information, making management-oriented audits impossible. Instead, audits have been concerned only with financial security and integrity.

The committee found that the C.I.A.'s Inspector General has, on occasion, been denied access to certain information regarding proprietaries. This has sometimes inhibited the ability of the inspector office to serve the function for which it was established. Moreover, the General Accounting Office has not audited these operations. The lack of review, by either the G.A.O. or the C.I.A Inspector General's office, means that, in essence, there has been no outside review of proprietaries

One of the largest current proprietaries is an insurance-investment complex established in 1962 to provide pension annuities, insurance and escrow management for those who, for security reasons, could not receive them directly from the U.S. Government. The committee determined that the Congress was not informed of the existence of this proprietary until "sometime" after it had been made operational and had invested heavily in the domestic stock markets—a practice the C.I.A. has discontinued. Moreover, once this proprietary was removed from the Domestic Operations Division and placed under the General Counsel's office it received no annual C.I.A. project review.

The record establishes that on occasion the insurance-investment complex had been used to provide operational support to various covert action projects. The Inspector General, in 1970, criticized this use of the complex because it threatened to compromise the security of the complex's primary insurance objectives.

COVER

The committee examined cover because it is an important aspect of all C.I.A. clandestine activities. Its importance is underscored by the tragic murder of a C.I.A. station chief in Greece, coupled with continuing disclosures of C.I.A. agents' names. The committee sought to determine what, if anything, has been done in the past to strengthen cover, and what should be done in the future.

The commitee found conflicting views about what constitutes cover, what it can do, and what should be done to improve it. A 1970 C.I.A. inspector general report termed the agency's concept and use of cover to be lax, arbitrary, uneven, confused, and loose. The present cover staff in the C.I.A. considered the 1970 assessment to be simplistic and overly harsh. There is no question, however, that some improvements and changes are needed.

The committee found that there is a basic tension between maintaining adequate cover and effectively engaging in overseas intelligence activities. Almost every operational act by a C.I.A. officer under cover in the field—from working with local intelligence and police to attempting to recruit agents—reveals his true purpose and chips away at his cover. Some forms of cover do not provide concealment but offer a certain degree of deniability. Others are so elaborate that they limit the amount of work an officer can do for the C.I.A. In carrying out their responsibilities, C.I.A. officers generally regard the maintenance of cover as a "nuisance."

The situation of the Athens station chief, Richard Welch, illustrates the problem of striking the right balance between cover and operations, and also the transparency of cover. As the chief of the C.I.A.'s cover staff stated, by the time a person becomes chief of station, "there is not a great deal of cover staff left. The chief of the cover staff identified terrorism as a further security problem for officers overseas, one that is aggravated by the erosion of cover.

RECOMMENDATIONS

49. By statute, the C.I.A. should be permitted to use proprietaries subject to external and internal controls.

50. The committee recommends that the intelligence oversight committee(s) of Congress require at least an annual report on all proprietaries. The report should include a statement of each proprietary's nature and function, the results of internal annual C.I.A. audits, a list of all C.I.A. intercessions on behalf of its proprietaries with any other United States Government departments, agencies or bureaus, and such other information as the oversight committee deems appropriate.

51. The intelligence oversight committee(s) of Congress should require that the fiscal impact of proprietaries on the C.I.A.'s budget be made clear in the D.C.I.'s annual report to the oversight committee. The committee should also establish guidelines for creating large proprietaries, should these become necessary.

52. By statute, all returns of funds from proprietaries not needed for its operational purposes or because of liquidation or termination of a proprietary, should be remitted to the United States Treasury as Miscellaneous Receipts.

The Department of Justice should be consulted during the process of the sale or disposition of any C.I.A. proprietary.

53. By statute, former senior government officials should be prohibited from negotiating with the C.I.A. or any other agency regarding the disposal of proprietaries. The intelligence oversight committees of Congress should consider whether other activities among agencies of the intelligence community, the C.I.A. and former officials and employees, such as selling to or negotiating contracts with the C.I.A., should also be prohibited as is the case regarding military officials under 18 U.S.C. 207.

· · ·

OVERSIGHT AND THE INTELLIGENCE BUDGET

The committee finds that a full understanding of the budget of the intelligence community is required for effective oversight. The secrecy surrounding the budget, however, makes it impossible for Congress as a whole to make use of this valuable oversight tool.

Congress as a body has never explicitly voted on a "budget" for national intelligence activities. Congress has never voted funds specifically for C.I.A., N.S.A. and other national intelligence instrumentalities of the Department of Defense.

The funding levels for these intelligence agencies are fixed by subcommittees of the Armed Services and Appropriations Committees of both houses. Funds for these agencies are then concealed in the budget of the Department of Defense. Since this department budget is the one Congress approves, Congress as a whole, and the public, have never known how much the intelligence agencies are spending or how much is spent on intelligence activities generally. Neither Congress as a whole nor the public can determine whether the amount spent on intelligence, or by the intelligence agencies individually, is appropriate given the priorities.

Because the funds for intelligence are concealed in defense appropriations, those appropriations are thereby inflated. Most members of Congress and the public can neither determine which categories are inflated nor the extent to which funds in the inflated categories are being used for purposes for which they are approved.

Finally, the committee believes there is serious question as to whether the present system of complete secrecy violates the constitutional provision that:

"No Money shall be drawn from the Treasury but in Consequence of Appropriations made by Law; and a regular Statement and Account of the Receipts and Expenditures of all public Money shall be published from time to time."

The committee believes that the overall figure for national intelligence activities can be made public annually without endangering national security or revealing sensitive programs. The committee carefully examined the possible impact of such disclosure on the sources and methods of intelligence gathering and believes it to be minimal. The committee found that the primary concern about this level of disclosure was that it would lead to pressure for even more detailed revelation, which would compromise vital intelligence programs.

The committee believes that disclosure of an aggregate figure for national intelligence is as far as it is prudent to go at this stage in reconciling the nation's constitutional and national security requirements. Public speculation about overall intelligence costs would be eliminated, the public would be assured that funds appropriated to particular government agencies were in fact intended for those agencies, and both Congress and the public would be able to assess overall priorities in governmental spending.

RECOMMENDATIONS

77. The intelligence oversight committee(s) of Congress should authorize on an annual basis a "National Intelligence Budget," the total amount of which would be made public. The commitee recommends that the oversight committee consider whether it is necessary, given the constitutional requirement and the national security demands, to publish more detailed budgets.

78. The intelligence oversight committee(s) of Congress should monitor the tactical and indirect support accounts as well as the national activities of intelligence agencies in order to assure that they are kept in proper perspective and balance.

79. At the request of the intelligence oversight committee(s) of Congress and as its agent, staff members of the General Accounting Office should conduct full audits, both for compliance and for management of all components of the intelligence community. The G.A.O. should establish such procedures, compartmentation and clearances as are necessary in order to conduct these audits on a secure basis. In conducting such audits, the G.A.O. should be authorized to have all access to all necessary files and records of the intelligence community.

CHEMICAL AND BIOLOGICAL AGENTS AND THE INTELLIGENCE COMMUNITY

The committee investigated the testing and use of chemical and biological agents by agencies within the intelligence community. The testing programs originated in response to fears that countries hostile to the United States would use chemical and biological agents against Americans or our allies. Initially, this fear led to defensive programs. Soon this defensive orientation became secondary as the possibility of using these chemical and biological agents to obtain information from, or to gain control of, enemy agents became apparent.

The committee found that United States intelligence agencies engaged in research and development programs to discover materials which could be used to alter human behavior. As part of this effort, testing programs were instituted, first involving witting human subjects. Later, drugs were surreptitiously administered to unwitting human subjects.

The agency considered the testing programs highly sensitive. The committee found that few people within the agencies knew about them: There is no evidence that Congress was informed about them. These programs were kept from the American public because, as the inspector general of the C.I.A. wrote, "the knowledge that the agency is engaging in unethical and illicit activities would have serious repercussions in political and diplomatic circles and would be detrimental to the accomplishment of its [C.I.A.'s] mission."

The research and development program and particularly the testing program involving unwitting human subjects involved massive abridgements of the rights of individuals, sometimes with tragic consequences. The deaths of two Americans resulted from these programs; other participants in the testing programs still suffer residual effects. While some controlled testing for defensive purposes might be defended, the nature of the tests, their scale, and the fact that they were continued for years after it was known that the surreptitious administration of LSD to unwitting subjects was dangerous, indicate a disregard for human life and liberty.

The committee also found that within the intelligence community there were destructive jurisdictional conflicts over drug testing. Military testers withheld information from the C.I.A., ignoring their superiors' suggestions for coordination. The C.I.A. similarly failed to provide information on its programs to the military. In one case the military attempted to conceal their overseas operational testing of LSD from the C.I.A. and the C.I.A. attempted surreptitiously to discover the details of the military's program.

RECOMMENDATIONS

80. The C.I.A. and other foreign and foreign military intelligence agencies should not engage in experimentation on human subjects utilizing any drug, device or procedure which is designed, intended, or is reasonably likely to harm the physical or mental health of the human subject, except with the informed consent in writing, witnessed by a disinterested third party, of each human subject, and in accordance with the guidelines issued by the National Commission for the Protection of Human Subjects for Biomedical and Behavioral Research. Further, the jurisdiction of the commission should be amended to include the Central Intelligence Agency and the other intelligence agencies of the United States Government.

81. The Director of the Central Intelligence Agency and the Secretary of Defense should continue to make determined efforts to locate those individuals involved in human testing of chemical and biological

agents and to provide follow-up examinations and treatment, if necessary.

GENERAL RECOMMENDATIONS

82. *Internal Regulations*—Internal C.I.A. directives or regulations regarding significant agency policies and procedures should be waived only with the explicit written approval of the Director of Central Intelligence. Waiver of any such regulation or directive should in no way violate any law or infringe on the constitutional right and freedom of any citizen. If the D.C.I. approves the waiver or amendment of any significant regulation or directive, the N.S.C. and the appropriate Congressional oversight committee(s) should be notified immediately. Such notification should be accompanied by a statement explaining the reasons for the waiver or amendment.

83. *Security Clearances*—In the course of its investigation, the committee found that because of the many intelligence agencies participating in security clearance investigations, current security clearance procedures involve duplication of effort, waste of money and inconsistent patterns of investigation and standards. The intelligence oversight committee(s) of Congress, in consultation with the intelligence community, should consider framing standard security clearance procedures for all civilian intelligence agencies and background checks for Congressional committees when security clearances are required.

84. *Personnel Practices*—The committee found that intelligence agency training programs fail to instruct personnel adequately on the legal limitations and prohibitions applicable to intelligence activities. The committee recommends that these training programs should be expanded to include review of constitutional, statutory and regulatory provisions in an effort to heighten awareness among all intelligence personnel concerning the potential effects intelligence activities may have on citizens' legal rights.

85. *Security Functions of the Intelligence Agencies*—The committee found that the security components of intelligence agencies sometimes engaged in law enforcement activities. Some of these activities may have been unlawful. Intelligence agencies' security functions should be limited to protecting the agencies' personnel and facilities and lawful activities and to assuring that intelligence personnel follow proper security practices.

86. *Secrecy and Authorized Disclosure*—The committee has received various Administration proposals that would require persons having access to classified and sensitive information to maintain the secrecy of that information. The committee recommends that the issues raised by these proposals be considered by the new legislative intelligence oversight committees of Congress and that, in recasting the 1947 National Security Act and in consultation with the executive branch, the oversight committees consider the wisdom of new secrecy and disclosure legislation. In the view of the committee, any such consideration

should include carefully defining the following terms: national secrets; sources and methods; lawful and unlawful classification; lawful and unlawful disclosure.

The new legislation should provide civil and/or criminal penalties for unlawful classification and unlawful disclosure. The statute should also provide for internal departmental and agency procedures for employees who believe that classification and/or disclosure procedures are being improperly or illegally used to report such belief. There should also be a statutory procedure whereby an employee who has used the agency channel to no avail can report such belief without impunity to an "authorized" institutional group outside the agency. The new Intelligence Oversight Board is one such group. The intelligence oversight committee(s) of Congress would be another. The statute should specify that revealing classified information in the course of reporting information to an authorized group would not constitute unlawful disclosure of classified information.

87. *Federal Register for Classified Executive Orders*—In the course of its investigation, the committee often had difficulty locating classified orders, directives, instructions and regulations issued by various elements of the executive branch. Access to these orders by the intelligence oversight committee(s) of Congress is essential to informed oversight of the intelligence community.

The committee recommends that a Federal Register for classified executive orders be established, by statute. The statute should require the registry, under appropriate security procedures, of all executive orders—however they are labeled—concerning the intelligence activities of the United States. Among the documents for which registry in the Classified Federal Register should be required are all National Security Council intelligence directives and all Director of Central Intelligence directives. Provision should be made for access to classified executive orders by the intelligence oversight committee(s) of Congress. Classified executive orders would not be lawful until filed with the registry, although there should be provision for immediate implementation in emergency situations with prompt subsequent registry required.

Suggested Further Readings

I. 1945 TO 1952

An important revisionist work critical of administration Cold War policy is Gabriel and Joyce Kolko, *The Limits of Power* (New York: Harper & Row, 1972). A more moderate, yet still revisionist, account is Walter LaFeber, *America, Russia, and the Cold War, 1945–1966*, rev. ed. (New York: Wiley, 1972). Dean Acheson offers his defense in *Present at the Creation* (New York: Norton, 1969). Alonzo Hamby has written the now standard book on the Truman administration: *Beyond the New Deal* (New York: Columbia University Press, 1973). See also the more critical anthology edited by Barton J. Bernstein and Allen J. Matusow, *The Truman Administration: A Documentary History* (New York: Harper & Row, 1966), as well as Bernstein's *Toward a New Past* (New York: Random House, 1967), and *Politics and Policies of the Truman Administration* (Chicago: Quadrangle, 1970).

II. 1953 TO 1959

The best book on Dwight Eisenhower is Herbert S. Parmet, *Eisenhower and the American Crusades* (New York: Macmillan, 1972). See also Emmet John Hughes, *The Ordeal of Power* (New York: Atheneum, 1963), and Arthur Larson, *Eisenhower: The President Nobody Knew* (New York: Scribner's, 1968). The standard work on Joseph McCarthy is Michael Paul Rogin, *The Intellectuals and McCarthy* (Cambridge, Mass.: Harvard University Press, 1967); still interesting is William F. Buckley, Jr., and L. Brent Bozell's defense, *McCarthy and His Enemies* (Chicago: Henry Regnery, 1954). Some outstanding works of social criticism are David Riesman et al., *The Lonely Crowd* (New Haven: Yale University Press, 1950); Daniel Bell, *The End of Ideology*, rev. ed. (New York: Free Press, 1965); C. Wright Mills, *The Power Elite* (New York: Oxford University Press, 1956); John Kenneth Galbraith, *American Capitalism* (Boston: Houghton Mifflin, 1956).

III. THE 1960's

A Thousand Days by Arthur Schlesinger, Jr. (Boston: Houghton Mifflin, 1965) is still by far the best book on the Kennedy administration, although it is too generous to the president. All recent books have been critical, even hypercritical, of Kennedy. See, for example, Henry Fairlie, *The Kennedy Promise* (Garden City, N.Y.: Doubleday, 1973); Louise Fitzsimons, *The Kennedy Doctrine* (New York: Random House, 1972); and Nancy Gager Clinch, *The Kennedy Neurosis* (New York: Grosset and Dunlap, 1973). A book both critical of and sympathetic to President Johnson is *Lyndon Johnson and the American Dream* by Doris Kearns (New York: Harper & Row, 1976). A good book on Martin Luther King, Jr., is John A. Williams, *The King God Didn't Save* (New York: Coward-McCann, 1970); a statement by a more radical figure is Eldridge Cleaver, *Soul on Ice* (New York: McGraw-Hill, 1967). A good historical account of the Vietnam War is Arthur Schlesinger, Jr., *The Bitter Heritage: Vietnam and American Democracy, 1941–1966* (Boston: Houghton Mifflin, 1967); a more recent examination of America's role is Frances Fitzgerald, *Fire in the Lake* (Boston: Little, Brown, 1972). A good account of the election of 1968—and of the events of that startling year itself—is Lewis Chester et al., *An American Melodrama* (New York: Viking, 1969).

IV. THE 1970's

The best book on Richard Nixon is still the rambling *Nixon Agonistes* by Garry Wills (Boston: Houghton Mifflin, 1970). On the economy see Robert Lekachman, *Inflation: The Permanent Problem of Boom and Bust* (New York: Vintage, 1973). On Watergate there are Jonathan Schell, *The Time of Illusion* (New York: Alfred A. Knopf, 1975) and John Dean, *Blind Ambition* (New York: Simon & Schuster, 1976). On politics generally, see Kirkpatrick Sale, *Power Shift: The Rise of the Southern Rim and Its Challenge to the Eastern Establishment* (New York: Random House, 1975), and Sidney Verba, *Political Participation in America* (Ann Arbor, Mich.: Inter-University Consortium for Political Research, 1975).